new relations

the refashioning of british poetry 1980-1994

new relations

the refashioning of
british poetry
1980-1994

DAVID KENNEDY

seren

PR
601
.K46
1996

seren is the book imprint of
Poetry Wales Press Ltd
Wyndham Street, Bridgend,
Mid Glamorgan, CF31 1EF
Wales

© David Kennedy, 1996

A CIP record for this book is available at the
British Library Cataloguing in Publication Data Office

ISBN 1-85411-162-0
1-85411-163-9 paperback

*The publisher acknowledges the financial support of the
Arts Council of Wales*

Cover design by Simon Hicks
Background reproduced from the *Oxford English Dictionary*
2nd edn. (1989) by permission of Oxford University Press

Printed in Plantin by
WBC Book Manufacturers, Bridgend

Contents

7   Preface
9   Introduction

24   1. Voice and Ownership: Ideas of Individual Voice
     and Dominant Culture from 'Middle Generation'
     to 'New Generation'

55   2. 'England Gone': The Rhetorical Imagination
     and Ideas of Nation in the Poetry of Simon Armitage
     and Glyn Maxwell

79   3. 'Just the facts, Just the': A Rough Guide to British
     Postmodernism

120   4. Elegies for the Living: The Poetry of Peter Reading

153   5. The Noise of Science

185   6. Home Thoughts From Abroad

214   7. "Finding an Adequate Measure": Poetry as Media

236   8. "Everyone Agrees": How British Poetry Joined the
      Culture Club

253   Appendix: *The New Poetry* — A User's Guide
276   Acknowledgements
278   Bibliography
291   Index
295   About the Author

In Britain today, two parallel movements of unravelling can be discerned beneath the topical ephemera of political life — an unravelling of the current form of the union between Britain's component nations, visible in swift and dramatic political changes in Northern Ireland and in immobility and the decaying legitimacy of Westminister rule in Scotland, and impelled by the ongoing and deepening crisis of the monarchy; and an unravelling of English national culture itself, as the English struggle to shake off the inherited mythologies which distort their perception of themselves and their relations with neighbouring peoples. These two movements are accelerated by the deformation, and consequent decline in legitimacy, of many of the institutions of government in Britain, which is the principal legacy of fifteen years of neo-liberal policy.

John Gray: 'Whatever happened to Englishness?'(1994)

Preface

This book of essays sets out to complement *The New Poetry* (1993) and, like that anthology, it intends to be suggestive rather than encyclopaedic. It is aimed at the interested general reader as well as the teacher and student of contemporary British poetry. Don Paterson has likened poetry to "a strange little town for which no reliable streetplan exists, full of all-night cafés, tiny specialist libraries, tango bars, Zen gardens and Balti houses"; and the essays collected here might be said to describe a number of possible routes through the town. Nevertheless, I believe it is important to ask some hard questions about the present state of British poetry and have framed the book with an Introduction which addresses the critical status of poetry and with a final chapter which attempts a detached view of British poetry's public profile in the late 1980s and early 1990s.

My epigraph describes "two parallel movements of unravelling" and portrays British culture and society undergoing not radical instability but a prolonged process of adjustments, re-examinations and realignments; and it is my belief that British poetry in the 1980s and 1990s is best understood as a similar process of reorientations, revisitings and shifts. Consequently, the essays which follow do not serve a single thesis but are oriented by a number of defining ideas. There is the conception — developed from a remark by Sean O'Brien — of poets exploring 'the earned surplus' of the previous generation; the image of an 'energetic mismatch' of apparently exclusive or traditionally hostile elements; and the blurring of lines between realism and postmodernism. As such points might suggest, it is also my belief that British poetry in the 1980s and 1990s is most susceptible to a series of 'double readings'. For example, any account of British culture and society in the last quarter of the twentieth century must describe the erosion of the post-war consensus and greater economic and social division; and at the same time recognise that the erosion of that consensus can also be described as the collapse of a master narrative which many commentators would find characteristic of the wider condition of postmodernity in Western societies. This prompts some uncomfortable questions: are we living through a period of fragmentation or pluralism? does the so-called 'poetry boom' of the late 1980s and early 1990s owe its existence to the forces of the free market? I do not presume to have answers to such questions but I hope to offer some approaches to them. The Introduction sketches out the defining ideas referred to above. Chapter

One discusses the defining tensions between individual voice and dominant culture in the poetry of Eavan Boland, Douglas Dunn, Tony Harrison and Seamus Heaney and traces their influence on and reverberations in the work of younger writers like Sean O'Brien. Chapter Two examines the work of two of British poetry's brightest young stars, Simon Armitage and Glyn Maxwell, in terms of the relation between their conception of poetic language and impoverished ideas of nation. Chapter Three asks if there is a characteristically British 'postmodernism of the real' through an exploration of the poetry of John Ash, Peter Didsbury and Ian McMillan. Chapter Four is devoted to a full length study of Peter Reading and argues that his work functions as a microcosm of many of the key aspects of British poetry after 1980. Chapter Five looks at the increasing interfusion of poetry and science in the work of poets such as Robert Crawford, Pauline Stainer and Lavinia Greenlaw. Chapter Six looks at the way British poets have, in recent years, sought their inspiration from non-native poetries. Case studies include the influence of post-war American poetry on Northern British poets. Chapter Seven examines the resurgence of interest in public or political poetry or, as I term it, 'poetry as media'. Chapter Eight attempts to take a detached view of recent British poetry and the ways in which it has moved closer to the rest of the British arts industry and has been influenced by wider commercial trends.

Although this book does not aim to be comprehensive I feel it is important, with the teacher and student of poetry in mind, to explain some omissions. First, Irish poetry — North and South — seems to me to be more than adequately covered and theorised in existing books by, among others, Neil Corcoran, Edna Longley and Clair Wills; there seemed little point in opening the ground again. The exception is the poetry of Seamus Heaney where I believe I have made an original contribution. Second, I have chosen not to write about Black British or Afro-Caribbean poetry not only because it seems inappropriate for a white critic to do so but because these poetries are still being theorised through perspectives of language and difference. Third, I have not devoted a separate chapter to women's poetry: to do so seems to me complicit with consigning women poets to a literary ghetto and with perpetuating conceptions of poetry by women as a kind of cultural sideshow. The result is, I hope, a collection of essays which will not only offer a record of an important period in British poetry but will also contribute to a wider debate about the relations between culture and society in late twentieth century Britain.

Introduction

In a special issue of *Poetry Review* (Winter 1994/5) called 'The Reviewer' the magazine's editor Peter Forbes characterised the current state of poetry reviewing as "compromised", "incestuous" and marred by "the invention of spurious interest". The remarks were essentially variations on a theme first introduced two years earlier in another special issue entitled 'Going Critical':

> What poetry most needs now is good criticism ... [G]iven the vast amounts of published poetry today, the lack of major books of criticism is troubling. It's not that our most distinguished critics have given up on poetry — quite — but if you look at books on poetry by Frank Kermode, Christopher Ricks, Barbara Everett etc, you'll find that Larkin and Geoffrey Hill are the most recent poets considered.

When this sort of analysis appears in a populist journal like *Poetry Review* it is safe to assume that it reflects a widely held view within the British poetry scene. If we take this view on its own terms, it appears that the reasons for a co-existence of poetical glut and critical famine are clear and straightforward. There is an understandable problem with, say, cut-off dates which makes it difficult to evaluate new and still-developing writers. A critic preparing an essay on, for example, Michael Hofmann would certainly have to consider his first two collections, *Nights in the Iron Hotel* (1983) and *Acrimony* (1987) on which his considerable reputation is based; but what is he to do with *Corona, Corona* (1993) which has been less well received and is clearly in many respects a transitional work? Similarly, as this collection of essays was nearing completion and going to press several of the poets discussed in it published new collections which it was too late to include but whose exclusion may render the assessments of their work here incomplete or partial. The nature of poetry publishing and dissemination itself — the two tier split between a declining number of major publishers and innumerable magazines and pamphlet presses — complicates matters still further because it means that a poet's work of necessity appears fugitively and relatively invisibly between collections. Many writers publish either significant work or significant quantities of work that they later choose not to collect but which may nevertheless be fundamental to an evaluation of their oeuvre. A recent article in *P.N. Review* (Ellis 1994, 51-4) sought to assess the small body of work that Geoffrey Hill has published in magazines and periodicals in the ten years since his last collection but even this proved to be a problematic undertaking as the author had to acknowledge in a footnote an inaccessible — for British readers — American *New and Collected* which not only prints altered versions of the few works discussed but a further handful of new work.

The invisibility of an established writer to the critic is perhaps problematic enough but invisibility can also be described in another way: when you don't know something how do you know that you don't know it? Two comments, by Lawrence Sail and Neil Astley respectively, illuminate this point:

> What if, in this age of relentless publicity and promotion, no one had really discovered the foremost writer of the time?
> (1995, 13)

* * *

> ... the poets who are receiving most of the current coverage are the same poets: I don't mind that they've become fashionable, but I would like to hear more about other poets whose work is just as strong.
> (1994/5, 3)

Both comments connect with the understandable reluctance of some critics to deal with poetry that is not yet sufficiently distanced from its period of origin. As one reviewer of *The New Poetry* (1993) put it: "We live too close to the literature of our own time to know for sure whether it is any good or not" (Powell 1993, 59). Leaving aside the continuing confusion about the standards by which cultural products may be measured, it is clear that what is prized today may be unread and remaindered tomorrow. Criticism, on the other hand, seeks the longer view, a context beyond current fashion. F.R. Leavis's proposal in the 'Epilogue' to *New Bearings in English Poetry* of William Empson and Ronald Bottrall as leaders of the coming generation of innovators is merely the most notorious example of how history can wrongfoot the critic. If, then, we take the *Poetry Review* line on the current state of poetry and criticism, the dearth of criticism may be largely explained by the image of the critic of the contemporary, haunted by fears of his or her own provisionality, turning aside to Eliot, Wordsworth or Yeats who are dead and safe. However, I said "*if* we take" and I want to go on to sketch an alternative view which suggests that *Poetry Review's* portrayal of critical famine is incorrect; that it largely contains the answers to its own bewilderment; and that the current state of poetry and criticism can be traced to the state of contemporary British poetry itself as manifested in the attitudes of many of its commentators and practitioners.

Simply put, the poetry scene's view of its own art and of the severely truthful art of criticism are matters of deliberate and self-serving misconceptions. Just as Douglas Dunn once wrote that "There are many many worlds, there are many laws" so there would seem to be many varieties of 'good criticism'. In the canon of Kermode, Ricks and Everett there is clearly no place for such critics as Alan Robinson who produced a ground-breaking study *Instabilities In Contemporary British Poetry* in 1988 or for Edward Larrissy whose *Reading Twentieth Century Poetry* (1991) offers original readings of everyone from Eliot to Ashbery. As this exclusion suggests, the poetry scene's definition of good criticism expresses a body of undeclared and unanalysed opinion: what poetry most needs now is good criticism by critical authority figures; good criticism by those who are public intellectuals as opposed to mere academics; and good criticism by those who make either no or very little visible engagement with critical theory. One finds the same variety of good criticism being praised in the Editorial to *P.N. Review* 103 (May-June 1995) which recommends the American poet Louise Glück's book of essays, *Proofs And Theories*, for going against "a time of poetic *laissez-faire*" and for offering theories that "are not those that find favour in modern seminar rooms but those that grow from observation and practice". This combines two other undeclared and unanalysed assumptions implicit in the pages of poetry magazines: that poetry is in the front line of a battle against the Academy; and that only poets know how to write about poetry. Anyone else attempting the art of criticism is met with instant hostility. Here are some typical comments from *Poetry Review's* special issue 'The Reviewer':

> Unfortunately, very few critics other than poets are capable of understanding how and why poems are made.

* * *

> As the most personal of genres, the *why* of poetry affects the *how* pretty directly ... I get bored with critics who write chiefly about the how.

* * *

It seems pointless to review poetry unless you can write it
yourself ... I'm very careful in my condemnations or recommen-
dations; it's not just several years' work you're representing
but the whole medium.

* * *

Where evaluation cannot be kept out ... it should be based
as far as possible on lived experience rather than comparison
with other texts. Which brings me to my least favourite
category of reviewers — literary academics, who seem to
combine, to an almost perfect extent, vast textual erudition
with a quite appalling ignorance of life.

Transposing these attitudes to other cultural genres highlights
their essential eccentricity. Peter Fuller, for example, was neither a
painter nor a sculptor but this did not prevent him from writing with
sympathy and insight about artists as diverse as Willem de Kooning,
Jackson Pollock, Henry Moore and Cecil Collins. In fact, the world
of fine art offers us innumerable examples of the difficulty and
perhaps even inadvisability of searching for the 'reality' or 'experience'
behind a work. The Arnolfini Marriage Portrait by Van Eyck in the
National Gallery continues to divide critics over whether it is a
straightforward portrait or a symbolic representation of Christian
ideas of matrimony. Taken together, the four extracts from *Poetry
Review's* symposium suggest that poetry is defensively and quite
deliberately misconceived by both practitioners and pundits through
cults of the personal and the real. Both readers and writers are
continually enjoined to seek out and prize what the author of our
fourth extract calls elsewhere in his piece "the still, small voice of
authentic feeling". Poetry, in this manifestation, somehow gets away
with being paradoxical to the point of self-destruction. Poetry, the
argument goes, is personal, intimate but is somehow a recognisable
discourse. Poetry is personal but at its best universal. Poetry is an
essential part of culture but somehow exists above the usual systems
of cultural exchange and valuation. After all, the argument contin-
ues, everyone writes poetry, don't they? And if everyone writes
poetry then poetry becomes almost sacrosanct. How dare you
criticise the poems I wrote about the death of my wife or my pet
gibbon: they are how I really felt. Peter Sansom goes right to the
heart of the matter in his useful handbook *Writing Poems* (1994, 8-9)
when he observes that "We tend to feel that poems are true". He
goes on to say of Simon Armitage's poem 'Gone' — from his first
collection *Zoom!* (1989, 36) — which describes the events before

and after a funeral, that it is "so accurately observed, so convincingly felt, it's hard to believe that Simon Armitage hasn't actually suffered such a bereavement". The point is, of course, that it really doesn't matter if he has or not; and that a poem about a funeral whose first words are "Heaven, at last" is clearly asking us to respond not to its apparent authenticity but to a knowing and highly self-conscious literary performance. Cults of the authentic and the personal do poets and poetry no favours. One of the great enigmas of the age must be the way that Glyn Maxwell, who is an extremely *difficult* poet, is consistently portrayed as if he writes the poetic equivalent of a suburban soap opera. Limited ideas about poetry manifest themselves in other ways. Time and again, in article after interview after review, one reads the same old phrases, piously parroted, from Coleridge, Keats, Wordsworth, Eliot and even Pope. This is not to say that ideas such as 'negative capability' do not have an eternal relevance but just consider how strange it would be to open the latest issue of *Art Monthly* and find contemporary painting or sculpture discussed in terms borrowed from John Ruskin and Sir Joshua Reynolds.

The worst aspect of the current state of the poetry scene's view of itself and of criticism is the fact that it is a kind of self-fulfilling prophecy. The readers of *Poetry Review* and *P.N. Review*, the leading periodicals, can be forgiven for agreeing that there's a dearth of 'good criticism' because both magazines choose to ignore the majority that gets published. One would have thought, for example, that since Seamus Heaney is one of the most widely read and studied of contemporary poets there would be considerable interest in books about him. Neither *Poetry Review* nor *P.N. Review* noticed Michael Parker's excellent *Seamus Heaney: The Making of the Poet* (1993) which not only allows one to see all Heaney's writings to date as one continuous oeuvre but also demonstrates an at times surprising continuity between his life and his work. Henry Hart's study *Seamus Heaney: Poet of Contrary Progressions* (1991) was similarly ignored as was Luke Spencer's recent book on Tony Harrison. As I've suggested above this seems to be symptomatic of a 'love-hate' relationship with the Academy for, whether poets and poetry pundits like it or not, poetry needs the attention of the Academy in order to enjoy and maintain the high cultural prestige that is out of all proportion to the actual size of its readership. (In much the same way, the cultural position of Shakespeare has little to do with timeless genius and everything to do with a combination of subsidised theatre and examination syllabuses.) The poetry scene, in fact, wants the endorsement of the Academy but thinks it can avoid the fundamentals of contemporary critical enquiry: the exposing and upsetting of undeclared and unanalysed assumptions; the refusal to ignore the problematics of discourse brought into play when, for example, one gender writes in the persona of the other; or an alertness to questions of sexuality or nationality. And when the poetry scene finds that it can't have its cake, chew it and then spit it out, it goes firmly on the defensive. Poets, one is told haughtily, don't write about issues — they just invite us to share in the magic of language.

My point is that the current state of poetry and criticism, the love-hate relationship between the two, is based on a fundamental misconception about poetry: that the emotional and the imaginative can somehow be separated from the discursive. One of my reasons for writing this book is precisely because much of the most interesting and perhaps most important poetry of the last fifteen years is distinguished by a dominance of the discursive mode. I would even go so far as to argue that it is one of the major sources of energy in what William Scammell (1992, viii) rightly identified as "a flourishing contemporary poetic culture with something of the brio and ambition once thought lost to the novel and to more exciting poets overseas". What is equally undeniable is that brio and abundance have gone hand-in-hand with *apparent* fragmentation and incoherence. Alan Robinson (1988, ix) takes for granted "the radical destabilisation of British poetry at present"; and Neil Corcoran (1993, 196-203) draws persuasive connections in British poetry since 1970 between the destruction of political consensus, the decentralised nature of the poetry scene and the influence of postmodernism. It seems to me, however, that at any number of points since 1960 British poetry can be portrayed in varying degrees of destabilisation; and I intend to demonstrate that while there are indeed serious difficulties in imposing uniform coherence, much of the most interesting poetry since 1980 may be traced, wholly or partly, to a number of defining ideas. These ideas, I submit, amount to a reoriented consciousness about poetry and the poetry produced under their influence to events in that consciousness. It is the nature of this reoriented consciousness that I intend to sketch in the remainder of this Introduction.

The background to this reorientation is perhaps best understood by considering the work of Philip Larkin in which we can identify, albeit residually, broad areas of agreement about poetry and, by extension, about culture and nation. The relations between poet and subject, dialect and dominant pronunciation and speaking voice and poetic cadence can be said to represent the belief that while individuals may have varying backgrounds, attitudes and aspirations such differences can be smoothed into a common style and forgotten in a set of shared values. The allusion to the Laurence Olivier film of *Henry V* at the end of Larkin's poem 'The Whitsun Weddings' is a clear emblem of such a belief. On a more subtle level, *Henry V* is an imitation that invites the tears of the true patriot so that the allusion also stands for a conception of culture and nation in which artificiality is recognised and then deliberately ignored. This suggests that Larkin's place in the argument is more complex and, indeed, it can be argued that his continuing influence depends not only on the way his work exhibits the successes of an all-purpose social realist style but also on the degree to which it worries about the reality of consensus and the style's apparently easy rewards. 'The Whitsun Weddings' is, at a simple level, a 'traditional' English poem in which emotion is held in check by formal precision; but, on another, it is an updating of that tradition that both acknowledges and pays it debts with its references to "floatings of industrial froth", "a cooling tower" and "acres of dismantled cars". Larkin's scrupulous concern to portray the true circumstances and moment of inspiration and to acknowledge, however uneasily, the poet's connections with society at large can be described as the reorientation of poetic consciousness in embryo. His example was seized on by what Douglas Dunn has termed 'the middle generation' of poets — including himself, Tony Harrison and Seamus Heaney — as a spur and a permission to write poetry whose strengths are based on a literal 'truth to origins' (Astley [ed.] 1991, 129). The communities living in the shadow of Larkin's cooling tower, in the blighted urban pastoral of its industrial froth and dismantled cars — and, in Heaney's case, beyond the immediate metropolitan landscape — are explored as rich resources of affiliation, tradition and symbolism in their own right.

The poetry of Dunn, Harrison and Heaney rewrites the agreement that still existed for Larkin — and is symbolised by 'Church Going's' and 'Going, Going's' invitations to share in things that have effectively lost their meaning or disappeared — as a recognition that the individual and acts of culture are defined by issues of access, ownership, property and rights; and this recognition is, in turn, combined with some elements of the confessional mode's autobiographical poetic and cult of the authentic self. The initial reorientation that the early work of 'the middle generation' represents is, however, more than the same poetry but in regional accents; and to understand its continuing resonances we need to look briefly at the 1970s, bearing in mind as we do so a comment Sean O'Brien made about the relationship in his own poetry between realist and non-realist elements: "[W]hen things get weird, get strange, or the poem goes into overdrive, that seems to me to be *the earned surplus of all that realism*"(1992, 53 — my italics). The comment seems to me highly suggestive of the way in which the key collections of the 1970s — collections such as Douglas Dunn's *Barbarians* (1979), Geoffrey Hill's *Mercian Hymns* (1971), Tony Harrison's *The Loiners* and *From The School of Eloquence* (1970, 1978), Seamus Heaney's *Field Work* and *North* (1979, 1975) and Anne Stevenson's *Correspondences* (1974) — may be viewed in two ways. First, as events in an ongoing struggle to redefine the traditional canon of British poetry — traditional in the sense of being realist, lyric, social and largely novelistic — by subjecting it to maximum stress in order to admit previously excluded voices, histories, classes and genders. Second, as explorations of the fictional and the historical as modes of accommodation by which the outsider is able to gain access to an existing discourse or structure and preserve his sense of history, language and place as inherited struggles. The struggles to redefine the canon culminated in 1982 with the publication of *The Penguin Book of Contemporary British Poetry* edited by Blake Morrison and Andrew Motion. The anthology was careful to defuse the genuinely radical nature of much of the poetry it collected by denying any abrupt break with the past and proclaiming that the twenty poets it presented belonged "in the mainstream of British poetry". Similarly, the distinct areas of activity the anthology identified such as 'martianism' and narrative poetry were, with the exception of poetry from Northern Ireland, divorced from a wider cultural, political and social context by being subsumed under the vague appellation "the spirit of postmodernism".

By limiting its selections to twenty poets the Morrison/Motion anthology was inevitably partial but the fact that its editors felt unable to accommodate the work of Peter Reading — who had published five full collections between 1974 and 1981 — or Michael Hofmann — who had published widely in magazines since the mid-seventies — showed just how far their conception of a revised mainstream was being overtaken. The period 1982-1984 saw the following first collections appear: John Ash's *The Goodbyes*; Peter Didsbury's *The Butchers of Hull*; Michael Hofmann's *Nights in the Iron Hotel*; Sean O'Brien's *The Indoor Park*; Selima Hill's *Saying*

Hello at the Station; and Frank Kuppner's *A Bad Day For The Sung Dynasty*. The collections share a number of important characteristics.[1]

First, many of these first collections convey very strongly a sense of an ending, of being in a kind of cultural and historical 'afterwards' or in an unreal parallel universe which results in feelings that hover ambiguously between freedom and statelessness. John Ash in 'The Future Including The Past' (1982, 23) writes "My civilisation has ended, / and I liked it so much". Sean O'Brien in 'The Disappointment' and 'Walking' (1983, 22 and 10) describes a present where "From windy plinths The Great outstare / The disappointment of their will" and in which "We came late / To trespass on ourselves among the furniture". Peter Didsbury sets his poem 'Back of the House' in an "English garden" where "Language, fat and prone beneath her fountain / idly dispenses curling parchment notes, / her coveted, worthless licences to imitate" (1982, 20). Selima Hill uses an exotic and psychologically intense lyricism to suggest mysterious connections between home and family and the Gods and rituals of Ancient Egypt; and Frank Kuppner purports to give us a complete picture of an ancient civilisation but does so in such a way that forms and registers coexist as they never could as a civil reality. Finally, Michael Hofmann presents us with the ellipses and tentative statements of a world-view where the acute observations of a highly politicised imagination lead neither to commitment nor privileged judgement. It is not difficult to draw connections between this body of new poetry and the erosion of the cultural and political consensus that had been accelerating since the Seventies, and the backgrounds of some of the poets reinforce the feeling that such work is inexorably the product of its age. John Ash, for example, was born in Manchester but relocated to New York at the start of the 1980s; Frank Kuppner is a Scot of Polish extraction; and Michael Hofmann is an Anglo-German. Just as the work of these writers hovers between freedom and statelessness so, collectively, their first collections suggest something that is not quite fragmentation and not quite pluralism.

Second, in all these collections the dominant realist surface is being broken down, re-examined, reassembled and treated in ways that resist closure: that is, the contemplation of an object or the description of an event or a situation is not used to arrive at a conclusion such as Heaney's "The end of art is peace" (Morrison and Motion [eds.] 1982, 36) or Hugo Williams's observation that the butcher's "smile / Is the official seal on my marriage" (Morrison and Motion [eds.] 1982, 65). The new poets of the 1980s are more likely to end poems with lines like "*It depends what you mean*"

(O'Brien 1983, 54), "We jostle in the dark for a better view" (Hofmann 1983, 15) or "you heard someone call / for a light, and the door / of your room stood open"(Hill 1984, 26). Paradoxically, this resistance to traditional closure goes hand-in-hand with a highly developed narrative and fiction-making sensibility which is markedly different from the 'secret' or 'new narrative' school of Andrew Motion or James Fenton. Narrative becomes a way of exploring the arbitrariness of the imagination but it also connects with the sense of 'afterwards' identified earlier. The narratives and structures of history are, in a sense, 'running on empty', deprived of a clear destination. It is a perception that underlies, for example, the prevalence of maps in O'Brien's poetry or Michael Hofmann's "Fifty years late, you finish *Love on the Dole*"(1983, 48).

Third, as the Hofmann quote might suggest, narrative also connects with an aspect of all the collections under discussion which many commentators would type as characteristically postmodern: the aestheticisation of history and, by extension, cultural and political struggle. Peter Didsbury looks at a photograph of workers leaving a shipyard at the beginning of the century in 'Building the Titanic' (1982, 18): "We work a black change on you //... you are free, now, to consort like wolves on the snow". Didsbury's note to the poem invokes Keats's 'Ode on a Grecian Urn' and terms the photograph "a 'cold industrial'". In his prose poem 'The Building' (1982, 43-4) John Ash surveys some of the great cities of the world and reinvents them:

> And these are no longer centres of government, military operation or bureaucracy. They exist solely to be enjoyed, — places of rose-bushes, vines and lawless amusements, gentle and barbarous towns ...

Michael Hofmann's 'Shapes of Things' (1983, 39), which with its Wellsian echoes promises apocalyptic warnings about the future, uses the banality of its opening line "We are living in the long shadow of the Bomb" as the impetus for a narrative of jouissance of cultural signs which mocks the possibility of such a function for art. The poem is also typical of a common strand in poetry since 1982: the way the self and experience are indivisible from the discourses of culture and the media. The aestheticising impulse towards culture, history and politics is perhaps typical of a period when in both Britain and the USA 'nation' was reinvented as an aesthetic construct. However, it also has a particular meaning in terms of the relation of the poetry of the 1980s to that of the 1970s.

Sean O'Brien has said of Simon Armitage that his poetry "proceeds very confidently from the assumption that there is no battle to be won about where he comes from — he is a generation on from Tony Harrison — this battle has been fought and won and it's not something he has to concern himself with" (Interview 1992, 62). We might say that rather than *wishing* to be the poet his father reads, Armitage simply gets on with the job of *being* that poet. Another younger poet, W.N. Herbert, goes so far as to cast doubts on the continuing, wider relevance of the whole project of 'the middle generation':

> I remember once in the Poetry Workshop ... there were several poets who were strongly interested in this, with Tony Harrison for example, with the whole sort of angst of becoming middle class through education. I never felt any angst about it! I never felt there was any sundering whatsoever.
> (Interview 1990, 90)

Herbert's remarks suggest another way in which history may be over and poets living in an 'afterwards': the poet is released from the previous generation's struggle over rights and is free to follow the dictates of his imagination. But if the poet has no battle to win about where he comes from, the structural problems of British culture and society still remain and, many would argue, have been made worse in the last ten to fifteen years. If we are not to accuse the new poets of the 1980s of complacency and / or wilful ignorance, we need a clearer sense of what comes after the 'battle'.

A glimpse is given by W.N. Herbert's poem in synthetic or dictionary Scots 'Mappamundi' which was originally written c.1983:

> Eh've wurkt oot a poetic map o thi warld.
>
> Vass tracts o land ur penntit reid tae shaw
> Englan kens naethin aboot um. Ireland's
> bin shuftit tae London, whaur
> oafficis o thi Poetry Sock occupeh fehv
> squerr mile ...
> (1994, 123)

At first sight, the poem seems to be making a straightforward satirical complaint about English cultural imperialism and a radical rebuttal of it by being written in Scots. The last line of the poem — "In this scenario Eh'm a bittern stoarm aff Ulm" — which seems to return to a position of marginalisation and cultural impoverishment is, in fact, doing something more complex. After all, to have worked a poetic map of the world as this poem has is no great feat; such a map, it might be argued, is obvious to anyone. What the poem satirises is the complete arbitrariness of culture and the resultant impossibility of consensus and what its last line inscribes — in embryo — is a poetry of displacement in which displacement is recognised as inevitable but not disabling. If Ireland can be "shuftit tae London" then any cultural origin or position is available and equally valid. Thus, Herbert feels free to write in both English and Scots just as Simon Armitage feels free to use whatever models — English or American — seem appropriate. Poets originating from the areas that "Englan kens naethin aboot" are not going to waste time and energy opening an argument with that nation and its ignorance.

This perhaps sheds some light on the fourth area of commonality between these first collections: a consciousness of and engagement with European culture and history. On one level, this can be understood as a very late, positive feedback with modernism. Peter Didsbury's *The Butchers of Hull* pays homage to Paul Klee and Max Ernst (11, 28). Sean O'Brien's syntax and narrative sense are clearly indebted to Conrad and *The Indoor Park* also refers to Matisse — albeit in an ironical manner — and contains an ode to that characteristic product of the Bauhaus, the anglepoise lamp. Selima Hill's use of Ancient Egyptian gods has clear parallels with High Modernism's use of myth and ritual; and Michael Hofmann's work is visually informed by Expressionist painters of the Weimar Republic. Such references may seem more than a little paradoxical in the context of the quiet but determined anti-modernism symbolised by a poem like Simon Armitage's 'It Ain't What You Do It's What It Does to You' (1989, 20) but, on another level, the residue of modernism is characteristic of the period code of postmodernism. Hutcheon (1988 passim) argues that "the presence of the past" is a sign of "a critical revisiting, an ironic dialogue with the past of both art and society" and of an "ironic rethinking of history" (4, 5). It is one of the many contradictions of postmodernism that it can both aestheticise the past *and* mount a critique of it. Similarly, it can both use modernism as a model of permission for the contemporary to seek out new forms *and* comment on the unreality of its legacy of art's non-engagement. Alan Robinson (1988, 52) interprets Michael Hofmann's references to Weimar art in his poems about 1980s Britain as suggestions that the present is "a more extreme version of the crisis in capitalism of the inter-war years"; and it seems likely that the residue of modernism in other new poets of the 1980s points to a shared sense of crisis. The presence of postmodernism can be felt in other aspects of their work. Edward Larrissy (1990, 177-9) makes a persuasive case for understanding postmodernism in psychological terms, arguing that its subject is typically "the erosion of the boundaries between the objective and the subjective" and "the erosion of the difference between 'inside and 'outside'" (177) and that, as a consequence, "organising principles ... [are] treated with a certain ironic levity" (179). A title like *The Indoor Park* clearly fits with such an analysis as does O'Brien's poem 'In the Head' (1983, 35) where the blurring of fantasy and reality is mirrored in the intermingling of discourses of desire and politics. Peter Didsbury's poem 'The Web' (1982, 50) which I discuss in greater detail in Chapter Three presents the individual as a node on a species of linguistic and historical 'internet' while 'During a Storm' (1982, 16) seems to reject any distinction between inner and outer: "I'm the cause of all this. Of all I see". Similarly, Larrissy's identification of different organizing principles can be seen in *The Goodbyes's* numerous references to music; in Frank Kuppner's reinterpretation of and expansion on images in a book of Chinese paintings; and in Michael Hofmann's assertion — if one can call it that! — in the title poem of his first collection, "We are fascinated by our own anaesthesia, / our inability to function".

To return to Sean O'Brien's remark, all these aspects may be considered as 'the earned surplus' of the realism of 'the middle generation'. However, as such an image suggests, there was not a radical break and if British poetry throughout the 1980s can be seen incorporating aspects of postmodernism, it can also be seen enacting what one critic has termed "a characteristically British refusal to eschew realism. This has meant that postmodernism has not been used as an excuse to disavow political responsibility or the need to comprehend experience. So even John Ash and Ian McMillan — the most thorough [of] postmodernists ... — display a powerful social awareness and sense of place"(Gregson 1993, 78). The sense of a dialogue taking place between realism and postmodernism is brilliantly exemplified by Michael Hofmann's poem 'Eclogue' (1986, 29) which begins

> Industry undressing in front of Agriculture —
> not a pretty sight. The subject for one
> of those allegorical Victorian sculptures.
> An energetic mismatch

and concludes

> A quarry is an inverted cathedral: witchcraft,
> a steeple of air sharpened and buried in the ground.
> — All around these dangerous sites, sheep graze,
> horned and bleating like eminent Victorians.

"Dangerous sites" refers both to the ruins of the post-industrial landscape and to traditional cultural discourses. The former symbolise the destructive, dehumanizing power of industrial and technological advance; and the latter mask the true face and consequences of that power. Reading cultural signs in this way is typical of many poets of the 1980s and 1990s and so too are 'Eclogue's' "energetic mismatch" of discourses and its imaginative "witchcraft". The lack of an identifiable, populated locale or of an easily identifiable speaker is also typical. The inhabitants of the early poems of Hofmann, Didsbury, O'Brien and Hill, for example, are usually isolated or separated individuals, found in their rooms or their own heads, at their desks or on solitary excursions; or silent halves of couples. It is as if, as the 1980s opened, a new generation of poets no longer felt obliged or, perhaps, no longer felt able to write as citizens of 'the society of the poem'. As the decade progressed this resulted not only in the voice speaking a poem being left open to question but to that voice being placed, as it were, in inverted commas. Who is speaking in, say, Jo Shapcott's poem 'Phrasebook' (Hulse, Kennedy and Morley [eds.] 1993, 205) which mixes excerpts of an intimate individual narrative with TV news flashes from the Gulf War and lines from an old-fashioned travellers' phrasebook? A poem which begins "I'm standing here inside my skin" and ends "Let me pass please. I am an Englishwoman" moves from apparent confessional authority to a bewildering assertion of the speaker's complete fictionality. The reader is most emphatically not being invited to share in an easily recognisable and commodifiable experience but to explore something that cannot be smoothed into any consensus about the common life. The artful confusion of discourses in the poem invites the reader to speculate on the relation between the impossibility of a bourgeois poetry of commodified confession and the uncertainty of Britain's rôle in the post-imperial age. The continuities provided by ideas of nation have been replaced by the flickering, contingent realities of the media and for many poets the term 'energetic mismatch' would also describe the way the world and the individual's experience of it are formed by and / or mediated through an almost infinite number of information systems, linguistic or otherwise. It is a conception that informs the poetry of, amongst others, Carol Ann Duffy, Glyn Maxwell and Peter Reading. Indeed the work of Peter Reading offers an extreme but socially comprehensive vision of Britain in an age when consensus seems to have been irrevocably eroded and sustaining 'meta-narratives' of community, culture and nation placed under erasure.

Note

1. The changing landscape of British and Irish poetry at the start of the 1980s is further exemplified by the appearance of the following collections: Nuala Ní Dhomhnaill: *An Dealg Droighin* (1981); Paul Durcan: *Jesus, Break His Fall* (1980); Eavan Boland: *Night Feed* (1982); John Hartley Williams: *Hidden Identities* (1982); Paul Durcan: *Ark Of The North* (1982); Duncan Bush: *Aquarium* (1983); Helen Dunmore: *The Apple Fall* (1983); Grace Nichols: *i is a long memoried woman* (1983); Matthew Sweeney: *A Round House* (1983); Paul Durcan: *Jumping The Train Tracks With Angela* (1983); David Dabydeen: *Slave Song* (1984); Tom Leonard: *Intimate Voices* (1984); Paula Meehan: *Return And No Blame* (1984).

1. Voice and Ownership:
Ideas of Individual Voice and Dominant Culture from 'Middle Generation' to 'New Generation'

As its title is intended to indicate, this chapter deals with the way that contemporary British poetry — by which I mean poetry that began to be published from the late 1960s onwards — is defined by a process of 'occupation' by which the work of previously marginalised or excluded constituencies has come to dominate; and the way this process has meant the working through of particular conflicts between the voice of the individual and cultural norms. The conflicts arise from a taking for granted of what Seamus Heaney (1980, 43) calls "a connection between the core of a poet's speaking voice and the core of his poetic voice, between his original accent and his discovered style"; and a simultaneous recognition, in Derek Walcott's words that "when you enter a language, you enter a kind of choice which contains in it the political history of the language, the imperial width of the language, the fact that you are either subjugated by the language or you have to dominate it. So language is not a place of retreat, it's not a place of escape, it's not even a place of resolution. It's a place of struggle" (in O'Brien 1990).

Alvarez's 1962 anthology *The New Poetry* is one place where ideas of what I term 'voice and ownership' appear in embryo form. Alvarez's introduction characterised the history of twentieth century English poetry as "a series of negative feedbacks": the Modernists against the Georgians, the Apocalyptic poets of the 1940s against Auden, and the Movement against the Apocalyptics and the worst excesses of the Modernists:

> All three negative feedbacks work, in their different ways, to preserve the idea that life in England goes on much as it always has, give or take a few minor changes in the class system ... [The] concept of gentility still reigns supreme. And gentility is a belief that life is always more or less orderly, people more or less polite, their emotions and habits more or less decent and more or less controllable ...

Poetry, in this model, is therefore complicit with the status quo and, by implication, debates about style, form and authenticity are a series of systematic evasions of the fundamental structural problems of English society. The seed had been cast. If poetry is not about order or decency or control then it becomes increasingly difficult to conceive of it dealing with the eternal, the lyric or the moral. Or, to put it another way: if the eternal, the lyric and the moral are tainted by an association with the status quo then the poet's first subject becomes the language he thinks and feels and writes in; the production of poetic voice and who owns the means of its production. This shift was very explicitly re-formulated by poets of 'the middle generation' of Douglas Dunn, Tony Harrison and Seamus Heaney and their contemporaries — a generation who were coming to poetry around the time of *The New Poetry*'s first publication — as a quarrel and a struggle and in precisely those terms. In what follows I shall examine how 'the middle generation' brought this quarrel and struggle, the issues of voice and ownership, into the mainstream and made them one of the fundamental subjects of post-war British poetry; and I shall go on to suggest that the work of younger poets enacts, as a result of that generation's example, not a continuity with tradition but with a set of ideas about culture, language, poetry and authority and authenticity. I shall, where appropriate, inform my discussion with comments on and models of colonial and post-colonial writing taken from, amongst others, Edward Said, Frantz Fanon and Derek Walcott.

In a lecture given in 1990 and subsequently published as 'The Topical Muse', Douglas Dunn characterised his generation's engagement with poetry as follows:

> It is noticeable that the demography of poetry has changed in such a way as to make it look as if the energy of the language has been over-refined at the posher end of the social scale. It would be wrong to generalise too self-confidently on this issue, but the 'middle generation' is populated by more writers from Ireland, Scotland and the North of England than could have been predicted in 1944 when the Education Acts entered the statute books.
> (Astley [ed.] 1991, 129-132)

Dunn goes on to argue that the 'middle generation's' members "share a perception of how their voices are not those of the proprietorial language of the literature to which they have devoted themselves". It is this perception that animates much of Tony Harrison's poetry, particularly a poem like 'Them & [uz]' (1984, 122-4) which rediscovers Cockney Keats and the fact that "Wordsworth's *matter / water* are full rhymes"; and the following lines from Seamus Heaney's 'The Ministry of Fear' (1980, 129-130) which Dunn's lecture quotes approvingly:

I tried to write about the sycamores
And innovated a South Derry rhyme
With *hushed* and *lulled* full chimes for *pushed* and *pulled.*
Those hobnailed boots from beyond the mountain
Were walking, by God, all over the fine
Lawns of elocution.

The poem first appeared in Heaney's collection *North* (1975) and
the last line of the extract connects with Dunn's poem 'The Come-on'
from his 1979 collection *Barbarians* (13-14), where a dominant
"culture of connivance / of 'authority'" is seen as a walled garden
which might contain those same "fine lawns":

To have watched the soul of my people
        Fingered by the callous
Enlivens the bitter ooze from my grudge.
        Mere seepage from 'background'
Takes over, blacking out what intellect
        Was nursed by school or book
Or has accrued by questioning the world.
        Enchanting, beloved texts
Searched in for a generous mandate for
        Believing who I am,
What I have lived and felt, might just as well
        Not exist when the vile
Come on with their 'coals in the bath' stories
        or mock at your accent.
Even now I am an embarrassment
        To myself, my candour.
Listen now to the 'professional classes'
        Renewing claims to 'rights',
Possession of land, ownership of work,
        Decency of 'standards'.
In the bleep-bleep of versicles, leisure novels,
        Black traffic of Oxbridge —
Books and bicycles, the bile of success —
        Men dressed in prunella
Utter credentials and their culture rules us,
        A culture of connivance,
Of 'authority', arts of bland recoveries.
        Where, then, is 'poetry'?
Brothers, they say we have no culture.
        We are of the wrong world,
Our level is the popular, the media,
        The sensational columns,
Unless we enter through a narrow gate

In a wall they have built
To join them in the 'disinterested tradition'
Of tea, of couplets dipped
In sherry and the decanted, portentous remark.
Therefore, we'll deafen them
With the dull staccato of our typewriters.
     . . .

'The Come-on' can be interestingly and usefully glossed by a reading of an editorial entitled 'The Grudge' which Dunn contributed to *Stand* magazine some four years earlier which outlines the special predicament of the working class writer: "His work is ... directed at an audience who do not receive it; instead, it is received by an audience of those he is against". The working class writer's dilemma is that he is writing a literature of revolt but doing so in a bourgeois discourse i.e. 'Literature' itself. As the poem asks, "Where, then, is 'poetry'?". 'The Grudge' argues that this dilemma may be negotiated by "commitment ... the idea under which a working-class poet can organise the sundry circumstances which belong to him and which cohere in the form of beliefs about the world". This not only keeps "the grudge intact and pure"; it enables him to redress the 'coals in the bath' stories and oppose the 'disinterested tradition' with another that is passionately *interested* in what 'The Hunched' calls (1986, 47) calls "the lives of other people" that "will not leave me". This double commitment gives the poet strength to struggle to recover "poetry as the vision of its own classless society and not as the instrument of class ascendancy" (Editorial 1975, 4-6). It would be wrong to assume however that Dunn's poem and editorial are interchangeable polemics. What makes 'The Come-on' such a complex and interesting poem and gives it a centrality in this chapter is that Dunn supplies, if I can so put it, the political dimension complacently glossed by Alvarez and so powerfully present for Walcott.

The poem can in fact be read as a compressed version of some of the arguments Edward Said advances in his study *Culture and Imperialism* (1993). For Said, culture has two central meanings. One is "all those practices, like the arts of description, communication, and representation, that have relative autonomy from the economic, social and political realms and that often exist in aesthetic forms, one of whose principal aims is pleasure". The other meaning is that of "'a concept that includes a refining and elevating element, each society's reservoir of the best that has been known and thought as Matthew Arnold put it in the 1860s'". Here, certainly, is the culture of "Enchanting, beloved texts / Searched in for a generous mandate".

However, Said argues that the Arnoldian meaning of culture also carries with it connotations of national identity and superiority and in this account becomes bound up with imperialism. Imperialism Said defines as "'the practice, the theory and the attitudes of a dominating metropolitan centre ruling a distant territory'". It is this aspect of culture that the speaker of 'The Come-on' encounters when he asserts bitterly that the "enchanting, beloved texts ... might just as well / Not exist"; and the next lines of the poem make clear that one consequence of this 'doubleness' of culture is a conflict within the individual himself which mirrors the struggle between the coloniser and the colonised, the oppressor and the oppressed. The writing of the poem and the voicing of the sentiments within it become 'embarrassments' because revenge and complicity uneasily co-exist.

It is this that also prompts the question "Where, then, is 'poetry'?". The poetry in question is partly that of "couplets dipped / In sherry" but also, more crucially, the poetry which the young Scottish poet W.N. Herbert has called "fundamentally anarchic", possessing "dangerous aspects, aspects of play, aspects of moral structuring — whatever people dread"(Interview 1990, 89-95). It is also the poetry which Joseph Brodsky, in his inaugural address as Poet Laureate of the USA (1991/2, 4-9), sees as synonymous with society's evolutionary potential. 'The Come-on' ends with a call to what Said terms resistance. The culture that underwrites and promotes imperialism also, inevitably, produces resistance to that imperialism. The process that leads from identification with "enchanting, beloved texts" to a resistance of the values they embody and impose can be best understood by reference to the model of colonial and post-colonial culture outlined by Frantz Fanon in *The Wretched of the Earth*, first published in 1961. Fanon models the cultural consciousness of the colonial subject in three "levels" or "phases". The first phase is a "period of unqualified assimilation" in which the native intellectual "gives proof that he has assimilated the culture of the occupying power. His writings correspond point by point with those of his opposite numbers in the mother country" (1985, 178-9). This corresponds with the opening section of Dunn's poem when "a generous mandate" still seems possible. In the second phase, the native comes to realise that oppression goes hand-in-hand with "the best that has been known and thought" and seeks to counter this with a rediscovery of the cultural and linguistic forms that imperialism devalues, ignores or suppresses altogether. Fanon adds, however, that this identification with native traditions is only superficial and is, in fact, as disabling as the previous period of assimilation; or in the words of 'The Come-on', "Mere seepage from 'background' takes over". The third and final phase Fanon terms "the fighting phase" (1985, 180-1). In this the native comes to understand that while cultural archaeology is valuable, it is complicit with views of the people as uncivilised and backward: "The truths of a nation are in the first place its realities"(1985, 180-1). The existence of a nation and its people is only substantiated "in the fight which the people wage against the forces of occupation" (1985, 179). This corresponds with the final section of the poem which calls for deafening typewriters and goes on to imagine infiltration and eventual entry into the garden and the tearing down of its walls.

An important part of the process of resistance is the production of what Said calls "counter-structures" or "counter-narratives". In terms of 'The Come-on' this does not only mean writing the true versions of "'coals in the bath' stories" but also appropriating and 'occupying' the discourses of the oppressor. I would argue that it is this that underlies the group of words and phrases that appear in quotation marks. These are words and phrases that have been appropriated by the "culture of connivance" and given class-specific meanings which are bound up with Said's second definition of culture as the means of transmitting and reinforcing superiority over others. Quite simply, they have become corrupted into components of a discourse of cultural hypocrisy. The project of redressing this imbalance of meaning explains why much of the poetry of 'the middle generation' can be described as Adamic writing in which naming is at once a re-appropriation and a revelation of networks of correspondences, meanings and relationships. The placing of words such as 'background' and terms such as 'coals in the bath' in quotation marks connects with the way a character in Walcott's poem 'The Schooner *Flight*' calls himself a "nigger". In a valuable essay called 'The Sigh of History' James McCorkle (1994, 106) draws attention to "the complex irony of naming [oneself] with the language of colonials' scorn" which "refuses to allow a forgetting a history ... and recalls immediately [one's] condition". It becomes another way of keeping the grudge intact and pure. Placing words in inverted commas — particularly 'authority' or 'disinterested tradition' — is also an enactment of 'The Come-on's' "honesty is cunning" and of the "revenge theft" which Roland Barthes advocates in his essay *Sade-Fourier-Loyola*:

In fact, today, there is no language site outside bourgeois

ideology: our language comes from it, returns to it, remains
closed up in it. The only possible rejoinder is neither con-
frontation nor destruction, but only theft: fragment the old
text of culture, science and literature and change its features
according to formulae of disguise, as one disguises stolen
goods.
    (1976, 10)

'The Come-on' remains, along with a later trio of poems on
Scottish literature — 'Green Breeks', 'John Wilson in Greenock
1786' and 'Tannahill' (1986, 177-192) — one of Douglas Dunn's
clearest poetic statements of precisely what is at stake in the rela-
tionship between a working class writer and the dominant culture
and its discourses and forms. It stands almost as a kind of manifesto
or 'guerilla handbook' which holds in a particular tension a pessimism
of the intellect and an optimism of the will. 'The Come-on's'
"cunning", like Barthes's "theft", "disguise" and "stolen goods",
seems to underlie the fact that Dunn's poetry — like Tony Harrison's
and Seamus Heaney's — never strays very far from the formal.
Indeed, the Barthian model becomes explicit in Dunn's poem 'The
Disguise' (1986, 96) in which "the finest insult" is to use formal
prosody and not free verse. But the 'finest insults' are clearly not
without their price. Dunn has spoken of finding that "I want verse
in my work all the time, and fight against it before it gets out of
hand" (Interview 1990, 12-13) and throughout his work one can
detect a tension between the dictates of the individual imagination
and what 'Green Breeks' (1986, 177) calls "the quicklime ... of
ordered literature". The tension is a productive one and underwrites
the enactment in many of Dunn's best poems of what he has termed,
in reference to Larkin, an "earned lyricism":

> One minute he's talking about an awful pie, and the next he
> walks along a railway platform in Sheffield and sees 'the
> ranged / Joining and parting lines reflect a strong / Unhin-
> dered moon'. How many poets since 1950 or so have deserved
> the right to put a word like 'unhindered' before the classic
> property of 'moon'? It's this idea of lyricism being *earned* that
> should attract our attention. I know it can sound risible, but
> it's that swift transition from something as banal as a bad pie
> to the moon that in its eccentric, unnerving way, guarantees
> Larkin's lyricism as true.
>   (Interview 1991, 10)

But why must lyricism, post 1950 or so, be earned and be seen to be earned? And *how* is it to be earned? Regarding the *why*, there would seem to be a number of coincident and/or symbiotic issues concerning the English language and English poetic language which, for Dunn, are unavoidable. First, there is what he has defined as "the post-imperial status of the English language" (Interview 1990) which perhaps rewrites his assertion in 'The Topical Muse' that "the demography of poetry has changed". Second, there is the sense that when any contemporary poet uses English he does so conscious that, as Heaney writes of Larkin (1980, 164) "what accrues in the language is not 'a golden and stinking blaze', not the rank and fermenting composts of philology and history, but the bright sense of words worn clean in literate conversation". Third, there is a particular manifestation of self-consciousness in contemporary poetry which Dunn, in an illuminating essay on Norman MacCaig, calls "the sense that poetry has of itself ... as devotional ... What it comes down to is the love and concern which poetry bestows on its subjects" (1990, 68). What all these statements engage with is a sense of the English language losing its natural authority and evocative power and of the corresponding need of poets to work harder in the language, to remake it as an active instrument. The English language has become a place of diminished energy because it is has dissipated itself in "arts of bland recoveries" and, more importantly, because it is now the language of an historical 'afterwards', a period which may be described as a coda or postscript to either the end of Empire, the collapse of the post-war consensus or the project of the Enlightenment depending on one's perspective. It is this consciousness that lies behind Heaney's estimate of Larkin and behind Dunn's comment in 'The Local' (1986, 169) that "we stand / In this armpit of English vernacular, / Hopelessly in touch with where we are". What is left is the quality of attention focused through the language, "the love and concern".

How lyricism is to be earned is just as complex. It begins with the subjects the poet chooses — working class life and industrial land-scapes — none of which are naturally associated with the lyric and other traditional forms. Such subjects set the poet — and his audience — a kind of test. Dunn has remarked (Interview 1990) that "What most poets want, I suspect, is the enlivened bravery that pulls poetry even more directly from life and experience and con-viction, passion and rage, not less. The problem of candour is one of psychological and social tact as well as technical". Neil Corcoran (1992, 213) quotes Seamus Heaney making a similar remark that he wanted "to take the English lyric and make it eat stuff that it has never eaten before ... and make it still an English lyric". The combination of tact, bravery and challenge is at its subtlest in a poem such as Dunn's 'The Butterfly House' (1985, 10) (from the book *Elegies* written after the death of his first wife) where the poet, looking round his house, sees not only the "objects implicated in my love" but also "the slave trade in its raw materials". "The properties of the world", the poem continues, "make a world, a viewpoint of the heart".

The dual consciousness and even wider 'perspectivism' of 'The Butterfly House' can also be discerned in Dunn's first collection *Terry Street* (1969). 'Close of Play' is a suburban elegy at nightfall which opens with a simple, lyric observation:

> Cricketers have the manners of ghosts,
> Wandering in white on the tended ground.
>
> They go in now, walking in twos and threes.
> This sight is worth a week of evenings.
>   (1986, 23-5)

The implication is that a week's watching has somehow 'earned' such a moment; but it is one that is progressively undercut as the poem proceeds. First, we get a portrayal of "Behind the trees, toughminded fops // In sports cars roar like a mini-Bacchus" which then modulates into an image of banal suburban order and contentment, through images of wild nature, until at the end of the poem "The golf course // Becomes a desert, a place without manners. / The rapists gather under hedges and bridges". At its simplest level, the poem opposes poetic fantasy with everyday reality but it also demonstrates how, through such an opposition, lyricism can be earned. The poem does not end with a lyrical disclosure but opens with one whose neat order is then simultaneously subverted and paradoxically guaranteed by the admission of the banality and disorder that coexist with it and within it. It is this that Dunn has called "a right, true measure of vulgarity" (Interview 1991, 11). Co-existence is crucial to the issue of voice and ownership, for the poem criticises its own initial lyricism by seeking to include all the lives, events and agendas that occur during and after its apprehension. No one person or class can lay claim, finally, to ownership of "the gap before the night" or the following darkness; and the opening image of the cricketers, for all its chilly perfection, is revealed as complacent, complicit in a fiction of order.

'The House Next Door' (1986, 59) suggests that the relationship between the individual voice and the accepted norms of language is not only difficult per se but is further complicated by the poet's own ambivalent feelings. The house stands for a whole world or class perspective where "garage is pronounced gar*age* / strawberries never known as strawbs, but *fraises*":

> Why do I love them, that milieu not mine,
> The youngest, laughingly, 'last of the line'?

> No answers. They have given me
> Too much for answering.

However, Dunn's poetry also offers the possibility that the rift between those who speak in their own voice and those who are perceived to own culture and language need not remain an open wound. 'The Harp of Renfrewshire' (1986, 160), subtitled "contemplating a map", looks at how that wound might at least be partially salved by an active relationship with the individual voice's origins in a particular place, with one's personal vision or what Seamus Heaney (1980, 17) calls "omphalos, meaning the navel, and hence the stone that marked the centre of the world":

> Annals of the trilled R, gently stroked L,
> Lamenting O of local literature,
> Open, on this, their one-page book, a still
> Land-language chattered in a river's burr.

> Small-talk of herdsmen, rural argument —
> These soft disputes drift over river-meadows,
> A darg of conversations, a verbal scent —
> Tut-tutted discourse, time of day, word-brose.

Language is seen and heard here at the centre of life, perhaps even *as* the centre of life. Dunn's native shire is revisited as the place where his voice is both made and sustained and where language remains in touch with its derivations. We might note here that "brose" is a dish of oatmeal with boiling water or milk poured on it — simple but slow-burning fuel; and that "darg" is a dialect word for 'day's work' but is also, as Geoffrey Hill's 'Mercian Hymn XXV' (1985, 129) reminds us, a primitive forge. The redemptive revisitation and re-identification of 'The Harp of Renfrewshire' runs through Dunn's collection *Northlight* (1988) which celebrates his return to Scotland:

> Innermost dialect
> Describes Fife's lyric hills,

Life, love and intellect
In lucid syllables.

    ★ ★ ★

In the hollows of home
I find life, love and ground
And intimate welcome:
With you, and these, I'm bound
  To history.
           'At Falkland Place' (1988, 1-2)

The identification of voice with the very soil of a particular place allows us to follow the voice and ownership argument from Douglas Dunn to Seamus Heaney. Of all the members of Dunn's 'middle generation', it is Heaney who explores the difficult but ultimately redemptive power of such an identification most deeply. His poetry, like Dunn's, is marked by memories and consciousness of the injuries done by the "culture of connivance" and its "bland recoveries" but it also writes out the debt to that culture that enables the primacy of a different order of experience to be asserted:

> I ... knew the whole of Keats's ode 'To Autumn' but the only line that was luminous then was "To bend with apples the mossed cottage trees", because my uncle had a small orchard where the old apple trees were sleeved in a soft green moss ... The literary language, the civilized utterance from the classic canon of English poetry, was a kind of force-feeding. It did not delight us by reflecting our experience; it did not re-echo our own speech in formal and surprising arrangements. Poetry lessons, in fact, were rather like catechism lessons: official inculcations of hallowed formulae that were somehow expected to stand us in good stead in the adult life that stretched out ahead.
>   (1980, 26)

Heaney here gives a detailed account of how the gentility, politeness, decency, control and goodness described by Alvarez are transmitted, of how the dominant culture offers one mode of being as absolute when it is, in fact, merely one choice out of many. The process of inculcation gives the individual a divided cultural inheritance that can lead to various forms of alienation and dissociation; or as 'The Badgers' (1979, 25) asks rhetorically: "How perilous is it to chose / not to love the life we're shown?". The point that it is our local speech that first shows us life is made explicitly in the relatively minor poem 'The Guttural Muse' (1979, 28). The poet, at his "window over the hotel car park", listens to the sounds of the summer night and the voices of young people leaving the disco-theque: "Their voices rose up thick and comforting". Heaney has said (Haffenden 1981, 58) that the poem grew out of "a vision of the kind of life I had in the Fifties, going to dances and so on, and I felt the redemptive quality of the dialect, of the guttural, of the illiterate self". Poet and poetry must find a comfortable place between what 'Song' (1979, 56) calls "the mud-flowers of dialect / And the imortelles of perfect pitch". "The life we're shown" — local, primal — exists as a kind of 'deep grammar' but because language is not abstract and works by association and correspondence the relationship between illiterate and literate, guttural and refined, is always being remade.

Local speech and place of origin as the foundations of a set of choices opposed to the dominant culture inevitably have meanings peculiar to an Irish and Northern Irish context. Many twentieth century Anglophone Irish writers share a sense of a cultural and linguistic identity crisis, a crisis stated explicitly in Chapter Five of James Joyce's *A Portrait of the Artist as a Young Man* (1916) when Stephen reflects on a conversation with his English Jesuit teacher:

> The language in which we are speaking is his before it is mine. How different are the words *home, Christ, ale, master,* on his lips and on mine! I cannot speak or write these words without unrest of spirit. His language, so familiar and so foreign, will always be for me an acquired speech. I have not made or accepted its words. My voice holds them at bay. My soul frets in the shadow of his language.
> (*EJJ*, 1972, 200)

Just how different the word 'home' sounds is demonstrated in the scene that opens the chapter where Stephen breakfasts at home before classes: "The yellow dripping had been scooped out like a boghole" and someone is asked to fetch him water for washing with the words "Fill it out, you, Maggy" (1972, 188). Here is English spoken as a 'familiar and foreign' language; and here too is country — rural and national — at the forefront of consciousness. The identity crisis not only a matter of negotiating, in Heaney's terms, the conflicts between "South Derry rhyme" and "elocution": Stephen's "soul frets" because to be Irish and think, speak and write in English is to become aware, sooner or later, of the lost Gaelic past and the oppression of Ireland by England, and of Irish by English. Just as Dunn has spoken of "the post imperial status of the English language" so Heaney has made a similar diagnosis in relation to Ireland generally and to 'the troubles' specifically:

What we have is the tail-end of a struggle in a province
between territorial piety and imperial power.
(1980, 57)

The local and the regional, far from being remote from or irrele-
vant to a larger context of economic and political struggle, in fact,
give imaginative access to it because they keep the writer in touch
with the roots and history of language and the collective experience
of its speakers; or, in the words of Frantz Fanon, "men of culture
take their stand in the field of history" (1985, 168): Fanon's words
were originally written in the context of an unresolved struggle and
Heaney's portrayal of Irish history, past and present, also makes
plain that once the writer positions himself historically he takes up
a role in a continuing process; and that the 'voice and ownership'
issue becomes even more complex. First, in seeking a way of writing
that preserves "the redemptive quality ... of the illiterate self" the
poet runs the risk of replicating the imperial project, the subjection
of piety by power, because the illiterate must inevitably be fitted into
the literate and the formal. The poet risks alienating himself from
the sources that sustain his inspiration. Second, if the local and the
guttural give the poet access to and standing in Fanon's "field of
history" then the resultant sense of commitment and responsibility
lead to a poetry that is public and universal, responsive to present
imperatives. Again the poet risks distancing himself irretrievably
from his roots but, more crucially, his new rôle puts those roots to
the ultimate test. For example, can a voice that is authentic, faithful
to origins, address the public and the universal convincingly? Can
the local and the guttural 'compete' in this larger arena?

It is in an attempt to explore and answer such questions that
Heaney's poetry often inscribes exhilaration in the individual
creative power and a corresponding recognition of the real status of
that power; and works through a dialectic of empowerment and
subjection. 'The Toome Road' (1979, 15) makes an explicit
presentation of "territorial piety" usurped or infringed by "imperial
power". The speaker of the poem meets early one morning a convoy
of armoured cars: "How long were they approaching down my roads
/ As if they owned them?" The answer might be 'since the time of
Cromwell at least' and the image of "headphoned soldiers standing
up in turrets" implies that imperial power can be seen in terms of
phallic intrusion. But the very fact that the question is asked at all
suggests a kind of unworldliness, a condition of historical ignorance
or naivety. The line "The whole country was sleeping" demands to
be read both locally and nationally:

Whom should I run to tell
Among all of those with their back doors on the latch
For the bringer of bad news, that small-hours visitant
Who, by being expected, might be kept distant?

These lines imply that the local is essentially powerless because it is
not a culture per se but a collection of customs and, to quote from
Fanon again, "custom is always the deterioration of culture" (1985,
10). The ancient nation has been reduced to the "rights of way" at
the beginning of the poem. It is a point made graphically at the end
of the poem, when the poet (as opposed, I think, to the speaker of
the poem) steps forward and apostrophises the soldiers in a manner
that verges on self-parody: "O charioteers, above your dormant
guns, / It stands here still, stands vibrant as you pass, / The invisible,
untoppled omphalos". Heaney asserts the power of myths of origins
and an ancient sense of nationhood at the same time as he presents
us with the powerlessness of the vernacular; and he makes this
assertion, uneasily, self-consciously, in the vocabulary and tone of
"the hallowed formulae" of "the civilized utterance" (1980, 27).
The literate has had to stand in — usurp — the illiterate in a way
that parallels the struggle between piety and power. Heaney is not
quite saying, with Walter Benjamin, that "there is no cultural
document which is not at the same time a record of barbarism" but
he is offering an implicit argument that acts of culture, sooner or
later, reveal the connections between the two. It is an argument
glossed in another way by 'Bog Oak' (1980, 56) which reminds us
that Edmund Spenser composed that quintessential English poem
The Faerie Queene on his Irish estate and suggests that the poem is
animated by a distinctly Irish sense of place and landscape. It does
not take much research to discover that Spenser's estate was a
reward for services in the conquest of Ireland and that the poet also
wrote a pamphlet proposing the most brutal possible subjection of
the Irish people.

'The Harvest Bow' (1979, 58; and Morrison and Motion [eds.]
1982, 36) makes a similar point by criticising the variety of lyric
poetry that reaches easily after neat conclusions and morals, through
appearing to offer that variety, questioning it and offering an alter-
native. The poem opens on a moment of shared creative contem-
plation as the poet remembers watching his father plait the bow of
the title, "a knowable corona / A throwaway love-knot of straw".
The poem could almost have ended here but what follows enacts
something that lies between a withdrawal from and justification of
metaphorical extravagance. The second stanza suggests that not

only is the making of such bows a skill from a bygone age but that the bow is a product of a largely inarticulate or culturally inexpert class or milieu. As in Tony Harrison, poetry and the arts in general are related to craft and labour. The third stanza shows the questioning of the lyric impulse at its most explicit:

> And if I spy into its golden loops
> I see us walk between the railway slopes
> Into an evening of long grass and midges,
> Blue smoke straight up, old beds and ploughs in hedges,
> An auction notice on an outhouse wall —

These lines offer us another reading of the first stanza's "mellowed silence" with Dunn's "right true measure of vulgarity" added in in the form of old beds. The passage also suggests a narrative of a decaying or disused rural landscape in which the reader is left to ponder the precise nature of the auction notice. The next stanza reinforces the impression of a deserted scene: "your stick / [whacks] the tips of weeds and bushes / ... but flushes / Nothing". At the end of the poem we seem to have journeyed from lyric contemplation to moral tale:

> *The end of art is peace*
> Could be the motto of this frail device
> That I have pinned up on our deal dresser —

Such a motto, as Corcoran (1986, 150) points out, inevitably echoes the end of Keats's 'Ode on a Grecian Urn' and its "Beauty is truth, truth beauty"; but Heaney's "could" alerts us to the fact that he is playing with and subverting the commodifying expectations of and impulses in such poetry. Heaney's possible motto belongs to Dunn's "culture of connivance" and its arts of "bland recoveries" for, as the last three lines make clear, experience cannot be captured in this way. As with language at the close of 'Alphabets' there is always something that escapes materialism; and the plaiting of the bow, done apparently in a pre-reflective state, is a way of positioning the self and the creative act outside systems of cultural commodification and exchange. These systems are evoked by the way the harvest bow "pinned up on our deal dresser" picks up on the earlier image of the auction notice "on an outhouse wall". The harvest bow, like the notice, comes to stand as an emblem of transferred ownership and the way that transfer changes the nature of the thing transferred. The poem describes a transaction in which a simple gift rooted in everyday custom becomes a craft object which when it enters the system of cultural exchange and value represented by the poem becomes a cultural icon. To divorce the harvest bow from the circumstances of its making and the complex history of its maker and of the traditions it expresses is to participate in an 'unearned lyricism'. The conclusion of the poem expresses Heaney's recognition of the difficulty in holding the guttural and the literate or the pre-reflective and the cultural in a proper relation.

Dunn has characterised Tony Harrison's style as one of "a Scholarship Boy's Revenge" (Astley [ed.] 1991, 130); and of all the 'middle generation' poets Harrison is the most thorough and uncompromising in his project "to fashion truly oppositional meanings out of fundamentally bourgeois establishment poetic forms" (Spencer 1994, 16). The fact that his work can be described in such terms sets it apart from Barthian 'theft' and 'disguise' and from the subversion of commodified and/or commodifying forms; rather, as he has said, "I like to subject them [artistic frames and regular metre] to a sort of maximum strain" (Interview 1991, 87). Harrison's continuing — or as the title of an early collection has it 'continuous' — engagement with conflicts arising from issues of class, voice and ownership have been widely discussed — see for example Astley (ed.) (1991), Corcoran (1993) and Spencer (1994). What I want to focus on in the space I have here are the points where Harrison's poetry relates to my preceding argument and thereby allows a perspective on how the poetry of the 'middle generation' starts to cohere; and particularly where his work overlaps with colonial and post-colonial writing and models of such writing.

The lines "So right, yer buggers, then! We'll occupy / Your lousy leasehold Poetry" which open the second part of 'Them & [uz]' (1984, 122-4) encapsulate not only the direction and register of Harrison's project but also the way his poetry, alert to the smallest ambiguity, double meaning or irony, writes its own commentary and displays ambivalence towards that project. Language is literally a place of struggle as variant meanings suggest themselves and force the reader to consider them in a dynamic relationship. "Lousy leasehold" typifies both alertness and struggle. The sense of limited and transferable tenure is crucial here: 'poetry' like 'literature' is a relatively recent bourgeois invention (see Raymond Williams 1983, 187) which is closely connected with the rise of the leisure class in the nineteenth century. Literature and poetry are products of the same historical period which created concepts of 'standard language', concepts which continue to reverberate in culture, education and society. It was the age of popular guides to grammar and pronunciation. *Poor Letter H*, for example, was first published in 1854 and had reached its fortieth edition by 1866.

The connections and conflicts between literature, speech and standards are evoked by the poem's references to "Cockney Keats", Daniel Jones — author of an early twentieth century pronouncing dictionary — and to "Wordsworth's *matter / water* [being] full rhymes". In this context, "lousy" not only carries the sense of neglect and infestation but also of abundance which in turn suggests neglect from a kind of well-heeled complacency. 'Occupation' becomes not merely a case of the working-class entering the garden as at the end of Dunn's 'The Come-on' but of taking up tenancy and ownership to make a better job, to restore what the "buggers", speakers of RP, have edited out or suppressed. 'Occupation', with its echoes of squatter's rights implies that language and literature are under-used properties; but equally it reminds us of the precarious status of the squatter or 'sitter-in'.

Linguistic conflict in Harrison's work as part of a larger struggle is illuminated by examples from colonial and post-colonial writing. Rick Rylance (in Astley [ed.] 1991, 114-128) makes a valuable reading of the African background to poems such as 'On Not Being Milton' and 'Dichtung and Wahreit' (1984, 112 and 170). Although 'Them & [uz]' does not place itself explicitly in this context it does have some interesting points of overlap with it. The opening of part I —

> aiai, ay, ay! ... stutterer Demosthenes
> gob full of pebbles outshouting seas —

offers a powerful image of the physical struggle involved in speaking as others wish, portraying it as a literal discomfort to or even violence on the self. In a useful introduction to Anglophone African poetry, Chris Miller (1994, 69) reports the experience of Kenyan Marxist novelist and playwright Ngugi wa Thiong:

> Ngugi was educated in a missionary school. When a student used a native language, he was forced to place a ball of paper in his mouth. He had to keep it there until another student spoke in his mother tongue; the ball of paper was then placed on that tongue. Thus was the native language and culture suffocated.

Education, identity and language in a colonial context might even be evoked by Harrison's 'buggers'. The writing and first book publication of the poem are contemporaneous with the staging of

Howard Brenton's play *The Romans in Britain* with its notorious portrayal of imperialism as homosexual rape. To return to one's own tongue, to find the confidence in means to be able to "tell the Receivers where to go" as Harrison puts it, becomes a revolutionary act in an unresolved, never-ending struggle:

> My first mention in the *Times*
> automatically made Tony Anthony!

The closing lines of the poem demonstrate the necessity of a kind of linguistic *lutta continua* and the difficulties involved in fashioning oppositional meanings out of bourgeois forms or positioning them within bourgeois discourses or structures. For if Harrison's project is to 'occupy' or inhabit various discourses or voices then he is, equally, occupied or inhabited by them.

The second half of 'Them & [uz]' shows that the individual's relation to and position in culture is always precarious, always renegotiable. To chew up and spit out "Littererchewer", to reassert one's real name and tell the Receivers where to go may only lead to another imposed identity. Language is simultaneously the place in which one's status is located and the means by which it is constantly being redefined, brutally or subtly upgraded or downgraded. To appropriate may also involve being appropriated, a point perhaps indicated by the slightly unnatural position of 'yer buggers'. The way many of the poems in *The School of Eloquence* sequence mix both 'standard' and dialect English not only mimes this process but show that in being true to his 'bilingualism' Harrison's own identity and status are a continuing process of adaptation. Walcott's comments about his own conflicts over choosing between patois and English are pertinent here:

> In trying to seek a combination of the authentic and the
> universally comprehensible, I found myself at the center of
> a language poised between defiance and translation ...
> (Interview quoted in Terada 1992, 34)

In an essay that quotes at length from this interview, Susan M. Schultz argues that Walcott's eventual decision not to choose between languages, "to remain poised between defiance and trans-lation", creates "a third language" or "third" or mingled voice: "Between the oral tradition and the literary one, we hear the voices of the two traditions interfused" (Schultz 1994, 94). However, where Walcott's refusal to choose leads to the individual, the poet and his poetry being offered as a means of mediating between traditions, cultures and languages, Harrison's similar refusal leads to a recognition that it is the anger and hurt of the individual consciousness that prevents mediation taking place. The memory of personal experience and the need to be truthful to it means that cultural fictions cannot suffice. The individual poem is not an accommodation or a healing but more often, in the words of Dunn's 'The Come-on', "the bitter ooze from my grudge" (1979, 13).

The refusal to choose the poem as the means and site of mediation has other consequences. A poem from *The School of Eloquence* typically enacts an obsessive reckoning of the distance between Harrison's background, education and achievements; and, thereby, revisits his ambivalence about the benefits of education. Education has taken him out of his class but it has also enabled him to record the stages of exile and so refuse complicity in the oppression of his class and in the suppression of its history. Poetry as a narrative of ambivalence is one point where Harrison's poetry coheres most obviously and most readily with that of Dunn and Heaney; and it is also where the 'middle generation's' debt to Larkin comes into focus. Harrison's self-conscious facility with languages, Heaney's use of linguistic, phonetic and other expert terminologies and Dunn's adroitness with intricate forms and rhymes inscribe an awkwardness that comes from what Harrison has called (Interview 1991, 86) "becoming a master of something, of learning skills ... partly to show off to them". This relates to what Andrew Crozier (in Sinfield [ed.] 1983, 219) identifies in the way Larkin's speaker in 'Church Going' shows off his knowledge of church fitments. Words like "pyx" disturb the language of the poem and its avowed agnosticism "so that we are uneasily aware of the incomplete adjustment of the poet's intentions and the serviceability of his persona; at best we might feel *his 'wit' is a form of discomfort"* (my italics).

Wit as discomfort is particularly to the fore in poems that deal with Harrison's classical education and his resultant skill in Greek and Latin. For example, Neil Corcoran (1993, 158-9) shows how his use of lines from Milton's Latin poem *Ad Patrem* as one of the epigraphs to *The School of Eloquence* registers filial gratitude and debt; implies the poet's own class exile and freedom from the oppression of his class; and gives the reader — unlikely nowadays to read Latin — a lesson in cultural and linguistic alienation. The complex ironies of a classical education are further explored in 'Me Tarzan' (1984, 116) where they are informed by perspectives of colonialism and gender. The young Harrison, prevented from joining his mates by Latin homework, is "against / all pale-face Caesars, *for* Geronimo". Education and language are seen in terms of judgements about civilization and barbarism; and of a choice between written, urban history and the unrecuperable legends of a displaced nomadic people. At the end of the poem, the boy shouts to his friends through the skylight:

> *Ah bloody can't ah've gorra Latin prose.*
>
> His bodiless head that's poking out's
> like patriarchal Cissy-bleeding-ro's.

Here the boy is unmanned, made a cissy by his education and takes his revenge by bestowing the same insult on one of the authors he's set to study. However, as usual in Harrison's poetry, one word articulates many arguments. The word 'Cicero' is translated, broken apart and remade into dialect in a manner reminiscent of Walcott in *Omeros*:

> I said, 'Omeros,'
>
> and *O* was the conch-shell's invocation, *mer* was
> both mother and sea in our Antillean patois,
> *os*, a grey bone, and the white surf as it crashes
>
> and spreads its sibilant collar on a lace shore.
>   (1990, 14)

Just as Walcott takes a name from the Western tradition and places it in the Antilles in a reversal of the naming of slaves after classical figures, so Harrison splits a classical name in a way that parallels and repays the personal 'splitting' that 'Me Tarzan' and other poems portray. This instance of appropriation and renaming is one of many in Harrison's oeuvre which together signpost that part of his project is, like Walcott's, Adamic. Paradoxically, what emerges out of both of the broken 'Homer' and the broken 'Cicero' are instances of indestructible humanity. The appropriation of meaning and the subjecting of "the looms of owned language" ('On Not Being Milton', 1984, 112) to maximum strain, register what 'Self-Justification' (1984, 161) calls the

> aggression, struggle, loss, blank printer's ems
> by which all   eloquence   gets justified.

which returns us once again to something akin to Dunn's earned lyricism.

'Blocks' (1984, 156) finds the poet refusing to use the oratorical skills of "all my years of Latin and of Greek" at his mother's funeral and reflecting instead that it is

> *A time to* ... plough back into the soil
> the simple rhymes that started at her knee.

The image of ploughing recurs in a two part sonnet 'Lines to my Grandfathers' (1984, 177-179) where the poet apostrophises his ancestors: "fell farmer, railwayman and publican". Again, the title is both literal and metaphorical as Harrison's connects the poet's craft with his grandfathers' work. The poem begins with an image of "Ploughed parallel as print the stony earth" and, by the end, Harrison is telling us "I strive to keep my lines direct and straight". Remembering "grampa Horner" he tells us

> He cobbled all our boots. I've got his last.
> We use it as a doorstep on warm days.
> My present is propped open by their past.

This inevitably echoes Heaney's comment about the importance of "[keeping] open the imagination's supply lines to the past" (1980, 151) and the images of ploughing in both Harrison's poems can also be read in the context of Heaney's 'Glanmore Sonnets' I and II (1979, 33-43). The sonnet sequence describes the period when Heaney and his family moved to County Wicklow after he had resigned from teaching at Queen's University. Heaney has said of the period that "Spiritually I felt terrifically steadied" (Haffenden 1981, 59) but the sequence involves more than a celebratory return to roots. The first line of the sequence is "Vowels ploughed into other: opened ground" which echoes the closing lines of an earlier poem 'Act of Union' — "the big pain / That leaves you raw, like opened ground, again" (1980, 125-6). In this context, consciousness, particularly the cultural or literary variety, is something unnatural done to the self by an outside agency and "vowels" and "other" can be interpreted in a number of ways: self and culture, dialect and standard speech, Irish and English, speech and literary form. The second sonnet, by repunctuating the line, suggests how that raw wound might be salved:

> Then I landed in the hedge-school of Glanmore
> And from the backs of ditches hoped to raise
> A voice caught back off slug-horn and chanter
> That might continue, hold, dispel, appease:

> Vowels ploughed into other, opened ground,
> Each verse returning like the plough turned round.

The lines not only describe the sustaining interrelation of local and cultural but also argue that passivity is an essential part of creation. Passivity is very usefully glossed by Douglas Dunn in an interview with John Haffenden (1981, 16) when he describes it as "not passivity in the way it would be used in contemporary humbug as a put-down — that it, not being 'active' enough — but the writer allowing his own mind to happen in the face of other things that were happening round him". In the light of this definition, 'vowels' and 'other' might also stand, in Heaney's work, for the poet's dual commitment and responsibility: to his own imagination and to the public sphere.

A further overlap can be found in Heaney's and Harrison's use of 'O' and circle images. Heaney's poem 'Alphabets' and the first two poems in Harrison's sequence 'Sonnets for August 1945' and 'The Morning After, I, II' (1992, 9, 10), modulate the circle into the globe and the universe in a similar manner. In Harrison's poem the circle is the one scorched by a victory bonfire on VJ Day and its ending makes a lament for something lost at the start of the post-war period: "that, now clouded, sense of public joy"; but there is "still that dark, scorched circle on the road". This leads into the second poem which reminds us that VJ Day was the result of the horrors of Hiroshima and Nagasaki and that the modern world starts here:

> That circle of scorched cobbles scarred with tar's
> a night-sky globe nerve-rackingly all black,
> both hemispheres entire but with no stars,
> an Archerless zilch, a Scaleless zodiac.

The 'scorched circle' also alludes to Harrison's work in the theatre. The images of Leeds folk dancing round a bonfire remind us that drama and many other aspects of culture have their roots in ancient festivals and rituals, the sort of primitive celebration that Eliot imagines in 'East Coker' (1974, 197) where figures "round and round the fire" keep "The time of the seasons and the constellations". This explains why Harrison's image of a post-holocaust world is "an Archerless zilch" but the Eliot passage also highlights Harrison's implicit argument that cultural activity must not lose touch with its affirmative roots. And to return to Heaney, his "slug-horn and chanter" and "opened ground" perhaps rewrite Eliot's "music / Of the weak pipe and the little drum" heard in an "open field".

Dunn, Harrison and Heaney were the keynote poets of Blake

Morrison's and Andrew Motion's *Penguin Book of Contemporary British Poetry* (1982) with its assertion that "what we are struck by powerfully is the sense of common purpose: to extend the imaginative franchise". It is not my intention to warm over cold controversies but the 'voice and ownership' argument I have been developing gives "franchise" a peculiar aptness. Leaving aside the echoes of monetarist politics and the early years of Thatcherism, "imaginative franchise" continues to be a problematic phrase. The Concise OED gives six distinct meanings for 'franchise' which all involve the granting of rights by one person or body to another person or body. In Morrison's and Motion's conclusion it still remains unclear, after all these years, precisely who is supposed to be granting what to whom. Similarly, the alienation they detected in the Northern Irish poets they collected, "the attitude of the anthropologist or alien invader or remembering exile" (12), was not confined to those poets or formed only by responses to a political situation. The poetry of the 'middle generation' can be said to enact a kind of 'double encoding' beautifully but painfully described in Seamus Heaney's 'Exposure' (1980, 136):

> Rain comes down through the alders,
> Its low conducive voices
> Mutter about let-downs and erosions
> And yet each drop recalls
>
> The diamond absolutes.

In the second half of this chapter I want to examine how the 'middle generation's' agenda has remained a defining influence, sometimes overt, sometimes tacit, on the poets who began to publish in the 1980s or whose best work was done in that period. I shall explore how the 'voice and ownership' conflict has, in many ways, moved on from the ground-breaking confrontations of Dunn, Harrison and Heaney — we might recall Sean O'Brien's comment that the "battle has been fought and won"; and I shall also look at the work of Eavan Boland to show how the conflict has particular meanings for the woman poet. Sean O'Brien (b.1952) clearly takes the work of Douglas Dunn as a starting point but just as some commentators have seen the seeds of surrealism in the more extreme descriptive passages of Zola's naturalistic prose, so O'Brien pushes Dunn's Northern anti-pastoralism to the point where its realist urban details begin to blur and dissolve under the pressure of what O'Brien (Interview 1992, 53) terms "a sort of imaginative energy

that seeks out shape". O'Brien's poetry typically combines a pow-
erfully strange sense of "what Peter Porter calls the arbitrariness of
the real imagination" (Interview 1991/2, 167) with a similarly strong
conviction that "the imagination is historically shaped" (Interview
1992, 62). It is not surprising that O'Brien has identified (Interview
1992) Dunn's poem 'The River Through The City' (1986, 37) as
one of his touchstones. In Dunn's poem an initial hallucinatory
realism gradually modulates into dark fantasy: "the uncatchable
black fish / ... know where Hitler is hiding". 'The River Through
The City' combines the 'arbitrary' and the 'historical' aspects of the
imagination in a way that clearly underwrites O'Brien's observation
that, in his own work, "when things get weird, get strange, or the
poem goes into overdrive, that seems to me to be the earned surplus
of all that realism" (Interview 1992, 53). While such a remark relates
to Dunn's conception of an earned lyricism and to the wider 'dual
consciousness' of the 'middle generation', O'Brien's engagement
with such questions is what one might term a residual confrontation;
that is, it is more of a nervily exploratory habitation of them which
has particular implications for both the forms and subjects of his poetry:

> ... the poems I write are intended in a specific sense to be
> dramatic — that is to say they are not supposed to be talking
> about their subjects, they are supposed to be their subjects.
> (Interview 1991/2, 167)

The relationship between the arbitrary and historical aspects of
the imagination and its implications for form and subject can be
seen most notably in 'Dry Sailors' from O'Brien's collection *H M S
Glasshouse* (1991), a book he has said is concerned with "the point
of view of a private occupancy of history, the way in which events
make themselves felt in the private life" (Interview 1992, 54). As its
title makes clear, 'Dry Sailors' sees this occupancy of history in terms
of an historical inheritance of unobtainable realities and inoperable
myths. The poem begins with the word "Becalmed" which refers to
"the water-clerks" who are sailing "theoretical oceans"; what is left
to them is "the glamour of not setting out" and a quite literal
fictionality of existence.

'Dry Sailors' shows one way in which the arbitrary, 'real' imagination
is related to the 'historical' imagination. It enacts, in one sense, the
energy of the former trying to find a place within the limits of the
latter. It also helps us to start to see how conflicts arising out of issues
of voice and ownership are rewritten in O'Brien's poetry as questions
of ownership and history, private occupancy and public myth.

Images of our essential fictionality and of the 'pre-written' nature
of everyday existence, of being an actor in an inherited and
predetermined script, combine with a sense of the end of history to
give O'Brien's work its characteristic tones and flavours. What is
distilled is a kind of historical melancholy which produces an
undercut lyrical elegance that another age might have called ennui.
In 'The Disappointment' (1983, 22) the narrator's apparently
motiveless existence has a distinct historical derivation:

> All afternoon I trudge around
> Inventing tasks. I look and sniff
> And find Victoria and Albert
> Brilliant white and everpresent.
> From windy plinths The Great outstare
> The disappointment of their will
>
> As dusk elaborates the park.

History, like the sound of "pianoforte being taught and loathed"
which ends the poem, has "unwarranted effects / Not brave enough
for sorrow but still there". The question the passage begs is: surely
the present is more than the past's disappointed future? But the
question surely has an ironic twist in the context of Thatcherite
Britain since the dominant ideology claimed roots in the previous
century's values. The effects of history are characterised explicitly
in 'Walking' (1983, 10) whose location is, once again, a park:

> The planthouse is the room within the room
> And all this is England,
> Just left here and what's to be done?
> ...
> We were not invited. We came late
> To trespass on ourselves among the furniture.

Parks are a recurring location in O'Brien's poetry and he has
drawn attention to them as "[models] of nature, nature used to
resemble itself, manipulated to resemble itself. And you can see
analogies between that and all kinds of artistic activities" (Interview
1992). Here, it is the past that is both manipulated and manipulating,
a discourse that has specific implications in the wider context of
Britain in the 1980s and the rise of the heritage industry, the
aestheticisation of the past and revisionist interpretations of the
value systems of both the pre-1945 period and the last century.
What results is a present that 'resembles itself', a mode of existence

as fictionalised as a park: "You are condemned to live this script /
Until the gestures make you retch, / And then forever ...". The
English present as a kind of ghostly, Sisyphean limbo is a picture
painted again in 'The Park by the Railway' (1983, 16) in which
another couple are meeting and perhaps also 'unmeeting':

> Coal and politics, invisible decades
> Of rain, domestic love and failing mills
> That ended in a war and then a war
> Are fading into what we are: two young
> Polite incapables, our tickets bought
> Well in advance, who will not starve, or die
> Of anything but choice. Who could not choose
> To live this funeral.

The "Adulterous cortège of cars around the park" in 'Walking' has
become an inclusive condition, although the poem seems undecided
whether history is really over or whether the present is just de-
historicised. If part of our English destiny is to be characters in
search of an author, 'The Mechanical Toy Museum' from O'Brien's
second collection *The Frighteners* (1987, 30) suggests that the English
respond to history itself as if it is an addictive commodity that "keeps
you fingering your change, / This taste for proofs of entropy".

Fictionality, entropy and the desire for hierarchy come together
powerfully in the events of the Second World War and the central
position they continue to occupy in English cultural and political
life. 'Propaganda' (1991, 12-13), arguably one of O'Brien's finest
poems to date, makes a comprehensive engagement with this defining
myth. The setting of the poem is a deserted railway station in the
middle of summer, a setting that has loud resonances in terms of
poems about England for it inevitably recalls, among others,
Larkin's 'The Whitsun Weddings' and Edward Thomas's 'Adlestrop'.
Indeed, O'Brien is clearly asking us to think about the meanings of
such poems: for example, not only is 'Adlestrop' a form of propaganda
in its pleasing rural description but its characteristically English
procedure of hiding the sad and the personal in the humorously
anecdotal might also be thought of as a kind of aesthetic and poetic
propaganda. I think O'Brien takes his setting from Thomas but,
more importantly, he investigates its sense of timelessness and
stillness, the "minute a blackbird sang" which is both an ending and
a beginning; and he tries to 'write out' in full what flits behind the
attractive equivocations of Thomas's original: that ideas of England
are located, almost unobtainably, between the private and the

public. We might also note here that railways function in particular ways in the collective English consciousness. Their condition is often taken as a parable of the condition of the country as a whole and used as a means of determining its position on a line between action and inaction, sickness and health. The unsigned editorial in Issue 4/D of the magazine O'Brien co-edits, *The Printer's Devil* (Spring 1994), makes exactly this kind of analysis, referring to the impending privatisation of the railways as a symptom of "the same warped DNA as you'll find in any other diseased part of the body politic" and as "a terrible failure of the imagination".

'Propaganda' sets its scene of a timeless summer with images that relate to earlier poems like 'Walking' and 'The Park By The Railway':

> It seems that at last we have come to the place
> That described us before we were thought of.
> We stand on its sweltering, porterless platform
> And wait in the time-honoured manner.
> The stalled afternoon's like a story
> Once left on a train with a chapter to go ...

In contrast with the two earlier poems, 'Propaganda' is at pains to explore just exactly what is involved in the elusive / illusive sense of being players in a pre-determined scenario. The first stanza ends with a sense of "the perfect assurance that somewhere / Close by it is quietly happening". I think we can take "it" in two ways: first, as England, its history and myths; and, second, as the Second World War, the past that is always present in England, present in locutions such as 'Dunkirk spirit' and the old war films that are shown virtually every Sunday afternoon, year in, year out, almost as a kind of surrogate religion. The Second World War remains such a powerful and sensitive 'site' because it combines, uncomfortably, the proofs of both glory and entropy O'Brien identifies in 'The Mechanical Toy Museum'; or, in O'Brien's terms, the workings of the arbitrary and the historical imagination. It combines proof of national character and strength with a suspicion that the Second World War was decisive in hastening Britain's — or more correctly — England's decline from its already precarious position as a Great Power. The controversy and loathing which greeted Clive Ponting's 1994 biography of Winston Churchill centred on the book's picture of the War. John Charmley (*TLS*, 13.5.94, 8) summarized Ponting's revaluation as follows: "It may comfort the British to believe that they played a crucial part in defeating Hitler and that without them the world would have fallen to Nazism, but the balance of the evidence suggests otherwise ...". The continuing cultural and collective psychological returns to the Second World War are a way of avoiding unpleasant truths by reliving action but not its consequences. The timelessness of the English scene is a kind of historical limbo, divorced from temporality, where we allow ourselves anything but the facts. The idea of comforting myth is emphasised in the poem's third and final section which begins "How easy to know where we stand" and then turns that knowledge on its head:

> When Hammerpond enters, no longer a tramp,
> To deliver the long explanation
> Whose end we will miss when the radio coughs
> And announces that all roads are flooded,
> The sovereign's in Canada, Hitler in Brighton,
> And no one will leave here tonight.

The meaning of England, "the long explanation", remains forever elusive. The radio announcement emphasises not only the manipulative, ungenerous nature of historical and political myths and the impotent superfluity of our part in them but also implies, through the idea of a parallel universe, that the greatest of all fictions may be England itself. There is something badly askew with a country whose present gives way so readily to an unobtainable and increasingly remote past.

Much of O'Brien's most recent poetry has concentrated on the 1940s and 1950s as the source not only of myths about England and Englishness but as the point at which the post-war consensus, now effectively destroyed, was established. The period, therefore, can be said to tie together and locate the central, defining tension in O'Brien's poetry between transformation and immobility. It is this that underwrites his constant returns to snow, harbours, the sea, pubs, parks, maps, charts and atlases. *H M S Glasshouse* paints a detailed picture of England's relationship with its past and tacitly argues for a different kind of relationship, similar perhaps to that which Robert Hewison (in Tredell 1994, 169) calls "a critical connection ... I think we have to understand the past in terms of change and in terms of competing discourses, of competing powers really, and until we understand that, we won't understand the extent to which we continue to exist in competing discourses with competing powers". O'Brien does not offer any answers except to explore historical detachment as both blessing and curse; and to reiterate that "The way out may involve seeing clearly what you're in" (Interview 1992, 56). Or, to put it another way, the way out may involve letting the arbitrariness of the real imagination catalyse and transform the immobility predetermined by the historical imagination. 'Ludic' may be another way of saying 'lucid'.

Sean O'Brien takes the voice and ownership conflict in the poetry of Dunn and both expands and relocates it. If a major part of Dunn's 'project' in the overtly political poetry of *Barbarians* (1979) and *St Kilda's Parliament* (1981) is, as Alan Robinson argues (1988, 82-100), to counter England's "continuing political and artistic hegemony" (ix) over Scotland, then a fundamental part of O'Brien's is to reveal that hegemony as it is exercised over the English themselves; and just as Dunn dramatises the verbal and "visual negotiation of deferentiality and mastery" to epitomise "the wider nexus of power relationships in society" (Robinson 1988, 82) so O'Brien uses the fictionalising impulses of the imagination to dramatise the 'master narratives' of English culture and to explore how the deferentiality and mastery implicit in those narratives determines the individual's everyday and historical experience. Similarly, we can say that where Harrison is subjecting traditional forms and metres to maximum stress, O'Brien is doing the same with an inheritance of poetry that is largely social and realist, amplifying its fictive elements to engage with larger discourses and powers.

A discussion oriented around Dunn, Harrison, Heaney and O'Brien might suggest that the 'voice and ownership' argument is exclusively male and working-class. Indeed, Rick Rylance (in Astley [ed.] 1991, 126) argues that the post-war history of the British working-class, Harrison's poetry and, by extension, the poetry of the rest of the 'middle generation', "has been a characteristically male discourse and has stressed ... achievement [and] loss". However, Dunn, Harrison and Heaney all to some extent personify the sources of their inspiration as feminine and all three recognise the need for what Virginia Woolf in *A Room of One's Own* (1977, 99) calls "some collaboration ... in the mind between the woman and the man before the art of creation can be accomplished. Some marriage of opposites has to be consummated". This recognition hardly claims the 'middle generation' for feminism but it does demonstrate that the poetry of its members responds to the changed nature of sexual politics from the Sixties onwards. If the poetry of the 'middle generation' tries to juggle truth to class origins, consciousness of exclusion from one's class, the need to find a way of life outside it and an anguished recognition of that class's virtual destruction, then it also, residually, tries to find a suitable role for the male outside traditional patriarchal structures. In this context, O'Brien's 'disappointment' and 'polite incapability' can perhaps be read back into the 'middle generation' as uncertainty over the relation of gender to status. Detachment from history and hierarchy can also be read as detachment from patriarchy.

The poetry of Eavan Boland (b.1944) shows that, while questions of permission and status are necessarily more fundamental to a woman poet, the same conflicts over class, education and voice drive and define it. Boland's starting point is best expressed by the title of a Michèle Roberts poem, 'women's entry into culture is experienced as lack' (1986, 27); and her poetry works to redress exclusions and impoverishments in order that a counter-narrative can be written, a project explicit in collection titles like *In Her Own Image* (1980), *Night Feed* (1982) and *Outside History* (1990). Boland summarises her position in the Ronald Duncan Lecture for 1994:

> I am an Irish poet. A woman poet. In the first category I enter the tradition of the English language at an angle. In the second, I enter my own tradition at an even more steep angle.
>   (1995, 10)

Boland's poetry seeks to redress a set of compound exclusions. We have already encountered one of these several times in the course of this chapter and it appears in 'An Irish Childhood in England' in the form of the London schoolteacher "who when I produced 'I amn't' in the classroom turned / and said — 'you're not in Ireland now'" (1987). This subjugation of self was not answered by being back in Ireland. In Boland's accounts (1990, 21-8 and 1995, 10) her time as an undergraduate at Trinity College, studying English Literature and beginning to write poetry, found her unaware of the partial nature of prevailing accounts of Irish history and literature. This unawareness is the subject of 'The Achill Woman' (1990, 27-8) which is itself another version of an anecdote in Boland's essay 'Outside History' (1990, 21-8). The poem describes how the undergraduate Boland spent an Easter alone in a cottage on an island off the west coast of Ireland studying the Elizabethan court poets of the Silver Age. Each evening, the old woman who looked after the cottage would bring Boland a bucket of water as there was no mains supply and the two would talk until nightfall. What the essay makes explicit and the poem does not is that the old woman talked about the Irish famine. Montefiore (1994, 211-24) gives a detailed account of the complex ironies of the story — that Boland is studying English poetry on the anniversary of the Easter Rising; that two of the court poets, Raleigh and Spenser, were instrumental in

the Elizabethan conquest of Ireland — but the point of the poem is
the young Boland's ignorance:

> ... nothing now can change the way I went
> indoors ...
> ...
> and took down my book
> and opened it and failed to comprehend
>
> the harmonies of servitude
> ...
> the songs crying out their ironies.
>   (1990, 28)

English language and English literature are the discourses of
oppression and, consequently, give no sense of the struggles of
culture and history. Boland acknowledges (1995, 11) that there was
a counter-tradition available to her in which "language was a sign
of dispossession, and the authority of the poet was vested in the
record kept of such dispossession" but adds that this also leads to
alienation and exclusion. 'The Achill Woman' portrays the marginal-
isation of women but implies that this is inextricable from traditional
images of women as personifications of Ireland; or as Boland terms
it in the essay 'Outside History' "an alienating rhetoric of imagery;
a fusion of the national and the feminine which seemed to simplify
both" (1990, 22). The poem criticises the female personifications
of the Irish tradition and the English courtly love poem through a
snapshot of a real woman's life and its connection to a suppressed
history. In another sense, however, 'The Achill Woman' and the
whole of the 'Outside History' sequence are the achievements that
partially answer an initial sense of loss, of 'entry into culture
experienced as lack'. Boland has written of the time when she was
writing *In Her Own Image* and *Night Feed*

> I simply felt that I could not record the life I lived in the poem
> I wrote, unless I could find my name in the poetic past. And
> I could not find it.
>   (1995, 11)

Boland's work to date makes an overt argument that the poet's
permission and authority come from the example of the individual
life lived and written against myth and in the service of history; or,
in terms of Dunn's poem 'The Come-on', from placing "what I have
lived and felt" against the enchantments of the "beloved" canon and
"'coals in the bath' stories".

2. 'England Gone':
The Rhetorical Imagination and Ideas of Nation in the Poetry of Simon Armitage and Glyn Maxwell

The poet Elaine Feinstein, reviewing *The New Poetry* (Hulse, Kennedy and Morley [eds.] 1993), said of its contributors: "These poets work to the eye and mind rather than to the ear" (1993, 10). Peter Porter made a similar point when he wrote of a sense "of recitative being favoured over aria" (1993, 37). Both reviewers were responding to the evidence of a number of shifts that can be said to characterise British poetry since 1980. As I argued in Chapter One, one of these involves ideas about individual poetic voice and its relation to the dominant culture. The dominant culture also manifests prevailing ideas about nation and nationality, England and Englishness. Neil Corcoran valuably points out (1993, xv-xvi) that English poetry in the post-war period is inseparable from "persistent ideas of 'Englishness' in a period in which Britain lost its empire and most of its colonies"; and that it often portrays "a coming to terms among English writers themselves with a national individuality newly and differently defining itself in relation to a vastly altering historical circumstance and political status". It is the relation between individual poetic voice and prevailing ideas about and perceptions of nation that I want to explore in this chapter. I want to suggest that what Feinstein and Porter detected are manifestations of what I shall term 'the rhetorical imagination'; and, through an examination of the poetry of two of Britain's most acclaimed and prolific younger poets, Simon Armitage and Glyn Maxwell, demonstrate not only its workings but its connections with the parallel movements of unravelling described in this book's epigraph.

To understand how the rhetorical imagination comes about we must consider, briefly, what preceded it. When Seamus Heaney wrote his essay 'Englands of the Mind'(1980, 150-169) on three of the most important poets of the immediate post-war period, Ted Hughes, Geoffrey Hill and Philip Larkin, he was able to use and expand on T.S. Eliot's formulation of 'the auditory imagination' to illuminate their work:

> 'the feeling for syllable and rhythm, penetrating far below the conscious levels of thought and feeling, invigorating every word; sinking to the most primitive and forgotten, returning to the origin and bringing something back', fusing 'the most

ancient and the most civilised mentality'. I presume Eliot was
thinking here about the cultural depth-charges latent in
certain words and rhythms, that binding secret between
words in poetry that delights not just the ear but the whole
backward and abysm of mind and body; thinking of the
energies beating in and between words that the poet brings
into half-deliberate play; thinking of the relationship between
the word as pure vocable, as articulate noise, and the word
as etymological occurrence, as symptom of human history,
memory and attachments.
      (Heaney 1980, 150)

One can also assume that Eliot was thinking of the model of critical
and poetical experience that had preoccupied him since 'Tradition
and the Individual Talent' (Kermode [ed.] 1975, 37-44) and which
he described in a letter to Stephen Spender: "You have to give
yourself up; and then recover yourself, and the third moment is
having something to say, before you have wholly forgotten both
surrender and recovery. Of course, the self recovered is never the
same as the self before it was given" (Tate [ed.] 1971, 55-6). 'The
auditory imagination' describes a sensuous alertness underpinned
by a similarly active combination of the conscious and subconscious
minds. It mirrors the three moments of surrender, recovery and
saying and their inter-relation in its 'penetrating', 'sinking', 'returning'
and 'bringing something back'. Most importantly, Heaney expands
Eliot's model to give surrender, recovery and saying cultural, historical
and national dimensions. The relation between the wholly sensual
moment of surrender and the intellectual process of saying are
indentifiable with the fusing of "the most ancient and the most
civilised mentality".
      A powerful sense of this fusing is, Heaney argues, crucial to the
very different poetries of Hughes, Hill and Larkin. The work of all
three poets draws its identity, originality and vitality from a largely
deliberate concern "to keep open the imagination's supply lines to
the past" (1980, 151) and from an ear for the roots of the English
language and the associative resonances that make up ideas of
England. Heaney goes on to argue that "their separate voices are
guaranteed by three separate foundations which, when combined,
represent almost the total resources of the English language itself"
(1980, 151). Consequently, we can 'hear' pre-English elements and
the middle English alliterative tradition in Hughes; English becoming
Latinate and subtler in Hill; and, finally, the roots of modern,
standard English in the Renaissance, Tudor and Augustan periods

in Larkin. Crucially, Heaney points out that all three, because of their active and sustaining relationship with the past, were able to move from a regional or class-specific experience to a national and universal one; and that the two positions were mutually nurturing.

The original date of Heaney's essay — 1976 — is highly suggestive in itself for it marks a particular historical moment when ideas of England and its history were on the brink of radical change. The poetries of Hughes, Hill and Larkin suggest that, for the native born speaker, England, English and Englishness are still bound up with inclusiveness. A whole range of experiences can, it seems, be accommodated. It is an inclusiveness that is underpinned by what one might term 'Platonic' ideas of England, as when Charles Tomlinson looks out into the plain of York:

> It is no tyranny
> To the cycle a hedge hides and whose rider
> Slotted into the scene, drifts by
> And, making the will of the land his own,
> Is wing-swift land-bound.
> 'Near York' (1986, 45)

However, as the Tomlinson poem makes clear, such ideas of England are essentially aesthetic ones which, in a very large sense, 'stand in' for both engaged political theory and fundamental philosophy. What they describe is merely a vague but powerful assumption that a particular form of life embodies certain values. Heaney's essay provides the starting point for my discussion of the rhetorical imagination because it comes in the middle of a period, 1974-9, which may be seen as a 'hinge' between the post-war consensus *and* Thatcherism; and between 'aesthetic' England and its attendant liberalisms *and* the political and economic realities of a revisited and re-invigorated nationalist Great Britain. This change was a response to widespread feelings of economic, cultural and political exhaustion. The country was governed by a minority Labour government; inflation had, in 1975, reached twenty-five per cent; and unemployment was increasing. The publication in the same year of Malcolm Bradbury's novel *The History Man* which satirises the sociological excesses of the post-war consensus and liberal social policies, showed that the dominant wisdom was starting to change. The election of Margaret Thatcher in 1979 and her subsequent eleven years in power resulted in an 'England of the mind' that became narrower, single-perspective and exclusive of many. It is hardly surprising that "one of us" became one of the key phrases of

Thatcherism: a mark of approbation and a badge of membership whose precise meaning was known only to the bestower.

The real shock of Thatcherism, in retrospect, was that it retained 'aesthetic' England while ridiculing any ideas that values are embodied in specific forms of life. It sought to replace the imperatives and lessons of history and tradition — often uncomfortable and inconvenient — with the powerful currents of the free market. It also created a climate of opinion in which a particular conceptual framework could be dismantled and junked. It is this that Philip Larkin foresaw in his poem of 1972 'Going, Going' (see Heaney 1980, 168):

> And that will be England gone,
> The shadows, the meadows, the lanes,
> The guildhalls, the carved choirs ...

Sustaining cultural traditions — local, pastoral and social — were to be replaced with commodified and marketable concepts such as 'heritage'; or, as Larkin imagines earlier in the poem, "the tourist parts". The underpinning social setting of law and custom was exhausted and could therefore be either ignored or sold off. In this context, a local or regional perspective — the rootedness Heaney identifies in Hughes, Hill and Larkin — could no longer have the same meaning, could no longer serve to bring the individual into an active, reciprocal relationship with his culture or with the past.

The radical changes in British politics after 1979 and their consequences for culture and society mean that Heaney's argument can only be expressed *negatively*. His conclusions that Britain's loss of status on the world stage had resulted in "a kind of piety to local origins ... a new valuing of the native English experience" still assumes the existence of a consensus. He refers approvingly to Donald Davie's *The Shires* as an example of this return to origins. However, what happens in poetry of the 1980s is that local piety does not lead to an English experience but remains a local one; and that a view of England as a nation seems impossible. For example, John Fuller's poem 'The Shires' (1991, 24-34) founders in whimsy and in postures of self-congratulatory marginalisation expressed in an imagery of "footnotes", "dubious information" and "an unimportant story, now forgotten". More revealingly, many of the descriptions of English counties seem interchangeable. The poet who comes to maturity and to poetry in a period when consensus has been irrevocably eroded, history commodified and the relation between values and forms of life derided will, in Heaney's terms,

inevitably acquire an impoverished account of how he come to be
as he is and where he is. He may lack, if one can so term it, an
historical self and will therefore struggle to develop an imagination
whose supply lines to the past are kept open. He will be at least
partially deaf to the associative resonances between his own voice
and the body of his native language. He may find it difficult to see
his own life beyond its immediate context and his work may explore
species of isolation and discontinuity. What results is an imagination
that places its emphasis on and draws its energy from the forms
rather than the noise of language; that is not auditory but rhetorical.
I have, however, used the conditional tense in the preceding account
because while the rhetorical imagination can be described as the
product of an impoverishment, it would be wholly incorrect to
assume that it is itself a form of impoverishment. Indeed, one of the
paradoxes of the poetry of both Simon Armitage and Glyn Maxwell
is that carefully husbanded resources of containment and circum-
spection go hand-in-hand with exuberant enjoyment, prolific out-
put and a wide range of occasion and inspiration.

How, then, can we model the rhetorical imagination and the
poetry it informs and produces? First, it is important to stress that
I am not using the term rhetorical pejoratively but, as I proposed at
the start of this chapter, to attempt to describe a change of emphasis
from the latencies and nuances of language to its forms and surfaces.
It is a change that takes great account of the means of transmission.
Simon Armitage has been praised by Peter Reading for creating
"a muscular language of his own out of the slangy, youthful,
up-to-the-minute jargon and vernacular of his native northern
England"; and for writing "poems with an energy which comes
directly from life now and the living language". This last remark
(from a review of Armitage's first collection in *The Guardian* by
Carol Ann Duffy)[1] is a particularly telling one for it implies a
conception of language not as a rich inheritance or an instrument
but as something that exists only in the mouths of its speakers; exists,
in fact, as a commodity in a kind of linguistic free market. Poetic
language, it is implied, exists in a kind of eternal present and
becomes quite literally *timeless*.

Second, as these two estimates of Armitage make plain, the poetry
of the rhetorical imagination is full of received linguistic elements.
Both Armitage and Maxwell share, for example, an interest in the
use of cliché for both comic and ironic effect and as an available,
convenient resource. Their poetries also borrow from both non-
literary (media, advertising) and non-cultural (commerce, sport)

discourses. This makes it less likely that poetry can be, as Paul Muldoon suggested in 'The Frog' (1986, 83) something that "comes to mind as another small upheaval / amongst the rubble" or is born, in Les Murray's memorable phrase, "at the back of the head". As we shall see, the work of Simon Armitage and Glyn Maxwell is usually dramatic in conception or framing and is concerned to justify its existence with an account of the occasions of its own making. The poem, it seems, is not proof enough on its own but needs 'circumstantial evidence' as well.

Third, the use of cliché and non-poetic vocabularies in the traditional sense 'foregrounds' the rhetorical operations involved in both writing and reading that enable one to move from surface to meaning. A process of 'translation' takes place in which, for example, the expected decorations of the genre (simile, metaphor, etc) can be understood as both versions of prosaic facts *and* pleasures of the text. Armitage and Maxwell, in common with many of their contemporaries, put the whole process in quotation marks so that the reader is often forced to concede that an individual poem is about language before anything else and, indeed, may *only* be about language. Armitage's poem 'Ivory' (1989, 74) is essentially a list of synonyms for inconsequential chatter. It may also, through its oblique reference to Craig Raine's 'An Enquiry into Two Inches of Ivory' (Morrison and Motion [eds.] 1982, 170-171) and its own manifesto of linguistic purity, be a satire on 'martian' *ostranenie* but such a possibility is secondary to the poet's exhilarated enjoyment in wielding quaint words and phrases. In a similar way, Maxwell's titles — for example 'In Herrick Shape For Her' — are an invitation to share in and admire the poet's own pleasure and expertise in form. The result is that subject and idiom or subject and form are placed in a relationship that seems to be shifting, being constantly renegotiated throughout the course of a poem and remaining unclear at its close. It is as if a poem could be described as two waves oscillating at different amplitudes, sometimes moving apart, sometimes coming close, sometimes coinciding. A similar type of relationship is set up in other areas: between attitude or pose and authentic feeling; assertion and argument; form or system and organic development; syntax and the resonances and echoes of language. Such procedures inevitably make questions such as "who is speaking?" difficult to answer and ask us to consider the artifice involved in poetic discourse. They also raise much more fundamental questions. It becomes harder, for example, to conceive of language as the place where aesthetic and moral concerns meet and interfuse and this increased difficulty leads us to examine the nature of the times that produce such problematic writing.

Fourth, the use of what one reviewer termed "slangy, youthful, up-to-the-minute jargon and vernacular" highlights another crucial difference between the auditory and rhetorical imaginations. Heaney's expansion of Eliot's conception employs terms such as "latent", "secret" and "backward and abysm". G.W. Turner, in a useful account of stylistics, reminds us, in contrast, that "the slang and colloquialism of familiar speech ... are always partly protective of the inner self" (1973, 191). If slang and jargon protect the personal then a poetry that draws on their energies involves particular conceptions of rôle and audience and may well be telling us something about the particular engagements it favours. Heaney's line "The end of art is peace" ('The Harvest Bow', Morrison and Motion [eds.] 1982, 36), however tentative its formulation and context, is not something one expects to find expressed by one of the younger poets of the 1980s. As John Bayley has written: "Simon Armitage and other virtuoso performers have acquired the post-modernist trick of putting poetry, like a clever TV advertisement, in inverted commas, of being clever whilst amusing us about the process of being clever, using cliché or romance with a streetwise grin" (1993, 15). 'Clever cleverness' has implications for the persistent cults of the authentic and the personal which I referred to in the Introduction when examining Peter Sansom's comments on Armitage's poem 'Gone'. If the poetry of the rhetorical imagination is truly a product of the last ten or fifteen years, then one begins to wonder about connections between the age's divorce of values from forms of life and the way much contemporary poetry seems to have managed to divorce the authentic from the personal.

Finally, as I intend to demonstrate, the workings of the rhetorical imagination are closely bound up with a changed relationship with England or with ideas of England. Like Hughes, Hill and Larkin, Armitage and Maxwell are sustained by precise locales but Armitage's Pennine north of England and Maxwell's Welwyn Garden City are seen in an impoverished and unequal relationship with the larger idea and reality of England or portrayed as either totally excluded from or indifferent to such a relationship. Indeed, it is interesting to note here that Simon Armitage's home village of Marsden appears in the footnote to Tony Harrison's sonnet 'On Not Being Milton' (1981):

> An Enoch is a sledge-hammer used by the Luddites to smash
> the frames which were also made by Enoch Taylor of Marsden.

The cry was: Enoch made them and Enoch shall break them!

The connection is highly pertinent not only to a better under-
standing of Heaney's conception of how the local gives access to the
historical and the universal but also to Sean O'Brien's portrayal of
younger poets being uninvolved in the struggles of 'the middle
generation'.

I want to start my discussion by suggesting that the rhetorical
imagination has two sides, active and passive; and that Glyn Maxwell's
poetry demonstrates the former and Simon Armitage's the latter.
This is partly confirmed by the circumstantial view Armitage takes
of the moment of a poem:

> The place where I live offers the urban and the rural, both at
> very short notice. The moors behind our house are some of
> the bleakest and most extreme in the country, but at the same
> time we are within an hour of about five major cities and a
> handful of big towns. Perhaps that's why a lot of my poems
> exist at that uncomfortable intersection where the back street
> meets the sheep dip. The swineherd talking back-slang.
>   (Interview 1991, 94)

The ending of 'Canard' (1989, 55) makes a similar point — albeit
in the context of a rebuffed homosexual advance:

> Our liaisons, he suggested, could be purely ironic,
> like the coming together of two great rivers:
> productive, creative but not embryonic.

The idea of the intersection — a place where things or people meet,
divide, cut across each other — is a crucial one in Armitage's poetry.
His work is full of both deliberate meetings and chance encounters,
the consequences of which are not any earth-shattering change but
a resonance, a nagging echo, a recognition not quite made, like the
thoughts of the waitress at the end of Raymond Carver's story 'Fat'
(1985, 16):

> That's a funny story, Rita says, but I can see she doesn't
> know what to make of it.
>   I feel depressed. But I won't go into it with her. I've
> already told her too much.
>   She sits there waiting, her dainty fingers poking her hair.
>   *Waiting for what*? I'd like to know.
>   It is August.
>   My life is going to change. I feel it.

Or like the wind in 'Bylot Island' (1989, 35) in which the protagonists imagine they hear "the traces of strong, familiar voices / calling our names. Our names. This is serious". The importance of intersections also does much to explain the obsessive interest Armitage's poetry takes in the occasions of its own making, its habitual self-conscious announcements of them. Here are a few examples: "I interviewed him twice ..." ('Social Enquiry Report', 1989, 58); "You pull onto the soft verge" ('Bempton', 1989, 59); "Heard the one about the guy from Heaton Mersey?" ('Snow Joke', 1989, 9); and "At the Working Men's Home Produce Auction" ('Untitled with Flowers', 1992, 28).

The concern with occasions is symptomatic of a particular relationship with poetry and experience, language and imagination. It is one in which the poet is as much recorder as maker and in which not only his subjects but the language used to describe them come from outside the self and are verified outside the self. Language, far from being Heaney's "total resource", becomes localised and guaranteed by local use. There is little that can be 'made new' except things like clichés, a favourite Armitage strategy. Similarly, once poetry comes to be seen purely in terms of a 'socialised' language, a particular set of constraints comes into play. For example, any conviction a poet might have that *anything* which has a genuinely present meaning and importance to him is a good and legitimate subject to write on is put under question. Armitage has remarked: "I feel obliged in some way to consider writing in terms of a situation and what its human consequences are, rather than just write about a bowlful of flowers for the sake of it. For me, there's no point in that, unless the writer's dealing with how he or she feels about it, or how that's going to be for other people" (Interview 1991/2). Taken together, the intersection, the circumstantial, the social, amount to a very different relationship with language to that defined by Heaney in 'Englands of the Mind'. If we agree with Heaney that Larkin's voice is the "stripped standard English voice" of the "urban, modern man, the insular Englishman, responding to the tones of his own clan, ill at ease when out of his environment" yet holding to a "composed and tempered English nationalism" (1980, 167), then Armitage's voice is stripped back even further. In its enactment of Wordsworth's "plainer and more emphatic speech", the clan is all. There is no sense of a larger society and England has ceased to matter or even, quite possibly, to exist. The references to the 'outside', to England or to English in Armitage's poetry are few but telling. For example, the drug in 'The Stuff' (1989, 68) "arrived in our town by word of

mouth // ... It came from the South". Similarly, in the title poem of
Zoom! (1989, 80), "before we know it it is out of our hands: / city,
nation"; while in 'The Visitor' (1989, 67) "my guest's impeccable
English might ring out / and deceive you". The England that does
exist in Armitage's poems is an anonymous countryside between or
around cities that gives nothing and receives nothing: "It will right
itself, that square / of flattened grass where we laid the blanket"
(1992, 71).

The 'myth of origins' that Armitage posits against this is stated
most explicitly in 'It Ain't What You Do It's What It Does To You'
(1989, 20):

> I have not bummed across America
> with only a dollar to spare, one pair
> of busted Levis and a bowie knife.
> I have lived with thieves in Manchester.
>
> I have not padded through the Taj Mahal,
> barefoot, listening to the space between
> each footfall picking up and putting down
> its print against the marble floor. But I
>
> skimmed flat stones across Black Moss on a day
> so still I could hear each set of ripples
> as they crossed. I felt each stone's inertia
> spend itself against the water; then sink.
>
> I have not toyed with a parachute chord
> while perched on the lip of a light-aircraft;
> but I held the wobbly head of a boy
> at the day centre and stroked his fat hands.
>
> And I guess that the tightness in the throat
> and the tiny cascading sensation
> somewhere inside us are both part of that
> sense of something else. That feeling, I mean.

The poem is at once a warning against misconceptions of significant
experience; an existential 'design for living'; and an *ars poetica*. It
appears to work as a simple opposition: the heroic / romantic isolation,
the danger and silence of America and India contrasted with the
more prosaic realities encountered in Manchester, at Black Moss
and at the day centre. However, there is more to the poem's
argument than a plain statement of the fact that imaginative challenges
and rewards may be found on one's own doorstep. 'It Ain't What

You Do ...' contrasts an exploratory selfishness with life in a recognisable and verifiable community and it is possible, in this context, to read the poem politically and argue that it is grounded in the sort of values that have been largely discarded or denigrated since 1979. But if we read the poem in terms of the rhetorical imagination then its contrasts become more problematic. What is most striking, I think, is the final stanza's simultaneous enactment of the intervention of language into experience and its immediate failure. If we view the poem in terms of Eliot's process of 'surrender-recovery-something to say' then Armitage seems unable to get very far beyond the 'surrender' stage. The end of the poem represents a winding down to a vaguely assertive shrug. In contrast to Eliot's belief that "the self recovered is never the same as the self before it was given" and in spite of the poem's apparent account of 'outside' working on 'inside', the poem implies a model of experience in which the self remains essentially unchanged; and significant experience obscurely assimilated as a "sense of something else".

It is a model of experience that may be traced to the way the poem flirts and plays with expectations of conventional mimesis. The intensely personal key experiences of the poem — the stones skimmed across Black Moss, the boy at the day centre — are to do with silence and withdrawal and, like the grammatical structure of the stanzas that describe them, they remain closed. If the experience of Black Moss is to be weighed against that of the Taj Mahal, if tourism is to weighed against roots, then there must, one feels, be more involved than just silence and space: a comparable sense of history and grandeur perhaps. Similarly, the exact nature of the opposition in stanza four seems largely unavailable. The curious thing here is that the poem is careful to employ a language of 'use' — bummed, Levis, busted, wobbly — to invite us into "that sense of something else". The fact that this remains largely undefined can be traced to the picture of nation that emerges alongside it. If we contrast Armitage's England with, say, Larkin's "meadows, ... lanes // ... guildhalls [and] carved choirs", we can see that these places of work, commerce, exchange and community have been replaced by the criminal inner city, an isolated tarn and the artificial community of the day centre. The implication is of a changed social fabric underlying a different model of experience and needing a less resonant language to express it. The poem relies for its energy and effects on undercut negative assertions: its shape and movement are determined syntactically rather than verbally. The sounding of the deep resonances of English that, for an earlier generation of poets, seemed to go hand-in-hand with access to larger ideas of self and nation seems almost alien to the world of 'It Ain't What You Do ...'. The poem is crucial, then, because it not only displays the workings of the rhetorical imagination in its passive mode but exemplifies how confidence in it moves into the gap left by the absence of shared ideas about experience, language and nation. The ending of the poem points to an uncertainty about its fitness to compensate totally that also prompts self-conscious remarks about experience elsewhere in Armitage's work: "but it will not stop there" (1989, 80) and "Which left a taste / of starting something that wouldn't finish" ('Parable of the Dead Donkey', Hulse, Kennedy and Morley [eds.] 1993, 333). Experience or life in Britain in the 1980s and 1990s is either uncatchable or discontinuous.

'True North' from Armitage's second collection *Kid* (1992, 3) gives a more explicit portrayal of why continuity with the past through language and shared ideas is no longer possible. The subject of the poem is a return home for Christmas "from one term at Portsmouth Poly / all that Falklands business yet to come":

> In the Old New Inn two men sat locked
> in an arm-wrestle — their one combined fist
> dithered like a compass needle. Later,
> after Easter, they would ask me outside
>
> for saying Malvinas in the wrong place
> at the wrong time.

Here is the same silent physicality which is at the heart of 'It Ain't What You Do ...' but the narrator finds himself excluded from it by the acquisition and use of a language that symbolises a wider world-view. However, it would be a mistake to read the poem in terms of 'the middle generation' as inscribing the angst of the class exile. The exclusion of the poet is, in fact, universal. The "Old New Inn" makes an oblique reference to the faking up and commodifying of history and tradition that has characterised British culture in recent years. The "composed and tempered English nationalism" that Heaney identifies in Larkin has given way to an inward, reactionary violence. The "one combined fist / [dithering] like a compass needle" is typical of the barely contained forces that seem to run through much of Armitage's work but it also stands for a strength and energy which, denied a relation to anything beyond its own immediate context, becomes self-destructive. At the end of the poem "As the guests yawned their heads off I lectured / about

wolves" which refers the reader back to the poet's first view of his
home village

> ... the village looked stopped; a clutch of houses
> in a toy snow-storm with the dust settled
>
> and me ready to stir it, loaded up
> with a haul of new facts...

England and English are no longer the sites of shared experience.
More importantly, England in its post-imperial period seems unable
and/or unwilling to enter into a new relationship with the world at
large as is indicated by the trouble over Malvinas. The narrator's
"haul of new facts" is unwanted and unwelcome. Significantly, in
terms of the rhetorical imagination, it is a lecture that becomes the
poet's chosen medium. The lecture may be an allegory or a parable
or merely part of the haul of new facts but the poet, his audience
and the reader no longer have any way of knowing. And as in 'It
Ain't What You Do ...', 'True North's' colloquialisms seem to work
against their own presence as signposts to an easily recognisable and
shareable linguistic environment. "A bummed ride", "that Falklands
business" "ask me outside" and "in the wrong place / at the wrong
time" are casual phrases that register displacement and conflict. It
is perhaps not too surprising to find Armitage, his tongue at least
half in his cheek, writing in 'Speaking Terms' (1992, 64)

> words being what they are
> we wouldn't want to lose the only sense
> we can share in: silence

'True North' portrays England as a fragmented nation of isolated,
passive communities where Portsmouth seems as foreign as Bothnia
and where comfortable inertia occasionally gives way to outbursts
of clannish, nationalistic violence; and where if available experience
is limited then so is the language needed to describe it. It is a measure
of Armitage's originality that he makes a reduced palette into a
strength and virtue. His button-holing openings — "Which reminds
me ..." (1992, 1), "So that's that ..." (1992, 42) — show a concern
to make the best possible contract with the reader under difficult
circumstances. Nevertheless, his reliance on rhetorical strategies
and on over-used resources such as colloquialisms and clichés may
also be read as symptomatic of a period when disillusionment with
and distrust of nation have, in the work of many poets, manifested

themselves as linguistic doubt. Similarly, while Armitage's poems' precise Northern locations — Hyde, Newton-le-Willows, Huddersfield, Manchester — suggest that if most people ignore England it is because England ignores most people, the constant journeying in many of the poems suggests indirection and dissipation of energy; the local, cut off from the national, slowly exhausting itself.

Glyn Maxwell also writes out of a particular geographical location, South East England, the very heart of what Terry Eagleton has called "the depthless, technocratic, dehistoricised sensibility of Thatcherite Britain" (1989/90, 46). Like the poetry of Simon Armitage, Maxwell's work seems to exist in a species of eternal present, the only available past being that of the author's own lifetime: "the third digit / of the year I live in / will never be 7, / will never be 6 ..." ('Hyphen', 1990, 77). Maxwell's poetry also relies heavily for its effects on rhetorical strategies and, as with Armitage's, this may be traced to its relation with the matter of England. However, Maxwell comes to poetry expecting to make England his subject and to find English a resonant resource and as a consequence his work comes to exemplify the active side of the rhetorical imagination:

> I smoked under
> our giant oak,
>
> our Charles II oak, I followed its arms
> through calm, gradual argument, towards
> the smaller points, the versions, the odd forms,
> the dead ends, and a single one towards
> a bud on the white sky,
> then out, away.
> 'Stairs and Oak' (1990, 16)

The concluding stanza of this poem of childhood and early adolescence describes the emergence of the self, of individuality; but it also reads as England disappearing into nothingness; leaving the poet nowhere. 'Drive To The Seashore' (1990, 25) explores this marginalisation further:

> We passed, free citizens, between the gloves
> of dark and costly cities, and our eyes
> bewildered us with factories. We talked.
>
> Of what? Of the bright dead in the old days,
> often of them. Of the great coal-towns, coked
> to death with scruffy accents. Of the leaves

whirled to shit again. Of the strikers sacked
and picking out a turkey with their wives.
Of boys crawling downstairs: we talked of those

but did this: drove to where the violet waves
push from the dark, light up, lash out to seize
their opposite, and curse to no effect.

The first stanza, with its rolling, almost Biblical rhythms, func-
tions as a kind of linguistic and poetic past. Its resonant, elevated
language is an enactment of the "old days" with their "bright dead"
and of the possibility of an active, sustaining relationship with
history and language. The second and third stanzas, in contrast, give
us the short, superficial 'soundbites' of late twentieth century English
speech, its captions and bulletins. The last stanza mirrors the first
in both form and register but describes marginalisation and passivity.
As at the end of 'Stairs and Oak' the present seems "stopped" like
Armitage's home village at the opening of 'True North'. Knowledge
and language do not lead to action and change just as conventional
poetic modes — in this case lyric and pastoral — have become
useless instruments which can record but not fully apprehend. The
last phrase of the poem, "and curse to no effect", returns us to the
beginning and invites us to reflect on the true meaning of "free
citizens". However, what is most interesting in terms of the poetry
of the rhetorical imagination and its relation to previous generations
is that 'Drive To The Seashore' can be seen to rewrite and update
much of Geoffrey Hill's sequence 'Of Commerce and Society'
(1985, 46-51). A number of things point to this. First, there are a
number of recognisable Hill 'trademarks': the presence of the sea
and the dead, the locution "the [adjective] dead", the use of colons,
distinctly peculiar phrases such as "scruffy accents" and "gloves of
costly cities". Second, we have the same combination of short
phrases and rolling, elegiac periods as in Hill's sequence; and the
elegiac mode applied to economic realities. Third, we have Hill's
characteristic anxiety about the making of poetry which Maxwell
expresses residually in "we talked of those // but did this". But if
Maxwell uses a Hillian framework he does so to make points about
changes in art, politics and society. Where Hill is concerned to
commune with the dead, Maxwell's poem founders on the unavail-
ability of history; where Hill's sequence, for all its anxiety and
embarrassment over poetry, argues that art works as a corrective to
time and to official history, Maxwell's poem suggests that such a
conception is increasingly problematic; and where Hill's sequence

stresses the intimate interfusing of the commercial and the personal, Maxwell's poem describes the excluding realities of industrial and post-industrial society. The most telling difference is in the fact that both Hill and Maxwell mix and scramble register and vocabulary; but where Hill does so to emphasise the difficulty of the creative act, of making a personal response to history, Maxwell does so to underline the problematic nature of poetry and experience. The rolling periods and short phrases, the lyric mode and media-informed visualisations, suggest the ambiguous status of "free citizens".

'Citizen' is a term used throughout Maxwell's poetry. It is a word which, with its Roman and French revolutionary associations and consequent connotations of an active relationship with the state guaranteed by law, is bound to sound heavily ironic in an English context. It is also a word which, like 'heritage', prevailing political ideologies have made into a marketable commodity through such things as *The Citizens' Charter* (HMSO 1991) and exhortations to the populace to become 'active citizens'. Hence, in Maxwell's poetry, it becomes a kind of 'doublethink' term for a passive, powerless relationship to both government and country. In 'The Gap' (1990, 70) "A class of ordinary citizen will pay for this" and, more graphically, in 'Mild Citizen' (1990, 57), the speaker describes himself as "mild citizen / of what's suggested, what's appropriate because it saves my neck". Similarly, in 'Blacksong' (1990, 78) the sinister Mrs Sable is observed "dusting off a citizen / for his own good"; and other poems refer to "the forgotten citizens" and "a single what-luck citizen". Less frequent than 'citizen' but just as suggestive are 'sons'. The term is often used in an ironic or, occasionally, sneering way and is, I would argue, another 'double-think' term. Far from implying a continuity with the past through family, it is used to describe an immature, infantile relationship with it and an inability to act. Like "the first and second sons of kings" in 'Plaint of the Elder Princes' (1992, 74), Maxwell's 'sons' generally "serve to do the right thing wrong / or do the bad thing first, / or stagger along ...". 'Son' also has the meaning of 'person viewed as inheriting an occupation, quality': Maxwell's are usually either disinherited or, like the Mayor's son, ridiculous mimics of those qualities or occupations. With concepts such as 'citizen' and 'son' debased and open to derision, "what that leaves are blokes" ('Breath', 1990, 59). 'Blokes' and 'blokishness' are central to the milieu and tone of Maxwell's poetry. A colloquial term like 'bloke' is, of course, notoriously difficult to define but one starting point might be the Mayor's son himself (1990, 10-14), able to "make such alert decisions to impress" but the next minute go over "on his arse". A bloke, it would seem, is a kind of imago adult with an emotional world undeveloped beyond, at best, his late teens. A bloke swaggers, "curses to no effect", knows "two dozen unfunny jokes" and, in the crudest sense, has a big heart. But if 'blokishness' is a kind of immaturity, then it inevitably displays all the other shortcomings of the emotionally undeveloped and can be ungenerous, sneering, selfish, even vengeful and mad. As the narrator of 'Out of the Rain' puts it (1992, 44), "... we weren't about to sully our hands with politics. / Anarchists we weren't. Arseholes maybe". One can almost hear a blokish laugh after the last phrase.

Citizen, son, bloke: their meanings are central to an understanding of the conceptual, emotional, political and social world Maxwell's poetry describes and inhabits and, consequently, to an understanding of its reliance on rhetorical strategies, dramatic form and foregrounded syntax. Powerless, passive and immature personae will necessarily have an unequal relationship with language. Experiments in improvised theatre have demonstrated that our behaviour largely depends on the recognition of the status of the other and the playing of our own status as a response to it:

> ... [E]very inflection and movement implies a status, and ... no action is due to chance, or really 'motiveless' ... Normally we are 'forbidden' to see status transactions except when there's a conflict. In reality status transactions continue all the time.
> (Johnstone 1982, 33)

Maxwell — who also works as an actor, director and playwright — writes a poetry informed not only by an awareness of status play and transaction but also of the linguistic consequences and effects produced by adjustments to that play and transaction. It is this that partly underlies his concern with syntax and with the positioning of words and phrases. Again, an example drawn from theatre improvisation is instructive: "I might then begin to insert a tentative 'er' at the beginning of each of my sentences, and ask the group if they detect any change in me. They say I look helpless and weak ... Then I move the 'er' into the middle of the sentences and they say that they perceive me becoming a little stronger. If I make the 'er' longer, and move it back to the beginning of the sentences, then they say I look more important, more confident" (Johnstone 1982, 42-3). We can see Maxwell's awareness of status play and transaction at work in 'Poisonfield' (1990, 56):

> We thanked. We stopped at a dance-hall for tea,
>   discussing politics, and our new friends
> we couldn't shake off. Then I think I said
>
> Is it time to move to a vote? And the dance
>   failed, the disapproving children heard
> apologies that sidled out of me ...

Maxwell uses weak language assertively to suggest the fictive nature of autonomy and democracy, hence the deliberate positioning and resultant oddity of "we thanked". Similarly, the narrator of the poem attempts to take charge of the situation but fails to because he asks a tentative question instead making an authoritative statement. By the end of the passage his true status is revealed by the "apologies that *sidled* out of me ..." (my italics). 'Mild Citizen' (1990, 57), referred to earlier, represents a more complex working through of status. Its opening suggests the narrator's omniscience: "birds, / shit and circle over these charlatans / who haggle in the field". This continues in the next lines which find the narrator "scotching short words / I really want, the ragged and berserk / in favour of a point of view". In other words, position is being asserted over the content of the communication. At the close of the poem, the narrator leaves his work:

> When it gets late
>   I walk, mild citizen
> of what's suggested, what's appropriate
> because it saves my neck. Only, again,
> I see the pale, shock-haired Delegate
> emerging from the Chamber, and I hear
>   the moaning on the lane,
> where the mild citizens keep moving, where
> empty musicians play in endless rain.

Again, we move from low status paraded as authority to the reality of life as a 'mild citizen'. When terms like citizen become heavily ironic or even derogatory and the matter of England becomes — as at the end of 'Stairs and Oak' — a series of metaphors going nowhere, and the playing of status games and a concomitant concern with precision of expression move centre-stage. Just as Armitage's poem 'Nightshift' (1989, 19) is defined by the absences of the two people whose relationship it describes, so Maxwell's poetry seeks to

compensate for the now problematic nature of England as natural
subject and of English as the language of authority and status. As I
have suggested, Glyn Maxwell's poetry exists in a kind of eternal
present. "What those people do / now is everything" says the
narrator of 'The End of the Weekend' (1990, 27). Thus, the
language itself becomes dehistoricised, turned in on itself. It is this
that underlies what Brodsky endorses on the cover of his first
collection as the poetry's "tendency to draw metaphor from the
syntax itself". Maxwell's titles more often than not refer us to their
own grammar than to any recognisable subject: 'Grown And Who
Means', 'And Leaves Astonishing', 'Two Old Ones Did It', 'Once
Was, Is Now', 'The Hang of It'. The poetry's invitation is in the
questions such titles prompt: who? what? where? Similarly, many
poems end abruptly with words such as 'it', 'that', 'so' and 'up'.
The English language is reduced to its smallest, least expressive
particles and then asked to do as much work as possible. Language
does indeed become a set of utensils as when the Mayor's son feels
"Love working with the utensils / he generally called his heart and
soul" (1990, 13). The reductions of the language connect with the
favoured but reduced milieu of much of Maxwell's poetry: his
hometown of Welwyn Garden City (founded 1919):

> I always try and defend it when I can because it was planned
> by decent men who were trying to plan something that people
> could live in decently.
>   (Interview 1990)

Conceptually, however, things are a little more complicated. A
garden city, like a prose poem or dry cleaning, is a conjunction that
seems likely to cancel itself out and end up neither one thing or the
other. The garden city movement, with its idealistic project to
combine the best of town and country and thereby 're-ruralise' an
urban environment determined by the Industrial Revolution, seems
a typically English vision in its belief that the prelapsarian pastoral
can be recreated and nurtured by the lapsarian industrial. The result,
in Welwyn's case, is a place which Maxwell has also characterised as

> ... a very quiet place which is however right in the centre of
> things, of what's going on ... it's uniform, it's psychologically
> quite untaxing to live in — I've always thought of it as an
> easel one can paint things on. About the state of England at
> the moment.
>   (Interview 1990)

In the same interview, Maxwell refers to Welwyn as a 'limbo', a place "where you can be terribly happy with what you've got except you haven't really got anything at all". The idea of England as a state of "not really having anything at all" echoes Maxwell's ironic use of the term 'citizen' and is echoed further in 'Mine' (1990, 62) which talks of "a promise, an / obedience and, finally / a helplessness"; and that 'limbo' is evoked in a different way by the line "The middles of my afternoons in England" (1990, 11). Simon Armitage's Pennine towns and villages and the bleak spaces between them portray a fragmented country; Glyn Maxwell's Welwyn Garden City is a place that, like England itself, appears to give access to sustaining ideas and values, to embody a concept like decency in a form of life, but reveals itself to be empty, its essence elusive and illusory. England has become a country where, like the Andersons in 'The End of the Weekend' (1990, 27), people "[vote] when they could". It is the empty forms of life that Maxwell's poetry yearns to fill; and he has said, revealingly, that "the form helped create something when I didn't have anything to say"(Interview 1990).

We have seen that Maxwell's poetry is characterised by many of the same things we find in Simon Armitage's work: the use of cliché and colloquialism, the reliance on rhymes which Armitage has called "slant / near / para / loose / or half, or whatever" (Interview 1991) and a generally dramatic presentation. What distinguishes Maxwell's work is its 'foregrounded' syntax and grammar. A particularly rich example of what Maxwell does and — most crucially for the my argument — how it *sounds* can be found in the first two stanzas of 'Helene and Heloise' (1992, 34):

> So swim in the embassy pool in a tinkling breeze
> The sisters, mes cousines, they are blonde-haired
>   Helene and Heloise,
> One for the fifth time up to the diving board,
> The other, in her quiet shut-eye sidestroke
> Slowly away from me though I sip and look.
>
> From in the palace of shades, inscrutable, cool,
> I watch exactly what I want to watch
>   From by this swimming pool,
> Helene's shimmer and moss of a costume, each
> Soaking pony-tailing of the dark
> And light mane of the littler one as they walk

The two stanzas are organised so that the reader's attention is focused on the positioning of particular words and phrases and on the movement and structure of the sentences. In the fourth and fifth lines of the first stanza, for example, we are denied the expected completing verb for the sisters' actions and have to rely instead on the close patterning of 'i' and 's' sounds. These not only hold the stanzas together texturally: they mimic the poolside noises and the way the scene — in Thom Gunn's memorable phrase — 'comes and goes on the brain' of the narrator. Indeed, "tinkling" suggests the presence of windchimes which in turn suggest the intermittent stirrings of sense and apprehension. This 'coming and going' or intermittent stirring is closely related to typical Maxwell play with the status of his narrator. "Though I sip and look" and "I watch exactly what I want to watch" are placed and phrased to portray the narrator's all-seeing eye; but "though" — one of the subtlest things in the passage — undercuts this by hinting at both a lack of aesthetic control and the narrator's exclusion from full participation in the lifestyle before him. In this light, the second phrase is heavily ironic, another instance of Maxwell's strategy of presenting low status in high status terms. It implies that the exercise of our 'want' is usually the result of another's allowance or sufferance of it. "I sip and look", in one sense, symbolises how the stanzas work as a whole, marrying one of the passage's key sounds with a point of view. By the end of the second stanza, this 'marriage' has become all-important as both eye and ear are drawn to the deliberate strangenesses of "light mane of the littler" and "moss of a costume". David Morley (1993, 55) points out that the unconventional mimesis of these phrases produces "more of a tactile than an aural effect". It is a comment that could be applied to much of Maxwell's work in its identification of his move away from the conventionally poetic. The phrase "shimmer and moss" is typical of a poetry where verbs of seeing, looking and observing predominate and often stand for speaking; and where the electronic and other news media are never far away. Maxwell not only chooses titles such as 'Video Tale of a Patriot' — written as a screenplay — or 'Sports Story of a Winner': he constantly reminds us how our experience is filtered and how complacent we are about it. The protagonists of 'We Billion Cheered' (1992, 22) miss "some threat" through "eyes, lenses, screen and angle of view" while the narrator of 'In Herrick Shape For Her' (1992, 79) remarks casually "So poll me".

Maxwell is not translating poetic practice into almost literal spectacle merely in the interests of some postmodern jeu d'esprit. 'Helene and Heloise' shows the particular relation between language as subject and actual subject which I proposed at the start of this discussion. The first two stanzas show the gaze that desires as it commodifies as it desires and what results is a 'doubling' of voice that makes for a complex play, in Barthian terms, between the idiolect of the author and the institution of literature (Barthes in Chatman [ed.] 1971, 3-10). This, in its turn, produces the 'poetry in quotation marks' which is typical of the rhetorical imagination. Another example is the "forever / Trevor" rhyme that closes 'Sports Story of a Winner' (1992, 29). Where an Armitage poem plays off the colloquial and the poetic to imply criticism of prevailing models of significant experience, origin and value, Maxwell's rhyme, in its simultaneous enjoyment and mockery of a specific cultural discourse — sports commentary — amounts to a 'trebling' of voice that opens onto concerns that are moral as well as linguistic. We might recall here some lines from 'Plaint of the Elder Princes' (1992, 74): "... we serve to do the right thing wrong / or do the bad thing first, / or stagger along ...". The goodness or badness of our behaviour is a haphazard affair, something barely in our control. The complex textures of Maxwell's poetry with their competing linguistic elements mirror what Jonathan Culler calls "the absence of [an] unambiguous referential foundation" which means that we can no longer assume that "a change of expression is a change in thought" (Culler 1980, 135). Contemporary culture and its systems of dissemination and transmission — "lenses, screen and angle of view" — implicates us all in a generalised relativism of experience and judgement:

> The traffic lights were either green or red —
>
> it doesn't matter. Look at the Mayor's son,
>   no girl, no hat, under the sodium-
> lamps of his home town. (Elizabeth
>
> was born here too. Actually, so was I,
>   but Alison moved here in '83.)
> Change, traffic-lights! Go, hatchbacks of the time,
>
> the buses, and the other cars!
>   'Tale of the Mayor's Son' (1990, 10)

Maxwell's inflation of the trivial into the mock epic in this poem and in 'Tale of a Chocolate Egg' (1990, 96-111) and 'Out of the Rain' (1992, 42-64) makes a complex argument about the difficult of distinguishing between the trivial and the significant, of making the translation from the surfaces of a culture and society to their deeper meanings. The passage above also implies that the way our culture and society are structured make it impossible to concentrate on any one thing long enough to decide whether it is trivial or significant; and Maxwell's frequent use of repetition, interpolation, asides and unnecessary explanation works to subvert the idea of language signifying anything beyond the immediate context of its social use. We are, it seems, formed by and exist in a kind of experiential and linguistic free market.

Seamus Heaney concluded his essay 'Englands of the Mind' by arguing that

> English poets are being forced to explore not just the matter
> of England but what is the matter with England ...
> (1980, 169)

This assumes a consensus exists about England, the matter of England and the English language but even as Heaney was writing consensus was being irrevocably eroded and would be followed by polarisation and fragmentation. Since 1979, successive Conservative governments have worked to dissolve the idea of consensus and the institutions that enshrine and sustain it and to put in their place the forces of the free market and the cult of the individual. In doing so, however, Conservatism under Margaret Thatcher and John Major has, in the words of Ferdinand Mount, misunderstood "the fact that the common life ... arises out of ... traditions and makes possible the free market and not the other way about" (*TLS*, 15.10.93, 12). Similarly, Heaney's essay partly expresses the project of 'the middle generation' and other British regional poetries of the 1960s and 1970s to explore the problematic nature of ideas of nation and models of cultural and linguistic dominance. For the new poets of the 1980s, it is accepted that such ideas are debased or redundant. Significantly, when Glyn Maxwell writes of England, of the shires in the sense that Heaney identifies in Hughes, Hill, Larkin and Davie, he uses the medium of an elegy for an MP from a marginalised political party:

> He had
> a sense of human life, a sense of light
>
> and his old picturesque and ruined shire
> was richer than my own,
> where lawns are trimmed, and mild intelligent sons
>
> mention the past, and plan the bright to come.
> For him, this Cornishman,
> no such accident. Only a memory
>
> warm enough to keep his party in.
> 'I.M. David Penhaligon' (1990, 64)

England has become a fragmented country of quite distinct economies, lifestyles and, even, time zones. The decay of Liberalism from a once nation-defining ideology to a marginalised political position whose constituency is located in a part of the country which once had a distinct linguistic identity is, it is implied, typical of a country which is dehistoricised and urbanised and where the past is only 'mentioned'.

Note

1. Quotes from Reading and Duffy taken from blurb on *Xanadu*.

3. 'Just the Facts, Just the':
A Rough Guide to British Postmodernism

> Above all, though, what has made postmodernism such a
> positive influence ... is that it has not taken the form of
> extreme and paradoxically unquestioning scepticism that it
> does in John Ashbery, but has been linked with a charac-
> teristically British refusal totally to eschew realism. This has
> meant that postmodernism has not been used as an excuse
> to disavow political responsibility or the need to comprehend
> experience. So even John Ash and Ian McMillan ... display
> a powerful social awareness and sense of place.
> (Gregson 1993, 80)

There now seems to be a broad agreement about the importance
of postmodernism for recent British poetry. Alan Robinson
(1988, 49) asserted that Michael Hofmann's collection *Acrimony*
(1986) "consolidated him as the outstanding voice in British poetry
of an emergent Postmodernist sensibility". Neil Corcoran (1993,
201) has written of British and Irish poetry after 1970 that "the
fragmentation of a purportedly once unified or organic tradition into
separate and often mutually hostile variant kinds is, on one reading,
itself the most profound feature of the postmodern". Finally, Ian
Gregson, taking a more extreme position in a review of *The New
Poetry* (1993) — which also supplies my epigraph — comments that
the anthology reveals "the far greater influence that Paul Muldoon
has had with his hybrid poetic of playful but at the same time deadly
serious fictiveness — as compared with Seamus Heaney with his
atavistic poetic of rootedness and his naively mimetic view of
language" (1993, 80). However, none of these writers — with the
exception of Gregson — attempts to suggest whether British post-
modernist poetry merely reproduces the distinctive characteristics
of postmodernism or whether a distinctively British postmodernism
can be said to exist.

It is my intention in this chapter to suggest, taking some but not
all of my bearings from Gregson, that such a postmodernism may,
in fact be very clearly identified in recent British poetry; and that
while British postmodernist poetry does indeed share general char-
acteristics with other postmodernist art, its most accomplished (and
thorough) practitioners combine to sketch a poetic that assumes
a healthy scepticism about postmodernism itself and a wide
degree of selectivity about the practices it involves. Consequently,

this chapter will work through what I believe to be the most important characteristics of a British poetic postmodernism as they are exhibited in the work of a number of key writers of the 1980s and early 1990s, rather than present totalizing discussions of individual poets per se. Before doing so, I feel it is important to put on record what I understand by the notoriously dynamic term postmodernism; or rather, to say which of the numerous available definitions I accept and find useful.

First, I believe it is important to understand the essential condition of postmodernity as the sense of an ending of what Lyotard (1986, 15) calls the "master Narratives" or "grand Narratives" of our culture and society. These "master Narratives" take on any number of forms: they may be traditional poetic forms, models of class and gender, ideas of nation or theories of economic practice. In the area of poetry, for example, Larrissy (1990) has described late twentieth century poetry in Britain, Ireland and America as enacting both "the erosion of boundaries between the objective and the subjective" and taking as its subject "the erosion of the difference between 'inside' and 'outside'" (177). In the sphere of economics, Harvey (1989) has shown how the rigid ideas about labour processes, the workings of the market and patterns of consumption made possible by high employment and the post-war boom have given way to "flexible accumulation" founded on much more flexible work regimes; and Charles Handy (1990; 1994) has argued that we can no longer expect to work at one job or profession all our lives but must learn to develop a "portfolio" of different activities, some waged, some feed and some unwaged. Philosophically, we can say that postmodernism performs a wide-ranging critique of essentialist and foundationalist assumptions derived from Enlightenment discourses which assert the progressive amelioration of the human condition and the rationality, separateness and autonomy of the individual. In this context, Waugh (1989/1990, 64) argues that postmodernism shares with feminism a centrality of "subjective transformation" which operates as "the deconstruction of individualism within theory and the dissolution of character within aesthetic practice".

Dissolution, erosion, transformation: these are, I would argue, key terms for they underline that, despite the hysterical claims of some commentators, postmodernism is emphatically not a matter of decisive breaks or of radical ruptures. Indeed, it can often seem, at its simplest, to be the product of a confused self-consciousness brought about by that sense of an ending, an erosion of the boundaries between poetry — or art — and philosophy as defined by the French philosopher Stanislas Breton: "Poetry celebrates *that* the world exists; philosophy asks *why* the world exists" (Kearney 1986, 101). The erosion of boundaries and the end of "master narratives" lead not only to questions about the world but to questions about those boundaries and narratives themselves and, beyond that, to questions about the creation of meaning. Hutcheon (1988, 35) writes that "In Charles Russell's words, the greatest contribution of postmodernism has been a recognition of the fact that 'any particular meaning system in society takes its place amongst — and receives social validation from — the total pattern of semiotic systems that structure society'".

The recognition of the social construction of 'meaning' and 'world' and the foregrounding of that construction as aesthetic practice underline a particular relation between the postmodernist artist and late capitalist society, one that is neither exclusively oppositional or supportive. I follow Hutcheon here in her identification in postmodernist art and theory of what she terms "a model of double encoding" (1988, 222) in which that art and theory "both install and subvert prevailing norms — artistic and ideological. They are both critical and complicitous, outside and inside the dominant discourses of society". This 'double encoding' helps us to understand why parody and pastiche are such important and recurrent characteristics of the postmodern. Again, it is possible to read their use as a sign of radical rupture or conservative complicity. Lyotard, discussing postmodernist architecture, writes that "The disappearance of the Idea that rationality and freedom are progressing would explain a 'tone', style or mode specific to postmodern architecture. I would say it is a sort of 'bricolage': the multiple quotation of elements taken from earlier styles or periods, classical and modern" (1993, 47). David Harvey, on the other hand, sees the whole process as inseparable from socio-economic changes: "The rise of the new white-collar occupations ... provided a powerful source of demand for new cultural forms based on fashion, nostalgia, pastiche and kitsch — in short, all that we associate with postmodernism" (1989, 348).

There is some truth in both views but neither tells the whole story of postmodernist parody and pastiche. I would argue that, just as Larrissy (1990) points to the erosion of boundaries between 'inside' and 'outside', parody and pastiche are symptomatic of a similarly complex interfusing of heresy and reverence, irony and deference, distance and involvement.

Parody, in fact, relates to and underwrites many key indicators of the condition of postmodernity. First, as Hutcheon (1988, 23) argues, postmodernist "artworks share one major contradictory characteristic: they are all overtly historical and unavoidably political, precisely because they are formally parodic". To employ what Lyotard (1993) terms "'bricolage', the multiple quotation of elements", whatever the date of those elements, is to enter into a dialogue with a particular period and with the economic, social and political circumstances of the production of those elements. Second, parody relates to the erosion of the boundaries between art and philosophy I cited earlier, to a transformation in the relationship between what Breton terms "the classical metaphysics of identity and the modernist poetics of difference" or "the speculative principle of the *logos* and the poetic principle of the *mythos*" (Kearney 1986, 102). A reference to modernism in a discussion of postmodernism and parody should alert us to a particular transformation. It is a transformation defined most succinctly and persuasively by Brian McHale in his study *Postmodernist Fiction* (1987) where he identifies the move from Modernism to postmodernism as a move from poetics "dominated by epistemological issues" to "a poetics dominated by ontological issues" (xii). Steven Connor (1989, 125) states the move in different terms, arguing that "subjectivity gives way to textuality". Parody, then, signifies postmodernism as a move from interpretation to performance. As we shall see, it is inextricably bound up with postmodernism as transhistorical, intertextual and as the meeting place of high and low culture; and as an aesthetic practice concerned not with *production* but with *reproduction* (Crimp 1983, 44-5).

However, parody and pastiche are marks of something else that is crucial not only to postmodernist art in general but to British postmodernist poetry in particular. Again, I follow Hutcheon (1988) here who writes that "Parody seems to offer a perspective on the present and the past which allows an artist to speak *to* a discourse from *within* it, but without being totally recuperated by it. Parody appears to have become, for this reason, the mode of what I have called the 'excentric', of those who are marginalised by a dominant ideology ... [P]arody has ... been a favourite postmodern literary form of writers in places like Ireland and Canada, working as they do from both inside and outside a culturally different and dominant context" (35). The postmodernist artist recognises that the "master narratives" inscribe totalising and universalising impulses which either seek to homogenise difference or, simply, to exclude it and, consequently, works against these impulses.

The centre or the idea of a centre similarly becomes open to question. Lyotard, with characteristically overblown rhetoric, proclaims "Let us wage war on totality" (Waugh 1989/1990, 64).

McHale argues that postmodernist fiction often privileges "subuniverses of meaning" over "paramount reality" (1987, 20) and Hutcheon (1988, 58) writes "If the center will not hold, then, as one of the Merry Pranksters (in Tom Wolfe's *The Electric Kool-Aid Acid Test*) put it, 'Hail to the Edges!'". Confining ourselves to a discussion of recent British poetry, we can say that it is now something of a commonplace to point to the shifts from a metropolitan to a regional and from a native born to a non-native position and perspective as the most significant occurrences of the 1980s and early 1990s. Not only is Britain's largest poetry publisher, Bloodaxe Books, an independent company based in Newcastle upon Tyne; a glance through the twenty poets chosen for the Poetry Society's 'New Generation Poets' promotion (May 1994) shows them to comprise, among others, an Irish-American, a West Indian, an Asian and seven poets either born or based in Scotland. In much the same way — and I discuss this in greater detail in Chapter Eight "Everyone Agrees" — a poet's origins and/or angle of opposition to the actual or perceived centres of cultural and political power have become powerful elements in the marketing and valuing of British poetry. Indeed, if McHale (1987, 6-11) can argue that postmodernism is characterised by a shift of 'dominant' —— the focusing component of a work of art — from the epistemological to the ontological, it is possible to read much recent British poetry as the product of shifting geographic and phonic dominants; and I intend to show in this chapter that British postmodernist poetry is indivisible from ex-centricity.

Parody and pastiche are also, of course, essential components of the period code of modernism and this brings me to the next assumption I make in my understanding of the term postmodernism: that it exists in a particular relationship with modern art and modernism. I should emphasise that in employing the term 'modern art and modernism' I am not confining myself to the twentieth century or to the period 1914-1940 but intend to describe a cultural and historical period spanning roughly the mid-points of the nineteenth and twentieth centuries, beginning with Impressionism and ending with Abstract Expressionism. Again, there are as many opinions on the precise nature of the relation between postmodernism and modernism as there are writers on postmodernism but I find the following particularly suggestive. Lyotard (1993, 49) writes in 'Note on the Meaning of "Post-"' that "We know that in the domain of art, for example, or more precisely in the visual and plastic arts, the dominant view today is that the great movement of the avant-garde is over and done with. It has, as it were, become the done thing to indulge or deride the avant-garde — to regard them as the expression of an outdated modernity". For Lyotard, modernity is "outdated" because it represents the final episode in the 'master narrative' of the belief in humanising progress which may be traced back to the Enlightenment. "The great movement of the avant-garde" is similarly outdated because it represents the culmination of art as critique or, in Lyotard's words,, "a long, obstinate, and highly responsible work concerned with investigating the assumptions implicit in modernity" (1993, 49). In this context, then, the post-modern with its bricolage and apparent nostalgia becomes not "a movement of *comeback, flashback,* or *feedback* — that is, not a movement of repetition but a procedure in 'ana-': a procedure of analysis, anamnesis, anagogy and anamorphosis that elaborates an 'initial forgetting'" (1993, 50).

David Harvey makes a more complex and problematizing reading of the history of modernism which makes the reasons for the end of art as social critique more explicit. The shift from Europe to the USA as the centre of the international avant-garde during World War II not only coincides with the canonization of great modernist art and literature; it also shows, Harvey argues quoting Guilbaut

> international modernism [becoming] 'confounded with culture more broadly and abstractly defined' ... The depoliticization of modernism that occurred with the rise of abstract expression-ism ironically presaged its embrace by the political and cultural establishment as an ideological weapon in the cold war struggle. The art was full enough of alienation and anxiety, and expressive enough of violent fragmentation and creative destruction (all of which were surely appropriate to the nuclear age) to be used as a marvellous exemplar of US commitment to liberty of expression, rugged individualism and creative freedom.
> (1989, 36-37)

The art and literature of alienation and fragmentation were no longer seen as revolutionary antidotes to and/or critical enactments of the realities of bourgeois capitalist hegemony; and by the 1960s, high modernist culture had become clearly identified with authority, oppression and the establishment. However, I do not follow Harvey to his conclusion that postmodernism is founded on anti-modernism for, while this may be true in architectural theory and practice, I do not believe the argument holds water when applied to literature in general or to British poetry in particular. The presence of the modernist in the postmodernist is, I believe, another instance of

Hutcheon's 'double encoding' in that it points to a desire to redeem the avant-garde in general and modernism in particular from their associations with the discourses, institutions and structures of liberal capitalism and reinstate them as social and political critique; and that modernist presence also expresses a corresponding unease and scepticism about whether such a project is still viable in a British context. I believe too that the continuing presence of modernism in postmodernism in a British context also points to a dissatisfaction with and distrust of the more apocalyptic claims made on behalf of postmodernist theory and practice.

In outlining what I take to be some of the most characteristic features of a cultural phenomenon that has already been widely analysed and discussed, I hope to have achieved a number of things. First, to have provided a referential matrix for the discussion that follows and to have suggested that postmodernism is best approached through an understanding of the convergence of a number of operations. Second, as that might indicate, to have stressed that my own conception of postmodernism involves a reading of changed emphases not radical rupture; and that these changes may be understood as species of dissolution, erosion, transformation, outgrowth and supplement. Third, to have demonstrated that my own position on postmodernism is one of neither fierce opposition or unconditional embrace. It is too complex a phenomenon to be discussed from simplistic positions of 'pro' or 'anti' but, as Harvey (1989) and others have shown, it is so closely interconnected with prevailing economic and social conditions that it must be engaged with in any reading of cultural activity in capitalist democracies in the late twentieth century.

In the discussion that follows I shall examine the work of three British poets active in the 1980s and early 1990s whose poetic practice seems to me to evidence the most accomplished and thorough engagement with postmodernism. These poets are John Ash (b. 1948), Peter Didsbury (b. 1946) and Ian McMillan (b. 1956). All three originate from the North of England: Ash from Manchester, Didsbury from Fleetwood and McMillan from Barnsley. However, origin does not necessarily relate to ex-centricity here for while Didsbury and McMillan are still resident in the North of England, it should also be borne in mind that both Ash and Didsbury are both Oxford educated and that Ash is now resident in New York. I shall also bring into the discussion, as appropriate, a number of other poets whose work has bearing on my argument but who would be ill-served by the suggestion that their work makes a comparable engagement with postmodernism. I do not include Michael Hofmann in my key group of poets because his work has, I believe, already been perceptively and persuasively discussed elsewhere (see Robinson 1988, 49-62). I also exclude Paul Muldoon for the same reason (see Corcoran 1993, 202-3, 205-12). My discussion is divided into two parts. First, in a series of headed sub-sections, I examine how the work of John Ash, Peter Didsbury and Ian McMillan gives a particularly British meaning to some of the key characteristics of the period code of postmodernism. These subsections are:

- master narratives : English narratives
- Parody, pastiche, intertext : "Ted Hughes Is Elvis Presley"
- Ex-centricity : Critical regionalism

Then, in a second series of headed subsections, I examine a number of characteristics which I believe are exclusive to British postmodernist poetry. These are:

- The dialogue with realism
- The ghosts of politics
- A Pinch of Scepticism By Way Of A Conclusion : Aesthetic Practice v. Social Reality

Master narratives : English narratives

I have already noted in my introduction how several of the British poets who began publishing in the 1980s express a sense of an ending, of existing in a kind of cultural and historical 'afterlife'. Before discussing postmodernism per se I want to suggest how this shared sense of an ending — and indeed the turn towards post-modernism — may be traced to a particular set of cultural, historical and political imperatives.

First, the shared sense of an ending has direct roots in economic and political events after 1970. Robert Hewison has written that: "There is no doubt that the oil crisis of 1973 and the recession that followed was a cultural, as well as an economic shock, coming as it did on top of the student upheavals of 1968, and contributing to the industrial troubles that brought both the Heath Government down in 1974 and the Callaghan Government down in 1979. While the value of money was being eroded by hyper-inflation, the idea of continual growth, such as had taken place ever since 1945, was replaced by the perception of recession and decline" (*Too Much*, 304-5). Similarly, Neil Corcoran has argued that the erosion of cultural and political consensus manifest in [the 1960s] ... had, by the mid-1970s, become normative in British life" (1993, 196).

Finally, Bryan Appleyard has shown the remarkable similarities that exist between right-wing philosophers and historians and left-wing dramatists from the mid-1970s on: "The New Right and the Old Left can ... be seen to share the imagery of a broken culture. The explanations and remedies are different; what they were determined to see in the world, the imaginary population and landscape of the kingdom, was the same" (1989, 314).

With the post-war consensus eroded and effectively dissolved under Margaret Thatcher, the poetry of that consensus — produced by it, sustained by it and enacting it — ceased to be authoritative, believable or reassuring. 'The middle generation' of Douglas Dunn, Tony Harrison, Seamus Heaney and others had already given British poets their own powerful insight into what Eavan Boland, writing from a specifically Irish position (1994, 13), has termed "the flawed permissions which surround the inherited Irish poem — in which you could have a political murder, but not a baby; and a line of hills but not the suburbs under them". 'The middle generation', too, in their playing off of regional and received pronunciation had made English poetic language a subject. Now, poets began to question poetry as an art of recuperation and as a discourse of scientific rationalism. They began to question received ideas about mimetic models of poetic language and about poetic language as the expression of an autonomous, individual consciousness. If 'the middle generation' always place their work in relation to a dominant wisdom, to ideas about authority and centre, then the poets who started writing or who came to creative maturity in the 1980s ask questions about the idea of poetic authority itself. This had, of course, happened before, most notably in the 1960s, but the difference in the 1980s is, I would argue, that such questioning loses its oppositional edge. The poet is no longer engaged in a kind of guerilla resistance such as is enacted by Heaney's poem 'Broagh' (1980, 66) with its "last / *gh* the strangers found / difficult to manage". The erosion and dissolution of the post-war consensus renders such a project largely meaningless and, in a very real sense, suspect.

Writing post-consensus, the generation of poets who started to publish in the 1980s have their own sense of 'the flawed permissions which surround the inherited British poem'. The flaws begin with the very word 'British', a fact pointed out by Seamus Heaney in his poem 'An Open Letter' which famously and controversially rejected the colonialist rhetoric implied by the title of Morrison and Motion's 1982 anthology. Some other 'flaws' might be described as follows: a poem may be empirical but it cannot be phenomenological and if

a poem must always be valued by how 'real' it is, this leaves little
room for experiment, play and pleasure. The inherited British poem
seems oblivious to the fact that poets, as living, thinking and feeling
beings, will respond not only to other cultures but to the full range
of their own culture. Lyotard (1986, 15) has written that "A *self* does
not amount to much, but no self is an island ... [One] is always
located at a post through which various kinds of messages pass".
Making a similar point in a specifically British context, Malcolm
Bradbury lamented — as long ago as 1971 — that "the centrality of
imaginative literature — that is, in other than its most popular forms
— has declined, becoming just one factor in the vastly growing
output of communications" (in Hewison, *Too Much*, 269). Finally,
if the inherited British poem is complacent about the primacy of
literature and literacy, it is similarly complacent about the authority
and interpretation of history. The new British poets of the 1980s,
perhaps taking their lead from novelists such as Carlos Fuentes and
Angela Carter, have shown themselves willing and able to treat
history as material to be reworked.

In the preceding paragraphs I have, of course, been playing devil's
advocate in my construction and criticism of the inherited British
poem in order to highlight the impulses underlying much of the
more interesting British poetry and, specifically, British postmodernist
poetry produced after 1980. The 'master narrative' of the post-war
consensus no longer needed to be attacked and undermined as it
had been by the 'middle generation': it had simply broken down,
giving way to a curious condition somewhere between empowerment
and powerlessness, imaginative freedom and a journey without
maps. Ash's lines "'My civilisation has ended, / and I liked it so
much'" ('The Future Including the Past', 1982, 23) are a lament
but their camp unseriousness also suggests an enjoyment, almost a
relishing, of the ensuing displacement. Ash says later in the poem
"it was as if all the old problems of friction and inertia had been
solved". In one sense, the line parodies the political 'truths' asserted
after 1979 and particularly after the Falklands war; but, on another,
it stands for a kind of imaginative truth which British postmodernist
poets may be said to test throughout the period under examination.
What, then, are the world-cultural and world-historical 'master
narratives' they transact with and what are the specifically British ones?

Appropriately enough for a poet who may be characterised as
postmodernist, the poetry of John Ash is full of references to
architecture and music and, typically, uses musical form as a structural
model. First, as Ash himself has remarked (see 'Every Story Tells

It All') "we value music because of its ability to say something and not say it". In a postmodernist context Ash's remark inscribes a desire for an art form that does not — to borrow Hutcheon's term — 'entextualize' and thereby fix experience. Second, our response to a piece of music is typically to attempt to imagine a world to go with it: whether or not it is the legacy of nineteenth century bourgeois art, we always tend to write our own 'programme'. Music, then, is at once a narrative and not a narrative, at once complete picture and blank canvas. Creating other possible worlds is crucial to the postmodernist project. Third, music in our period seems increasingly a matter of hybrid forms and mixing of forms is again crucial to postmodernism. Fourth, architecture is one of the main sites of origin of postmodernism and of the relation between modernism and postmodernism. Postmodernist architecture restores play, colour, decoration and, consequently, pleasure to buildings and to our experience of them. These lines from 'The Building' are typical of such an impulse:

> Vienna, Petersburg, dead Miletus, Anuradhapura and proud
> Tiganocerta ....
>
> And these are no longer centres of government, military
> operation or bureaucracy. They exist solely to be enjoyed,
> — places of rose bushes, vines and lawless amusements,
> gentle and barbarous towns!

Freedom is, then, a "new quality of attention ... needed to get below the surface" ('Great Sonata 2', 1982, 62) or a world which is "a TV / on which I change channels at will, / never moving from the bed ..." ('Croissant Outlets in Seattle', 1987, 15).

The new quality of attention is, partly, the awareness of the old 'narratives' either having broken down or having become so degraded as to be meaningless: "and this is not the nineteenth century / of novels and puddings, of novels *like* puddings ..." ('Croissant Outlets in Seattle', 1987, 15). Traditional sustenance is not possible because language itself is different and it is here that Ash's new quality of attention may also be located. However, Ash again seems uncertain whether language has just changed and bequeathed us that change or whether the change is the result of a desire for change. 'Party Damage' (1987, 18) states this particular of 'double encoding' quite clearly:

> 'Please understand I mean exactly what I say,
> no more.' A word is spoken, an ordinary word,

and it becomes an entire landscape, —
an open and illustrated city ...

Somehow the ordinary becomes a mysterious departure but the links
between the self and the experience remain tantalisingly elusive. It
seems clear language can no longer be used mimetically or realistically:
"Did you think / you could just pick up language and use it, // as if
it were a pen or a spade — / the one called *spade*?". It is tempting to
read here an allusion to Heaney's famous poem 'Digging' in which
a pen becomes a spade and the very act of framing such a question
implies a rejection of the poetic and the view of language he may be
said to represent. Typically, Ash leaves his argument ambiguous for
in 'Telephone Nights' (1984, 53) we learn how "The fridge talks to
itself all night. Unconcerned / by the things we need of language, it
has / its own idea of perfection". The fact that a fridge makes an
expressionless humming suggests that "what we need" is mimesis,
an expressive medium. Ash's point here is the same as can be
deduced from his other references to and descriptions of the breaking
down or corruption of 'master narratives'. "A general displacement,
an unexpected / shift of emphasis has occurred" ('Fervent Osculation',
1984, 38) but it is up to the individual self to decide how great that
shift is and precisely where it applies. Experience is more complicated
and, as a consequence, more pleasurable than the old models allow.
The important thing is to make that perception: "But the idea of
The End is utterly discredited / and the map of the city resembles /
the cross-section of a tree-trunk or an onion" ('Without Being
Evening', 1984, 116).

Where John Ash's poetry seems concerned to work out a compromise
between the freedoms offered by a 'general displacement' and a
desire to find workable updates of "the old style, / humanist,
figurative" ('Romanza', 1987, 71), Peter Didsbury begins with the
assumption that transactions with the master narratives of culture
are inevitable and, as such, should be treated as a source of unworried
enjoyment. "These old high cultures want to get in everywhere / and
don't care how they do it usually" remarks the narrator of 'The X'
(1982, 29). Similarly, the narrator of 'Eikon Basilike' (1987, 38) —
which may be the key poem of Didsbury's oeuvre — tells us "The
deep structures / I could cope with, but the surface ones / were
coming at me in Esperanto, and fragments of horrible Volapuk". As
the plurals 'cultures' and 'structures' suggest, Didsbury's engage-
ments are numerous and interfused / interdisciplinary and far from
outlining them all I propose to examine three, which seem to me to
give his poetry its essential orientations.

History, often in the sense of the remote classical past, is the most apparent 'master narrative' running through Didsbury's poetry: "Everything has a Latin name / or speaks with the hollow mouth of history ..." ('The Experts', 1982, 14). John Osborne has made a perceptive analysis of the way Didsbury characteristically plays off words with Saxon roots against those with Greek or Latin derivations (see *Bête Noire* 6, 12-14) but whole poems also work through a similar procedure. The title poem of *The Classical Farm* 'translates' an Horatian ode on the festival of Faunus into old men on evening allotments while 'The Coffin Factory' (1994, 33) moves from its opening juxtaposition of "zephyrs" in a "semi-industrial suburb" to a bizarre fantasy in which a wind-blown strip of veneer becomes a descendant of "those dragon-banners / which Ammianus describes as having been borne / by the household troops of the Emperor Constantius". We are given a number of worlds and through them an argument for the relativity of meaning. The classical past as a site of the uncertain interpretation of fragments also serves as the model for a particular way of experiencing the world as a place of strange inscriptions and partial remains: "the words / Ocean Derived Aggregates" ('Traffic', 1987, 18) or "The coloured marble forecourts / Of shops that vanished in wartime" ('The Surgery', 1987, 23). A Roman view of the world as a place of innumerable and specific deities also underwrites the central narrative of much of Didsbury's poetry: the location of God, religion and the transcendental in a largely atheistic historical period. Although God was pronounced dead over one hundred years ago, what pervades Didsbury's poetry is more a sense of dissolution, of dispersal: if God is 'nowhere' in terms of established theological discourses then the result might be that he is, or bits of him are, everywhere. As a character in 'Glimpsed Among Trees' (1987, 48) puts it: "'... There are temples everywhere'. He ended, / and the problems of narration started up all over again". The question mark hanging just over who exactly resides in these temples, by what authority and speaking what truth, confronts us once more with the relativity of meaning.

Earlier, I referred to 'Eikon Basilike' as possibly the key poem of Didsbury's oeuvre. John Osborne has made a detailed and penetrating analysis of how brilliantly and pleasurably it exemplifies Didsbury's essential concerns: intertextuality, displacement of authorial authority, the relationship between dreams, language and the unconscious. I do not propose to go over the same ground but to draw attention to the poem as a species of 'purgatorio'. The poem begins with a walk through a frozen landscape: "During the late and continuing

cold / I went for a walk in the empty heart of the City". The frozen
landscape is one we might recognise from Dante or the nightmarish
fantasies of the late Anna Kavan; it is also a symbol of a state of
emotional petrification which Jungians would associate with catatonic
conditions — hence "the empty heart". The poem becomes a quest
in which three hares — anthropomorphic guides common in fairy
tales and, in fairy tales, often signs of one's essential self — lead the
narrator "through the urban fields that surrounded / the Stalag or
temple or star-ship of the Power Station". The Power Station, then,
becomes a terrifying symbol of absolute power as it may be experienced
and manifested on earth: political tyranny, religion and the ability
of mankind to journey to other worlds. The fields themselves are
"powdery channels of grass / ... all of them rising in Hades". We are
in a landscape of despair.

Didsbury is not only parodying religious quest / salvation narra-
tives or simply saying that God has been displaced by science: the
cancelled name of God stands as a symbol of the fact that any
attempt to say who or what controls our world and the universe is
a self-deluding fiction. Our knowledge of the unworldly is incom-
plete since we perceive it in the realm of the worldly and the finite.
It is this that explodes, say, Anselm's ontological proof for the
existence of God as a being 'greater than which cannot be thought'
— but how can thought think beyond itself? — and underwrites
Wittgenstein's opening proposition in the *Tractatus Logico-Philoso-
phicus* "The world is all that is the case" (1974, 5). Here, indeed,
we are confronted with what 'Glimpsed Among Trees' calls "the
problems of narration": as the old certainties, the old narratives,
break down we are faced with a liberating relativity of meaning but
without agreed structures we are more quickly brought up against
the limits of meaning. In 'Eikon Basilike' the question is not so much
the existence of God but the possibility of knowing Him: without
the support of conventional theological narratives he becomes a
barely legible and quickly dismissed sign.

The dialogue between the rational and the irrational also under-
lines what I believe are Didsbury's most important and defining
transactions with an English master narrative: the Romantic poets
generally and the figure of Samuel Taylor Coleridge in particular.
This takes place most visibly in 'The Guitar' (1987, 34) which uses
an epigraph from Coleridge's poem 'The Aeolian Harp': "And what
if all of animated nature / Be but organic Harps diversely framed, /
That tremble into thought ...". Didsbury's poem begins as an
apparent jeu d'esprit set in the Humber estuary: "Aerial songs,

estuarial poetry. / An electric guitar is being played. / Its neck is five miles long, / and forms a margin of the River Humber". The neck of the guitar becomes a railway line and down it comes a train carrying Coleridge who has fallen asleep and is "dreaming of the advent of the railways / but will not remember, because I intend to / keep it from him". Other characters gradually enter the poem — the engine driver, the locomotive itself which turns out to be an anthropomorphised diesel — and the poem fades away. Coleridge, it is clear, is invoked to represent the embrace of wayward nature as active resistance to the erosion of the status of the imagination and of the poet as its mouthpiece by the rise of scientific rationalism in the seventeenth and eighteenth centuries. The poem makes a specific reference to the latter century: "The sky is like an entry in the Oxford English Dictionary. / The earliest reference for it is 1764 ...". Rationalism, then, represents a literal foreshortening and Coleridge, particularly in his work on the symbology of religions, an attempt to restore inclusiveness. Didsbury's poem is at once a foregrounding of this conflict and itself a resistance of rationalist narratives by mixing up time periods, technology and classical gods. At the same time the ending of the poem gives a critical account of the idea that nature, as in Coleridge's 'Frost at Midnight', is the repository of an "eternal language, which they God utters". The protagonists of 'The Guitar' know something is going on outside the train but they cannot see what is really happening. As at the end of 'Eikon Basilike' our experience of the eternal is an arbitrary mix of the readable and the unreadable. 'The Guitar's' reference to keeping the advent of the railways from Coleridge may, however, be read as an implicit rejection of the later Coleridge in favour of the earlier one. The advent of the railways (which may be located approximately in the period 1813-25) coincides with the last years of Coleridge's life from the years of despair after the break with Sara Hutchinson to his final rôle as a public commentator on religion and the relations between Church and State. Didsbury's poem — which may in fact be an opium dream — is a celebration of Coleridge's 'shaping spirit' and not his 'inquiring spirit'.

This particular engagement with Coleridge bears on Didsbury's poetry in a number of ways which indicate some intriguing points of contact between romanticism and postmodernism. First, we might say that Coleridge's — and other Romantic poets' — sense of the predicament of the artist at the beginning of the technological age is precisely mirrored by many postmodernist artists' sense of their own predicament at the beginning of the post-industrial age of the digital super-highway. Both Romaticism and postmodernism inscribe a rejection of Englightenment-derived narratives of rationalism and ameliorising progress and both represent not a single tendency or a shared aesthetic but the simultaneous pressure of different and often contradictory responses. Similarly just as the *Lyrical Ballads* of 1798 exhibit a dualism comprising a conception of a poetry as everyday speech and an aspiration to a controlled poetry of transcendence, so postmodernism has been anatomised as an interfusing of high and low. Second, as many critics have noted, one of Coleridge's particular achievements was the development of an informal mode of poetry deriving its unity from conversational tone and rhythm which culminates in the 'Letter to Sara Hutchinson' and 'Dejection: An Ode'. I would argue that it is the particular voicing of this poetry in its combination of conversational tone and formal metrics that lies behind much of Didsbury's best work. One can hear its clear echo in the opening of 'A Priest in the Sabbath Dawn ...' — "Wake up, my heart, get out of bed / and put your scarlet shirt back on and leave ..." — and these lines from 'The Jar' might be straight out of Coleridge:

> Although I grieve that the discursive mode
> is lost to me behind swords of conjoined fire
> I take the roads that open to other music.

Didsbury's poetry shows its engagement with Coleridge's 'conversation' poetry in another important way. John Beer (1978, x) has written that "Coleridge's interest in the human heart extends to its physical workings — a fact which helps to develop the form of his poetry in a curiously apposite manner. Some years ago Albert Gérard pointed out that in many of the conversation poems an effect of 'systole' and 'diastole' could be traced". The poem begins with an immediate, often domestic, scene, moves to wider concerns, and then returns to its starting point which is now freshly illuminated by the poem's journey beyond the immediate. This is a characteristic Didsbury practice, as in 'The Hailstone' which moves from personal experience of weather through a wider socio-political narrative and back to a new consideration of a particular locale. Third, Coleridge symbolises the Romantic interest in the romance, the creation of exotically 'other' worlds which has come to be part of the period code of postmodernism. Finally, as John Beer (1978, xxvi) has pointed out, Coleridge "was fascinated by all the processes of light" believing "that in studying the behaviour of light man was closest to points of possible correspondence between his own powers and those of nature" and was brought "to the very border of language, the point where it merges with the mystery of perceptual process itself". Didsbury shares this fascination and, one feels, largely for the same reasons: "The red industrial nights of summer" ('Red Nights', 1987, 26); "Light from the horn windows / Or which falls through greaseproof paper / Or which whispers words like 'oilcloth'"('A Shop', 1987, 51); "The moon was dark; but the stars were like the hearts of birds, on fixed and acceptable journeyings" ('Running', 1982, 17). Didsbury's fascination may be taken to stand for a poetry which, like Ash's, subjects the mimetic practice of the inherited British poem to maximum stress; just as the early Coleridge sought to enact an emotional inclusiveness rejected by the prevailing Augustan neo-classicism of his own period.

Of the three poets under discussion, Ian McMillan may be said to have travelled the furthest distance from statements about post-modernism to practice of it. The majority of his work seems to take it for granted and get on with it, as an epigraph taken from Paul Bowles for his second collection *Now It Can Be Told* (1983) makes clear: "Each time I go to a place I have not seen before, I hope it will be as different as possible from the places I already know ... The concept of the status quo is a purely theoretical one; modifications occur hourly ...". His cartoon-like poems evidence not so much a dialogue with master narratives as a series of reports on the lived experience of postmodernity; or, as the early poem 'Responses To Industrialisation' puts it: "The roads to Hell were paved; / that much we could deduce. / The rest was guesswork" (1983, v). A *new* narrative is in place, a narrative not of the hermeneutic anarchism of an Ashbery but rather of hermeneutic autonomy: as 'Time Taken Out' (1983, 19) reminds us, "we are responsible // for our own reading and listening, / always". It is useful at this juncture to consider Jean-Francois Lyotard's remarks on the connection between postmodernism, new methods of communication and new concepts of the self: "Young or old, rich or poor, a person is always located at 'nodal points' of specific communication circuits, however tiny these may be" (1986,15). As I shall show, McMillan invariably conceives of both poem and self as a 'nodal point' but as the quotations above suggest he does not provide commentary on what is received. This makes him unique amongst British postmodernist poets in that he does not inscribe a dynamic narrative that tests the relations between empowerment and powerlessness in any overt way. However, because McMillan is also concerned to "[mine] the common miracles of poetry" ('A Village-Mentality Poem', 1988)

and to do so in a particular time and a particular place — northern
English mining country in the 1980s — he is inevitably forced into
a series of transactions with English 'master narratives'.

McMillan's poetry makes a particular set of transactions with
twentieth-century English poetry, informed by his enactment of the
poem as 'nodal point'. 'Responses To Industrialization' (1983, 10)
contains the following isolated line: "Purity of diction is one thing,
but". The line refers to Donald Davie's *Purity of Diction in English
Verse* (1966) which may now be read as something approaching a
manifesto of the Movement and its rejection of modernist-derived
experiment and permissiveness. A poem which, as I've already
noted, opens with an assertion that "The rest was guesswork"
questions the rational structure of language and the rational structure
of poetry as the only way open to the poet. Indeed, McMillan's
opening — "The roads to Hell were paved; / that much we could
deduce. / The rest was guesswork" — may be said to satirise Davie
by taking him completely at face value, particularly his assertion that
"the distinguishing excellence of pure diction [is] the practice of
refurbishing old metaphors gone dead, rather than hunting out of
new ones" (Hewison, *In Anger*, 109).

Viewing McMillan's work as reports on the lived experience of
postmodernity sheds useful light on his departure from one of the
most fundamental poetic narratives of all: the poem as page work.
More than anyone else of his generation, McMillan consistently
produces work which blurs the distinctions between page poem and
performance poem just as his readings typically combine elements
of traditional poetry readings and stand-up comedy routines. He
has worked a lot on radio and is clearly attracted to the idea of "instant
and disposable" poetry that is heard by millions (see the introduction
to *Yakety Yak*). This does not mean however that his work is either
one thing or the other: in common with younger poets like Glyn
Maxwell his poetry often works equally well as both things. This
may offer us linguistic fireworks at the expense of the kind of emotional
truth we are taught to expect from poetry but, again, this is typical of
McMillan's determination not to produce poems that look and "sound
like / poems" ('Jesus Died From Eating Curtains', 1994, 32).

Parody, pastiche, intertext : "Ted Hughes Is Elvis Presley"

I have already outlined how parody, pastiche, bricolage and inter-
textual play have been identified as key characteristics of the period
code of postmodernism as a world-historical and world-cultural

phenomenon. John Ash, Peter Didsbury and Ian McMillan employ all or some of these strategies but, as I intend to show, all three poets do more than criticise particular discourses or models through what, in Bakhtinian terms, may be termed a reversal of their evaluative 'directions' (McHale, 21); rather, all three poets use deliberate deformations of discourses and models to create what McHale defines (58), in postmodernist fiction, as "a kind of between-worlds space — a zone". This, in turn, may be related to the shift from an epistemological to an ontological dominant and is a way of phrasing the 'post-cognitive questions' McHale (1) borrows from Dick Higgins: "Which world is this? What is to be done in it? Which of my selves is to do it?"

Ian McMillan's 'Propp's Last Case' (1987, 76) is preceded by a quotation from a non-existent work of literary criticism: "Occasionally, during the late '50s and early '60s, the dominant position of the realist Yorkshire novel was challenged by a number of American-influenced works known as the *hardboiled* school of Yorkshire prose" (McMillan, *Trends in't Yorkshire Novel*, unpublished). McMillan both invokes and subverts academic authority but he also invokes a particular period in British fiction which might be best represented by a novel like John Braine's *Room at the Top* (1957). Braine has said of its hero (see Hewison, *In Anger*, 158) "My job in writing about Joe Lampton was to look at him clearly. It's not the job of a novelist to pass moral judgements". By suggesting that such a tradition was challenged, McMillan is arguing against a kind of typecasting by origin and also against the disaffected materialism of novels like Braine's. The title 'Propp's Last Case' also alludes to a well-known detective novel of the early 1900s, *Trent's Last Case*, and to Beckett's play *Krapp's Last Tape* and, as if these were not enough, the poem's opening lines pile on further allusions to Ted Hughes's poem 'The Thought Fox' — "I imagine this midnight moment's forest" (1982, 13) — and to Heaney's essay in praise of Hughes, Geoffrey Hill and Philip Larkin, 'Englands of the Mind'. This has a number of effects. First, it enacts a resistance of language as depiction and poem as coded autobiography and acts instead as an invitation to active reading and to a method of producing cultural objects that functions through inclusion. Second, the majority of McMillan's allusions invoke not only a particular period in recent English literature but a particular model which continues to reverberate and to bequeath standards of 'authenticity' for native writers. McMillan's intertextual play suggests another model in which the poem and even the narrator are 'made' by existing texts and not through engagements with narratives of nature or social reality. What Heaney's essay calls 'the matter of England' is, in fact, a fiction made new by each of us, by each act of writing. Finally, by parodying detective fiction, McMillan parodies what McHale (16) calls "the epistemological genre *par excellence*" thereby asserting text as pleasure in itself, not road to truth. Or, as the poet's interlocutor puts it in 'Death's Feet' (1994, 15), "'I hope it's one of your / Inspector McMillan novels. I just // love his jutting jaw, and the way / he solves it on the penultimate / page, leaving the last page free // for recipes".

If 'Propp's Last Case' uses complex intertextual play to make passing criticism of particular models of English writing, then 'Ted Hughes Is Elvis Presley' uses the same strategy to more direct effect. Other poets such as Steve Ellis in 'To Ted Hughes' (1986, 32) and Peter Sansom in 'A Dream Mistaking A Person For What He Has Come To Represent' (Carcanet 1994, 39) have suggested that the present Laureate may be the poetic equivalent of a popstar: McMillan's poem makes that identification directly. It is an engagement with Poet Laureate Superstar and is a surreal fantasy in which Elvis Presley reincarnates himself as Ted Hughes; and which ends with a reference to Hughes's poem 'Pike':

> I sit here,
> I can feel the evening shrinking me
> smaller and smaller.
> I have almost gone.
> Ted, three inches long, perfect.
> Elvis, Ted.
>   (1994, 19)

Elsewhere there are other references to Hughes's work, both pre- and post-Laureateship, as in "I look up. Outside a fox peers at me" and "I am writing a poem / about the death of the Queen Mother / but it won't come right". Beneath the surreal mockery are some serious questions about poetry. What is the meaning of poetry and what kind of poetry has meaning for a generation for whom the cheap potencies of popular culture have more meaning than the eternals of High Art? When McMillan writes "I am Elvis Presley. / I am Ted Hughes. // At my poetry readings I sneer and rock my hips" he is asking us to reflect on different kinds of cultural authority, on different accounts of experience and on the possibility of poetry as a truly popular art. 'Ted Hughes Is Elvis Presley' also questions the kind of poetry Ted Hughes has come to represent by imagining a scene in which the poet, Orpheus-like, serenades the Hughes menagerie of foxes, jaguars, pigs and crows. The event is, of course, impossible and the implication is that the animal poetry on which Hughes's reputation rests is a kind of impossibility too. As the last words of the poem suggest, Hughes's poetry, like Presley's rock and roll and despite its intensely puritan aesthetic, is all about self.

Both 'Propp's Last Case' and 'Ted Hughes Is Elvis Presley' pose Higgins's 'post-cognitive' questions in cultural terms: what literary / cultural world is this? To what does it allude? How does this determine my actions in it? And my self in it? The poem becomes a fictional zone in which the poet is free to play around with the dominant and any number of answers to those questions can be made, explored and enjoyed. The poem as 'zone' is developed further in Peter Didsbury's homage to Lawrence Sterne, 'A Winter's Fancy' (1987, 16):

> A winter's fancy.
> I look out of my window
> and perceive I am Lawrence Sterne.
> I am sitting in Shandy Hall.
> It is raining.
> I am inventing a Bag,
> which will accommodate everything.

Larrissy's erosion of the difference between inside and outside here becomes the means by which the narrator's fictionality is recognised and Sterne is located inside his own fiction. (There may, as Osborne has pointed out, be a literal truth here for Sterne did name his home Shandy Hall.) Sterne, then, becomes the precursor of the resistance of apparently totalising but actually selective discourses and the aesthetic of inclusiveness that are key indicators of postmodernism. Just as crucially, *Tristram Shandy*, "the greatest shaggy-dog story in the language" (Ricks, Intro, 7), may be taken as a precursor of the shift from epistemological to ontological dominant. Tristram, we may recall, is confused as to exactly where his 'life and opinions' begin: he chooses not to begin with his birth but with the moment of his conception, only to decide later that it is with the death of his brother, "from this point properly, that the story of my LIFE and my OPINIONS sets out". This, and Tristram's father's reference to "the creation of the world" in the novel's opening scene, reminds us that the book, any book, is its own world. As the heroine of Pynchon's novel *The Crying of Lot 49* writes in her memo book "Shall I project a world?" (56). 'A Winter's Fancy' develops the idea of a projected world by not only alluding to other

authors and texts — the poem mentions Thucydides and Osborne
has also suggested Borges, Plath and T.E. Hulme — but by expand-
ing the narrator's identity: "I am also John, an elderly bibliophile".
At the end of the poem, the scene outside the window of Shandy
Hall passes "before the eyes / of Peter Didsbury, in his 35th year. /
I consider other inventions of mine, / which rise before me in the
darkening pane. / Light me that candle, oh my clever hand, / for it
is late, and I am admirably tired". Didsbury is the creation of his
own narrator.

John Ash's use of parody, pastiche and intertextual play is much
more illusive. Ash's characteristic is to allude quite casually to
European authors — often symbolist or surrealist — and thereby
invoke non-native aesthetic procedures which, in turn, makes an
implicit criticism of inherited British models and the expectations
they underwrite. Ash's allusions also function as he once defined
Debussy's *Jeux*: "coherence is achieved through discontinuity. Or,
to put it another way, distant constellations reveal themselves
through windows suddenly thrown open, mirrors expose their
vacancy, fans palpitate in unknown hands, ecstatic flights are
abruptly cut off ..." ('Reading Music', *P.N. Review* 50, 48). Present
reality is suddenly disturbed by an allusive but illusive otherness.
'Glowing Embers: Paraphrases & Fictions — for Blaise Cendrars'
(1984, 56) inscribes an impressionistic biography of the French poet
and novelist (1887-1961) whose work conveys the excitement of
travel and adventure through a jumble of simultaneous impressions
and surprise effects: "The idea was to be at the centre of things, —
/ but where was the centre?":

> I was nostalgic for all places and all times
> and I was eager to push forward
>
> my every action cast the shadow which is contemplation
>
> and I sang

Not only is the poem a zone where the Russian Revolution co-exists
with discotheques; if action stands for contemplation then episte-
mology has become ontology. The relationship between 'here' and
'elsewhere' becomes a kind of nostalgia for cultural co-existence and
the possibility of a choice of models. Abroad is a 'zone'.

'Little Variations for Natalia Ginzburg' (1987, 62) invokes a
different kind of aesthetic but does so to make a similar point about
the shift from an epistemological to an ontological dominant.
Ginzberg's novels have been noted for their depictions of people

isolated both from the world and from themselves and for their particular procedure of 'cumulative characterisation' by which protagonists are gradually revealed. Ash's poem mocks the mimetic model of fiction as investigation leading to revelation. The poem follows this procedure of suggestion and concealment by becoming a pattern of repeated words and phrases which convey, ultimately, the impression of both an epistemological and an ontological cul de sac. The mystery cannot be solved but the impressions attendant on its non-solution go on accumulating and this accumulation may in fact be the only solution. Understanding as felt illusiveness leads us to Ash's most important but most subtle intertextual engagement, the poetry of John Ashbery. Ashbery's presence is easily discerned through direct echoes of both phrase and cadence but Ash does not merely copy him: the American poet's importance is felt most fundamentally as practice, as a way of behaving in language. An Ashbery poem, typically, enacts a mime of meaning, rejects a poetry of persons and objects and speaks in singular and plural voices simultaneously:

> Heck, it's anybody's story,
> A sentimental journey — "gonna take a sentimental journey",
> And we do, but you wake up under the table of a dream:
> You are that dream, and it is the seventh layer of you.
> We haven't moved an inch, and everything has changed.
> 'More Pleasant Adventures' (1987, 317)

Such a passage invites interpretation but mocks and frustrates it just as "story", "journey", "adventure" and the "you / do" rhyme suggest but do not disclose both a narrative continuity and destination and a structural coherence. The passage describes nothing but its own processes, offers nothing, in fact, save "the odd contiguity", "the way everything is mashed together and somehow gives one a sense of elation" which Ashbery has remarked he so loves about New York ('In conversation with John Ash', *P.N. Review* 46, 31-34). As I've already pointed out, Ash's work often contains direct echoes of Ashbery: "I could tell you about the rain: it is not raining" ('Unwilling Suspension', 1987, 11) and "It had been raining but / It had not been raining" ('A Boy', Ashbery 1987, 10). He just as often mimics Ashbery's odd, contiguous garrulity:

> There are still more hairs on my head
> Than there are croissant outlets in Seattle.
> People tell me I'm looking good, but should I believe them?
> Is anyone more trustworthy than a newspaper?
> 'Croissant Outlets in Seattle' (1987, 15)

However, just as Ash's poetry generally seeks an accommodation between the anarchistic extremes of contemporary US models and European modernism — a search symbolised by his many invocations of late nineteenth and early twentieth century avant-garde literature and music — so his use of the 'international style' of postmodernism which Ashbery may be said to embody is a way of writing poetry that does not reject meaning but insists on its provisionality: "This is not exactly what I mean. / It is all approximate things" ('Becoming a Berceuse', 1987, 24). Or as Ash wrote of Debussy, "It is a form that instantly renews itself..." ('Reading Music', *P.N. Review* 50, 45-48).

Ex-centricity : Critical Regionalism

Hutcheon (1988) has argued persuasively that postmodernism has been decisively shaped by minoritarian, or what she calls "ex-centric" discourses. A sampling of collection titles since 1980 would also seem to confirm this: Peter Didsbury's *The Butchers of Hull* (1982); Douglas Dunn's *Northlight* (1988); Eavan Boland's *Outside History* (1990); Ciaran Carson's *The Irish For No* (1988) and *Belfast Confetti* (1990); Robert Crawford's *A Scottish Assembly* (1990); W.N. Herbert's *Anither Music* (1991); Geoff Hattersley's *Slouching Towards Rotherham* (1987) and Ian Duhig's *The Bradford Count* (1991). All these titles offer us writing from a traditionally marginalised perspective and, indeed, so prevalent was this trend throughout the 1980s that one reviewer of *The New Poetry* was moved to title his notice 'Provinces plenty, London nil'. What I intend to argue here is that in the work of British postmodernist poets this "ex-centricity" is used as the basis for 'critical regionalism'.

Critical regionalism is a term I borrow from postmodernist architectural practice and was coined by Alex Tzonis and Liliane Lefaivre in 'The grid and the pathway' (1981). It is a way of distancing architecture from both Enlightenment progressivism and reactionary nostalgia for pre-industrial forms. Kenneth Frampton (1983) defines it as follows: "The fundamental strategy of Critical Regionalism is to mediate the impact of universal civilisation with elements derived indirectly from the peculiarities of a particular place. It is clear ... that Critical Regionalism depends upon maintaining a high level of critical self-consciousness. It may find its governing inspiration in such things as the range and quality of the local light, or in a *tectonic* derived from a peculiar structural model, or in the topography of a given site". A desire to mediate the universal is something we encounter throughout postmodernist theory but, as Frampton points out, Critical Regionalism should not be interpreted as a simple-minded and potentially reactionary yearning for a populist or a vernacular architecture. The key word in his formulation is 'tectonic' in its sense of 'wholeness', for Critical Regionalism seeks to counter "that which Heidegger has called a 'loss of nearness'" brought about by the privileging of perspective over "the sense of smell, hearing and taste" and to bridge the "consequent distancing from a more direct experience of the environment".

At first sight, such a theory may itself seem to be distanced from contemporary British poetry but the work of Ash, Didsbury and McMillan can be shown to have a commonality of practice with Critical Regionalism in ways that are surprisingly literal as well as figurative. Critical Regionalism, when applied to British poetry, becomes not only the opposition of a Heaneyesque 'rootedness' to what Eagleton has termed "the depthless, technocratic, dehistoricised sensibility" of late twentieth-century Britain but a 'usage', a way of structuring the impulses and products of the imagination. It is a usage that can, in part, be traced to some of the work of 'the middle generation', particularly a poem such as Douglas Dunn's 'Land-scape With One Figure' (1987, 28):

> If I could sleep standing, I would wait here
> For ever, becoming a landmark, something fixed
> For tug crews or seabound passengers to point at,
> An example of being a part of a place.

At first sight, the stanza appears to hold a number of elements — the real and the fictive, the local and the universal — in a kind of congenial balance, but a closer examination reveals the 'rootedness' of 'the middle generation' starting to become unstable, ambiguous. Documentary realism accesses hallucinatory fiction, the grounded self gives up its identity. It is this that younger poets have been more interested in than a 'sense of place' per se. In fact, the local as a 'usage' can be traced further back to Roy Fisher's seminal *City* (1969) which, as Gregson has shown (*Bête Noire* 6, 186-196), not only blurs the objective and the subjective and offers a model of representation without moralising but dramatises "doubts about where the self ends and its environment begins". The local becomes the site of a discontinuous self: "the self has made the city a part of its emotional life ... the city has been internalised through the distortions of memory and feeling". This, in its turn, underwrites a dramatisation of a conflict over representation which is visible in the way 'City' combines the documentary — "A hundred years ago this was almost the edge of town" (Fulcrum edn, 28) — and the expressionist nightmare: "The city at night ... could be broken like asphalt, and the men and women rolled out like sleeping maggots" (Fulcrum edn, 35). As these examples show, 'City' also enacts an intensity of vision that is surprisingly impersonal. Finally, Gregson's analysis of 'City' is pertinent to my borrowing of Critical Regionalism in its demonstration of how "each bit of subject matter ... is a stubbornly diffuse and singular material derived originally from the local environment" and is used in a way that preserves its diffuseness and calls into question the city as a single, fixed idea. The cumulative effect of the poem is to call into question the inherited, 'traditional' relationship between landscape and poet.

Peter Didsbury's poem 'Three Lakes by Humber' (1982, 21) asks similar questions about the representation of landscape. The first lake appears as a lagoon of industrial pollution and its colouring suggests the real becoming hallucinatory, a suggestion which is developed in the second section about a neighbouring boating lake which Didsbury imagines contaminating by means of "a conspirators' canal dug overnight". The third and final lake is "an Iron Age mirror". The local both structures the imagination and is structured by it: Didsbury turns the two lakes he does not want against each other in order to gain the freedom to enjoy the third which becomes internalised and then transformed by feeling. As in Fisher's poem 'City', an environment becomes imaginative space rather than representable reality.

John Ash makes overt homage to Fisher's poem in two prose poems dedicated to its author (1984, 31, 54). Ash, like Didsbury, sets up a complex play of absence and presence in which the urban landscape becomes a work of art that is botched or unfinished. Plastic flowers are "not even symbols anymore only a drained colour". The first piece ends with dawn — "a denial" — breaking over the shores of the reservoir where mud "dries out and cracks: a glaze badly fired". In the second piece, we begin with a statement of disintegration — "It's not going to come together" — move through images of fictiveness, scenes from an unstaged opera, and end with a painting where "the central figures" have been overlooked in favour of "the marginal detail". However, "the smudged white space draws us in" suggesting that, as in Didsbury's poem 'The Shore', the city is a 'spacing', a place of intervals and 'unselfhood' where the imagination can claim free play and decide for itself the degree of absence and presence that attaches there. The effect of these poems comes close to what McHale identifies in postmodernist fiction (32) as a matter of "ontological oscillation, a flickering ... or, to use Ingarden's ... metaphor, an effect of 'iridescence' or 'opalescence'". According to Ingarden, "in a manner of speaking, two different worlds are struggling for supremacy, with neither of them capable of attaining it". Ash writes an extreme version of this in several poems that interfuse Paris and Manchester — 'Nostalgia' (1987, 52); 'Early Views of Manchester and Paris: Third View', (1982, 52) — and in 'The Didsbury Elegies' (1984, 26). A suburb of Manchester becomes a fictional zone in which 'reality' is absurdly and nightmarishly 'extended': autumn becomes permanent, the thinning gardens reveal something that is perhaps a skeleton, perhaps a sculpture, perhaps a mechanism.

Where Didsbury and Ash write a version of 'ex-centricity' that often seeks to defamiliarise the local by isolating particular elements, Ian McMillan's poetry is unmistakably set in a specific region. His work is full of references to Yorkshire generally and to the South Yorkshire mining region specifically. 'Wharram Percy, North Yorkshire' (1983, 17) offers the local as access to a wider experience, albeit with McMillan's characteristic humour:

> A sky, 'lined with worry
> and fatigue' is dark
> over the coast. A damp
> wind jostles old ladies:
>
> this is the mystery
> of the modern world.

'Villages Without Mains Gas' (1988) gives us a version of the blurring of self and environment, of objective and subjective, which Gregson highlights in Fisher:

> Barnburgh, Marr, Hickleton; almost
> a denial of the past
>
> through a celebration of the past.
>
>   ★ ★ ★
>
> The years shift on a fulcrum of dirt roads
> and cars avoiding holes in roads
>
> and fields holding the smell of a ploughed soul.

This is, in one sense, McMillan's 'example of being a part of a place' and, like Dunn's poem, the passage enacts materialism becoming unstable, illusive. More importantly, though, McMillan's poem suggests, like Fisher's 'City', that places only truly exist as histories of feeling and memory. 'Denial' and 'celebration' are the poem's version of absence and presence. This conception of place comes to the fore in the poems that deal with South Yorkshire specifically, for they inevitably engage with the fundamental changes brought about there by the progressive dismantling of the coal industry throughout the 1980s. The most interesting of these is 'The er Barnsley Seascapes' (1994, 82-87), a surreal fantasy in which parts of South Yorkshire not only become coastal but also an historical tourist attraction. The eight sections of the poem accumulate into a complex piece of writing which deals with the destruction of working class life and the replacement of grounded ethics and politics with a kind of moveable, entrepreneurial aesthetics. Close-knit communities have become fictional zones whose inhabitants have purses "from Habitat, in the shape of a bath / filled with coal", can rent videos called "Barnsley is Basingstoke!" or "Barnsley is Japan!" and work, if at all, for what used to be the NCB but is now called "British Smile". Through its fantastic and ludicrous exaggerations, the poem suggests that reality has overtaken theory: the dismantling of the coal industry was the breaking up of a 'master narrative' which resulted not in generalised feelings of displacement and loss but the lived experience of postmodernism.

The poem describes what Foucault (McHale, 44) has termed a 'heterotopia', "the disorder in which fragments of a large number of possible orders glitter separately ... without ... a common *locus* beneath them all" — indeed, section 6, 'er from a Learned Paper about the Seascapes', details how some of the surviving South Yorkshire Coastal Mining Settlements "have worked loose from the earth // and slither around the countryside". In a very real sense, life after coal seems to prove that a materialist aesthetic is ill-advised and unworkable and to confirm the provisionality of ontological status. The repeated use of "er" underlines this as well as emphasising a condition of helplessness in the face of irrevocable change. It is, in fact, an excellent example of the status play referred to in the preceding chapter (see pages 71-72). The poem sets up an oscillation between the presence of Barnsley as tourist seascape and the absence of Barnsley as a community with a literal bond with the earth. However, just as the use of "er" also implies a residual local identity, so this absence still seems capable of supplying a 'tectonic', a topographical shaping:

Only the water, solid
and glinting. Only
the noise of the water,

and the noise of the moon
slowly deflating, and
only the noise of the stars

being sold, clinking,
keeps me awake
all day.
    'Seascape could er be anywhere around here'

Just as celebration can almost be denial so a parodic report of the death of a heterogeneous tradition may approach, if not its salvation, then at least an argument for its importance. Critical regionalism, like parody, provides a means of criticising a discourse from within without being completely assimilated by it.

"Just The Facts, Just The" : The Dialogue with Realism

McHale (5) argues that the very term 'postmodernism' emphasises an "element of logical and historical *consequence* rather than sheer temporal *posteriority*". Such an emphasis questions how far, if at all, postmodernism can be read as a "radical rhetoric of rupture" (Hutcheon, 50). However, if we accept Hutcheon's thesis that postmodernism is a mode of formal self-consciousness in late twentieth century capitalist culture, then it seems inevitable that it will be characterised by major paradoxes of form and ideology. We have already seen, for example, how John Ash's poetry both flirts with the exhilaration of the sense of an ending and simultaneously attempts to update classical liberal humanism. In the preceding section I used terms such as 'oscillation', 'flickering' and 'iridescence' to describe the effect of such 'double encoding' and a similar irresolvable ambivalence underlies British postmodernist poets' transactions with the inherited discourse of traditional realism. The nature of these transactions may be summed up by lines like "the weather ... / came in over the towers like perdition / like a paragraph in the densest type" (John Ash, 'The Cascades N.Y.', 1987, 36) or "The sky is like an entry in The Oxford English Dictionary. / The earliest reference for it is 1764" (Peter Didsbury, 'The Guitar', 1987, 34). They suggest, yet again, that the characteristic British postmodernist poetic 'project' does not — to borrow from

Hutcheon (229) — "'liquidate referentials' so much as force a rethinking of the entire notion of reference ... It suggests that all we have ever had to work with is a system of signs and that to call attention to this is not to deny the real, but to remember that we only *give meaning to* the real within those signifying systems".

Peter Didsbury's poem 'The Web' (1982, 50) makes the dialogue with realism explicit through its dedication to Douglas Dunn. The poem sets up other resonances with Dunn, particularly his collection *Terry Street* (1969). 'The Web' uses the same·stopped, two line stanzas as Dunn's 'South Bank of the Humber' and 'Late Night Walk Down Terry Street' (1969, 56, 25). Where Dunn's poem 'Young Women in Rollers'(1969, 29) has its narrator listening to "Mozart playing loudly // On the afternoon Third", Didsbury's poem begins with "A summer noon ... // Brahms is on the Third". Similarly, Didsbury's "Literary tropes. A passing Chinaman" echoes Dunn's "Chinese characters / In the lower sky" ('On Roofs of Terry Street', 1969, 21). However, this is a debt one quite expects to see being repaid — Didsbury was, after all, one of the poets in Dunn's excellent anthology of Hull-based poets *A Rumoured City*. What is more interesting is how Didsbury's poem expands on Dunn. Dunn's poem 'Young Women in Rollers' ends with the line "There are many worlds, there are many laws" and where Dunn offers this observation in economic and social terms, Didsbury takes the 'classic' Dunn location of the terraced street and reveals it as a zone, a 'world' in McHale's terms, shaped by a number of discourses and a blurring of divisions between them — Brahms may be on the Third but "So is last night's pain".

In fact, in purely psychological terms, the whole of Didsbury's poem may be said to function as a series of 'delusions of reference'. The line "Picture windows make me sick" may function as a rejection of documentary realism but the poem takes more interest — confirmed by Didsbury's note — in the derivation of 'window' from the Old Norse *vindauga* or 'wind's eye'. Later lines — "Lady Etymology, teach me how to cry" and "Language and history make me tender" — and the play with the name of Job's last daughter Keren-happuch meaning 'horn of eye paint' not only suggest that our ways of feeling are culturally determined but make clear that "last night's pain" is not lovesickness but the agony of poetic creation. The poem's final image — "A pole with wires, that serves the street. / The Web, where all our voices meet" — gives us a surprising echo of Lyotard's conception of the self as a 'nodal point' or 'listening post' (see Larrissy, 182). Indeed, the last line inevitably conjures images of the cyberspace of telecommunication and computer networks which some commentators see as a new kind of social space. The community of the terraced street is changing. "All our voices" may also refer to a meeting of discourses — music, language, the Bible — as enacted by the poem and also as a meeting of all the constituent 'voices' that make up each self.

Didsbury's poem, then, seems in many ways to grow quite naturally out of Dunn's practice, taking its fictive, hallucinatory and surreal touches and expanding them into a full-blown poetic of defamiliarisation. Even an urban sketch is a meeting of signifying systems; even a terraced back-street is entirely 'of the mind', something made plain by the way each pair of lines contrasts two worlds: real and discourse, fact and relativity. Once 'world' becomes 'language' it enters a medium which, Bahtkin argued (in Hutcheon, 80), is not "neutral" or "the private property of the user: it is 'overpopulated' with the intentions of others". It is these 'intentions' which Didsbury teases out of real events and actual places. 'The Web' stands as a model of what John Ash has termed in his own poetry (*P.N. Review* 47, 38) "'orchestral objectivity' — a species of *polyphony* if you like, and not some reedy, solo voice eternally practising the monotonous scales of its 'feelings', 'memories' and 'impressions'". Or, as Didsbury writes in 'The Flowers of Finland' (1982, 42), "telling the truth about the world / mightn't be the best way / of getting some things down". Realism is not valueless but it is only valuable when it leads to a mode that Ash calls "configural".

A configural poetic suggests the relationship of a number of positions or views. Ash, typically, moves from the real to the imaginary as in 'Streets' (1991, 77):

> Doesn't the whole city cry out to him
> that he must do something remarkable today?
> One assumes (one can assume anything)
> that behind the charming pediment of a smile
> there is an interior to be explored,

The passage does more than offer a disdainful burlesque of the way we experience reality through making up stories about it: it suggests that, just as objects, people, and places in a narrative are only ever partially revealed to us at any given point and we unproblematically fill in the rest, so our experience of reality takes the part for the whole in the same way. McHale (1987, 32) is useful here for he quotes a passage from Gilbert Sorrentino's novel *Mulligan Stew* (1979) which foregrounds these assumptions:

> At the side of the living room, a staircase leads 'nowhere'.
> Oh, I don't mean to say that it disappears into empty space,
> it simply leads to a kind of ... haziness, in which one knows
> there is *supposed* to be a hallway and bedroom doors: but there
> is absolutely nothing.

The architectural imagery of Ash's poem suggests that we are deluding ourselves if we think we are clever enough to tell the real from the fictive. To return to Hutcheon, Ash is not 'liquidating referentials': he is perhaps suggesting that to understand their complexity and the complexity involved in that understanding may in some way serve to 'liquidate' us. Conventional realism may be frustrated in its desire for mimetic precision but the world is still describable: the difference is that description has no responsibility except to the logic of the imagination.

It is a point that Ian McMillan makes overtly in 'Form Without Implicit Moral' (1983, 26):

> The only word I can think of
> to describe the scene
> is 'outfit'
> and that is the wrong word,
> is completely the wrong word.

The passage plays with the meaning of completeness and the possibility of a totalising aesthetic or discourse. Not only is 'outfit' completely the wrong word, its rejection highlights the inherent absurdity in assuming that the various elements of a scene can be made to fit together like a suit of clothes. Like Didsbury, McMillan may be said to take Dunn's line "There are many worlds, there are many laws" at face value as 'permission' to produce what Barthes (see Hutcheon, 80, 81) termed 'text as social space' in which no single thing dominates. The world demands to be treated as something approaching an aleatory score.

Reality, then, is too complex to be documented according to an 'A=B' model but this does not mean that British postmodernist poets have followed Ashbery in offering us language itself as the only reality, or the poem as a self-reflexive parody that mocks the hermeneutic impulse and enacts little more than *kenosis* or self-emptying. Specific cultural conditions play their part in this: British poets have not, by and large, made much engagement with French and Russian writers of the period 1900-1940; and, similarly, there is no native phenomenon comparable in influence to Abstract Expressionism and its ideas of 'all-over' surface, formal and imaginative *flatness* and what Fuller (1980, 85) terms a self-critical program which produced works that give "pleasure of a kind which [is] dissociated from considerations of meaning, truth or history". However, to argue that British poets have been carrying on a sustaining dialogue with native realism is not to suggest a project that seeks to uncover / recover the essential Englishness of native maverick talents; rather, it is simply to suggest that British poets do not see postmodernism as a matter of simple rejections and dependent choices. The dialogue with realism underlines that they engage with postmodernism not as rupture but as processes of erosion, transformation and dissolution, as a poetics that problematizes but does not necessarily deconstruct. In Hutcheon's words (230) "The postmodern still operates ... in the realm of representation, not of simulation, even if it constantly questions the rules of that realm".

The Victim of a Recent Bombing : The ghosts of politics

The inherently contradictory nature of postmodernism is perhaps nowhere more apparent than in the critical debates over its political 'colour'. Hutcheon (4) asserts that postmodernism is "inescapably political" but also observes (201) that "it has been accused of everything from reactionary nostalgia to radical revolution". The radical extreme may be found in writers such as Arthur Kroker and David Cook who, with characteristic silliness, see postmodernism as a poetics of the apocalypse, "the terrain of a new political refusal" as "western culture runs down toward the brilliant illumination of a final burn out" (1988, xvii). Jameson has made the most influential statement of the opposing view which sees postmodernism as an articulation of the free-market logic of late capitalism. It is a view that continues to have wide currency and lies behind such state-ments as Luckhurst's, for example, that postmodernism's "sexual politics are in fact 'pre-postmodern'" (*Bête Noire* 8/9, 181) and Harvey's that "postmodernism comes dangerously close to complicity with the aestheticising of politics upon which it is based" (1989, 117). At first sight, Harvey's remark would seem eminently applicable to these lines from John Ash's poem 'Nympheas' (1984, 39):

> On the wall above the table a print,
> predominantly mauve, displays
> the victim of a recent bombing
> dissolved into luscious water-lights and lilies: it looks
>
> good enough to eat ...

However, I want to argue that, as in the case of their continuing dialogue with realism, the presence of such material in the work of British postmodernist poets is bound up with their particular sense of what the postmodernist project involves. A decisive factor here is what I take to be the poets' sense of what Docherty (26) has termed "the basis of an ethical demand in the postmodern": "The demand is for a just relating to alterity, and for a cognition of the event of heterogeneity. In short, therefore, we must discover — produce — justice. It is here that the real political burden and trajectory of the postmodern is to be found: the search for a just politics, or the search for just a politics." What must also be borne in mind is the flowering of postmodernism in British poetry against the background of the Thatcher era. I would argue, however, that what connections may exist do not necessarily underwrite a Jamesonian view of post-modernism in British poetry but rather that the nature of the political material present in that poetry — generalised images of oppression, oblique critiques of the class system, non-specific barbs against the status quo — may in fact reflect the largely ineffectual nature of opposition during that period. Finally, the presence of political material usually works to disturb a fictive, typically post-modern surface which suggests that, as with realism, British poets do not view the problematizing poetics of the postmodern as unproblematic 'manna'.

John Ash's first major collection *The Goodbyes* (1982) contains a number of generalised statements of political import which relate to the postmodern's sense of the breakdown of 'master narratives' and which it is instructive to consider together as various sides of a single argument:

> The sentiment is questionable: regret for a vanished order
> which, if it still existed, we'd dream of destroying like any
> nation of the colonised.
>   'The Big House', 18

★ ★ ★

> Your world has ended ... again ... And that smile
> so carefully judged to deflect all criticism
> is the true sign that you are lost like the idea of a just
>   society ...
>   'The Grapefruit Segments: A Book of Preludes', 30

★ ★ ★

> The task ahead
> is momentous but pleasurable: you have to invent, or —

which may be the same thing — remember
the language of this place, its peculiar history ...
              ... whether it is
appropriate to talk of 'serfdom' after the close of its
    nineteenth century,
the ambiguous relationship of this to the rise of a
    bourgeoisie ...
          'The Stranger in the Corridor', 36

The three passages clearly relate to the dynamic account of the postmodern condition already identified in Ash's poetry in the first section of this chapter, and the questions they imply about our relationship with a vanished order may be taken as typical of the 'double encoding' we have seen elsewhere. The location of generalised political observations in generalised accounts of the condition of postmodernity may also be taken as an indication of how thoroughly the political permeates the Ash poetic. While the second passage seems to yearn for justice overtly in the sense of Docherty's "ethical demand", the three passages together imply rather than state a complex view of the present. In one sense, the political here seems closely allied with Ash's conception that "pleasure's not simple": the invention of the past and the corresponding desire to aestheticise politics does not sidestep inconvenient historical imperatives. The passage from 'The Stranger in the Corridor' may be read as an oblique commentary on the rise of the British heritage industry and the links between its commodification of the past and a political philosophy which worked from the assumption that the majority of the British people had not approved of and had certainly not enjoyed the years from 1960 to 1975.

What problematizes this reading is that Ash recognises that the commodification of the past is indeed very pleasurable and that while no-one would want the old order reinstated, the present seems quite happy to collude in a order that, in its own way, is just as hierarchical and unjust. In *The Branching Stairs* (1984) and *Disbelief* (1987) this generalised commentary has become a full-blown meta-narrative of political oppression which remains tantalisingly un-located. In 'The Sudden Ending of Their Dream' (1987, 56) "The police were not watching them / although their vans rushed past hissing in the rain, / and black princesses sheltered nervously in doorways" and in 'Men, Women, and Children' (1987, 47) "life is a festive march ... until // we are forced to think of our destination, — / the oppressive portals of the capitol, / the altars still smelling of blood". Similarly 'Bespalko's Devotions' (1984, 105) has a whole section devoted to a description of what appears to be life under a totalitarian regime, and 'The Poem of Arrival' (1984, 152) describes an afternoon becoming "permanent / like a monument for which forgotten slaves had died / under the oppression of a repulsive dynasty". The cumulative effect of such passages is to imply that while the condition of postmodernity may permit a dandyish devotion to pleasure there is one master narrative that has not broken down as irreparably as we might hope and that postmodernism may, indeed, be a form of complacency that allows its resurgence. To invoke the end of capitalism and the dawn of the post-industrial age may, in fact, be a seductive and largely aristocratic fiction which ignores that millions of people continue and will continue to lead lives of fruitless toil and that postmodernism may be a 'space' in which only a very few can properly orient themselves.

The impulse to aestheticise is confronted by Ian McMillan in 'Pit Closure As Art' (1994, 12). The poem is set at a "major retrospective" at whose centre "there is a door / which you open" and which gives access to a world of total powerlessness. The responses of the viewer — smiles, tears, — "become the property of The Artist" and at the end of the poem the viewer has become part of The Art: there is, quite literally, no way out. As is often the case with McMillan, a surreal surface masks a complexly allusive — and illusive — argument. 'Pit Closure As Art' is not merely a simplistic presentation of the fact that aesthetics and politics are inseparable or even that they are products of the same prevailing set of material conditions. The poem asks us to consider the sado-masochistic nature of the trans- action between viewer and artist; the possibility that the same sort of transactions occur in both the aesthetic and the political spheres; and that art may be used as a masquerade to hide political realities.

The title of the poem and its setting at a "major retrospective" also sets up a play with ideas of heritage culture and the way that old industrial sites — wharves, warehouses, factories — have been reinvented into luxurious dwellings and business accommodation for the professions and the new 'service industries'. On this level 'Pit Closure As Art' can be closely related to 'The er Barnsley Seascapes' (see pages 106-107) and McMillan himself has traced both poems to an earlier piece 'Title (Northumberland June 11/12th 1987)' (1994, 74). 'Title' is a collage of various notes on a summer holiday and the General election of 1987 which the poet has described as "one of those Kurt Schwitters things made out of bus tickets". The fact that the poem presents half of its material upside down allies it with Modernism but an autotelic avant-gardism is unsettled by notes such as "The boys ran into the trees", "How do you paint terror?" and "Redraft me, I am / frightened, bud". The effect is to ask the reader to fill in the rest of a narrative that may be about political oppression and the statelessness of opposition. Art, particularly postmodernist art, occupies an ambiguous position, moving between complicity with the prevailing order and resistance to it; or, as McMillan puts it in 'Why We Need Libraries' (1994, 10). "You never know what will happen, though, // because the future is a book in a private library. Unless we can request that book // and borrow it and read it and read it."

Where Ash and McMillan foreground a dynamic discussion of the possibility of satisfying Docherty's "ethical demand", Peter Didsbury is more subtle, enacting an inclusive poetic in which politics is but one of many inseparable discourses. Indeed, to borrow two of Docherty's key terms, Didsbury's characteristic procedure may be said to involve an unpacking of 'alterity' and 'heterogeneity': "With more than one world / it might be easier. / I could watch us from the others" ('Hermetic', 1982, 12). In Didsbury's poetry, an alertness to the construction of cultural codes is one way of giving a sense of "more than one world". 'The British Museum' (1987, 63) attempts to view the institution 'innocently':

> We dream of the British Museum.
>
>   *   *   *
>
>   We're busy dreaming ourselves political.
> An elegant system of sleep is constructing
> A complex lodge for a free and scholarly people.
> A state of grace that lies sleeping within the State
> Is emptying its present halls of plunder.

At first sight, this reads as an indictment of culture as a mask for the true nature of political order: a 'great British institution' is viewed, in Osborne's words, "not as an object of veneration, but as a monument in the history of booty" (*Bête Noire* 6, 25). This is, I believe, only a partial reading for Didsbury's subtlety lies in asking us to consider how culture can be simultaneously a seductive, elegant 'dream', "a complex lodge" and "A state of grace" and how culture depends for its existence on a species of 'doublethink' which means we can still be seduced, put to sleep by monuments to booty or documents of barbarism. Indeed, the poem may even go so far as to suggest that the self-congratulation involved in "dreaming ourselves political", in learning the 'truth' about culture and, consequently,

picturing ourselves as citizens of "a free and scholarly people" is part
of the seduction. Our own knowingness may be one of the fantasies
we bring to transactions with culture.

Finally, I want to look at 'The Hailstone' (1987, 60) which is, to
date, Didsbury's most ambitious poem politically in its suggestion
that even our most mundane everyday experiences may be somehow
connected to culturally and, therefore, politically constructed codes.
The poem opens in a thunderstorm, "in the kind of rain we used to
call a cloudburst", a line which immediately sets up echoes of a
genteel and ordered world. The nature of such order is explored in
the next section:

> A woman sheltering inside the shop
> had a frightened dog,
> which she didn't want us to touch.
> It had something to do with class,
> and the ownership of fear.

Osborne (*Bête Noire* 6, 25) asserts that "In the twenty-first century
an astute reader might deduce the entire Thatcher era from these
five lines" but again, I would argue, this largely misses the point.
Didsbury is making generalised connections between gentility, class
and "the ownership of fear" in a British context as the poem's long
central section makes plain:

> It was like being back
> in the reign of George the Sixth, the kind of small town
> which still lies stacked in the back of old storerooms in
>   schools,
> where plural roof and elf expect to get very wet

The poem evokes not only a lost age of order — symbolised by
plurals, titles and "nouns of congregation" — and of cultural
pessimism and caution but implies a similarity between it and the
present, in this case 1984, the date of the poem's first publication.
The passage mimes the nostalgia which was at the heart of British
politics in the 1980s. The line about "a usable language" fore-
grounds the self-delusion involved in such a project, both politically
and culturally. The self-delusion is that language and, by extension,
cultural and political activity, gives what Belsey (Tredell 1994, 220)
terms "a transparent access to something beyond it". As with the
earlier image of the woman with the frightened dog this is definitely
not the case; the best that can be achieved is a kind of illusive,

associative resonance. Reading 'The Hailstone' in the light of Docherty's "ethical demand" suggests that,' for Didsbury, "the search for a just politics" begins with language itself, with a recognition of its materiality and of the randomness of the imagination. The image of the woman with the dog as an apprehension of political order can also be related to postmodernism in general. Docherty (25) describes the beginning of "a shift in emphasis away from what we could call scientific knowledge towards what should properly be considered as a form of narrative knowledge. Rather than knowing the stable essence of a thing, we begin to tell the story of the event of judging it and to enact the narrative of how it changes consciousness and produces a new knowledge. Barthes once advocated a shift 'from work to text'; the postmodern advocates a shift 'from text to event' ... The postmodern prefers the event of knowing to the fact of knowledge, so to speak." Such a preference can prove dangerously seductive and lead to Harvey's 'aestheticising'. British postmodernist poets' understanding of the interlocation of the political and the aesthetic has enabled them not only to avoid this danger in postmodernism itself but also to warn against it in the wider social and political contexts of Britain after 1979.

A Pinch Of Scepticism By Way Of A Conclusion : Aesthetic Practice v. Social Reality

The Daily Telegraph Saturday Magazine (26.3.94) carried an article entitled 'Front Line E14' which investigated how the Bengali community of London's East End reacted to racist terror and violence. The article is pertinent because it highlights the gap between postmodernist cultural activity and critical theory and everyday social and political reality. The article featured a colour photo of "Andrew Mackay, a music producer, with the daughter of an Asian singer he works with, walking in Limeharbour on the Isle of Dogs. 'It's weird, really,' he says. 'Here we are creating this wonderful crossover music, mixing Indian rhythms with western styles, and yet the girls I'm working with live in a street on the island where none of the white people talks to them'." Sarah Maguire, one of the poets featured in 1994's 'New Generation Poets' promotion, has made a similar point (Poetry Review — New Generation Poets Special Issue, 69): "Frolicking in a boundless ocean of contingency is not an activity open to the (increasing numbers) of poor, homeless and exploited". References elsewhere in Maguire's piece to the election of Ronald Reagan as an example of ethics being replaced by aesthetics and to the end of Fordism suggest a debt to Harvey's account of the condition of postmodernity but Maguire's particular choice of emphasis provides a useful crystallisation of the way British poets have responded to the challenge of postmodernism. Maguire argues that

> there are 'left' and 'right' versions of postmodernism. The former (at its best) places a postcolonialist and feminist stress on difference and otherness which, whilst emphasising the deconstruction of meta-narratives (such as notions of gender and race) can retain a materialist and political analysis of inequality and injustice. The 'right' version of postmodernism, whilst having a similar stress on the deconstruction of metaphysics, revels unashamedly in the seamless free-play of signifiers which leads to an idealisation of the signifier deprived of the signified.

Resistance of idealisation is readily located in Ash's poem 'The Ungrateful Citizens' (1991, 81) which begins on a whim: "It occurs to me that I would like to write a poem about Naples". The poem is clearly inspired by Ashbery's 'The Instruction Manual' (1987, 5) in which the speaker fantasises about visiting "Guadalajara! City of rose-coloured flowers!" but whereas Ashbery's poem merely presents us with a sequence of seductive imaginings and then returns to its opening reality, Ash's poem ends with the citizens of Naples attacking the poet for having made "the amorous ballet the tourist requires for a backdrop" out of "a place of ordinary wretchedness".

Ash's poem, like Maguire's distinction between 'left' and 'right', suggests that British poets are only too well aware that postmodernism can seduce the artist into the kind of self-absorbed unwatchfulness that Prospero falls victim to in front of the masque of goddesses and spirits he conjures in Act IV of *The Tempest*. Indeed, the postmodernist poetic represented by Ashbery can often appear as a species of élite and impenetrable masque whereas British postmodernist poetic practice has been closely associated with wider currents of 'populism' and 'democratization' in British poetry of the 1980s and early 1990s. The postmodernism of Ash, Didsbury and McMillan — or of Crawford, Herbert and Kuppner — is emphatically not what Harvey (336) castigates as a narrowing of the field of social vision and "a passive depiction of otherness, alienation and contingency". However, I do not want to suggest by this that British poets are merely producing a kind of 'postmodernism with a social conscience' but that their work embodies a sense of what Harvey (358) terms the "dangers in releasing an unknown and perhaps uncontrollable aesthetic power into an unstable situation". This has meant we have seen nothing of postmodernism in its guise of "neo-Nietzschean celebratory lament" (Hutcheon, 223) as exemplified by the writings of Baudrillard or Kroker and Cook.

British poets since 1980 may often have felt they were living in an old country in which 'master narratives' were either breaking down or being actively deconstructed. As I hope to have shown, postmodernism continues to be such a positive influence for a number of British poets because it has liberated them from the totalising and consequently exclusive impulses of the inherited British poem. Just as 'the middle generation' of Dunn, Harrison and Heaney subjected 'traditional' British metrics to maximum stress, so postmodernism has enabled a younger generation to 're-envision' the poem as a 'laboratory' of the systems and codes that structure culture and society. What has resulted has not been élite language games but a generous inclusiveness; or, as Ash puts it in 'Advanced Choreography for Beginners' (1984, 40): "the point is: // to establish a new lyricism in which all ... things will find their place".

In a review of recent books by American novelist E.L. Doctorow, Stephen Fender observed that "technology has institutionalised the efficient production and distribution of every civic good save one: information, charity, law enforcement, power and light are organised; only wealth remains undistributed" (*TLS*, 27.5.94, 20). David Harvey has some characteristically uncomfortable things to say about the relationship between the condition of postmodernity and the 'technocratisation' of late twentieth century capitalism. I want to end this essay on a more speculative note: it may not be going too far to suggest that postmodernism as practised by contemporary British poets may start with a realisation that if redistribution of wealth is not possible literally then it can at least be achieved 'culturally'.

4. Elegies for the Living:
The Poetry of Peter Reading

Peter Reading is a largely solitary figure in British poetry in the last quarter of the twentieth century. Tom Paulin (1992, 287) has pointed to Reading's "amazed and unflinching discovery of a subject few English poets have been able to confront — Junk Britain"; but the fourteen collections Reading has published since 1974 have also dealt increasingly with what Alan Jenkins has termed "Reading's dark, often appalled and appalling vision ... [of] the ways of *H.sap*" (1986). The reviewer who titled his notice of a recent Reading volume 'Desperanto' was at once bleakly complimentary and startlingly apt (Maxwell 1992). Reading himself has said (Interview 1985) that he started out wanting "to write in as *hard* a way as I could" and that "art has always struck me most when it was to do with coping with things, often hard things, things that are difficult to take". Just *how* difficult some people have found Reading's poetry is underlined both by the *TLS* receiving gifts of excrement after it published his poem 'Cub', about a terrorist incident in the Lebanon, and by another reviewer's bewildered cry, "What does Peter Reading, fine poet of our age, yes absolutely, what does Peter Reading want?" (Whitworth 1989). Indeed, a large section of the poetry reading public would presumably be in agreement with Gavin Ewart's amicable parody 'The Peter Reading Poem' (1989, 99), part of which goes:

Teenag|ers rum|tum || titty|tum-titty | head-bashing | babies
Tum-titty,|umtitty |um ||hominoids | aliens, | oicks

Reading is, however, set apart by much more than his subjects and the responses they provoke. First, as the Ewart parody makes clear, his work makes an overt and self-conscious engagement with metre and form. The last line of *Final Demands* (1988) is a crossed-out notation of metrical feet and his work as a whole is characterised by the use of and reference to such forms as alexandrines, elegaics, distiches, Alcaics, Alcmanics and Anglo-Saxon alliterative forms at a time when most poets have continued in traditional English forms or vers libre. Second, as such an engagement indicates, in a period when many British poets have either looked abroad for inspiration or negotiated with such twentieth century figures as Auden, Eliot, Hughes, Larkin and Pound, Reading's formal and conceptual poetic models remain either classical or those of the earliest English poems.

This is a point I shall return to later in this chapter and it is important to bear in mind that Reading's work is always concerned to measure the human and, particularly, its late twentieth century manifestation, against the largest possible temporal perspective. Third, since his first book *For The Municipality's Elderly* (1974), Reading has worked exclusively in sequences in which multiple narrators and stories orbit round a central concern: cancer in *C* (1984), for example, or mental illness in *Tom O'Bedlam's Beauties* (1981). This highlights the powerful narrative / novelistic drive in Reading's work of which he has commented (Interview 1985), "The concision of poetry appeals to me, but the novelist's job — big scale serious tacklings of things, as in Dickens or Smollet — is something I try in a smaller way to get into what I do". The references to Smollet and particularly to Dickens are significant because many of Reading's books can be read as residual novels in Leavis's 'great tradition' in which society is a complex organism. Accents, dialects and class-specific discourses notated with scientific accuracy, as well as letters, journals, and newspaper reports offer a complex commentary on each book's chosen concern. What makes Reading's 'residual' novels so remarkable is that their continuity is located in exuberant technical invention: 'concision' relates to 'big scale serious tacklings' in that a particular book's subject is inseparable from a particular formal challenge Reading sets himself. Thus *C* (1984) deals with cancer in "100 100-word units" while *Ukulele Music / Going On* (1985) offers a sustained bravura performance in the use of distiche. Finally, Reading is unique in that although his books deal graphically with particular subjects, his underlying concerns — the smallness of human endeavour, the uselessness of poetry, the conflict between social codes and actual behaviour — have remained unwaveringly consistent. It is one of the typical paradoxes of his work that as his texts have become ever more provisional and polyphonic so these concerns have become clearer and clearer. There is perhaps no other poet currently writing whose work demands to be read as a single oeuvre, as a kind of gigantic, spiralling narrative. From *Ukulele Music* (1985) and *Stet* (1986) onwards, Reading's books have been characterised by obsessive revisitings and recastings of earlier work, a process which dominates his most recent collection *Last Poems* (1994). The book reprints the title poem from *Nothing For Anyone* (1977) — once in a 'frame' which bemoans its neglect and again at the end of the book as an illegible photocopy — reworks material from *Stet* and *C* and returns to Reading's first collection.

All this must, however, serve as 'signposting' only for I do not propose to confine myself to a discussion of what sets Peter Reading apart from the rest of British poetry in the 1980s and early 1990s: rather, I want to argue, at the risk of appearing paradoxical, that his extremities may be taken as exemplary. Tom Paulin (1992, 287) has described Reading as "the unofficial laureate of a decaying nation". I want to go further and argue that Reading's work may be read as nothing less than a microcosm of British poetry from 1980 onwards for it contains many of the key currents in the period, among them: intertextuality, narrative, the polyphonic poem, the last of England and the end of history, the interfusion of the media and of science, the relocation of the pastoral. My argument is grounded in two places. First, in these two passages from Reading's book *Evagatory* (1992) which I believe may be taken as a summary of his abiding concerns:

> Cranial voice loquacious/inadequate
>   (translationese from life to lingo):
>
> Only a troubled idyll now possible,
> pastoral picnic under an ozone hole,
> England, *The Times* screwed up in a trash-bucket,
>   gliding astern, the Thames, the old prides,
>   end of an era, nation, notion,
>   Albion urban, devenustated
>   (one of those routine periodic
> faunal extinctions [cf. the Permian]),
> anthropod aberration (posterity).
>   (14)

* * *

> nothing on earth can abide forever,
> illness or age or aggression takes us,
> striving for fame beyond death is futile
> (none will be left to celebrate heroes' *lof*),
>
> days and delights depart, and inferior
>   beings infest and despoil earth, each one
> greys and grows grave and, pallid, passes.
>   (20)

I shall use words or phrases in these passages as keys to Reading's concerns and their interfusion with British poetry of the 1980s and early 1990s. As the two passages make plain, any reading of Reading's work involves an engagement with and understanding of what Neil

Roberts (1995) has identified as species of 'rupture' or 'fragmentation'. "Loquacious/inadequate" is merely one of the tamer instances. Elsewhere, for example, *Ukulele Music* (1985) fills up metrical space with the irritating "plinkaplinka" of its eponymous instrument; its companion book *Going On* mocks itself as the "slick prestidigital art of Not Caring/Hopelessly Caring" (*ER*, 226); and the "bilge" and "mawkishness" of tombstone inscriptions can still somehow "[prompt] a sharp intake of breath" (*3 in 1*, 127). The second grounding of my discussion, therefore, will be the detailing of the particular ruptures or fragmentations involved in each of the areas suggested by the two passages from *Evagatory*. Finally, I do not propose to detail every instance where Reading's work may be related to the wider currents of British poetry. I shall refer to the more interesting of these and leave the others to resonate with other chapters in the book.

"Troubled idyll / pastoral picnic / Albion urban" : From pastoral to municipal

The published poetry of Peter Reading begins in a particular place: a locale that is geographically provincial; that is at some precarious point between the pastoral and the urban, the idealised and the blighted; that is sometimes a transition, sometimes an interfusion, sometimes a clash. The title of his first collection signals this in particular ways. *For The Municipality's Elderly* (1974) announces the urban reality of everyday life and perhaps suggests as well a sense that larger ideas of nation have shrunk to an all too temporal and material dispensation. This is made problematic, however, by the word "for" which sets up echoes of elegiac form as in, say, Lowell's 'For The Union Dead' (*SP*, 62) or the first of Geoffrey Hill's 'Two Formal Elegies' which is subtitled 'For the Jews in Europe' (1985, 30). Elegies are for the dead but Reading's title suggests, paradoxically, elegies for the living. Elegiac echoes are further problematized by their particular associations in an English context, as in Gray's 'Elegy in a Country Churchyard'. Elegies are at their most powerful when they combine a lament for the dead with a pastoral setting and recuperate the dead in an idealised landscape, as in Heaney's 'The Strand at Lough Beg' (1979, 17). Again, Reading's title suggests the opposite: the world of corporations, councils, city halls and libraries. The problematics of Reading's title also inform 'Embarkation' (1974, 8) in which a journey on a suburban commuter train in summer appears to evoke something akin to

Edward Thomas's 'Adlestrop' "Something today evokes ... / a
summer ending and a country halt" (1978, 71) — but ends with a
purgatorial vision which would not be out of place in *The Waste
Land*: "And I have been among them on the quay, / placed pennies,
at the turnstile, on our tongues". 'Embarkation' not only makes
plain that the relationship between pastoral and municipal is not
just one of an unfavourable contrast but foregrounds an inescapable
fictionalising involved in our responses to both. The pastoral, par-
ticularly, is indivisible from The Pastoral as cultural construct: 'A
two inch square of Botticelli, held / up to the light, reveals a greener
world / than I see daily or can hope to move to" ('Spring Letter
(Primavera)', 1974, 28). It is a point that is made even more
graphically in 'Raspberrying' (1974, 22):

> Nature
> itself as anachronistic today
> as a poem about it.
>
> Yet one feels almost justified still to acknowledge
> the deeper reflection of, albeit hackneyed,
> the Human Condition in Nature (reduced
> as she is from the nympho once over-extolled
> for ad-nauseam cyclic fecundity, to
> today's stripped-bare and thorny old sod half-heartedly
> whorily pouting a couple of blackening nipples.)

The loss of sexual appetite and potency has, of course, particular
relevance in a collection concerned with old age but Reading gives
other connotations to this lapsarian state which resonate throughout
his work. First, the decline from pastoral to municipal is inextricable
from the decline from youth to age, a relation highlighted in
gruesome detail in *Diplopic* (1983) and *Ukulele Music* (1985) where
the elderly are both frontline casualties of urban atrocities and
bewildered chorus. Second, and perhaps, more contentiously, the
decline from pastoral to municipal is further problematized by the
suggestion that it is indivisible from a political decline, from left to
right. 'Juvenilia' (1974, 30) gives us some reflections in a river and
a particular sense of why both 'Nature' and 'poems about it' are
anachronistic:

> But having found love I am left with nothing to say.
> And I find, in place of Socialist leanings,
> a ninety per cent misanthropy,
> which once expressed gains nothing by repetition.

Trouble at t'idyll, indeed. The pastoral no longer exists as either a cultural or ideological resource: all that remains is the possibility of enjoying it on a purely personal level on a country trip or a picnic: "a pastoral souvenir — the closest we ever / can hope now to get to the ruined original" ('Removals', 1974, 33).

For all Reading's mockery of Nature and the Pastoral even 'souvenirs' of 'ruined originals' retain a surprising power. The first of our key passages from *Evagatory* is but one of a number of descriptions of picnics made in various places around the world — Australia, Yugoslavia — which despite their co-existence with "ozone", "pulsing UV" and "Greenhouse meteorology" act as windows onto what a similar passage in *C* (*3 in 1*, 86) calls "something irrevocably ~~pleasant~~ lovely". The picnic in *C* is, in fact, described from four separate points of view: that of 'C' himself, his wife, their young daughter and a passing gipsy (*3 in 1*, 70, 71, 76, 86). The point remains the same as in *Elderly*: whatever power we invest in the pastoral can only be personal, intimate. *C*, surprisingly, gives further clues to the exact nature of the relation between the pastoral and the municipal in Reading's work, suggesting that what is portrayed is not a decline but a relocation of the former in the latter; and that while Reading's work may often seem at first sight merely a correlative to TV documentaries on urban anomie and inner city collapse, its obsession with the city is founded on a sense of it as 'troubled idyll' or what one critic of popular culture has identified as 'the urban pastoral' (Cottrell-Boyce, 1994).

The relevant passages in *C* are those in which we are apparently presented with the drug-induced fantasies of cancer patients which conflate personal and social decay (*3 in 1*, 91, 97):

> (Not just me, but the public clocks in the cities are fucked-up — / the Building Society one, the one on the Bank, / the one on the Town Hall, the one at the Station, all stopped / at a hopeless time ... And this isn't / some crusty superannuated old Colonel / lamenting, saying 'Of course, it was all fields then...')
> (91)

* * *

> (Not just me, but also, out there, the cities whose shit / surges into the sea in tsunamis, / and Shopping Precincts whose shit of canines and rolling / Coke tins and paper and fag-ends and polystyrene / chip trays and plastic chip-forks rattle in bleak winds ...

> This isn't some crusty Colonel (retired) lamenting / 'Of
> course it was all fields then, you see, in those days ...', /
> but me, me ...)
> (97)

Despite the protestations of Reading's narrator to the contrary,
these passages are lamentations, not for the decline from pastoral
to municipal but for the collapse of the municipal itself. In an age
when the emphasis on heritage, leisure and service industries and,
perhaps, business sponsorship of the arts seem to confirm Britain's
status as a post-industrial nation, the concept of a rural Eden from
which its citizens have been cruelly cast out has little, if any, real
meaning. The majority of people — and several generations of their
forebears — know only an urban experience. The enduring
popularity of *Coronation Street* rests on its vision of both a close-knit
community and the essentially benign nature of urban living. What
this and the passages from *C* make clear is that images of order and
innocence have been relocated from the country to the city: as
Reading's narrator says of the stopped clocks, "whereas when I was
a child / they were constants to be relied on, now the resources / and
requisite knowledge to fix them are gone". Here, surely, one catches
an echo of a lament for lost country crafts and lore, for an irretrievable
local knowledge. The relocation of the pastoral in the urban is, of
course, an easily identifiable phenomena in late twentieth century
British poetry: it can be traced from Larkin's 'The Whitsun Weddings'
through Dunn's 'Horses In A Suburban Field' (1969, 43) to more
recent poems like Sean O'Brien's 'The Park By The Railway' (1983,
16), Simon Armitage's *Xanadu* and many of Glyn Maxwell's cele-
brations of life in Welwyn Garden City. What makes Reading's work
more than just a catalogue of present difficulties is, that like that
other isolated genius, Roy Fisher, he responds to the urban scene
with what Corcoran (1993) identifies in Fisher's 'Handsworth
Liberties' (*Poems 1955-1987*, 117-125) as "something of the intensity
of feeling associated with more 'natural' places in the history of
English Romanticism" (174). The lament for stopped clocks encodes
a nostalgia for a *mechanical*, pre-electronic age and by implication a
particular period in the history of cities in general and of urban
Britain in particular. References in *Ukulele Music* (1985) to "post-
Coronation disintegration" (*3 in 1*, 122, 156) suggest that period
may be identified as the time before cities became the ground of
hasty and ill-advised architectural, economic, and social experiments.
    The comparison with Fisher is instructive in other ways, not least
in the way it points up a relation between Reading's conception of

urban life and the essential modernism of much of his work. Reading's polyphonic sequences are works of collage in which apparently pre-existing voices and documents are incorporated but not assimilated in a manner that strongly recalls the modernism of Pound, Williams and Zukofsky. Reading's work also shares with modernism a self-conscious focusing on its own belatedness: just as one of *The Waste Land's* refrains is 'HURRY UP PLEASE IT'S TIME' so many of Reading's books seem to vacillate in the manner of Beckett's narrator in *The Unnameable,* "I can't go on, I'll go on". *Evagatory* (1992) ends with the silence of deep space while Reading's most recent collection *Last Poems* (1994) purports to be a posthumous work, the papers of a Shropshire suicide. I have already drawn attention to the echoes of Eliot in Reading's first book and it seems to me not too far-fetched to suggest that Reading's urban idyll is the modernist city, the 'unreal city' of *The Waste Land* derived from Baudelaire. The city evoked in *C* where "public clocks ... were constants to be relied on" is not far removed from the city "where Saint Mary Woolnoth kept the hours" as "a crowd flowed" or where "four and five and six o'clock" are marked by the tramp of "insistent feet" (*TWL*, Part I and Preludes-IV). 'Absentees', an early Reading poem from *The Prison Cell and Barrel Mystery* (1976) might almost be an extra 'prelude':

> Vinyl scoured of footmarks,
> office a mausoleum,
> typewriters muffled in hoods,
> a clerk's ghost stirs in the cistern
> and in the unoccupied cubicle,
> the chain still swinging, the seat warm.

This has in common with Eliot not only a conception of the city as fictionalised interior but also shares with Eliot — and through him with Baudelaire — the city as the place of the crowd even when that crowd is absent. The second conception of the city is important to an understanding of Reading's urban idyll because, as Walter Benjamin points out in 'On Some Motifs In Baudelaire' (1982, 170), it is one in which the crowd and the city are inseparable; that is, there is no rift between people and their environment. In contrast, Reading's work describes what Benjamin terms "a rift between the masses and the city": Reading's cities are not only places of filth and alienation but environments where individuals are at the mercy of each other or predatory groups. The mass has been replaced by "pongoid subspecies" (*UM, 3 in 1,* 123).

"Troubled idyll", "pastoral picnic under an ozone hole" and "Albion urban" appear to emblematize a nostalgic lament for an unobtainable pastoral utopia but a closer examination of Reading's poetry reveals a more complex argument. Just as "Nature [is] anachronistic", reduced from 'nympho' to decaying 'whore' so the potency and meaning of the rural idyll shares the status of sad joke. The phrase "Albion urban" is not, in fact, a lament but a statement of *relocation*: the recurrent attacks on modern architecture 'disfiguring' our cities, the rise of neighbourhood watch schemes and the growth of the 'ideal city' of the out of town shopping mall all point to a desire to romanticize and rhapsodize the urban. Reading's strategy of appearing to offer us one species of rupture or fragmentation only to offer us another that is even more uncomfortable is typical of his work.

[the Permian] / (posterity) / heroes' lof

I have already drawn attention to the way Reading's poetry combines "things that are difficult to take" (Interview 1985) with equally difficult technical challenges. *Going On*, Book II of *Ukulele Music* (1985), purports to offer the poet's own comment on this:

> [Bit of a habit, the feigned indignation,
> various metres, Alcmanics and so forth,
> ludic responses to global debacles.
> Just Going On remains possible through the
> slick prestidigital art of Not Caring/Hopelessly Caring.]
>   (*ER*, 226)

But 'ludic' will only do as a partial explanation: as the heading of this subsection suggests, Reading's poetry embodies a defining combination of metrical, formal and conceptual / temporal concerns.

Neil Roberts has noted that "early in his career [Reading] shifted from English pentameters to a variety of accentual approximations to classical quantitative metres, for which the only significant precedent in English poetry is Clough" (1995). Reading — on his own account — uses hexameters, Alcaic and Alcmanic stanzas, elegiac distiches and even murkier obscurities such as the Adonic line and the Choriambic foot. The comparison with Clough is instructive for just as Clough used hexameters in his long poems *The Bothie of Tober-na-Vulich* and *Amours de Voyage* to introduce the effects of colloquial speech into Victorian poetry so Reading (Interview, 1985) has commented that his attraction to English quantitative metre stems from its ability "to vary the texture between, not exactly the demotic, but between the conversational and the formal".

Such a texture or tension seems to be the crux of much of Reading's work but the use of classical metres also offers a particular set of freedoms: "for most of us no ghosts haunt the Alcaic stanza in the way that, say, Gray's 'Elegy' haunts Harrison's quatrains" (Roberts 1995). Geoffrey Hill (Haffenden 1981, 88) has remarked that "In handling the English language the poet makes an act of recognition that etymology is history". Similarly, Reading's use of classical metres involves a recognition and rejection of the inheritance that comes with using traditional English metres and forms in terms of tone and subject. As the epigraph to *C* (1984) has it: "Verse is for healthy / arty-farties. The dying / and surgeons use prose" (*3 in 1*, 59). *C* is punctuated every ten pages or so by harsh dismissals of poetry: "Verse unvindicable" (63); "pentameters, like colons, inadequate", "*no* metric is vindicable" (72); "(Great unvindicable idea: a 17-liner, 100-word, pentameter acrostic ...)" (83); "But is there, today, / one ghastly experience / that vindicates verse?" (92); and "— fuck-all / there is justify lyric / metre"(112). These dismissals have, of course, particular meanings within the narrative of *C* but an unsentimental self-consciousness about whether poetry is 'vindicable' or 'unvindicable' can be traced through the entire Reading oeuvre, and, in one sense, classical metres become 'vindicable' precisely because they're not 'haunted'. English quantitative metres also allow a precision and rigour which often seem to be lacking from the seductive beat of the pentameter. This connects with another essential characteristic of Reading's work: its impatient matter of factness. Roberts (1995) has noted that "One frequently gets from Reading's work a sense that, the note of pathos, tragedy or sympathy once struck, to prolong or repeat it would be a dishonest indulgence". The use of approximations of classical quantitative metres quite literally give the right 'quantity'.

The classical in Reading's poetry means more, however, than the search for metres which are not, in the memorable words from 'Removals' (1974, 33), 'ruined originals'. The true place of the classical may perhaps be discerned from this passage of spoof nineteenth century fiction in *Final Demands* (1988). The subject, typically for Reading, is illegible writing:

> She had thought that the hieroglyphs were similar to those shewn her by Mr Bancroft at the Horse Shoe Inn, where some skilful mason had incorporated one of the antique "Roony Stanes" from the derelict Priory into the steps of that

hostelry's mounting-block. *Like those forgotten, or not yet understood, utterances,* which one could not help but contemplate as one mounted to the saddle in Bancroft's courtyard, *these scripts seemed half to reveal and half conceal some strange sad mystery.*
     (8-9 — my italics)

At the simplest level, Reading's poetry makes a case for the enduring relevance of the classical. *Ukulele Music* (1985) conflates the corruption of Imperial Rome with the collapse of the inner city (*3 in 1*, 153-4) while *Last Poems* (1994) follows a poem entitled 'Bosnian' (5) with another entitled 'Homeric' (6-10) which gives us a version of Book XXII of *The Odyssey* as an unflinching description of murder and violence. Reading seems to derive from classical models both a particular world view and a set of conceptions about what poetry should be and should deal with. First, Reading's work expresses a powerful sense of the vanity of human wishes, the insignificance of human endeavour and the baseness and irrationality of human behaviour. He has gone on record (Interview 1985) saying that "I'm concerned with not being so *conceited* as to think that there's something special going on which we are somehow heirs to" and that whatever set life on Earth in motion "was all the same an extraordinary event that makes us look rather unremarkable, for all our books and bottles". I would argue that this world view makes Reading a pessimist in the sense that say, Juvenal was a pessimist. Indeed, it is instructive to compare Juvenal on marriage in Satire X (the source of Johnson's *The Vanity of Human Wishes*) with Reading on the same subject in *Nothing For Anyone* (1977):

> Led helpless
> By irrational impulse and powerful blind desires
> We ask for marriage and children. But the Gods alone know
> What they'll be like, our future wives and offspring!
>   (Penguin edn, 1970, 216-7)

> ... we are most of us perfectly capable
> of falling in love (to a fairly profound
> degree) with any or all of a larger
> cross-section of the opposite sex
> than normal social and matrimonial
> codes make it comfy to realize ...
>   'The John O'Groats Theory' (*ER*, 45)

In an atheistic — or at best agnostic — age Reading cannot invoke the Gods to demonstrate the true scale of humanity: his work uses instead the vast perspectives of astrophysics and palaeontology.

Second, Reading shares the classical writer's anxiety over permanence, the anxiety that prompted Horace to assert his poetry would be 'more lasting than bronze'. Reading shares the anxiety but not the 'conceit': "A speaker / crackles that history is that / which remains. This assumes historians" ('New Year Letter', 1974, 35). Here, again, palaeontology provides perspective but Reading returns obsessively to the barbaric ways of 'H.sap': "Few atrocities / of which H.sap can conceive / remain unfulfilled" (*UM*, 3 in 1, 118). In this light, why would anyone want to write a history of the 'Recent'? ('Ex Lab', *3 in 1*, 87). And if, as *Evagatory* has it, "all which we valued nears expiry" (5) there may, in fact, be no-one left to read it.

Third, I believe Reading shares with classical writers that particular world-view which displays no consciousness that the structure of society can be changed. The point of the interwoven nineteenth and twentieth century narratives in *Final Demands* (1988) is surely to support one of the larger arguments of Reading's oeuvre that society has not actually changed or improved but has merely mutated into a new form of the same old thing. However, whereas for a classical writer the status quo, whatever its faults, was somehow always tolerable, Reading's diagnosis of our condition is terminal. Juvenal, for example, might write from the perspective of a middle-class threatened with oblivion by historical process: for Reading the game is up for everyone. If I mention Juvenal again it is because there is a very strong sense in which Reading is like the Roman satirist in his unflinching portrayal of the worst of humanity and his acid comedy. Who else would put a poem into the mouth — beak? — of the tortured parrot of a battered old lady? ('Mynah Petrachan', 1983, *3 in 1*, 23). And like Juvenal's — and Tacitus's and Suetonius's — pictures of an age in which the *pax Romana* was underwritten by widescale corruption, so the bulk of Reading's work has been written in a period of apparent political stability in which a focus on 'traditional' values and individual freedom has led inexplicably to wider social division.

Reading remains an unmistakably English writer — in ways that, say, John Ash or Selima Hill are not — and it's no surprise to find his work has much in common with the earliest English poetry. Reading has remarked (Interview 1985) of *Piers Plowman, Sir Gawain*, and Chaucer that "I was attracted to the vigour of those works ... to what isn't messing about". The anxiety over permanence,

which may be traced in his earliest work and has become a matter-
of-fact acceptance of the absence of posterity, is expressed from
Perduta Gente (1989) onwards by references to and versions of
Anglo-Saxon poetry.

Evagatory (1992) contains a number of poems in which elders
sing species of 'the last of the lays'; uses language which is clearly
indebted to the Anglo-Saxon alliterative tradition ("farctate with
feculence", "flow from freshly sliced flesh") and borrows what
might almost be termed a fatalistic cliché, "flight of a sparrow brief
through the feasting hall" (11). Reading's most recent collection,
Last Poems (1994), contains versions of the burial of Beowulf, 'The
Ruin', 'The Wife's Lament' and a poem from the *Exeter Book*. The
imaginative sympathy between Reading and the Anglo-Saxon poets
may be viewed in a number of ways. Most importantly, Anglo-
Saxon poetry is primarily a poetry of exile, fragmentation and
rupture which is either located in or looks forward to what, to its
speakers, seems an inevitable 'worst of all possible worlds'. Human
endeavour is not only transitory but eminently vulnerable to what
'Fragmentary' (1994, 35) calls "Fate's onslaught" and what the
Anglo-Saxons themselves called *Weird*. This connects powerfully
and suggestively with Reading's sense that we have lost control of
our destiny not only in terms of the English nation but in terms of the
whole human species: "Two hundred years ago, when we would have
been able to exercise some control, something could have been done"
(Interview 1990/1). Just as Reading replaces a religious perspective
with a palaeontological and astrophysical one, so he gives us the latter
day manifestations of *Weird*: the cancer of *C*, the poisoned planet of
Evagatory, the nuclear accidents and waste of *Perduta Gente*. "Fate's
onslaught" becomes, in the words of *Final Demands* (1988),

> *Ave!*, impartial Viral Democracy
>   (heightening all shared vulnerability):
>   down-and-out/Duchess; meths bum / MP;
>   temp and autocratrix; Tongan / Taffy ...
>   (11)

Anglo-Saxon poetry's ruptures also relate to Reading's own
through the characteristic tension in his work between technical
means and subject matter. Reading is clearly attracted to the earliest
English poetry's "vigour ... to what isn't messing about" but he
borrows forms, language and metrics to produce work that, increasingly
since *Stet* (1986), plays with cancellation, expiry and decay. Here,
the poetry's sense of its own uselessness and belatedness acquires a

different, more ancient meaning. It is appropriate that our key passage puts posterity into brackets for Reading has stated that he doesn't believe it exists: "There's no posterity to write for. I'm writing now for mutated arthropods" (Interview 1990/1, 96). And yet, not only does Reading keep on publishing one more 'last book', his work after *Stet* demands to be read in the manner of a scholar collating corrupt and fugitive classical ms. The reader is cast very definitely in the role of one who comes after. The pages of *Stet* (1986), *Perduta Gente* (1989), *Evagatory* (1992) and *Final Demands* (1988) are unnumbered — although I have numbered them here for ease of reference — which suggests that their published order is provisional, random, undecided. The reader is at once all-powerful and impotent and is, therefore, complicit in Reading's own sense of "total impotence" (Interview 1985) and his sense that such a position is "comfortable" (Interview 1990/1, 96). Again, this relates to Anglo-Saxon poetry for its speakers share in this position and, like the classical authors who preceded them, show no consciousness that the world can be otherwise. The structures of experience are immutable givens and it is a typical 'Reading rupture' that his own updated consciousness of this is expressed in fragmentary works whose form is withheld. The rupture of text / cancelled text is paralleled in the position of the author in Reading's poetry: the classical and Anglo-Saxon provide models of texts whose authors are either unknown or, if known, have no presence as biographical realities. When Peter Reading does appear to be present in his work it is usually as the poet attacked by his critics or as 'Peter Reading', as in the title poem of *Fiction* (1979) in which he is the nom de plume of a character in someone else's novel: "Even one's self is wholly fictitious" (*ER*, 66).

"Translationese from life to lingo ... trash-bucket ... devenustated" : Language and etymology

If Reading has sought out 'unhaunted' forms and metres to under-pin a particular conceptual universe and set of ideas about poetry's subjects and uses, then he has also embarked on a similar quest regarding language. The early poem 'Raspberrying' (1974, 22), which describes the reduction of Nature from "nympho once over-extolled" to "stripped-bare and thorny old sod", appears to enact as well a corresponding 'reduction' of language from words with Latin derivations to those with Old or Middle English ones, and of poetry from abstract ideas to concrete particulars. But we have already seen that such 'reductions' or 'ruptures' are never as straightforward as they seem and while Reading's poetry makes use of words like 'kerry', 'skipper', 'piss' and 'shit' it also contains words like 'pediculous', 'logaoedic' and 'devenustated'. Similarly, another early poem seems as distrusting of the concrete as 'Raspberrying' is of the abstract: "Marvellous / things have occurred since then that can never / survive in a concrete sense" ('New Year Letter', 1974, 35).

Reading has famously (Interview 1985) rejected "art ... like Ovaltine" and his particular 'take' on language may be grounded there also. *Ukulele Music* (1985) identifies the key component of Englishness as "Carrying on as though things were O.K. is what we are good at" (*3 in 1*, 158) and, by extension, 'traditional' or acceptable art and poetry are complicit in this. Reading responds with a concern for accuracy: "I'm offended by wrong-headed duff gen" (Interview 1985). For example, the description of a tortured parrot in 'At Home' (*Diplopic*, *3 in 1*, 21) is careful to refer to "flight-feathers" and "primaries"; and a meeting with a gipsy leading a horse in *C* (*3 in 1*, 70) becomes an obsessive listing of equine anatomy. Accuracy has another function:

> It has not been without usefulness that the Press has administered wholesale mad slovenly filth, glibly in apposite prose,
>
> for it has wholly anaesthetized us to what we would either break under the horror of, or, join in, encouraged by trends.
>   (*UM, 3 in 1*, 155)

If this is the result of the cultural hegemony of 'carrying on' then Reading's linguistic 'mix' counters it with a version of what Neil Corcoran has suggested is, in Roy Fisher's poetry, "a new disorientation derived from the theories of *ostranenie* ('making strange') of the Russian formalists" (1993, 173). Or, as the early poem 'Earthworks' (1974, 9) puts it: "A fumbled pirouette in zipping-up / [results] in lost balance". Lost linguistic balance is also Reading's version of what Corcoran (1993, 165) reads in Christopher Middleton as an under-pinning hostility to 'the humanistic solecisms' of contemporary English poetry written largely in an empiricist tradition.

Reading's '*ostranenie*' employs a number of distinct strategies. The first is an uncomfortable mixing of registers as in 'At Marsden Bay', the opening poem of *Diplopic* (1983)(*3 in 1*, 5-6):

Gibbo grubs up a Magnesian Limestone

chunk and assails the ledges at random,
biffing an incubating kittiwake
full in the sternum — an audible slap.
Wings bent the wrong way, it thumps at the cliff base,
twitching, half closing an eye. Gibbo seizes
a black webbed foot and swings the lump joyously
round and round his head.

The passage portrays an act of brutal and indiscriminate violence
with a mixture of pedantic precision, glancing euphemism reminiscent
of Victorian prose ("assails the ledges at random"), and scientific
and onomatopoeic accuracy. "Magnesian" co-exists with "biff",
"thump" and "slap". The effect is to reject the idea of the poem as
either the site of a democratic and normalising discourse or as a
utopian structure. Just as the action of the poem takes place at an
isolated, extra-social location so the poem itself functions as a
questioning of the idea that the order of art mirrors the order of the
society which produces it, an idea that has overshadowed much
English poetry, as either comfort or irritant, since 1945. If society
is conspicuous by its absence here, so too are authorial voice and
position. The tone of the passage is 'unbalanced' by its various
registers and, aesthetically, it is uncertain whether we are witnessing
supreme control or complete mess. We cannot be certain who is
speaking; nor are we being invited either to condemn or sympathise.
It is left up to us to discover why the experience described should
matter to both poet and audience. As with Brechtian 'alienation',
the language of the poem works to keep the reader in a state of
alertness both to what is depicted and the means of that depiction.
Reading began his career as a painter and has made some sharp
observations on the prevailing presupposition, among both poets
and critics, that "poetry is some sort of tool to engineer something.
It can be, but it doesn't need to be as calculating as that. Paintings
don't do that; when you look at a Rothko or a Giotto, you're not
assailed with the question 'What does he want?'. There are certain
allegiances, but you don't ask that question ... you see the thing, and
a kind of vision" (Interview 1990/1, 95). References in the Reading
oeuvre to Rothko, Auerbach and Pollock suggest an artist as inter-
ested in texture as in form.

Reading's second distinct strategy is, as with his relocation of the
pastoral within the urban, a case of an apparent 'rupture' being
reversed. Mature Reading — by which I mean from *Diplopic* (1983)
onwards — is characterised by elaborate, Latinate usage: 'extravasate',
'tetrous', 'pediculous', 'uriniferous', 'anhydrous', 'farctate', 'feculence'.

In English, the polysyllabic word of classical derivation is usually associated with the abstract, with the realm of ideas, as with the following words introduced into the language by Sir Thomas Browne: *antediluvian, hallucination, incontrovertible, insecurity, precarious* and *retrogression* (see Potter 1982, 80). In contrast, words with what may be broadly termed an Anglo-Saxon derivation deal with the concrete, the literal matter of the universe: *dirt, earth, soil, ground*. With a method that is at once ludic and deadly serious, Reading takes the concrete and presents it in the guise of the abstract. 'Pediculous', for example, means 'louse-infested' while 'tetrous' is an insanely exact coinage — in the context of *Perduta Gente's* down-and-outs — with connotations of alcoholic fermentation. Similarly, 'devenustated' seems to be a word entirely Reading's own and derived from the archaic word 'venus' meaning (according to Webster) beautiful, comely, elegant and graceful. The use of such words relates to Reading's relish for clashes between the demotic and the formal — as in the line "tetrous, pediculous, skint" (1989, 4) — and to his concern for scientific-type accuracy, for avoiding 'duff gen'. 'Pediculous', for example, means not just 'louse-infested' but 'infested with lice of the genus *pediculus*' to which human lice belong. The anxiety over accuracy is expressed in the phrase "loquacious / inadequate" from the first of our key passages but, more interestingly, the care over accurate usages connects with what Book II of *Ukulele Music* calls "the / slick prestidigital art of Not Caring/Hopelessly Caring" (*ER*, 226). The expenditure of effort and language involved combines detachment and 'hopeless care' and, as in the opening poem from *Diplopic*, signposts that these subjects demand our attention. It is typical of Reading's presentation that such concern is dismissed as "translationese", that such invention goes hand-in-hand with hopelessness.

"Translationese" again reminds us that Reading's poetry involves a continual play with the degree of its own authority. The use of words so far removed from everyday "lingo" that most readers will have to look them up has the effect of making the meaning only partially present. Paradoxically, these usages are as decadent as they are inventive and accurate and resonate with the combination of modernist belatedness and Anglo-Saxon derived fatalism discussed above. Their presence in the most recent, most fragmented texts — *Perduta Gente*, say, or *Stet* — works to make them symptomatic of the present period of "anthropod aberration".

Such usages are not, however, unique in British poetry of the 1980s and some other brief examples will help to put Reading's work in context. A notable example is the opening stanza of Robert Crawford's poem 'Scotland' (1990, 42):

> Semiconductor country, land crammed with intimate expanses,
> Your cities are superlattices, heterojunctive
> Graphed from the air, your cropmarked farmlands
> Are epitaxies of tweed.

The unfamiliar language here is borrowed from the cutting edge of science. MacDiarmid certainly stands behind the poem and also, perhaps more remotely, Craig Raine's poem 'Flying To Belfast, 1977' (Morrison and Motion [eds.] 1982, 174) in which the city is likened to "a radio // with its back ripped off". Crawford uses the vocabularies of 'smart' technologies and industrial processes — many of which have made their base in Scotland — to set up a playful discussion of questions of size and its relation to power. The effect is as iconoclastic as Reading but to different ends for contemporary Scottish poetry searches for a 'classless' language that is free of the constraints of English and English models of poetry. The use of words such as "epitaxies" or "superlattices" should not be mistaken for an elevated linguistic 'martianism' but as a way of treating the poem as an artistic object as opposed to a sensuous recollection ending with a glum or even minatory moral. And where English poetry can often seem to be a death-obsessed art, Crawford counters this with work that hums with upbeat energy. Reading's particular usages, like Crawford's, seem part of a wider interest in British poetry post-1980 in exploring the physicality of language and in giving the physical equal status with the emotional. An extravagant version of this is found in the poetry of Ciaran Carson where language and objects become interchangeable, as in "it was raining / exclamation marks, / Nuts, bolts, nails, car-keys. A fount of broken type" ('Belfast Confetti', 1990, 31). If poetry is to avoid being "translationese" then it must involve a recognition that living and art are physical relationships with the world, a negotiation of the dramas of its objects and processes.

A plurality of Englishes / Polyphonies

The title of this subsection comes not from our key passages but from Neil Corcoran's valuable essay on Reading's narratology (1993, 254-7); for, while Reading's lexical mixes and shifts serve to frustrate and problematize expectations about such matters as poetic authority or the presence and role of the poet, they are usually indivisible from particular speakers with distinct class identities. Reading is, as Terry Eagleton wrote of Tony Harrison, "a natural Bakhtinian, even if he has never read a word of him" (Astley [ed.] 1991, 49), but where Harrison's poetry takes as its subject that language is a place of struggle, Reading's contending voices offer glosses on each other and competing judgements on a particular book's defining subject. Reading's particular strategy is, in fact, to treat each discourse as a highly specialized register in a way that recalls what McHale (1987, 168) has identified in postmodernist fiction as

> the strategy of antilanguage. An antilanguage is the specialized discourse of a deviant social group — either deviant in the usual negative sense (e.g. criminal and prison subcultures) or what we might call prestigiously deviant (e.g. military élites, religious mystics, perhaps even poets). Just as the group's behaviour deviates from social norms, so analogously its language deviates from the standard.

Where Harrison's work always contains a sense of the dominant wisdom, Reading's later radically disrupted texts — *Stet* or *Ukulele Music* — offer no sense of norms or standards. The effect of, say, pages 32 and 33 of *Stet* which appear to juxtapose at random a monologue by a saloon bar philosopher, 'Reading's' recollection of his childhood, an interview with a radio astronomer, and a fragment of chat from an ex-Empire type, is to render them all equally unlikely, abnormal and deviant. There is no 'straight man' and the reader is aggressively presented with the disintegration of the text and the limits of his own knowledge. The fact that all four passages are presented as fragments casts further doubt on their authority and importance. Indeed, it is arguable that what polyphony there is resists dialogue between its various components and exists purely as a plurality of discourses. The passages provoke only a series of baffled questions: what is the mimetic framework of the two pages? What subject can all these passages be relevant to? How do these voices co-exist? Do they?

Reading's fundamental pessimism about the ways of H.sap makes all behaviour equally suspect and, by implication, all discourse equally untrustworthy. What his polyphonies offer us, in fact, are competing levels of misunderstanding or powerlessness. *Ukulele Music* makes this point most graphically by making Viv, a semi-literate charlady, and her family both victims and perpetrators of horrific urban lawlessness: her sister is injured when a bus queue is 'bombed' with bottles from a pedestrian bridge and her son attacks a baby with a broken bottle. And despite the fact that these same events feature in poems by the poet she chars for and that she herself enters 'Ukulele Music's' elegiac distiches, the last words of the poem — as opposed to the "plinkplinka plonk" of the ukulele that actually end it — seem ludicrously inapt:

> Whatsisname says to me 'Viv you're the life and soul of the party'—
> Viv, he says MEANS life, you know (in Greek or Lating or French)
>   (3 in 1, 165)

The poem, like the juxtapositions of *Stet*, alienates understanding by offering a clichéd image of the working-class as the embodiment of unselfconscious and salutary vitality, an idea it has unflinchingly rejected. The point is that, *in English*, Viv has no such meaning. It is the final misunderstanding in a cumulative process and underlines that the ultimate effect of Reading's polyphonies is to reinforce his poetry's consciousness of its own belatedness. Where a plurality of voices and Englishes might be thought to presage democratic truth-telling, it only emphasises "a position of 'absolute impotence'" (Interview 1990/91, 96).

"England ... the old prides, end of an era, nation, notion"

The consciousness of such a position derives from Reading's perception of England or, more correctly, Britain, a perception that is more complex and less programmatic than Tom Paulin's (1992) and Neil Corcoran's (1993) emphasis on his portrayal of 'Junk Britain' might suggest. As with his relocation of the pastoral, Reading's account of 'Junk Britain' is more than just the detailing of "the ruined original". The early poem 'St James's' (1974, 47) helps us to gauge just how much more by virtue of its being a specific intertext with Larkin's 'Church Going':

> On Holy Thursday cycling in the Lakes
> I found St. James's on a pewter hill
> and force of habit rather than desire
> carried me on towards the wrought iron gates.
>
> The dusty Dunlops and the worn out brakes
> of my Rudge leaning on the lake-stone wall
> seemed more akin to Larkin than to me.

By opposing "force of habit" to "desire" Reading's poem problematizes not only a particular key poem of British post-war poetry but by extension the ideas of poetry and nation that underlie Larkin's enduring influence and popularity. In a later stanza Reading's speaker describes himself as "observing, not from interest but a sense / of having to have a sense of history". Just as 'St James's' opening lines mimic and then reject the opening mood of 'Church Going' so the phrase appears to parallel Larkin's characteristic disenchanted scepticism only to turn aside and discover an irrevocable gulf between speaker and subject. The agnosticism of Larkin's poem, it is implied, is a self-deluding luxury: Reading's protagonist is not so much 'less deceived' as completely undeceived. "A sense of having to have a sense" is a criticism and a rejection of other 'luxuries' implicit in 'Church Going'. 'Church Going', like many of Larkin's enduring poems, manages to extract a unified meaning out of a moment of exclusion and fragmentation and dignifies personal melancholy by placing it in a wider context. 'St James's' rejects this by emphasising that the church contains Saxon and Norman elements, referring to "the Western Tower / (added about 1248)" and to the discovery of Viking remains in the churchyard. Reading's account of 'church going' cannot ignore underlying discontinuities in the experience and in the making of England and, by implication, Englishness. This sense of discontinuity and haphazardness becomes a second level of criticism and rejection which engages with what Blake Morrison has termed Larkin's "post imperial *tristesse*" (in Corcoran, 1993, 87), the interlocking of a personal fatalism and insecurity with an equally unavoidable sense of England's loss of place in the post-war world. 'St James's' highlights various components of England and Englishness and thereby questions whether we can ever have a clear enough idea of England to lament its loss of place. It also questions and, I think, clearly rejects the Larkin characteristic of having it both ways: that is, the interlocking of personal and national become not just a mirroring but, as Corcoran has argued (1993, 91), a 'merging' in which melancholy, insecurity, dissatisfaction, etc, etc become essential to English life. Reading's poem ends:

> *but I was not there,* just a cardboard copy
> guiltily going through the motions of
> what all day-trippers do before they leave ...
>   (my italics)

The personal is only that; the inherent temptation to make an elegy in an English country churchyard into an emblematizing and mythologizing account of nation is to be rejected.

Reading's 'refusal to mourn' also informs another explicit

intertextual encounter with Larkin, in this instance with 'The
Whitsun Weddings' on pages 28-9 of *Stet* (1986). Reading's poem,
like Larkin's, describes a train journey but his is a blank verse
narrative set in a Buffet carriage and dealing mainly with the loutish
behaviour of a group of drunken, teenage Army cadets. There are
a surprising number of echoes of Larkin in Reading's text: where
Larkin's poem travels past "a cooling tower", "acres of dismantled
cars" and "canals with floatings of industrial froth", Reading's
describes "A cooling tower, scrap cars bashed into cubes, / a
preternaturally mauve canal". The context of 'mauve' is characteristic
of the way Reading's poem 'translates' Larkin's: "The lemons,
mauves, and olive ochres" of the weddings become in Reading the
"pretty canary-yellow" of SO_2 emissions, the mauve of pollution and
the "orange scoop" of a plastic seat. Similarly, Larkin's "uncle shouting
smut" is echoed by Reading's cadet bellowing at a teenage girl "Ara sexy
gerraknickersorf!" and both poems end with images of rain:

> And as the tightened brakes took hold, there swelled
> A sense of falling, like an arrow-shower
> Sent out of sight, somewhere becoming rain.
>   (Larkin 1988, 116)

★ ★ ★

> pretty canary-yellow against grey
> sweals from stark plant (the voguish acid rain),
> Long Lifes vibrate, totter towards the edge.
>   (Reading 1986, 29)

Such similarities make the differences between the two poems all
the more telling. Larkin's poem is about not belonging, about
happiness — life even — going on elsewhere. It is also a class-specific
narrative: "girls in parodies of fashion"; "The fathers with broad
belts under their suits"; "The nylon gloves and jewellery-substitutes";
"... from cafés / And banquet-halls up yards". Reading's poem is an
intricate piece of description but it is not obviously observation:
there is no 'I' and no sense of exclusion:

> The Buffet carriage lurches side to side
> causing a democratic crocodile
> (*Financial Timeses, Suns*, a *TES*,
> spinsterly, oil-rig drunk, a see-through blouse,
> two sikhs, a briefcased First Class parvenu)
> to jig like salts on storm-tossed quarterdecks.
> They're queuing up to be insulted by
> a truculent steward ...
>   (28)

This is society, for better or worse, and the confusion of ways in which its members are judged — intellectual, racial, marital, sartorial and by class — reinforces a sense of pluralist and multi-racial reality. The image of "salts" stands for the pervasiveness of empire and its complete inappropriateness. This is the second major area of difference. Larkin's poem explicitly travels through a changed economic and social landscape but only hints at a wider context:

> All posed irresolutely, watching us go,
>
> As if out on the end of an event
>   Waving goodbye
> To something that survived it.
>
>   * * *
>
>   and it was nearly done, this frail
> Travelling coincidence; and what it held
> Stood ready to be loosed with all the power
> That being changed can give.
>   (1988, 114-115, 116)

Reading's poem views society as much more than "coincidence" but it is also a place where change is impossible. His poem explicitly grounds this incapacity for change in the conflict between reality and myth: just as the "democratic crocodile" is played against the simile of "salts" so the bellowing recruit is likened to "a furious shepherd / [who] might bellow some remonstrance at his dog / when it is five fields off, recalcitrant"; spring lambs gambol in a polluted landscape; and the imperialist war comics the recruits read are contrasted with the realities of such adventuring in "some bloody fool / flag-waving bunkum like the Falklands do". *Stet* as a whole makes clear not only the failure of such myths but suggests that there may be greater continuity with them than we like to think:

> '55: comics (*better* class) offered us
> Decent Types it was hoped we would emulate —
>
> Shaftesbury, Gandhi, Dickens, Florence
>   Nightingale, Faraday, Curie, Elgar ...
>
>   '85: some of us clearly have been moved more by the *worse* ones —
>   Bloody-Nosed Basher, The Yobbs, Sheik Fist The Middle
>   East Nit ...

'Ukulele Music' suggests a similar relation between the plundering and wanton destruction of the 'Capting's' maritime tales and the free-market excesses of the mid-1980s.

Reading's engagement with the matter of England is nothing less than a seismographically sensitive charting of the shock waves rippling from the rupture between 'nation' and 'notion'. His account of 'Junk Britain' seems so 'shocking' and uncomfortable because it is in marked contrast to 'traditional' poetic presentations of nation such as 'Adlestrop' or 'The Whitsun Weddings'. It may often portray individuals at the mercy of economic, historical and social imperatives but it rejects the kind of socialised niceness that demands that the political is hidden in the personal. In the same way it rejects narratives of "post-imperial *tristesse*", nostalgia and decline. If the present may be related to the past then, in purely English terms, it is more on the level of just deserts and painful continuities. And, as our key passage makes clear, the present condition of England is inseparable from the present condition of humanity generally: all nations are working through their own versions of "anthropod aberration".

Spiral Narratives / Viral Referencing

I have already drawn attention to the centrality of narrative in Reading's work, both in individual books and across his entire oeuvre. I shall now look at this in greater detail and relate it to wider importance of narrative in recent British poetry.

In their Introduction to *The Penguin Book of Contemporary British Poetry*, Blake Morrison and Andrew Motion identified narrative as a fundamental part of the "shift of sensibility" and "transition" (11) their anthology documented. They pointed to the way "that contemporary poets write their stories with more reference to what the process involves. The fact of fictionalizing is relished as it is performed" (1982, 19). This 'jouissance' on the part of the poet, they argued, produces works which draw attention both "to the artifice and autonomy of [the] text" and "to the problem of perception" by presenting stories that are "incomplete" or which withhold "what might normally be considered essential information" (1982, 19). Critical writing on narrative in recent British poetry has largely followed this line of enquiry. Both Gregson (1993) and Corcoran (1993) use Andrew Motion's poem 'Open Secrets' (Motion 1984, 11) as paradigmatic of what another Motion poem calls 'secret narratives' and argue that the continuing importance of narrative is characterised by the exploration of the paradoxical nature of concealment and revelation in storytelling; the exploitation of 'unstable' or ambiguous narrators; and deliberate misprisions of the candid and the discrete. Larrissy (1990, 180-1) sees Paul Muldoon's 'Immram' (Muldoon 1986, 58-71) as the culmination of what one might term the anti-foundationalist school of narrative, "for its subject-matter, which revolves around the idea of the lost father, itself indicates the absence of a secure originating truth which could guarantee the identity of the narrator". As we've already seen (Chapter One) Sean O'Brien has shown himself particularly adept at locating this allusive, open type of narrative in a wider cultural and political frame.

More interesting from our point of view is the development of another type of narrative poetry which Morrison and Motion did not foresee and which their Movement-derived aesthetic of balance and assimilation did not perhaps allow them to entertain. Gregson has identified this in the work of such apparently diverse poets as Jackie Kay, Matthew Sweeney, Simon Armitage and Glyn Maxwell as a style which "[gives] high priority to the mimicry of a colloquial and vividly contemporary voice" (1994, 75). Gregson also draws attention to the way the work of the three male writers registers "how off-centre human awareness is, how it gets obsessed with trivia". In the case of Armitage and Maxwell — and to a lesser extent Sweeney — this produces work which is mock-heroic both in design and effect and which, in its detailing of trivia, inevitably reproduces "the way that contemporary experience is mediated through a bewildering variety of linguistic systems" (1994, 76). However, the most important thing about the work of these poets — which Gregson does not stress — is that it rejects the exotically detailed and Pynchonesque parallel universes of a Fenton or a Muldoon in favour of recognisable, shareable — often very painful — experiences set in a distinct regional location. Armitage's Northern England, Kay's Scotland and Maxwell's Welwyn Garden City reject the luxury of treating the poem entirely as a fictional space in the manner of the Morrison / Motion generation: their stories are about real places and, by extension, real lives. One might almost catch an echo of Reading's rebuff to his critics: "He don't *invent* it, you know" (*UM*, *3 in 1*, 131). This evocation of authenticity leads to another key difference between 'new narrative' and 'new new narrative': the narrators and protagonists are not ambiguous or questionable in the same way that those of Fenton, Motion or Morrison are. If these writers set up a complex play around expectations of the identity in a poem of 'I' specifically and of the speaker generally then a poem like Armitage's 'The Stuff' (1989, 68-69) about drug dealing, his more recent 'Brassneck' (1992, 5-9) about pickpocketing or Maxwell's 'Tale of the Mayor's Son' (1990, 10-15) leave us in no doubt about the identity of their speakers. The play on identity becomes a play on language in which an awareness of the 'variety of linguistic systems' counterpoints contemporary / colloquial / regional with poetic voice. Such mingling of discourse results not in ambiguous authors and narrators as in ambiguous readers: a straightforward, 'unhaunted' response is made impossible and this combines powerfully with the poems' regional locations to argue with ideas of consensus and centre.

Reading's approach to narrative combines aspects of both the 'new' and 'new new' schools. From his first collection, *For The Municipality's Elderly* (1974), the identity of 'I' has always been various and is certain to be different in any two successive poems. Importantly, these speakers are never ambiguous or shadowy but are always clearly defined until they become the full-blown fictional characters of 'Ukulele Music' or *Final Demands* whose lives we feel able to imagine completely as we do those in a conventional novel. The only uncertain identity — and this becomes a key 'rupture' in the Reading oeuvre — is that of the speaker in poems which claim to present Reading speaking to us directly: is he an autobiographical, verifiable Peter Reading or a parallel 'Peter Reading' who also happens to be a poet based in Shropshire? This uncertainty is pushed to side-splitting absurdity in the title poem of *Fiction* (*ER*, 65-6):

> In Donald's novel, 'Don' (whose nom de plume
> is *'Peter Reading'*) sues a man whose *real*
> name is 'Peter Reading' for having once
> written a fiction about a poet
> who wrote verse concerning a novelist
> called 'Donald' whose book 'Fiction' deals with 'Don'
> (a poet who writes satirical verse
> ...)

The passage comes remarkably close to one of the procedures of postmodernist fiction which McHale (1987, 114-115), borrowing from Borges, terms "infinite regress" brought about by "recursive structure". The story disappears into infinity. However, while this may seem typical of the 'secret narrative' poets in its use of unstable narrators and protagonists, it seems just as typical of Reading's maturest work that however many levels one travels up or down the 'story' remains the same.

For Reading the use of multiple narrators and his obsessively accurate notation of their idiolects is not a truly democratic form of

writing or proof that truth is something to be assembled from a
number of different perspectives: it is, I would argue, an enactment
of something much simpler and more poignant, namely that his
subjects — old age, terminal illness, urban decay and national
decline — involve us all. It is what *Final Demands* (1988, 11) terms
"impartial Viral Democracy" and, as such, it inevitably provokes a
response from all it touches. Reading's 'everyday' subject matter
and colloquial narrators reach us, as we have seen, through outland-
ishly inventive forms and metres. As Paulin (1992, 289) points out,
"in breaking with the predominantly iambic mode of English verse
Reading signals his distance from the State. His classicism has a
displacing effect ...". The counterpointing of poetic and colloquial
Gregson (1993) identifies in the narratives of Armitage becomes, in
Reading's, a way of demonstrating his protagonists' distance from
the State or, indeed, from the comfort of any central, defining ideas.
Where an Armitage poem — as Gregson points out — is usually
content to make a spectacle out of its linguistic displacements,
Reading's narratives always invoke the 'big picture'. The fact that
their various characters all voice the same lack or bewilderment or
whatever inevitably makes them 'deconstructions'. It should be
noted that Reading's 'deconstructions' are very different from those
of Muldoon or Fenton which Alan Robinson (1988, 15) sees as
"subverting our familiar empirical confidence in reality" and "self-
consciously deconstructing any pretensions to the formal coherence
of Modernist poetry". Of course, any long polyphonic poem in
English must in some sense recall the key works of High Modernism
but what Reading does is to retain their fragmented surface and
ground it, not on residual symbolic or mystical structures, but on
observable reality.

Place is very much a part of this reality and, therefore, another
means of grounding. Sometimes this is specific as in 'Duologues'
(*ER*, 34-6), 'Parallel Texts' (*ER*, 79) or 'A bloke with whom I once
worked at the mill' (*Stet*, 11) where rural life is powerfully evoked
through the rhythms of its labour and speech. However, Reading
more often than not creates a kind of geographic matrix instantly
recognisable as contemporary England. *Stet*, for example, plays its
narrative of post-Imperial reaction against a background of Telford,
Aberdeen, Wenlock, A5 and "the larger towns — / Liverpool,
Glasgow, London, Belfast, / Birmingham". It is recognisable as the
undetailed, uninformative shorthand of a news report: discontinuous,
unconnected, one place irrevocably 'other' to the next, another
variety of deconstruction.

I want to end this section by considering the method which Reading has made so memorably his own, the 'viral referencing' which we referred to at the start of this chapter. Reading uses the method both within individual books and increasingly, after *Diplopic* across his entire oeuvre. A comment by the novelist Jeanette Winterson, about her own work is, I think, illuminating here: "I do try and write a spiral narrative, a narrative which is continually returning to itself, both thematically and as far as the images and the ideas are concerned but primarily as far as the language is concerned ..." (1994).

I want to look first at how Reading's spiral narrative and viral referencing work within a single book. *Stet* (1986) must stand as Reading's most radically ruptured text: pages are presented as spaces containing perhaps a couple of discontinuous stanzas, a fragment of prose and a single line of verse. The effect of this is to imply that the text should be read across two pages but, as with double column works such as Ashbery's 'Litany' or Derrida's 'Glas', such a reading remains 'unauthorized'. As Culler (1982, 160) has written of the Derrida text: "Constantly at work in [it] is the problematical relationship between the two columns: always offered as a possibility but never affirmed and never, except by a wilful act on the part of the reader, giving rise to a synthesis". Such a wilful act and its resultant synthesis are encouraged in *Stet* by repeated and modulated references. On page 9 we are given the isolated line: "La bouche amère, cru gâté, sécheresse" (A bitter taste in the mouth, a ruined vintage, dryness). This description of a wine sits in the middle of a page between two unrelated stanzas dealing with astrophysics and a bracketed proof correction note. On the facing page is a long poem dealing with the public shaming and subsequent recluse existence of a French woman accused of fraternizing with the Germans. Fine wines are a potent emblem in the Reading oeuvre of what little 'H.sap' has produced of any lasting value, a point starkly emphasised by its relation to the French story of cruelty, isolation and eventual madness. The line recurs in a half-hearted translation five pages later — "Bad dégustation, puant the cru, short, séché the finish" — and as an echo even later: "nosing the cru, we remark its generous finish" (24). In what becomes a typical procedure of the later poetry, this 'viral referencing' cross-fertilizes with other patterns of reference to suggest not so much a structure as an organism that is perpetually breaking down and renewing itself. The description of a wine resonates throughout a book that is full of drinking and ends with a mawkish scene in a pub garden. The recurrent monologues of a saloon bar fascist interfuse with the book's central narrative — the condition of post-Imperial England — to suggest that all the obsessive drinking is emblematic of this wider loss of place and purpose and resultant decadence and inertia.

Reading's original isolated French pentameter has other reverberations for *Stet* abounds in similarly isolated lines of verse from "A lady's album of 1826 / in my possession":

> pentameter one-liner unexplained:
>
> *This waiting bravely to be badly hurt.*
>
> [Untrue. *You* scrawl the whining metaphor
> before the scalpel, can't now justify
> expiation. Call it a day at that.]

Unjustifiable expiation echoes the anxiety in *C* over vindicable verse and *Stet*'s unexplained one-liners all ultimately return the reader to the starkest of all: "Muse!, sing the Grotty [scant alternative]". The line also underlines how *Stet* may be taken as paradigmatic of how 'viral referencing' works across the whole Reading oeuvre to turn it into a gigantic spiral narrative.

Stet, in fact, might be taken as Reading's own commentary on his work up to that point since it revisits and reworks several previous collections. Page 2 ("Engines cut out ... / Those at the bank and the grocer's") is a distillation and a rewrite of 'Fall', the opening poem of Reading's first collection. The important difference is that the original poem's "peculiar brand of politeness / that only climactic extremes, / or a war, produce" has become "that peculiar fetial / brand of perniciousness". "Fetial" has a precise meaning (according to Webster) of dealing with matters affecting relations between nations such as a treaty or declaration and rules of war. The exhausted and relocated pastoral of *For The Municipality's Elderly* is reworked to underwrite the vision of Britain that finds its fullest expression in *Ukulele Music*: "But now they are on the streets the ARMY against thugs and Mugers as that is where the REAL war is on NOW. cities in two halfs ..." (*3 in 1*, 124). Page 15 of *Stet* repeats the previous book's "Grans are bewildered by post-Coronation disintegration", placing it opposite an 'in character' plea for the return of National Service and capital punishment and on the same page as a *Ukulele Music*-style couplet: "This isn't Socrates, Einstein or Bach but just the same species / bloodily on the front page kicking itself into mulch". Other revisitings include extracts from "a lady's album" which first appears in *Nothing For Anyone* (*ER*, 41), a reappearance of the misanthropic journalist from 'Editorial' (*3 in 1*, 7) and a development of the global / astrophysical perspectives of *Nothing For Anyone*'s title poem.

Stet, then, sets the pattern for what has come to be seen as *echt* Reading: a fragmentary text which obsessively reworks and revisits its previous incarnations through a small body of detail. Reading's skinheads, astrophysicists, beleaguered pensioners and urban blight give his work an unmistakable flavour and identity as Maxwell's citizens, sons and blokes and O'Brien's parks, railways and rundown ports do theirs. The spiral narrative of England that results has, for the moment, come to rest at its key 'site': the final poem of *Last Poems* (as opposed to text under erasure) not only returns to Reading's first book but stands at Housman's grave. The opening poem of *A Shropshire Lad*, '1887', powerfully fuses the rural idyll and the imperial dream whose respective exhaustion and relocation and disintegration Reading so unflinchingly portrays. Reading's narrative stands for a wider interest in narrative in poetry of the 1980s and early 1990s which seeks subjects other than its own fictionalising. It is, perhaps, no accident that Les Murray's poem 'The Quality of Sprawl' (*CP*, 186-7) gets written at the beginning of the period. If Jeanette Winterson (1994) can say of her own work, "I am trying to push into my fiction the discipline and denseness of poetry — that seems to me to be a proper late twentieth century challenge", then many contemporary poets have deemed it a proper challenge to open their work to the bagginess of fiction.

"Ozone hole … / [cf. the Permian]": Poetry and Science

If Reading's work can be taken as paradigmatic of a particular interest in narrative then it is equally emblematic of a use among younger poets of both scientific material and vocabularies. However, where poets such as David Morley, Paul Mills and Lavinia Greenlaw have been drawn to similarities between scientific practice and imaginative act or used the larger perspectives of science as a means of liberating their poetry, Reading's use of science is inseparable from his 'take' on both poetry and "the ways of H.sap". Paulin (1992, 290) points to Reading's "hatred of technology" but it is important to make the distinction that Reading attacks commercial excesses not pure enquiry. In fact, Reading's use of science closely relates to what Paulin elsewhere (287) describes as his "journalistic commitment to the present social moment and [his] scorn [for] an aesthetic idea that prizes the lapidary and the fixed".

Reading is an obsessively *accurate* poet: "I'm offended by wrong-headed duff gen ... I'm very shocked by anthropomorphism". (Interview 1985, 8). This perhaps pushes him to the opposite extreme of *Anthriscus sylvestris, Laridae, Larus novaehollandiae* and *Calyptorhynchus funereus*. It also allows him to extend the fiction that he is not writing poetry but merely collecting and annotating what *Ukulele Music* calls 'material'. Such vocabulary is part of Reading's wider 'aesthetic dissidence' and has the same "displacing effect" (Paulin 1992, 289) as his classicism and his wider linguistic *ostranenie*. Paradoxically, it is one of the details that gives his poetry its fragile continuity.

The use of science to 'make strange' has a wider meaning in Reading's poetry: a 'making strange' of "the ways of H.sap" by viewing them from the longest possible perspective. *Diplopic* (1983), as its title suggests, develops this into a more complex 'double vision' in which the detached, long view is contrasted with vulnerable, personal experience:

> On this diagram,
> the Holocene or Recent
> (last ten thousand years)
> is far, far, far, far too small
> to register on this scale.
>   'Ex Lab' (*3 in 1*, 37)

>   * * *

> you might lend the issue added poignancy
> by being distanced — describe the electrified
> overgrown line in cool, botanical terms,

The distance afforded by botanical or palaeontological perspectives connects with another key Reading rupture: either none of it matters or the most intimate and/or most painful fragments of individual experience do — "You stroke your lover comprehensively" ('Midnight', 1994, 37). Reading's assertion that "It *is* a fucking good job that it all doesn't matter" (Interview 1985, 11) fuels a desire for wider and wider perspectives so that the Black Holes of *Nothing For Anyone* become in *Stet* a fragmentary but full-blown astrophysical narrative in which radio astronomy, quasars and VLBI (Very Long Baseline Interferometry) give Reading his biggest scale yet on which to judge humanity's puniness: "[Stet; Ave!, Reasonless causal physics]" (21); "Ave! no-nonesense astronomers probing Reasonless physics". VLBI also provides an 'aspirational model' for the extreme detachment and authorial effacement that dominate Reading's work:

> Yes, well, in Very Long Baseline Interferometry a number of
> astronomers, maybe around the world, examine a common
> radio emission simultaneously. They keep precise track of
> the timings with an atomic clock — extremely accurate, you
> know. The tapes of their radio observations are then flown
> to an HQ where they're played back exactly synchronized,
> and they're then joined electronically. The effect is like a
> giant connected radio telescope.
>   (31)

This might even describe the way individual collections function
within the whole Reading oeuvre.

Evagatory (1992) enacts a farewell voyage around a planet where
"all which we valued nears expiry" (5) and where the poet and his
grotty nation approach "hyperborean bleakness / ... guideless,
directionless, lightless, silent" (31). The book ends on board the
Voyager spacecraft "drifting, 290,000 / years beyond launch-pad,
in towards Sirius". Far from unlocking the secrets of the universe,
the probe will have been silent since the year 2020. Here, science
not only provides a perspective on human puniness: it also becomes
emblematic of human endeavour. Science is used to bolster the
misanthropy of Reading the Swiftian satirist for whom all human
behaviour is either bad or, at best, pointless. In the words of a
character from Huxley's novel *After Many A Summer*: "Yes, you've
got to be cynical ... Specially cynical about all the actions and
feelings you've been taught to suppose were good. Most of them are
not good. They're merely evils which happen to be regarded as
creditable. But, unfortunately, creditable evil is just as bad as
discreditable evil" (1976 edn, 99). Reading does not waver from the
perspective he offered on humanity from the outset, the perspective
of "When the world ends and space-age / picnickers freeze to flint
or melt or / asphyxiate ..." ('Plague Graves', 1974, 10). Science
merely supports a view of humanity which, as Ian Milner has written
of Holub, is "nothing if not contextual. Neither cell nor man lives
alone" (1990, 13).

Tom Paulin (1992, 287) has described Reading as "the unofficial
laureate of a decaying nation" but, as I have argued throughout this
chapter, Reading's value and interest extend far beyond his role of
social and political commentator. Just as his work demands to be
read backward and forward as a total oeuvre so his own position in
British poetry of the last quarter of this century links him both with

the "transition" documented by Morrison and Motion and with the ferment of activity that followed it in the 1980s and which now seems to have cooled down into such things as the 'New Generation Poets'. If his work is full of contradictions or 'ruptures' then these surely stem from its sensitivity to a particular historical moment and its cultural aftershocks: the moment when images of one nation with a single purpose were reworked and remarketed and yet most people's experience of living in that nation became ever more fraught, fragmentary and precarious.

5. The Noise of Science

Time and again during my work as a co-editor of *The New Poetry* (1993) I was struck by how much a poet's distinctive voice seemed indivisible from some kind of engagement with either scientific subjects or vocabularies. In one sense, this should not be at all remarkable for, as John Heath-Stubbs and Phillips Salmon point out in the introduction to their excellent anthology *Poems of Science* (1984), "in all periods ... poets have employed an intellectual framework derived from the science of their day"; and "in practice, poets are considerably more concerned with science and its opportunities for their poetry than has been recognised" (18, 35). The French cultural and scientific historian Michel Serres goes even further when he calls poetry "the noise of science" (1983). Looking at the current century we can rephrase Heath-Stubbs's and Salmon's first remark and say that the greater part of our framework of living derives from science. Our homes rely on science as the means of subduing and keeping in check dirt, disease and disorder through the use of appliances and medical and hygiene products. This book has been produced using computers and computer-controlled processes and it's likely that you have paid for it by having a plastic card electronically 'swiped' and that the sale was recorded by scanning the barcode on the book's back cover. Science and technology not only structure our physical world but in a very real sense determine that significant parts of our activities and perhaps even identity exist in an intangible and barely obtainable electronic domain, now popularly called cyberspace.

However, as that last image perhaps suggests, while science benefits us and improves our lives in innumerable ways we can never quite escape the feeling that it is fundamentally inimical to our fundamental humanity and our relationship with it remains, at best, ambivalent. This uncertainty about exactly what form of knowledge science is can be said to account for much of the history of strained relations and intermittent hostilities that have existed and continue to exist between art and science. On the one hand we have Auden asserting that "Art is the spiritual life made possible by science" and describing feeling when among scientists like "a shabby curate amongst bishops"; and the anthology referred to above collecting poems by 116 poets from Chaucer to Bernard Saint. On the other, as work was beginning on *The New Poetry* a series of articles by Professor Raymond Tallis in *P.N. Review* seemed to signal a re-opening of 'two cultures' hostilities from the scientists' side. Even leaving aside the fact that Professor Tallis is something of a professional 'nay-sayer' it seems clear that lasting peace has yet to break out. In this light, the fact that a whole of generation of poets can so easily and willingly side-step or ignore one of our culture's most notorious and damaging antagonisms becomes all the more suggestive of the mood that has been afoot in British poetry in the last ten to fifteen years. It is a mood that *Poetry Review* caught well when it said that "whole slabs of historical and cultural reference jostle, butt up against, and slip over each other in a form of linguistic plate tectonics" (Forbes 1994, 5); and it is the 'poetry and science' aspect of that 'slip over' I want to explore here. I shall begin with a very brief historical survey of the decidedly mixed relations between poetry and science from the Romantics onwards. I shall then look at the work of three older twentieth century poets — Miroslav Holub, Hugh MacDiarmid and Peter Redgrove — in an attempt to sketch a model of some of the ways in which poetry and science most typically combine. I shall follow this with an examination of what science means — 'why science now?' — to younger poets and I shall then follow some of these ideas in the work of a number of Eighties/ Nineties poets, some featured in *The New Poetry*, some not.

In his study *The Mirror and The Lamp: Romantic Theory and the Critical Tradition* (1971, 298-335), M.H. Abrams traces the ambivalent and often hostile relations between poetry and science to the Romantic period. Raymond Williams makes the same point from a different perspective in *Keywords* (1983, 40-3, 276-280) when he discovers the first significant divergence of 'art' and 'science' occurring in the late eighteenth and early nineteenth centuries. If the Romantics — Wordsworth, Coleridge, Keats et al — embodied an ambivalence to science they were, in fact, responding to a shift of sensibility at the end of the eighteenth century. Many eighteenth century poets had borrowed freely from Newton's *Opticks* and Newton's discoveries, far from being seen as deleterious to poetry, were welcomed as a new, exciting and complementary resource. Poetry's traditional claims to be the discourse of ultimate truth could now be supported by scientific evidence. James Thomson's 'To The Memory of Sir Isaac Newton' praises the great scientist for "[Untwisting] all the shining robe of day" and "To the charm'd eye [educing] the gorgeous train / Of parent colours" (in Abrams 1971, 305). Erasmus Darwin developed theories of biological evolution in long poems such as *The Loves of Plants* (1789), *The Economy of Vegetation* (1791) and *The Botanic Garden* (1803) and had a great influence on the

Romantics. Desmond King-Hele (1987) detects his presence in such diverse works as Coleridge's 'The Rime of the Ancient Mariner' and Blake's 'Book of Thel'. But by the end of the century dissenting, more sceptical voices were also to be heard so that the laments of Thomas Campbell's 'To The Rainbow' only a few years after Darwin's last work come to stand for a wider feeling:

> When Science from Creation's face
>   Enchantment's veil withdraws
> What lovely visions yield their place
>   To cold material laws.
>   (Abrams 1971, 308)

My account is necessarily compressed but it serves to sketch the background against which Wordsworth and his contemporaries worked and the attitudes they inherited and shared. In their critical writings, these became a recognition of poetry and science as distinct discourses. John Stuart Mill, for example, asserted that the "logical opposite" of poetry is "not prose, but matter of fact or science". Wordsworth too rejected the "contradistinction of Poetry and Prose" in favour of "the more philosophical one of Poetry and Matter of Fact, or Science" and Coleridge, for his part, defined the "union of passion with thought and pleasure" as "the essence of all poetry, as contra-distinguished from science, and distinguished from history civil or natural" (Abrams 1971, 299). It is important to note, however, that all these writers were merely making a distinction not stating an antagonism. Keats's famous assertion that Newton has destroyed all the poetry of the rainbow by reducing it to prismatic colours and his toast "Confusion to the memory of Newton" are not typical of the Romantics. As Abrams points out (1971, 310) Wordsworth sets the pattern for resolving potential conflicts: "Some are of the opinion that the habit of analysing, decomposing, and anatomizing is inevitably unfavourable to the perception of beauty ... The beauty in the form of a plant or an animal is not made less but more apparent by more accurate insight into its constituent properties and powers". Shelley, similarly, spoke of "Science and her sister Poesy" and this all-inclusive conception of human knowledge was echoed by the scientists themselves. Newton had said at the end of his life that "to myself I seem to have been only like a boy playing on the sea-shore, and diverting myself in now and then finding a smoother pebble or a prettier shell than ordinary, whilst *the great ocean of truth* [my italics] lay all undiscovered before me" (in Westfall 1980, 863). Lionel Trilling, in his useful account of the Leavis/Snow 'two cultures' dispute, reminds us that "it is told of Faraday that he refused to be called *physicist*; he very much disliked the new name, as being too special and particular, and insisted on the old one *philosopher*, in all its spacious generality" (1966, 176).

Nevertheless, despite the Romantics' recognition of poetry and science as complementary discourses there was also a sense in which Wordsworth and his contemporaries remained ambivalent about the exact relation between them. First, there is an insistence on the pre-eminence of poetry. The "Man of Science", Wordsworth wrote in the Preface to *Lyrical Ballads*, engages only with "particular parts of nature" but the poet "converses with general nature". Second, this conception of the ultimate superiority of poetry over science becomes even more confused when Wordsworth describes the social function of poetry and the poet in a letter to John Wilson. Here, poetry becomes the "science of feelings" which will act as a salve against "great national events" and "the uniformity of occupations" and "the increasing accumulation of men in cities" which produce a mental "state of almost savage torpor". Science and poetry might well be equally useful means of navigating Newton's "great ocean of truth" but the results of applied science were to be resisted (see Abrams 1971, 330). Shelley makes a similar point in his *Defence of Poetry* when he rails against "the cultivation of those sciences which have enlarged man's material empire but circumscribed his mind".

It was views such as these which were picked up and amplified by later writers, particularly Matthew Arnold, and war was declared between poetry and science. The brutalising effects of the commercial society that had developed out of the Industrial Revolution were everywhere apparent. Tennyson's *Maud*, for example, presents a world in which the village "bubbles o'er like a city, with gossip, scandal and spite" and where "the wakeful ear" is kept from sleep by the grinding of "villainous centre-bits". More importantly, the natural sciences had become so closely identified as the discourses of ultimate truth that religion itself seemed under attack if not entirely appropriated. Roy Porter (1994, 3) draws attention to some of the later public statements of Thomas Huxley: "Science, he explained, was the way to persuade the labouring man 'that it is better' for him that 'he starve than steal'; time was when it had been theologians who had said things like that." Raymond Williams (1983, 278) quotes an anonymous statement from 1867 that "we shall ... use the word 'science' in the sense which Englishmen so commonly give to it ... as expressing physical and experimental science, to the exclusion of theological and metaphysical". In the words of Abrams

> It was only in the early Victorian period, when all discourse was explicitly or tacitly thrown into two exhaustive modes of imaginative and rational, expressive and assertive, that religion fell together with poetry in opposition to science, and that religion, as a consequence, was converted into poetry, and poetry into a kind of religion.
> (1971, 335)

We can hear echoes of this in our own century in I.A. Richards's claim in his *Science and Poetry* (1926, 60-1) that "poetry is capable of saving us"; and in Les Murray's remark to the effect that all religions are large poems (1993, 252).

Even this sketch of the nineteenth century, in which poetry becomes a refuge for sensitive souls who worship in religiose cults of Beauty and in which science and technology are blamed for what one of Arnold's poems calls "this strange disease of modern life" may not be the whole story. The historian Keith Jenkins offers another perspective on hostilities between the arts and science:

> [T]he view was widely held that science was the route to truth, and this idea went right across the board from Ranke to Comte to Marx. But none pressed the case so hard for history's scientificity as Marx. Accordingly, from the moment when Marxist socialism started to refer to itself ... as "scientific socialism", so bourgeois theorists were concerned to undercut the sciences as such in order to catch in their nets the scientific / certaintist pretensions of the left.
> (1991, 53-4)

Although this account is a little colourful and Jenkins can only be talking about the late nineteenth century as *Das Kapital* was not published until 1867, his comments, in the light of that date, do connect very suggestively with the account given by Michel Serres in which the rupture between the arts and science only starts to look irrevocable with sophisticated formulations of thermodynamic theory c.1850-70. Science in terms of Faraday's general philosophy became meaningless and science in its modern guise as professionalised and expert enquiry began. Indeed, it is likely that Douglas Bush comes nearest the truth in his pioneering if disappointingly anti-science study of English poetry and science published some thirty years ago:

"In the nineteenth and twentieth centuries the heritage of romantic optimism passed to scientists, leaving poets to the contemplation of a great void" (1950, 108). As the present century opened the divide between arts and sciences seemed unbridgeable. In 1908, we find Matisse in 'Notes of a Painter' rejecting attempts to formulate a scientific theory of colour and asserting that such a theory could only be based on the "instinct and sensibility" of painters (in Barr, 1975 119-123). At about the same time, T.E. Hulme was attempting to give poetry a philosophical foundation using ideas from Coleridge and Bergson to distinguish different types of mental activity. A fuller treatment of Hulme's ideas and of their implications for twentieth century English poetry can be found in Kermode (1976, 133-53) and Davie (1976, 1-13, 166-70) but, simply put, Hulme's starting point is the distinction between "mechanical complexities" which come from the intellect and "vital complexities" which come from intuition. Bergson supplies Hulme with the more precise distinctions of "extensive" or analytical thought and "intensive" or synthetic thought. What is important for our discussion is that Hulme not only represents the intellect (extensive) and intuition (intensive) as exclusive and opposite but illustrates this by arguing that they are the bases of divergent discourses: respectively the sciences and the arts. The intellect "can only make diagrams" (1924, 138) while intuition works with "mysterious" syntheses that "can't be definitely stated" (1924, 139). As Davie has pointed out these ideas have remained influential because "We still generally assume that it is the poet's duty to exclude abstractions in favour of concretions"(1976, 13).

Against this background, then, one could be forgiven for expecting the Modernists to be vehemently anti-rationalist and anti-scientific. After all, many of the great works of High Modernism — most notably *The Waste Land* — present man in a lapsarian condition which is compounded by the urban experience — at its worst apocalyptic, at best infernal — but which may be redeemable by the recovery of lost myths and the continuities they embody. Osborne (1989) has shown how little water such a view holds by tracking how "the subject of contemporary physics, especially the work of Einstein, features prominently in the Modernist canon" (131). Out of Osborne's comprehensive survey, it is worth noting MacDiarmid's wide-ranging references to mathematics, physics and quantum physics in 'In Memoriam James Joyce' (to which I shall return presently); William Carlos Williams devoting part of *Paterson* to a discussion of the splitting of the atom; and T.S. Eliot's comparison of Joyce with Einstein. Eliot is, in fact, an interesting case in point.

As early as 1919 in 'Tradition and the Individual Talent' he likened the poet's mind to "a *receptacle* for seizing and storing up numberless feelings, phrases and images, which remain there until all the *particles* which can unite to form a new *compound* are present together" (1975, 41; my italics). However, the most remarkable part of Eliot's oeuvre for my purposes is section IV of 'Little Gidding'. Eliot's poem combines the fires of the Blitz with the fires of sin and the cleansing fires of divine grace. The point of the passage is a stark one: man's choice has not altered. Science and its products have made the mutability of the world all the more apparent which makes the compulsion to seek grace beyond it, for the religious soul, even more powerful. But Eliot's point is, one feels, more complex than either the terrible fruits of science as an excuse for good old-fashioned *contemptus mundi* or a vision of redemption to be shared with fellow believers. If the fires of the Blitz can suggest the fires of the pentecost and of redemption then only in the modern, scientific world can modern man hope to discover and locate his particular images of the spiritual and the eternal. The celestial city and the apocalyptic city are one and the same. It is a point made in Pauline Stainer's poem 'Modern Angels' where once again military hardware produces something like divine fire: "and from the flightdeck, / with all the inconsequence / of revelation, / the crossing arcs of afterburn" (1992, 80).

However, those born after 1950 have grown up with the same ambivalence to science and the technologies derived from it as Wordsworth and his contemporaries, an ambivalence that has more often than not looked like rupture. It is a condition symbolised by the 'two cultures' dispute between C.P. Snow and F.R. Leavis in 1959. The dispute is no longer of any interest in itself but the political and social conditions surrounding it are for they allow us to see the sort of issues that get drawn into the poetry and science debate and also suggest why younger poets have found it easy to ignore the traditional 'war'. Writing of the earlier Festival of Britain, Bryan Appleyard has summarized the context of the dispute as follows:

> At the Festival of Britain the bright exercises in modernism and the worship of technology were viewed by men and women dressed in cloth caps, suits and dresses identical to those of their parents. There was a discontinuity between the modernity of the intellectuals and the sensibility of the masses. In the case of the Festival this simply made the masses that much more difficult to lead. In the case of the Bomb, it endowed the scientists with demonic attributes.
> (1989, 41).

Science, then, was at once creator and destroyer: the means to a better way of life for everyone but also of destroying mankind. As one might expect in an English dispute there was also a class dimension: science was an élite specialism, an example of 'them' telling 'us' what was good for us which was guaranteed to grate on the English character.

The humanities, on the other hand, were open to all and improved the quality of life without altering the material fabric of it. Now, it seems clear that as the post-war period progressed two things altered decisively. First, the threat of global nuclear conflict has seemed less and less likely until the collapse of the Soviet empire seems to have removed it altogether. The Bomb no longer serves as a useful symbol of science. Second, Western capitalist societies underwent profound changes so that the gap between élite and masses became largely meaningless. Culturally, the distinctions between 'high' and 'low', or art and popular culture, have become harder and harder to draw; while socially and economically, in the U.K. at least, there has been a marked increase in the percentage of the population that would call themselves middle-class. Another factor has surely been the rise of environmentalism or 'green' consciousness which, interestingly, has involved not a knee-jerk rejection of science and all its work but a recognition that environmental problems can be traced to the misuse and misapplication of science. A final influence, much less easy to define, is that of postmodernism which, as commentators such as David Harvey have argued, has decisively affected not only cultural products but attitudes to and theories of economics and politics. It seems highly likely that postmodernism's self-consciousness, ficitiveness and impulse to aestheticization have had an influence on attitudes to science. Appleyard (1989, 279) has shown how Martin Amis, writing about the workings of nuclear weapons in *Einstein's Monsters*, can relish both the 'otherness' of scientific vocabulary and "reveal the whizz-bang excitement of science as an inhuman threat". The same 'whizz-bang' excitement of science not as inhuman threat but as 'cutting edge' knowledge can be seen in the considerable media attention focused on the discoveries and postulations of contemporary physics and quantum mechanics. The theories of Hawking and others have had the paradoxical effect of estranging us from our traditional view of ourselves and the universe but at the same time showing us ourselves as inextricably embedded in that universe.

Leaving aside the grumblings of Raymond Tallis — mainly directed at other academics — there has been a demonstrable change in attitudes towards science in recent years. Younger poets have been influenced by this change being 'in the air' but they have also drawn on the examples set by a number of older writers and it is three of these that I now want to examine briefly. Hugh MacDiarmid is similar to Basil Bunting in being a great Modernist poet whose low profile and neglect during his lifetime looks like being redressed by his growing influence after his death. These lines from 'In Memoriam James Joyce' give some clues to this:

> I seek a ground where my personal vision seizes
> The individual who is of a certain race and no other
> (Ultimately the means of seizing any individual
> Of any race, and every individual of every race),
> The point where art and science can meet,
> For there are two kinds of knowledge,
> Knowing about things and knowing things,
> Scientific data and aesthetic realisation,
> And I seek their perfect fusion in my work.
>   (1985, II, 782)

This is perhaps better rhetoric than poetry but the passage is exemplary for its drive for inclusiveness and unity. MacDiarmid wrote, in an essay called 'Aesthetics in Scotland' (1984), that "It is the unification, the wholeness of an outlook on life, that is the sign of the maturity of a genuine culture" and, he would surely have agreed, the sign of the maturity of a genuine poet too. Science, for a number of reasons, is an essential component of the mature outlook of the genuine poet. First, it stands for a universal culture and an international language which, in theory at least, transcends cultural, political and national differences. Universal culture and international language also have particular meanings in terms of MacDiarmid's 'world language' poems of which 'In Memoriam James Joyce' is one of the best examples. Earlier in the poem, MacDiarmid asserts that "Instead of language meaning the material of experience / — Things, ideas, emotions, feelings — / This material means language" (1985, II, 752). The whole world is available to become a part of the poet's speech and, as Watson (1985, 98) argues, the 'world language' poems such as 'In Memoriam James Joyce' "offer us both the world-as-language and language-as-the-world". In this light, science with its impulse to classify and systematize stands for an awareness of and a means of accessing what MacDiarmid calls in *Lucky Poet* "the interdependencies of life" and, elsewhere, "man's incredible variation". If one accepts the

popular view of science as the source of new knowledge about
ourselves and the universe then MacDiarmid's use of science and
its vocabularies also begs questions about the impact of available
knowledge on poetry and whether available knowledge can, in fact,
function as poetry. Second, MacDiarmid's use of science and other
expert vocabularies functions as a means of escaping what is per-
missible, what Hayden White (1978, 126-7) describes as "every
discipline ... as Neitzsche saw most clearly, [being] constituted by
what it *forbids* its practitioners to do". Heaney makes the same point
from a different angle in his description of Milosz's quarrel with
classicism, which becomes "a protective paradigm of the way things
are" (1989, 52). Heaney goes on to quote this line from Brian Friel's
play *Translations*: "a linguistic contour that no longer matches the
landscape of fact" which pinpoints exactly MacDiarmid's escape
from protective paradigms in 'On A Raised Beach'. Here are the
opening lines:

> All is lithogenesis — or lochia,
> Carpolite fruit of the forbidden tree,
> Stones blacker than any in the Caaba,
> Cream-coloured caen-stone, chatoyant pieces,
> Celadon and corbeau, bistre and biege,
> Glaucous, hoar, enfouldered, cyathiform ...
> (1985, I, 422)

MacDiarmid is asserting the obstinacy of reality — what the poem
later calls "inoppugnable reality" — through his own version of
ostranenie, 'making strange' or desuetization. If the language seems
resistant to immediate understanding or explication then this is, in
part, deliberate, because 'On A Raised Beach' resists the bourgeois
mystification inherent in conventional poems of nature and land-
scape. MacDiarmid's vision is, in contrast, implacably, com-
fortlessly materialist, implying that the hard truth of nature may in
fact be indivisible from the nature of truth, but there is nothing
pessimistic about it. Watson (1985, 80) suggests that "the paradox
is that the poem tries to make the realization and acceptance of that
understanding [of materiality] an act of spiritual triumph in itself".
Science and scientific and other expert vocabularies may look like
the spoils of "adventuring in dictionaries" ('In Memoriam James
Joyce', 1985, II, 823) but they are indivisible from MacDiarmid's total
conception of poetry. In a fascinating parallel which would no doubt
have pleased MacDiarmid immensely his later poetry demonstrates
the paradigm shift advanced by the mathematician Norbert Weiner
in his 1948 work *Cybernetics*: the move from one dominant paradigm,

energy, to a new one, information. In the words of one commentator, "One major advantage of the new paradigm to explain thinking was that it dealt with open systems, systems coupled to the outside world both for the reception of impressions and the performance of actions; the older paradigm of energy dealt only with closed, conservative systems. Another, perhaps even more important, advantage of the new paradigm was that it dealt with the behaviour of symbols ..." (McCorduck 1988, 72).

The poetry of Peter Redgrove bears marked similarities to Mac-Diarmid's in its concern with scientific terminology and expert vocabularies; its delight in lists and catalogues; and in its rich stew of variant dictions (Corcoran 1993, 144). The essential difference is that Redgrove is a trained and practising scientist who has rejected conventional science:

> ... the scientists have given us a picture of nature which is competitive, alien, empty, mechanical, and a universe in which we are complete strangers, and in which — talking about continuums — there is no continuum between our-selves and nature. This is the great romantic quest, that a continuum between nature and mankind should be proved ... Science still proceeds on behaviouristic principles. Thirty per cent of the population are intensely weather-sensitive. There is a kind of feeling-knowledge of the world which arises from meteorological changes. There is a response, an invisible response which is not accounted for in medical science.
> (Interview 1987, 5-6)

In an attempt to counter what he sees as behaviouristic, 'partially sighted' science and restore a continuum, Redgrove has created an intensely personal symbology, as anti-Christian as it is anti-behaviourist, with goddess myths and sexual energy as its defining principles. Redgrove's intellectual and creative energies are, as the interview extract suggests, excited by glimpses of the invisible and by poetry's ability to make the invisible visible through its essential synaesthesia. His poetry is full of scents, smells, tangs and perfumes and of images of matter undergoing transformation and this is paralleled by science changing into something supra-rational and semi-mystical where science, proto-science and pseudo-science combine. 'Temptation of the Books — VI' (1979, 143) speaks of "An obstetrics which is a cosmogony" and 'Orion Pacing' (1979, 93-4) gives us a typical Redgrove combination:

> Computer circuits printed like Orion, tied
> In bright points which are full of information;

The stars rustling, the wheat twinkling,
White man-splash on velvet, bullets of electricity.

'After The Crash' from the same collection (34) makes the point
more explicitly:

I am all blurred, I am warm soapy water;
Hard edges are for dead people,
Like the breadloaf that cannot be holographed
Because it is moving, gently heaving ...

As Redgrove's project to make the invisible visible suggests and
such passages make plain, his poetry is, at bottom, paradoxical. As
I have written elsewhere, what, for example, are the wider meanings
of a poetry that remains steadfastly male in its materialist outlook
but through which its male author tells us about goddesses, periods
and tampons (1993, 86-7). Science, in its behaviourist manifestation,
is perhaps the essential paradox: it is to be rejected because it itself
rejects the possibility of any continuum between man and the
universe and yet it must always be present in order to highlight what
has been rejected. In this sense, it functions almost as the 'shadow'
of Redgrove's own symbology. Similarly, just as holographics
reveals the nature of matter so conventional science often provides
the means of seeing the invisible world and connections which the
poetry, as in 'Orion Pacing', intuits. As Redgrove has remarked in an
interview, (1987, 9) ideas about pheromones and body magnetism
— which have been consigned to the pseudo-science of the popular
press — were "first described in moths by pest-control scientists".

If there are similarities between Redgrove's use of science and
MacDiarmid's then there are also important differences. Both poets
use science to suggest and enact unity and synthesis, albeit of very
distinct kinds and both use it in the service of a poetry that rejects
irony and distance. However, Redgrove's use of science or, perhaps
more correctly, Redgrovian science is a means of attempting a
unique organising principle which some commentators have
mistakenly termed surrealism or dream-logic. Rather his work has
the feeling of a dream in its perpetual discovery that everything is
something else, but nothing of a dream's bizarre abritrariness. In
'The Silvery Old Goldsmith' (1992, 25-6) "a midget's hat-stand"
is actually "a model / To scale of a radio-echo engraving on the sky
/ For a split-second all of Chopin's / Funeral march in the one
figure". What this suggests, in fact, is the inexhaustible potential of
the universe and of man in it and, by extension, a rejection of
conventional ideas of ending and death.

Redgrove's poetry often deals with death but always in the sense of the song from *The Tempest*, as "a sea-change / Into something rich and strange". In its celebratory materialism and its enjoyment of interconnected processes, the poetry seeks to transcend the conventional boundaries and expectations of both poetic and scientific discourse. In 'Two Visions of Science' (1979, 86-7) a vision of "all the bridegrooms / Dazzling in white dresses and not a bride among them" is contrasted with "a darkened pharmacy" of medicines "Lacking only a prescriber — and here she comes. / 'Are you the Doctor?' 'Yes, I am your Doctress'". Redgrove's conception of what is wrong with conventional science and how it may be cured symbolises man's incompleteness and unrealized potential. Science becomes the starting point, the grit in the oyster, for Redgrove's supra-rational, anti-Christian symbology.

Miroslav Holub is Czechoslovakia's most renowned living poet and also one of her leading scientists, working as chief research immunologist at the Institute for Clinical and Experimental Medicine in Prague and best known for work on the common cold using colonies of nude mice. In marked contrast to both MacDiarmid and Redgrove, Holub's poetry does not offer any self-conscious program. He has described it as follows:

> There should be a poetic idea in *my* system, in *my* thinking which is far from being a common sense ethic, far from a philosophical idea, far from the scientific idea ... Maybe the description of the ethos is 'the poetry *aiming* somewhere'. I wouldn't define where, but aiming somewhere.
> (Interview 1994, 40)

Again, in contrast to MacDiarmid and Redgrove, Holub enacts a synthesis of poetry and science rather than striving to resolve opposition or heal rupture. Ian Milner (1990, 13) reminds us that Holub has asserted on many occasions the basic similarities of scientific and poetic method, as in this statement: "The emotional, aesthetic and existential value is the same ... when looking into the microscope and seeing the expected (or at times the unexpected, but meaningful) and when looking into the nascent organism of the poem". Holub has also remarked (Interview 1994, 40) that life under a totalitarian system in which everything is based on the class struggle teaches an interconnectedness of activity. Milner remarks that "Holub's poetic vision [is] nothing if not contextual. Neither cell nor man lives alone". However, such comments give only the broadest clues to why the science is in the poetry and what it is doing.

The early poem 'Pathology' (1990, 29) offers the perspective of "the absolute / of the microscope's lenses" which sketches a paradigm of poetry as an activity that begins with fact, inquiry and truthful observation and description. Science stands for a rigour and scrupulosity which enable the speaker in 'Lyric Mood' (1990, 125) to admit that "I haven't found anything / but I can say so". This is a particular type of discourse which we might describe as typically East European and laconic but its radicalism lies not in that instantly recognisable 'sound' nor in its difference from both traditional 'last line homily' poetry or postmodern play: its originality lies in its admission that sometimes poetry has nothing to say and that we should expect it, incorporate it. In the words of 'Suffering' (1990, 105-6), one of Holub's finest poems, "Experiments succeed and experiments fail, / Like everything else in this world". 'Injection' (1990, 104) puts it another way:

> we feel in our finger-tips
> the weight of life
> and a strange joy in
> > being free
> > > to ask
>
> Without answers.

Scientific enquiry characterises not only a way of looking but a way of feeling too. The French scientist Claude Bernard has remarked that "outside of my laboratory, I let my imagination take wing; but once I go into my laboratory, I put my imagination away" (in Tallis, 'Newton's Sleep (1)', 49) which emphasises that doubt is an essential component of science: only precision, proof and replication count. In poetic terms, this accounts for Holub's sceptical, ironical take on the word and the world: he takes nothing at face value. A little paradoxically perhaps he often writes poems which have the flavour of the fable or the epigram but which remain surprisingly open-ended as if the scientist is always reminding the poet how little is knowable in any finite sense. "Art is fidelity to failure" (1990, 132).

If science provides a paradigm of looking and feeling it also informs an existential dimension to Holub's poetry for the image of the scientist intent on the world through his microscope is also an image of the individual, unique but interconnected, empowered by the ability to chose from alternatives but vulnerable through the inability to foretell the outcome and through the feeling — perhaps inevitable in a period when communism has collapsed and the voyages of late capitalism have become increasingly stormy — that the greater part of human endeavour is doomed to self-destruct. In the words of a character in Aldous Huxley's novel *After Many A Summer*, all actions are tainted by "Time and craving ... craving and time — two aspects of the same thing; and that thing is the raw material of evil" (1976, 91). The image of man as free but bounded is clearly informed by the experience of being an artist and a scientist in a totalitarian state but is also indivisible from a scientific perspective in which boundaries and limits are tested and retested and new freedoms suggested or old ones redefined. As in MacDiarmid and Redgrove, science becomes a means of escaping cultural, political and social paradigms and conventions and of accessing that elusive continuum. In the words of 'Distant Howling' (1990, 203) "Only the virus / remained above it all" which suggests, if not higher truth, then some standard of obtainable reality.

The poetry of MacDiarmid, Redgrove and Holub, though very different in its essentials and surfaces, does collectively throw light on some of the ways science is working in contemporary British poetry. First, science symbolises a desire for and the possibility of synthesis and unity. It offers a paradigm of intellectual enquiry which assumes a universal referentiality or what Les Murray calls — albeit with a different emphasis — "the perpetual dimension" which "breaks through sequential time not to timelessness but to a sort of enlarged spiritual present in which no life is suppressed" (1992, 176). The scientist Stephen Hawking has described the same phenomenon: "There is another kind of time to the real time where the Big Bang initiated the created universe: imaginary time in which the universe has no beginning and no end" (Interview 1992). At its simplest, science becomes a badge of what MacDiarmid called 'the wholeness of an outlook on life'. Second, science is a way of avoiding or of improving on unsatisfactory aspects of inherited or 'traditional' poetic discourse. For some poets, this may mean rejecting English irony and distance or the bourgeois mystification that seems inherent in certain subjects. For others, the use of scientific or other expert vocabularies is a sign of poetry relished as a 'language game' for its own sake or of an attempt to reinsert poetry into the everyday world. Finally, science comes to stand for the condition of man and the nature and acquisition of knowledge. MacDiarmid, Redgrove and Holub, for example, all use science to some degree as the starting point for redressing the desacrilisation of the world. Other poets, as we shall see later in the chapter, take the procedures of science as a paradigm of perception and knowledge generally. Quantum Mechanics, particularly, has forced redefinitions of objectivity. "One of the simplest explanations of Heisenberg's Uncertainty Principle is that the act of measuring sub-atomic entities alters their behaviour to the extent of rendering the results imprecise. In order to see minute particles one has to direct at them a light wave which consists of a stream of much larger particles called photons; and such a bombardment inevitably interferes with the structure being observed" (Osborne 1989, 120). This clearly has wide-ranging implications for artistic method and intellectual enquiry.

Beyond these generalised and, to some extent, international meanings, science is inextricable from trends peculiar to British poetry of the last ten to fifteen years. We have already noted how Holub's poetry is concerned with authentic reality, what Alvarez (1984, 9) has called "the limpid air of his poetry [where] there is no place for evasion or illusion or fakery". Authenticity has been and continues to be an important concept in British poetry, not only in terms of marketing and public relations (see Chapter Eight) but also at the grass roots level of creative writing courses and poetry workshops. It is a conception of poetry that is best summarized by these lines from the Introduction to Peter Sansom's *Writing Poems* (1994, 7): "My main preoccupation in this book is with writing authentically. I mean by this *saying genuinely what you genuinely need to say*. I believe that when you write authentically the experience is the same as Keats's must have been when writing his great poems" (his italics). The reference to Keats — and the evidence of Sansom's own eloquent poetry — suggest a defining conservatism at the heart of the project to write authentically. This would not, in itself, have much bearing were it not for the number of younger poets who have 'come up' through the sort of courses and imbibing the kind of ideas that Sansom's book lays out in detail. We must consider whether 'writing authentically' is just another version of 'write about what you know' and, consequently, whether the use of science is a way of disguising a conservative poetic as postmodern and radical. This, in turn, opens onto the whole, predictably vexed question of the nature of the relationship and transactions between postmodernism and a native poetry of objects, persons and values. The 'New Generation Poets' promotion seemed to 'make official' the engagement of postmodernism and empiricism but the presence of science in contemporary British poetry begs some uncomfortable questions. What are the implications of a usage that appears to emblematize a questioning of or a rejection of empiricist ideas about language but in fact employs vocabulary from empiricist modes of enquiry and knowledge? Is science in British poetry just empiricism by another name? I hope to offer some answers in the second half of this chapter.

If the presence of science in contemporary British poetry connects with postmodernism then it also connects with a particular aspect of modern poetry which Wallace Stevens touched on when he wrote that "In the presence of extraordinary reality, consciousness takes the place of imagination". This may be found at its most extreme in the poetry of, say, Frank O'Hara but it also informs the work of a surprising number of poets in *The New Poetry* (1993). Eavan Boland makes an explicit identification between poetry, science and such a shift in the opening lines of her great poem 'The Journey': "And then the dark fell and 'there has never' / I said 'been a poem to an antibiotic' ... Depend on it, somewhere a poet is wasting / his sweet uncluttered metres on the obvious / / emblem instead of the real thing" (1993, 49). Lavinia Greenlaw, whose work is clearly shaped by science, often writes a poetry which is concerned to register the precise mood or tone of a particular moment of consciousness, as in 'From Scattered Blue' (1993, 13) where a description of a drive along the Thames at sunset ends:

> It reminds me
> of how we used to talk; how we want sometimes
> to do more than just live it.

The yearning for the transcendent reality offered by the imagination disturbs the rest of the poem's carefully unillusioned description. Similarly, the poetry of Simon Armitage and Michael Hofmann — while not sharing in such a yearning — is characterised by a concern to detail exact moments to the extent that the act of writing becomes more important than what is being recorded.

It seems to me that the use of science is inextricable from British poetry's anxiety in the 1980s and early 1990s about its authority, function and role. Is poetry an eccentric, marginalised activity or a popular art? Can it become popular without becoming lightweight? Does poetry make nothing happen or can it 'make a difference'? Is it a broad church or an élite discourse? These sorts of questions describe an anxiety over the gap between how poetry is perceived and valued by its practitioners and how it is perceived and valued in the world at large. Poetry has always had to contend with estimates such as I.A. Richards influential and damaging distinction between scientific statement where "truth is ultimately a matter of verification" and the poet's "emotive utterance" which produces sentences which look like statements but are in fact "pseudo-statements" (Abrams 1971, 323). George Steiner makes a similar, albeit kinder, distinction in *Real Presences* when he refers to science as "hard, fatiguing individual work" and non-scientific knowledge as "a spontaneous spiritual knowing" (Tallis 1991, 34).

The use of science is not only a badge of rational 'fitness' but a way of bolstering poetry's traditional claims to be the discourse of ultimate truth. Finally, I would like to suggest, in passing, that science in contemporary British poetry may perhaps be related to the prevailing scientism of literary theory and cultural theory in general; and that, in some cases, it may be a form of 'martianism' without its impulses to irresponsible reification.

I now want to look at the work of five British poets in detail. They are, in alphabetical order: Robert Crawford, Lavinia Greenlaw, Paul Mills, David Morley and Pauline Stainer. With the exception of Paul Mills, all began publishing poetry in the 1980s and all have been quick to establish recognisable styles and voices. In preparing this half of the chapter, I have paid particular attention to the poets' own statements about the presence of science in their poetry and about the wider relationship between the arts and the sciences and I have included these as appropriate. Unless otherwise indicated, these 'sound bites' are taken from my own correspondence with the poets.

David Morley (b.1964) seems the likeliest candidate to take up Eavan Boland's challenge of writing an ode to an antibiotic. He read Zoology at Bristol — where he also attended Charles Tomlinson's poetry tutorials — and later completed a PhD on the impact of acid rain on lakes and tarns in Cumbria. As well as working as a poet, critic, teacher and literature development officer, he has continued to do scientific research although this has been outside the usual academic structures. Like MacDiarmid and Holub — both of whom he acknowledges as major influences — Morley is essentially a synthesist and, in his recent work, often writes as if he has single-handed mission to restore a Platonic cultural 'body' of which poetry and science are unhappy, wandering halves. Essential to Morley's poetry is a conception of poetry and science as interchangeable discourses. He has said that "my initial trajectory into verse arose out of a need to detail natural history as precisely — as efficiently — as I could" and that, conversely, "Eliot's 'objective correlative' is a paradigm for how a creative scientist actually works". The link between the two is through an understanding and enjoyment of what a scientist calls 'variables' and this informs Morley's illuminating remarks on Wallace Stevens:

Wallace Stevens takes a blackbird and observes it in thirteen ways. Thirteen 'test conditions', each of which is loaded with multivariate data of perception. Yet, Stevens asks us to trust the poem, and we do because the blackbird isn't presented as final in any way. The blackbird has not shown 100% significant difference from the blackbird we know in our heart. The blackbird is a dynamic organism, as is the observer, and the poem that results from the collusion of the two is a dynamic, restless document.

I would want to argue that Stevens's famous poem is as much about the precise notation of states of consciousness as it is about blackbirds, but Morley's analysis makes plain his own conception of science as a fundamental human activity. One can also discern, behind his last statement, a recognition of the implications of the uncertainty principle for narrative which is something we can also see in the work of Paul Mills.

Science as an emblem of passionate intelligence and as a paradigm for accurate but dynamic observation inform Morley's first collection *Releasing Stone* (1989). The poems abound in images which both seek to surprise and be irreplaceable. In 'Baudelaire 1857' (18) "dawn contrives its thermometer ascent", 'Errand' opens on a scene where "Earth moved like sugar, boiling" (10) and in 'Metal-work' (11) the poet watches his father measuring material with callipers that "twitch / legs skinny, / an avocet's". It seems to me that this is wonderfully alert writing by any standards but the book makes increasing claims on re-reading through its underlying ideas. 'Long Division' is relatively 'quiet' in terms of its verbal effects and in its account of 'after hours' at a scientific conference:

After dinner, falling to print, *New Scientist*
warns me there is only this
last particle to uncover, (but goes on)
how we are just that one

unthought-of-matter multiplied:
think of a number, double it.

At the end of the poem the poet sees "A gang of punks / [exploding] from falling glass, / scattering fear ... // I want to run with them". The poem — which has earlier called the interrelation of macro and micro "Dada art" — gives us poetry and science as aspects of the same discourse. It is the poem that permits the closing, confident identification of self and other but only as a recognition and validation of a scientific hypothesis. The relation between 'I' and the punks is another version of the poem's earlier "just that one ... multiplied". The identification is inevitable because science insists on accounting for all the variables, however uncomfortable or unwelcome these might be in other terms. 'Long Division' is, perhaps, Morley's version of Murray's 'perpetual dimension' "in which no life is suppressed" (op cit). A similar conception underlies 'Movings: A Field Observation' (34-5) in which a concern with accurate natural history allows the apparently arbitrary interdependencies of nature to become the order of art and 'Runner' (38-40) in which alertness to deer reveals "there is no cease but / grace notes in their running".

Morley's more recent work, as represented by *A Static Ballroom* (1993) has been more concerned with telling than enacting a synthesis of poetry and science and, indeed, acknowledges the reality of cultural paradigms that work against it. 'Fantasia On Themes From *Scientific American*' ends with its protagonist holding that journal "with somebody's *Collected Poems* snug inside it. // And you're clasping the edges with all your power / to stop them slipping away, both together". Morley suggests two ways of resisting this slippage. First, in '"Hawk Roosting": Rewrite' (14) he attempts a genuinely scientific poetry in which the well known Hughes poem is reworked as a zoologically exact villanelle:

> Moves over identical zone in territory.
> Male: dominant, sexually.
> Rapid Eye Movement when dormant.
>
> Highly-pressured, enviromentally.
> Future absence from food web: probably.
> Predation strategies "rehearsed", i.e.
> Rapid Eye Movement when dormant.

There can be doubt that Hughes's original is the better poem but Morley's point is not, so to speak, to go fifteen rounds with the Laureate. His rewrite picks up on a key phrase from Hughes's poem — "in sleep rehearse perfect kills and eat" (1982, 43) — and, through a series of terse 'corrections' suggests that while Hughes may well, in Heaney's words, have "recalled English poetry ... from a too suburban aversion of the attention from the elemental" (1980, 153) his view of nature is as romantic as Keats's. The language of Hughes's poem — dream, manners, convenience, please — gives the hawk a consciousness it does not possess. Morley's rewrite shows us hawk as an organism responding to stimuli and one that is vulnerable to change. Nature is not a paradigm for eternity and neither is it somehow cordoned off from the human. However, while Morley's villanelle is a bravura technical performance it does, when compared to the Hughes poem, rather beg the question whether poetry and science are actually exclusive discourses. Morley's second strategy for resisting slippage suggests a way out: "I'm very interested ... in superscience, in which a number of concepts from different fields of investigation are synthesised. One of the most intriguing variables is, of course, time". 'Superscience' (1993, 25-8) is an attempt to explore that plasticity and, in the process, show "How things build up to things, / build down" and to answer "What is this about your history / that tears you to pieces in limbfuls? / What is this that won't let you get away with nothing?". The question is as much aesthetic and poetic as it is existential and the answer, rather in the manner of Ashbery's *Flow Chart*, is in the *procès verbal*. But Morley is not a disciple of the New York School, is not after an anti-referential but sensuous discursiveness. The terms of the poem — "The story ... / ... will go off like a horse from gunshot", "exponential", "parabola", "graph", "equation" — oppose measurement and the uncontainable. This, in turn, echoes the "dynamic, restless document" Morley finds in Wallace Stevens and suggests that the synthesis of poetry and science is a paradigm for *multi*-referential discursiveness.

Paul Mills (b.1948) is concerned to register the impact of astrophysics and quantum mechanics on the way we view our world and he has drawn attention to the fact that, in 1926, when Yeats was writing to Sturge Moore that "The discoveries of science can never affect reality" Heisenberg was arriving at his uncertainty principle which marked the decisive break with classic Newtonian physics. Many poems in his most recent collection *Half Moon Bay* (1993) point out the smallness and brevity of human history in terms of cosmological time. 'Search' (22) refers to it as "a blip" while 'Under The Moon Of Pluto' (44) pictures "Our human history, dangled at the end of a snapped thread / Of chance, [hanging] on in astonishment". This concern with the planet, informed by travels in the American deserts, produces a number of poems on overtly ecological themes. Surprisingly, perhaps, few poets of recent years have produced a body of work located in this area. The centre of Mills's achievement and, I think, his originality is, however, his exploration of contemporary science in terms of narrative and discourse. If the work of Heisenberg and others changes our view of ourselves and our world, it also brings into question *how* we talk about them. It "involves the question of the discourse, or discourses, available for such a discussion". Similarly, just as David Morley likened the poet and the scientist in their response to variables, so Mills links science to narrative:

> The Uncertainty Principle ... defers the position of reliable narrator. It has to do this because what it observes at one time, given the same set of circumstances, cannot be predicted for another. This gap in narrative is exactly what interests the newly-developing positions in postmodernist thought, and exactly what leads to a mixing of disciplines and discourses on narrative. Reliable narrative must, can only be, a narrative afterwards, which not only predicts events but somehow knows them, as if they had already happened. But since Heisenberg there appeared, for the first time in science, the acute possibility that no narrative *afterwards* can be found. The drive for mastery implies a continual repositioning, ever more outside, beyond or above the previous method of observation, in order to achieve the sought position of omniscience.
> (1995, 41)

Mills responds to this in a number of poems which experiment with shifting perspectives or use images drawn from film and television, the most notable of which is 'Climate Change' (1993, 88-89) in which the spectacle of people parachuting from a plane prompts a meditation on the nature of time. The poem contrasts the "secure time" in which the scene occurs and is observed and "another scene, filmed / at wind-speed, a mill-race of clouds / pouring like smoke for hours, years, / a minute's extent of years". Mills ends the poem with a stanza which resists conventional closure by picturing the plain of York "fiercely charged with squalls and rays / of space-light" and returning to the moment before the drop, the moment before "the air will swarm / with shapes together in a scene / no one observes from the ground". The poem both enacts the 'continual repositioning' of postmodern narrative and mocks 'the drive for mastery' by finishing, quite literally, at the top of its story, a position which has already been shown least likely to be the most illuminating perspective.

But if science has demolished its own classic narratives and is inseparable from a wider, postmodern dissolution of 'master narratives', is anything left apart from a perpetual perspectivism, a cancerous aesthetic of total relativity? Mills believes "A sense of incompleteness is crucial ... Although this kind of writing is a matter of possible direction rather than already assured certainty, a lead might be found in the work of Zbigniew Herbert, whose combinations

of science-perspective, philosophy, narrative, religion, ironic mono-
logue, remove discourses from whichever institutions own them ...".
Mills's poetry shows that this removal can be as stupefying as it is
empowering. In 'A Christening', an atheist couple have their children
christened during a thunderstorm which is taken as the voice of
God, the poet reads from the Bible in the dark and the poem ends
with a man explaining the workings of a motorbike to a small girl,
a clear image of the scientific as the miraculous. In 'The Steel'
however the liberation of discourses allows a reading of the two
Terminator sci-fi films which teases out worrying images of industrial
power and fertility. This widening of perspective connects with
Mills's assertion that the "new sense of observable limits in science
needs to have its poetry ... To borrow Emily Dickinson's phrase,
'its business is circumference'. It is hardly surprising, then, to find
the sequence 'Galactic Landscapes' (1993, 82-5) beginning

> Therefore let everywhere be an edge,
> circumference the limits of the known,
> earth, plants, rocks, the moon,
> star-masses and vapour a torn edge
>
> ravelled and knotted about in curves of shine.
>
> And looped with it a parallel thread
> of darkness, the negative, the shaper.

The sequence tracks both edge and shaper through "ice on
Titan", "luminous cathedrals", "ocean-time" and "ancient time".
This is reminiscent of Redgrove in its sense of interconnected
processes and in the poem's larger narrative of man being shaped
as much by what he doesn't know as by the acquisition of
knowledge. "Edge is all we know" but that edge is constantly open
to revision and redefinition. (Indeed, as this chapter was being
drafted, *The Times* [3.11.94, 7] reported that two separate teams of
astronomers have discovered a new galaxy, Dwingeloo 1, hidden
behind the Milky Way, and seven new moons of Saturn.) The poem
ends on a stony beach, in a scene that is unavoidably reminiscent of
MacDiarmid, where pebbles, shells and fossils "too / are an edge,
the core of darkness untouched". Science — "a grail story with no
grail" Mills has called it — stands for the neverending search of
human knowledge. Its value for the poet lies in what it does to that
sense of 'edge' not only in the glimpses it allows of the invisible,
unknown or irrecoverable but also through the way it appears to

authenticate the perspectivism of cultural products in an age without reliable narratives.

A very different sense of boundaries and edges is involved in Robert Crawford's (b.1959) explorations of poetry and science. It is a sense that is best understood by two comments from his recent critical study *Identifying Poets: Self and Territory in Twentieth Century Poetry* (1994). The first is a quotation from Bakhtin that "the realm of culture has no internal territory: it is entirely distributed along the boundaries, boundaries pass everywhere, through its every aspect" (11). The second comes from Crawford's discussion of poetic identity in twentieth century Scottish poets: "Identity for the Scottish identifying poets, and for identifying poets generally, is not a matter of purity but an amalgam of resources"(1993, 174). Both comments connect with the defining presence in Crawford's poetry of Scotland as a place where languages — English, Gaelic and Scots — and, consequently, discourses play and intermingle. Scotland becomes a paradigm for purposeful coexistence and plurality: "Just after lunch / I'm reading how the name of Henry Duncan // Links the savings bank movement to the first scientific treatise / On fossilized footprints" ('Accidents', 1992, 16). As that passage also implies, science is indivisible from Scottish cultural identity and from the species of nationalism defined by Margaret Atwood in a quotation that gives the epigraph of Crawford's first collection *A Scottish Assembly* (1990): "... our cultural nationalism has a very modest mandate — namely, that we exist. It seems to threaten some people". In the 'voicing' of that existence science offers a continuity between past and present that is, at the same time, a way of recovering and reinstating Scotland in international terms. The Scottish influence on and intervention in the history of the West, the argument goes, can only be understood as a matter of paradigm shifts. Existence becomes threatening because those contributions have been ignored or marginalised by the English.

Crawford makes a similarly bold re-reading in his study *Devolving English Literature* (1993) where his starting point, crudely put, is that it was the Scots who invented English Literature as an academic subject. The tragic cultural irony is that they did so by accident. The original project of Scottish scholars and rhetoricians was to empower Scots through the acquisition of educated speech but this was simultaneous with the establishment of the early London chairs of English. The unlooked for result was that the work of the Scots had the effect of exemplifying and, thereby, bolstering metropolitan standards of correctness and, finally, of reinforcing England's cultural and political domination of Scotland. Crawford writes Scottish scientists into a comparable narrative in poems which revisit such figures as Logie Baird, Patrick Miller, the inventor of the steamship, and Napier who invented an early form of calculator. This sense of being instrumental in the British Empire and then marginalised by it is central to 'The Saltcoats Structuralists' (1990, 10) but the poem's narrative of the move from mechanical to electronic, from Pax Britannia to post everything, emphasises how much of peoples' lives are formed by such shifts or lie on the fault lines between paradigms. It is this that informs the fascination of Crawford's poetry with the juxtaposition of traditional images of Scotland with those of the modern Silicon Glen, a place of "Scotlands running together" and where "Ayrshire's a mud database / Updated hourly by jets into Prestwick" ('Fiesta', 1990, 26).

Crawford's work may appear to have an exclusively 'political' agenda but it is underwritten by a sense of literary tradition. He places himself firmly in "that remarkable line of twentieth century Scottish poets who have used science and scientific terminology as part of their work; the principal poets are John Davidson, Hugh MacDiarmid, and Edwin Morgan". Crawford is clearly committed to MacDiarmid's conception of science and art as inseparable aspects of human creativity — his "amalgam of resources" rewrites the older poet's "wholeness of an outlook on life" — but is particularly interested in using science in the context of short lyrics. The two come together in a poem like 'The Dalswinton Enlightenment' (1990, 21) which describes a voyage in "the world's first steamship" by the landscape painter, Alexander Naysmith, and his friend Robert Burns:

> The painter will later invent
> The compression rivet, and work out the axial arrangement
> Between propeller and engine. The poet will write about the light
> Of science dawning over Europe, remembering how
>
> Cold sun struck Pat's boat that October day at Dalswinton
> When the churning paddles articulated the loch
> In triumphant metre

This picture of prelapsarian unity should also alert us to a central paradox in Crawford's poetry: the relishing of plurality and difference but a sense that these are merely the acceptable faces of larger forces of uncontrollable dislocation and discontinuity. 'Graid' (1992, 30), word which means both "to make ready" and "made ready", is a comic nightmare of interchangeable discourses — "the Peugeot manual quotes / Confucius" — which inscribes a desperate faith that the postmodern condition is going *somewhere*. The poem, of course, also plays, after Duchamp, with ideas of the 'ready-made'. At its heart though is a glum image: "In this gloaming languages capsize / Into one another". 'Capsize' implies a voyage abandoned or made impossible and the sense of travelling but never arriving as fundamental to the modern — or postmodern — age hangs over many recent poems. 'Technology Transfer' (1992, 50) describes a journey "Towards a New World that is already // Dated or being upgraded"; and 'Iteration' (1992, 60) uses the endless replications of fractal geometry on a computer screen as an image of our times:

> I don't want to
> move,
> Just have it all happen, the nuisance of another day
>
> Of childlessness, another day of being in love —
> One water droplet, then four, the singular
>
> That is also a plural, the true thing that always changes

The discoveries of contemporary science are involved in an apprehension that the fundamentals of our everyday lives are literally beyond us and that we are reduced to the roles of passive spectators, albeit without emotion or perspective. And behind this existential argument is, necessarily, an aesthetic one, for the poem's earlier identification of "cat's eyes on the ringroad" with "a fir tree's cone after cone" evokes two controlling analogues of the mind of the artist and the work of art, machine and plant, which can be traced back at least as far as Coleridge. To make an analogy between cat's eyes and fir cones is not merely to dissolve the organic and the mechanical into each other but rather to suggest that one of the givens of our times is a realisation — authenticated by science — that such categories are no longer capable of containing the whole truth. However, it is equally a given that, as yet, we are uncertain about what the susceptibility of apparent opposites to the same description — mathematical formulae, four-dimensional geometry, patterning, intervals — actually means. In the words of 'Simultaneous Translation' (1992, 14) "This is where we all live now, / Wearing something like a Sony Walkman, // Hearing another voice every time we speak". In aesthetic terms, we are indeed left with only an "amalgam of resources" and all that that implies about questions of form and value. At the moment, Crawford seems to suggest, all we can do is track that 'other voice' and 'enjoy the show'. The poems in *Talkies* show Crawford moving beyond the agenda of cultural nationalism to something more generalised. He has said that "In some ways I'd tend to see my use of scientific material as experimental rather than theoretical, in the way physicists use that distinction". One might also invoke a remark by Michel Serres that "criticism is a generalised physics" (1983).

In an interview given as part of the 'New Generation Poets' promotion, Crawford said that "Directly or obliquely, a good poem is faithful to the language of its age. If it sounds unidiomatic, it sinks" (1994, 40). Speaking more directly of poetry and science, he has argued that "it's very important that the language of poetry include the language of science, and that the materials of modern everyday (as well as arcane) science be included in verse. If that doesn't happen, poetic language will be more and more detached from most of our everyday lives, and eventually become only a place for weekending". It is a measure of Crawford's originality that in attempting to be faithful to the language of his age he has not ignored the problematics of either language or age but has made them uniquely energising for his poetry.

At first sight, Lavinia Greenlaw's poetry might be thought similar to David Morley's. Her titles confess an abundant fascination with scientific subjects: 'For The First Dog In Space', 'Science For Poets', 'Electricity', 'Galileo's Wife'. A closer acquaintance with the poems themselves reveals her use of science is much less 'committed' than such titles suggest and this relates to a defining play throughout her work between the world as both definite knowledge and product of total change, what 'Yosemite' (1993, 16) terms "a transient symmetry". This play becomes more expansive and more problematic in 'Linear, Parallel, Constant' (1993, 28) where the sight of a missile convoy is described as "an exact miracle" whose "mathematical beauty / filled me with the same / superstition and certainty / that sends a rocket / to meet the heavens / carrying the name of a Roman god". The passage is an uncomfortable one and not least for its entirely appropriate derivation of space exploration and military hardware from the same technology. First, we have the surprising spectacle of a contemporary woman poet apparently celebrating and certainly acquiescing to embodiments of phallic power. The female poem appears to need the sanction and inspiration of the male signifier. Second, 'Yosemite's' suggestion that science maps the symmetry and art records its transience is here made explicit: event and record

of event combine to form "an exact miracle". This seems consistent
enough but the following suggestion that art or imagination is
'superstition' and science 'certainty' seems unsatisfactory, even
confused. Even more uncomfortable is the way the poem, having
already acquiesced quite happily to phallic power, wants to have it
both ways by using the same passage to present technology as a
product of superstition *and* certainty. The effect of this is to sketch
a deconstruction of the typical male intellectual system in which two
terms would invariably be in opposition, with superstition the
second term understood as the devalued opposite of the first. Now,
to be fair to Greenlaw, it is also possible to read the poem in precisely
this way, i.e. poetry's power and value lie in its ability to deconstruct
and reformulate existing, probably male, discourse and structure.
However, I feel that, ultimately, such a reading must remain elusive
because 'Linear, Parallel, Constant' remains so ambivalent about
the terms of its "exact miracle".

If 'Linear, Parallel, Constant' suggests that the impulse to register
the play between fact and flux, symmetry and transience, leads to
doubts about the 'right' language — male or female, science or art,
superstition or certainty — to describe that play then many of
Greenlaw's more interesting poems are essentially 'variations on a
theme'. 'Galileo's Wife' (1993, 29-31) is a narrative in the tradition
of 're-womanising' history. The male scientist clings to notions of
observable truth and a flat earth and, having sent his wife to find
the edge of the world, ignores the truth she brings back. The poem
is unambiguous: the nature of truth is imaginative and poetic and
therefore liable to be unheeded. 'Science For Poets' (1993, 48-49) is
a coolly observed account of an encounter between the two cultures,
in which it is the poet who embodies 'superstition' with her desire
for the romance of "physics / in the force of a stiletto heel" and
musings about serial killers and nail polish removal. Her companion
the scientist goes about a highly professionalised activity of "decimal
places" and "molecular shifts". The poem ends by noting that both
poetry and science need an "eye for detail" in order to catch "some
wild enlightenment". The observation also returns us to what
remains problematic about Greenlaw's use of science, namely the
nagging feeling that it is often used to enliven an essentially conven-
tional poetic. 'Years Later' (1993, 5), in which stars in orbit around
each other, never touching but never parting, remind the poet of an
unconsummated relationship, is typical. The correlation is neat but
lacks inevitability. Elsewhere, the prevalence of images involving
maps, charts and atlases — unread, incomplete, abandoned —

suggests that science may stand for an empirical discourse that has to be in place, however negatively or absently, before the flight of the imagination is justified and permissible. When, at the end of 'Night Photograph' (1993, 54), Greenlaw tells us that "There is a slight realignment of the planets. / Day breaks at no particular moment" she is offering us poetry as a self-contradictory discourse, at once incredibly sensitive to the smallest change and ludicrously inept. It is Greenlaw's fraught dialogue with discourses of definition and power that makes her use of science so precarious.

Pauline Stainer (b.1941) has called the presence of science in her poetry "simply a way of looking. I have never seen any division between 'science' and 'art'. One charges the other, as it did for Donne; the particle physics of sacrament, if you like: that chemical release in the brain as Piero della Francesca foreshortens the angel in flight; the Pulsar Obligato to which Christ's wounds re-align their diagonals. I suppose it's the electricity of *redemption* I'm after — unfashionable but *haunting!*" Stainer's comments illuminate both her concerns and her means but they also indicate the complex and highly original nature of her project to write a sacred poetry for the late twentieth century. To bring this out, I want to place against Stainer's own words two passages by others: the first is from Eve Tavor Bannett's contribution to Berry and Wernick's *Shadow of Spirit: Postmodernism and Religion* (1992) and the second is from a French philosopher who shapes that essay, Jean-Luc Nancy:

> Every person, every thing, every text, every society, every moment, is a *Doppelgänger*, divided from what inhabits it, and participating in that from which it is divided. This *partage* is our historical double-bind, our opportunity and our disaster. It is from here, from this proximity and distance of heaven and earth in the same physical or social or linguistic body, that Derrida and Nancy propose that we rethink our sociology, our philosophy and our politics.
> (Berry and Wernick [eds.] 1992, 133)

> Light, presence: what in another language one might name the open [l'ouvert]. It is to the open that we have no access because the open itself is the access to all that is. Presence is not a form or consistency of Being; it is access. Light is not a phenomenon, but the limit-speed of the world, that of all appearance and of all exposition.
> (Nancy 1993, 120)

Bannett's summation of the religious subtext of contemporary Western thought helps us to see how Stainer's most characteristic formulations — "the particle physics of sacrament", "the drift of the dreaming gene", "specific gravity of the blood" — make her poetry so distinctively contemporary even as they return to the defining paradox of Christianity: eternal truth (God) embodied in human form (Christ). Or, to put it another way, the signifier is radiantly incarnate everywhere and this is precisely why we can't see it. What one poem calls "the luminous inconsequence of / the sign which suffices" (1992, 22) is compensated for by the recognition that "Revelation / is an angle of the light" (1992, 40). The world and the body become the site of "the immaculate desertion" (1992, 69) and part of the revelation of light comes from glimpses of the afterglow of that desertion. Thus the woman looking at an x-ray of her son in the womb some time after his birth sees "sacrament brightly stilled" (1989, 21) and another recovering from an eye operation sees ladies playing bowls as "radiant figures / at the scene / of an unidentified miracle" (1989, 17). Jean-Luc Nancy's remarks are not only pertinent to Stainer's conception of revelation but also to her use of art. Few contemporary poets approach the world through painting as much as she does but where poems about particular pictures often seem preciously inadequate in other poets, Stainer's are, in effect, critical readings of experiments with light as adventures in the spirit. The painter 'teaches' us how an angle of the light can become revelation as in 'Paul Klee At Pompeii' (1992, 12), 'The Blue Beret (after Rembrandt)' (1992, 14) or 'The Dressing Station (after Stanley Spencer)' (1992, 47). This, in turn, reveals him as a mediator between worlds. This mediation is to be understood, I think, in two senses: first, in terms of the synthesis which Klee referred to when he wrote that an artist must be a poet, a naturalist and a philosopher; and second, in terms of mediation between and synthesis of the material and the spiritual, the formal and the ideal. If this suggests a conception of dialectical processes at the basis of all creation, then the artist — and the poet — is concerned with equilibrium. 'Cocteau and the Equilibrist' (1992, 73) presents this in literal terms of a balancing act between art and life while another poem wonders how to catch the urgent axis "of Leda and the Swan" (1992, 72).

Painting also returns inevitably, inexorably to the world and, most importantly, to the body as the site of Bannett's "historical double-bind". Science, which in popular perception at least is concerned either with theories of the universe or with genetics and medicine, has the same effect. Stainer's use of science as subject is, in fact, invariably medical — 'Music For Invasive Surgery' (1992, 26) is a typical title. The concern that shapes these poems is that if Christ's body was at once human and divine then our own are probably the same. Any work involving the human body mediates between two realms. It makes the world more miraculous and takes us as close as possible to the elusive spiritual dimension. In 'Leonardo Dissects The Heart' (1989, 47) "despair is knowing / the certainty of the source / but finding the face of the angel / always averted". Another poem asks "Why is excision / the most haunting of disciplines?" (1992, 26) and yet another answers that it is because if the human body is like Christ's body then medical science becomes a version of the redemption offered by the Crucifixion: we "heal by making / the correct wounds" (1992, 62).

If art and science reveal the sacred and thereby change our perception of the human and the material, they have a similar impact on the feminine. However, Stainer is clearly not writing a radical feminist poetry in the manner of Rich and neither is she concerned with a naive biological essentialism in which the body offers a 'language' which enables woman to transcend enforced inarticulacy. We have already noted how it is a woman's body that is the source of "sacrament brightly stilled" and how a woman perceives the radiant site of "an unidentified miracle". This conception of woman is developed further in 'Woman Holding a Balance' (1992, 61) written after a painting by Jan Vermeer. The seventeenth century Dutch master enables Stainer to discuss both painting and woman in terms of her 'undivided' discourse, for Vermeer portrayed the subtleties of light and experimented with perspective in ways that evoke analogies with physics and metaphysics. Indeed, some authorities have drawn comparisons with the work of Vermeer's contemporary Leeuwenhoek, the maker of microscopes, and with Spinoza and others have argued that many of his paintings are the fruit of experiments with the *camera obscura*. The refined perception of Vermeer's art appears to suggest a union of the scientific and the mystical.

Vermeer has another resonance for the modern age in that the majority of his subjects were young girls or women in domestic settings, often in the act of reading or writing letters. This inevitably opens on to questions of female writing as well as offering a problematic discourse of female privacy rendered visible by the male gaze. Corcoran (1993, 224) has drawn attention to the presence of a Vermeer painting, *Girl with a Pearl Earring*, in Medbh McGuckian's 'The Flitting' (1982, 48) which says of Vermeer's subject "Her narrative secretes its own values". Stainer's poem, however, only *starts* from that point in its discussion of what I take to be *A Woman Weighing Gold*:

We x-ray the embryo;
tap the womb
for the sex of the unborn;
but are haunted by your composure.

Inclining your cool head,
you weigh
what we have found
questionable:
woman as diviner.

                    *   *   *

We cannot weigh
the serenity of genes
...
but when you
suspend the scales

You embody
such stillness,
we could believe
light from your high window
incarnates a child.

As in at least eight other poems, the female body is the site where
science operates. Medical science appears to have rendered 'ques-
tionable' the female mysteries of conception and childbirth *and*
stereotypes of woman as idealised other. It is typical of Stainer's
exploration of the problematic nature of looking and seeing that she
does not offer art as a means of restoring lost mysteries. She suggests
instead something more radical and uncomfortable: that the appar-
ent idealisation of Vermeer's painting is in fact a true representation
of female power. The poem makes clear that the relationship
between art and science is inevitable but certainly not as 'simple' as
Stainer's own remarks suggest. The recognition of that inevitability
is a consequence of a distinction she has made between looking
'obliquely' and looking 'directly' (1994, 82). The understanding of
axes of vision and the ability to look directly and accept what is seen
are the measure of a poetry founded on a belief that its value and
power are an unflinching engagement with human complexity.

6. Home Thoughts From Abroad

W.H. Auden said that in some moods a poet might find Gertrude Stein more apposite than Shakespeare. British poets of the last fifteen years or so have not only proved themselves particularly adept in the cultivation of such moods but have also shown themselves remarkably willing to look beyond the British Isles and the English language for spurs and permissions. When *Poetry Review* polled the twenty members of the 'New Generation Poets' "to try to flush out" influences and affinities, it was forced to conclude that "The only unifying feature of their responses was their relative disdain for English poetry of the 20th century and their enthusiasm for American and European poetry" (Forbes 1994, 4). Out of the seventy or so authors and individual volumes cited, only around a third were English. *Poetry Review's* editorial took this as grounds for arguing, rather belatedly, that "These poets are the true fruits of postmodernism: all cultures are now available to add to one's own inheritances" (Forbes 1994, 5). However, many poets have turned to America and Europe precisely because they find themselves unable to accept 'their own inheritances'. Geoff Hattersley's title 'Frank O'Hara Five, Geoffrey Chaucer Nil' (1994, 31) may be only partly serious but it does neatly encapsulate an attitude which can be detected, in varying degrees, in a surprising number of writers. However, a study which is in effect a list demonstrating this or that influence seems to me neither interesting nor useful so I shall explore the importance and prevalence of 'home thoughts from abroad' in three ways. First, I shall attempt to suggest how and why such rejections of or supplements to one's own inheritance have become so characteristic of recent British poetry; second, I shall examine a small number of specific areas of influence or engagement — e.g. the 'New York school' and Northern British poets — which seem to me to exemplify why poets might find the English tradition insufficiently nourishing; and, third, I shall look at how travel or residence abroad has been decisive in providing a combination of what Charles Boyle (1994) calls "a sense of displacement" and a step towards "the innocent eye" (letter to the author).

There is a very important sense in which both foreign influences and foreign travel are inextricable from prevailing constructions of poetic authority, poetic identity and perhaps even poetry itself. I discuss these constructions in greater detail in Chapter Eight so shall restrict my comments here to their 'foreign' aspects. Ideas of poetry and of culture as global are 'in the air', from Blake Morrison's identification of an international 'superleague' of poets writing in English to Edward Said's *Culture and Imperialism* with its conception of a criticism which follows "the contrapuntal lines of a global analysis" (1993, 385). Maps, which appear to offer inclusiveness, seem more comfortable and less problematic than canons or traditions. If current ideas of poetic authority and poetic identity can be described as elements of a particular discourse then it is a discourse which, as with any other, is itself best understood in terms of what *cannot* or is *not* allowed to be said in it. For example, we do not expect to see a contemporary British poet either acknowledging or being ascribed exclusively English models and influences; and if we do come across such a rare and fabulous creature it is likely that we shall also find him or her being described as a 'formalist' or a 'traditionalist' and the poetry being praised for its *virtu*. So we find Andrew Motion, whose lineage may be traced to Hardy and Thomas, praised by one reviewer as "the genuine article" (Harris 1991, 71). On the other hand, it is interesting to note that Glyn Maxwell, whose main influence appears to be Auden and whose principal subject to date has been English metropolitan life, is presented to us supported by comments from two of Morrison's 'superleague', Joseph Brodsky and Derek Walcott. Similarly, we are continually reminded that Simon Armitage, whose best work is deeply rooted in his Northern English background, owes some of his most significant debts to Weldon Kees and other post-war American poets. Maxwell and Armitage are clearly not "the genuine article" in the sense that the reviewer of Motion intended: they are clearly new and different. On one level, such presentations are, of course, simply marketing but on another they are symptomatic of anxieties about how the status of the poet and the value of the poetry are to be both earned and justified. Travel seems to function in much the same way. It seems to me to be completely irrelevant to an appreciation of, say, Linda France's poetry to know that she once lived in Amsterdam unless a case is being made for either original subject matter or a fundamentally defining engagement with Dutch writing and culture. To understand exactly what is being constructed we only have to consider the very different impact that Glyn Maxwell's poetry would make if supported by praise from Ted Hughes or Tony Harrison; or how odd it would feel to read that, say, Les Murray 'has travelled widely in Europe' or that Allen Curnow 'has lived in Brussels and now works in San Francisco'. In the case of contemporary British poets, it is clear that foreign influences and foreign travel give them a lot of what Pierre Bourdieu called, albeit in a different context, symbolic capital; and the corresponding implication is that their work gains in both authority and value through a kind of extended provenance.

The desire and perhaps necessity to accumulate symbolic capital might well be thought to be a cynical phenomenon of the age of the free market but it can, in fact, be traced to inherited ideas of poetic value which go back at least as far as the late 1960s and early 1970s. We should perhaps not be too surprised to find one of Britain's most important poets, Seamus Heaney, and one of Britain's most influential editors and publishers, Neil Astley, saying the same thing as both were to some extent formed by this period. Astley (1993, 18-19) describes discovering an antidote to the 'boring' world of English poetry of the early 1970s:

> Someone told me about a series of mostly unobtainable books called Penguin Modern European Poets. I wasn't sure how to pronounce the names of many of the writers, but that didn't matter. Even in translation they communicated far more than most English poets I'd come across. They seemed to achieve an eloquence, a purity of utterance, which I had not experienced in my reading of English poetry. They weren't concerned with how things looked, but how things *were*; like the English Metaphysicals, they were obsessed with ideas and human experience, not appearances.

Heaney, in an extremely valuable essay entitled 'The Impact of Translation' (1989, 36-44) argues that from the mid-1960s onwards translation has linked "new literary experience to a modern martyrology". The result has been not only a recognition by English poets that "the locus of greatness is shifting away from their language" but a model of poetic value in which writing from Russia and Eastern Europe "has implicitly established a bench at which subsequent work will have to justify itself" (38-9). And where Astley contrasts the "ideas and human experience" of European poetry with the "appearances" of its English counterpart, Heaney argues that Russian writing in "the indicative mood" is "a shadow challenge" to "the conditional, the indeterminate mood" of much contemporary poetry in English in the West. Heaney's comments also suggest that the new benchmark has much to do with wider anxieties about cultural value in the late twentieth century. His use of the term "martyrology" offers a model in which value is first located *outside* a cultural product and is then fed back in. A corresponding feeling that the post-war English historical experience has been somehow 'inappropriate', even inauthentic, in terms of what Heaney calls "the tragic scenario" (1989, 44) that has unfolded elsewhere makes us "all the more susceptible" to translations and consequent influence. These "arrive like messages from those ... further down the road not taken by us — because, happily, it was a road not open to us" (1989, 44). Heaney's conclusion is suggestive beyond the context of his discussion of translated Russian and Eastern European poetry for it alerts us to the fact that foreign affiliations and influences have provided some British poets with ways of engaging with things which British poetry since 1945 has worked hard to exclude or devalue. One of these things might be an all-purpose style which one finds at its most expressive in Keith Douglas but in few later poets; and another might be Franco-American Modernism which, as F.T. Prince has reminded us (1994, 37), has been one of the central modes of twentieth century poetry. It is arguable that British poets' engagement with Modernism's transatlantic reincarnation as the so-called 'New York school' has partially reclaimed it from Movement-derived attacks on its dislocated syntax, symbolism and excessive use of foreign tags and arcane references.

The Movement's rejection of Modernism is pertinent here because it continues to provide a defining context for British poetry. Peter Sansom (1994, 32), for example, seems to take for granted "the pendulum theory of literary history" and asserts that "Since we've just been through a period when anything went, the most radical thing is to be conservative". Sansom's observation is neither merely a product of its age nor as glib as it looks for it implies, albeit unintentionally, that the history of post-war British poetry has not just been about swings between free verse and formalism, élitism and common language or regionalism and centralism: a fundamental plot line has involved and continues to involve a troubled relationship with the self-congratulatory conservatism that the Movement represents. Appleyard (1989, 306-7) has argued that the Morrison and Motion Penguin anthology can be understood in precisely this way as "a careful balancing act" between Movement gloom and Modernist obscurity. Corcoran's proposal (1993, 2) that the history of British poetry since 1940 is largely indistinguishable from the history of reactions to Modernism seems to me to offer only a partial account. The simple fact that several generations have been introduced to contemporary poetry through Alvarez's *New Poetry* suggests that it is reactions to the Movement and to the Movement's reactions to Modernism that have the most bearing on poetry in the last quarter of the century. At its most basic, the use of foreign models may simply be a way of avoiding or of escaping altogether both old disputes and recent compromises.

The background and contexts outlined above may go some way to explaining how and why foreign influences are such a characteristic phenomenon of the last fifteen years or so but, as Charles Tomlinson (Interview 1991) reminds us, 'home thoughts from abroad' are in themselves nothing new: "It was the challenge of foreign poetries — and the possibilities found in translating them — put on *their* metal Chaucer, Wyatt, Jonson [sic], Dryden, Pope, Pound". Tomlinson — like his friend and mentor Donald Davie — exemplifies an earlier generation's pioneering engagement with other poetries at a time when Larkin's hostility to all things 'foreign' seemed to set the tone for what was happening in England. Tomlinson has been a prolific translator of poets such as Machado, Paz and Bertolucci but it is the impact of modern American poetry that may be traced most clearly in his own work: not only has he edited William Carlos Williams but his reading of and friendships with several American 'Objectivists' underwrite experiments with lineation and with ideas of the poem as 'field' (see Morley 1995, Tomlinson 1981, Corcoran 1993). However, Tomlinson's example, though highly suggestive, is, I feel, of limited relevance in the present discussion; for, like Davie's comparable assimilation of Pound, his American influences often compliment a native factuality, plainness and self-criticism. I want to go a little further back and look briefly at Eliot and Pound's mining of Laforgue which still offers some very useful clues to foreign influence as liberation.

Hugh Kenner has remarked, with characteristic asperity, that "Laforgue was first of all a *rôle*" (1971, 134), but if that was the whole story then as sensitive a reader as Eliot or Pound might reasonably have been expected to excavate the essentials of such a rôle from Clough, particularly *Amours de Voyage*, just as free verse could have been developed from the examples of Tennyson and Whitman. Rôle is only the most superficial manifestation of something else: "A poet like Donne, or like Baudelaire and Laforgue, may almost be considered the inventor of an attitude, *a system of feeling or of morals*" (Eliot 1975, 161 — my italics). Eliot's comment, from his 1921 essay on Marvell, suggests the particular interrelation of consciousness and poetry as behaviour-in-language that make one writer influential when another is merely admired or enjoyed. More than that, of course, Laforgue was obviously contemporary in ways that, say, Hardy and Yeats were not:

Over the towns, the drizzling night.
To shave the mask, to flaunt a pair
Of mourning tails, with art dine right,
And then with bilious virgins wear
    An imbecilic air.
        'Complaint of Prehistoric Nostalgias' (Laforgue 1986, 83)

David Arkell (1979, 152) has reminded us that in 1915 Aldous Huxley wrote of these lines "All modern life in that last stanza". It is interesting to note Peter Porter, some eighty years later, making much the same point about his own response to the poetry of John Ashbery: "It lives in a world I recognise; it shows how to go out of doors into the town, to turn on the TV, to read books, look at pictures, have opinions, play word games, and make art face the difficult opportunities of daily discourse" (1994, 77). Porter's last phrase can be related to Pound's estimate of Laforgue as a "verbalist": "Bad verbalism is rhetoric, or the use of cliché *unconsciously*, or a mere playing with phrases. But there is good verbalism, distinct from lyricism and imagism, and in this Laforgue is a master" (in Collie 1977, 117). What Pound evokes here, I think, is principally the energetic mixing of discourse and register that contemporary critical theory terms 'polyphony' but also the fragmented or unstable subject that such mixing inevitably suggests. Both polyphony and instability are the result of what Edmund Wilson (in Davie 1976, 149) identified as the symbolist poet's refusal to subdue "disordered feeling to the logic of consecutive statement" and to develop in its place "the habit of telescoping the whole thing by a few stenographic strokes ... [The] symbolist ... invents ... a vocabulary and a syntax as unfamiliar as the sensation itself". This also directs us to a clearer understanding of what Pound meant by his rather puzzling assertion that Laforgue speaks in "an international tongue" (in Collie 1977, 117). A poetry that is 'stenographic' and concerned with registering the difficult shape of a sensation is one that is unlikely to be concerned with working in a particular tradition and its attendant conventions. Donald Davie (1986, 4-5) makes a similar point when he contrasts the "fixed" speaker and particular context of "the meditative lyric", typified by Gray's 'Elegy' and Wordsworth's 'Tintern Abbey', with the poetry of Czeslaw Milosz in which the speaker occupies "no fixed point for the duration of his poem but on the contrary [is] always flitting, moving about" (1986, 4-5). Instability becomes not breakdown but mobility.

Eliot and Pound's admittedly selective readings of a neglected nineteenth century French poet may seem rather remote from

British poetry of the last fifteen years but their engagement remains suggestive. First, their borrowing from Laforgue, at its simplest, exemplified a very self-conscious 'leaving home' which inevitably characterises many poets' use of foreign models; and it shows how that 'leaving home' becomes, albeit paradoxically, a way of 'coming home'. In the words of Charles Tomlinson (Interview 1991) "I found myself as a British poet because I could bring other ways of 'doing it' to bear on the task". Second, the example of Laforgue makes clear how often the use of foreign models or susceptibility to foreign influence is determined by the search for a voice that is free from narrow ideas about poetic discourse. In Laforgue, Eliot found a style that was flexible enough to underwrite "a system of feeling or of morals" but also allowed the poet to "write simply" (Arkell 1979, 220). Third, as the idea of flexibility suggests, Eliot and Pound found through Laforgue how the same poem might accommodate wild swings from the lyrical to the banal and, indeed, how the lyrical might be located in the banal. Laforgue's highly idiosyncratic development of *vers libre* showed them that freedom from prevailing conventions need not mean a radical break but could be a refinement of the best elements of existing traditions. Finally, Eliot and Pound's reading of an aspect of the previous century's dandyism finds a curious echo in our own period. Peter Porter (1993) has remarked on the fact that many of the poets in *The New Poetry* (1993) can be described as provincial dandies in their sophistication, playfulness and wit. As we shall see, these are qualities that are often decisively lit by 'home thoughts from abroad'.

The poetry of Duncan Bush (b.1946) may be described as the fruit of a number of atypical displacements and engagements. First, he is an Anglophone Welsh poet who is at pains to resist the conventional constructions of such an identity in both Wales and elsewhere. He is concerned to avoid what he has called (Interview 1992) the "state of provincialism and immaturity" that still partly characterises Welsh literary culture and the "peculiar, ambiguous combination of patriotic pride and colonial servility" involved in being Welsh. Second, he has been equally concerned to position himself in European and international contexts. He not only divides his time between Wales and Europe but one of his most outstanding achievements to date has been *The Genre Of Silence* (1988), a novel in verse and prose which told the life, tribulations and eventual disappearance of an imaginary poet in Stalin's Russia. Similarly, his first full-length collection *Aquarium* (1983) contained not only a large number of poems set abroad but also translations and versions

of work by Baudelaire, Mallarme, Montale and Pavese. Third, Bush
has described himself (Interview 1992) as "committed to the rather
un-British idea of the writer as intellectual (rather than mere
'wordsmith')." Bush's poetry suggests that he conceives of the
intellectual in terms similar to those set out by Edward Said in
Representations of the Intellectual (1994). Said (16-17) uses the Gulf
War as an example of how "the intellectual always stands between
loneliness and alignment" and of how his or her task is "to unearth
the forgotten, to make connections that [are] denied, to cite alter-
native courses of action". One senses behind Bush's best work a
feeling of responsibility to the truth as complex and to the creative
act as something that involves fact and fiction, myth and history, art
and politics.

Responsibility and a courageous recognition of complexity propel
one of Bush's most interesting poems 'The Avatar of King David'
(1983, 42-3) whose first stanza is reproduced below:

> Sightseers now stroll Dachau, Auschwitz,
>> Where we slid in pits,
>> Live Jews already skeleton;
>>> Where troupes herd in
>> Under the showers still, as for the Sistine
>
> Roof. Marvelling faces lift, to stare upon
> These concrete ceilings fingers clawed,
>>> To die. The Lord
>> Was no sustain. No blessing flowed
>>> On millions. Smoke
> We rose as, and the elders' teeth they broke
> For fillings ... They came on this road
>
> I leave by

The poem explores whether there can be 'poetry after Auschwitz'
by dealing with the subject of Auschwitz itself and by letting itself
become a mouthpiece for the death camps' victims. The form —
like the poem's extensive epigraph and some of its vocabulary — is
taken from Milton's versification of Psalm III and the choice of a
Miltonic model is significant for a number of reasons. First, Milton
projects a particular image of the poet and of poetry, for his life and
work could be said to connect with Said's conception of the intellectual
standing between loneliness and alignment. His versification of a
number of Psalms occurred in the period 1641-60 when Milton
wrote little poetry and devoted his time and energy to pamphleteering

in the cause of religious and civil liberty and to public duty under Cromwell. Conversely, *Paradise Lost*, *Paradise Regained* and *Samson Agonistes* were composed after the Restoration and Milton's narrow escape from execution for treason. Milton may be said to exemplify the difficulties in acting on responsibilities that are felt equally but are apparently exclusive: religious and worldly, personal and political, artistic and social. Second, as Milton himself reminds us in Book IX of *Paradise Lost*, a major part of his 'project' is to celebrate "the better fortitude / Of patience and heroic martyrdom", noble themes which remain "unsung". These themes have particular resonances in the second half of the twentieth century and in the exploration of the possibility of 'poetry after Auschwitz'. Third, if Milton's life and work exemplify difficulty then his poetry suggests the means of discussing difficult or apparently 'impossible' subjects. As Eliot pointed out, Milton's style relies on the cumulative power of large syntactical units as the carriers of 'intellectual power'. Finally, Milton may be said to symbolise Renaissance Humanism modulating into humanism as it came to be understood in the eighteenth, nineteenth and early twentieth centuries. What Raymond Williams (1983, 150) terms "the double quality of the Renaissance; the 'rebirth' of classical learning; the new winds of interest in *man* and in human activities" becomes in Milton an attempt to offer a synthesis of classical and Christian learning as the basis for the development of individual and social freedoms.

At first reading, Bush's poem might seem to be concerned only with a simplistic 'showing up' of both religion and humanism. The poem presents us not only with the apparent uselessness of religion by rewriting Milton's "For my sustain was the Lord" as a survivor's bitterly factual "The Lord / Was no sustain"; but by juxtaposing its two stanzas with one of Milton's, Bush asks us to consider the relation between European civilization and the death camps, between humanism and barbarism. It is the question asked by Steiner in the preface to *Language and Silence* (1979, 16): "What are the links, as yet scarcely understood, between the mental, psychological habits of high literacy and the temptations of the inhuman. Does some great boredom and surfeit of abstraction grow up inside literate civilization preparing it for the release of barbarism?" If this was Bush's only point, it could be argued that he was questioning his own right to speak and agreeing that there can and should be 'no poetry after Auschwitz' and the poem would either self-destruct or be little more than the tourism it documents. It is the subtle invocation of another literary model that both offers a way out and enables the poem to become at once more troubling and more resonant. "Smoke we rose as" and the second stanza's "Their bodies weighed / By air, so light they rose as one" clearly recalls Celan, the Celan of 'Largo' and 'Todesfugue' in which, respectively, the dead are "our whitely drifting / companions up there" and have "a grave in the air" (Trans. Hamburger 1990, 60, 326). We might say that Celan functions as the 'shadow' to Milton. 'Todesfugue' was originally written and published in the late 1940s and, by its very existence, insists that there can and must be 'poetry after Auschwitz'. The nature of this poetry can be best understood in terms of what has been called Celan's "negative theology" (Hamburger 1990, 29). It is a poetry that, for example, maintains a dialogue with God even though its speaker has been forsaken by God; it explores blasphemy, negation and paradox as ways of understanding what can barely be thought or imagined; and it seeks to give being and meaning to people and things which have none. In Bush's poem, living in the aftermath of the collapse of the culture of presence — what Steiner (1979, 15) calls the condition of 'coming after' — can perhaps be borne and understood through a poetics of absence. Celan's 'Todesfugue' provides Bush with a model for the way 'The Avatar of King David' functions as a carefully patterned series of repetitions and variations; and for the way the poem is spoken now by the poet and now by others.

The form of the poem, then, is Milton's but the content is Celan's and, appropriately, it ends with something perhaps more difficult to take than its starting point: "As smoke / they rose to Israel ..." Bush asks us to reflect on the relation between the death camps and the establishment of the Jewish state, a state which suggests a new chapter in which humanism and presence can be reclaimed and made new. Ultimately, Milton and Celan might be judged not so different: the poetry of both offers formal sublimations of 'difficult' or 'impossible' material; is concerned with the physicality of language, with word as object; and takes for granted the necessity of making words and syntax work in new ways. 'The Avatar of King David's' dialectic of presence and absence supports Heaney's conclusions in 'The Impact of Translation' (1989, 36-45) that poetry in English has been set new benchmarks by the historical and literary experiences of others. In rising to the challenge Bush has found it necessary to make room for those "messages from ... much further down the road not taken by us" (Heaney 1989, 44).

The feeling, in Heaney's words, (1989, 43) "that our own recent history of consumerist freedom and eerie nuclear security [is] less authentic" is clearly a factor in the concern with 'earned lyricism' discussed in Chapter One and with wider embarrassments over "rights to write imaginatively" (Heaney 1989, xvi). In the poetry of Tony Curtis (b. 1946) it underlies the significant number of poems dealing with the experience of the two world wars or with subjects such as the Russian revolution, the British Empire and specific individual tragedies. It is, then, not at all surprising to find in his collection *Taken for Pearls* (1993) a group of five love poems translated from the Arabic of the Iraqi poet Mudhafer Al Nawab (b.1932). Arab poetry can be said to have "established a bench" just as much as Heaney's Russian and Eastern European poetries and it is important to understand its particular contribution as well as "the composite image" (Heaney 1989, 39) that the conduct of its poets has projected. Two observations are helpful here: the first by editor, translator and poet Abdullah al-Udhari; the second by the critic Nicolas Tredell:

> The strength of the Arab poet is that he writes about the misery and tragedy of individuals who suffer the effects of politicians obsessed with the old illusions of grandeur. The politician proclaims nationalism and promotes sectional interests. The poet proclaims the individual and promotes Arab dignity. One broadcasts propaganda, the other writes the truth. It follows that Arab poetry is a high-risk business.
> (1986, 25)

> ... the presence of those from the 'periphery', from what were once the domains of empire and/or 'underdevelopment', has come to serve as a focus for the problems of contemporary civilization as the working class once seemed to do ...
> (1993, 163-5)

Both these statements might appear complicit in locations of value outside cultural products (see above) or in suggesting that Arab and other Third World poetries are only of interest for their displays of commitment or political struggle. However, the simple fact is that Arab poetry is public in ways that Western poetry is not. Where we expect recurrent images in a poet's work to offer 'keys' to fundamental concerns or conflicts, such characteristics in a contemporary Arab poet are unlikely to be private at all. Wedde (1973, 15-16) shows how in the work of Mahmoud Darwish jasmine, which Western readers would invariably find exotic, comes to symbolise the poet's homeland in ways instantly recognisable to Arab readers. Another essential difference, as al-Udhari's comments make plain, is that the role of the poet and the function of culture is to provide models of continuity: as Wedde (1973, 8) points out "tradition is current ... primarily as a tone, not as detail".

Curtis's introductory note to the translations (1993, 42) made with Mustafa Hadi tells us that Mudhafer Al Nawab "started writing poems in a southern colloquial Iraqi when he was a young man" and "is regarded by many as the founder of the colloquial romantic school of poetry". Al Nawab's use of colloquial speech connects him with a particular development in twentieth century Arab poetry, a loose grouping of poets known as the Mahjaris or 'Emigrants'. Their work is characterised by beliefs in the necessity of reflecting social change and that poets should write about their times in everyday speech. It is a conception of poetry that finds clear parallels in Curtis's own work but it only partly explains why the translations of Al Nawab fit with a Welsh Anglophone oeuvre so seamlessly. A more suggestive parallel is in the fact that although Curtis is concerned with everyday speech and plain language, he is equally concerned with how highly they can be charged without becoming self-consciously 'poetical' or precious. His poetry is highly sensual and visual but its colours, sounds and scents often open onto abstractions and universal concerns. "The musk of rosemary and marjoram" in 'At the Border' (1993, 11) is, in its own way, as expressive of a way of life as "the sound of coffee grinding / And cardamom scent" in the first of the translations ('To the Train and Hammad', 1993, 43-5). Imagery of the natural world in Arab poetry is not present merely as background or colour but as a resonant symbology which enables a poet to emphasise both belonging and separation. Life is something written, literally, on the earth which in turn writes on the individual. Curtis's most recent poems — particularly 'Queen's Tears', 'The Eagle', 'Pembrokeshire Buzzards' (1993, 8, 53, 56) — offer an interesting parallel in their tacit argument that, if there can no longer be continuity between man and his natural surroundings, than some species of relation to them is still important for self-knowledge. Finally, as Curtis's note about Al Nawab makes clear, 'the composite image' projected by the contemporary Arab poet is one that involves alienation within one's native land, the experiences of war and civil war, and exile as the only means of survival. Without forcing the point, this inevitably suggests that one reason for both the impact of translation and contemporary poets' exploration of foreign poetries involves a search for a discourse that can contain a sense of living as what Heaney memorably termed an "inner emigré". Or as Curtis has written in 'Thoughts from the Holiday Inn' (1989, 45), "How arbitrary one's identity is: with voice and gesture we are / Challenged to make sense of where and what we find ourselves". For the purposes of the current discussion, the lines remain nicely ambiguous implying not only that finding a voice is part of an answer to the challenge but also, conversely, that the challenge of voice and gesture is all around. Charles Tomlinson (Interview 1991) makes a similar point:

> It seems to me that one's 'sense of place' ... is made more fruitful by being aware of the bigger place in which literature moves, one's local flavour having, in some sense, to measure up to the scope of all that, both technically and in terms of an adequate subject matter.

A sense of identity and a sense of place beyond the merely literary are at the heart of one of the most interesting examples of 'home thoughts from abroad': the influence of the 'New York school' — John Ashbery, Kenneth Koch, Frank O'Hara and James Schuyler — on the so-called 'Huddersfield poets'. A caveat needs to be entered immediately however against applying too rigorous collective descriptions to either grouping of poets. For just as John Ashbery once described the New Yorkers as a "bunch of poets who happened to know each other" so Ian McMillan (Introduction 1991) has observed: "There isn't a Huddersfield style, although if there was it would be to do with a denial of style, an insistence on noticing everything, a refusal to accept limits of poetic language, and so on". The *refusnik* aesthetic implied here finds immediate parallels with the 'New York school' and highlights why the American poets have been such an attractive model for many poets who began to group around magazines like *Joe Soap's Canoe*, *The Wide Skirt* and *The North* and The Poetry Business bureau from the mid-1980s onwards; poets like Geoff Hattersley, Peter Sansom, Simon Armitage and Martin Stannard. The 'New York school' was anti-programmatic and anti-manifesto, in marked contrast to other American groupings such as, say, the Black Mountain poets. In fact, as Ian McMillan implies of Huddersfield, perhaps the only aesthetic Ashbery, Koch, O'Hara and Schuyler shared was a distrust of outside identifications and theories. Frank O'Hara, for example, wrote in his jokey *ars poetica* 'Personism' (*SP*, xiii) that "you just go on your nerve" and "refreshment arrives" when you've "stopped thinking"; and James Schuyler said much the same thing in 'Empathy and New Year' (1990, 51):

> New Year is nearly here
> and who, knowing himself, would

endanger his desires
resolving them
into a formula?

Both quotations suggest an essential hedonism about 'New York
school' poetry, by which I mean a shared belief that poetry should
give pleasure both in the writing and the reading, as when Ashbery
and Koch once wrote a sestina together called 'Crone Rhapsody' in
which all the end words are pieces of office furniture. However, the
passage from Schuyler also suggests that this position can be inter-
preted, in the broadest sense, politically. If capitalism is a system
that relies on the manufacture and exploitation of desire, then
Schuyler's poem makes a statement of desire as individual, uncon-
tainable and free. Against the background of the 1950s and early
1960s — McCarthyism, the Korean War, Cuba — the New York
poets' avoidance of systematic *and* systematizing thought and their
search "for linguistic ways of being that are outside existing
formulations of life" (Ford 1994, 113) start to acquire meanings
beyond a fondness for the pantoum or the improvisatory long poem.
I should say here immediately that I do not believe for one minute
that the New York poets were writing allegorical, subtly subversive
political poems in the manner of Eastern European poets under
Communism; but rather that their work shows how poetry can be
alive to its times without being merely agitprop and/or social
commentary; and that such an example has clearly been instructive
to a number of Northern English poets writing under Thatcherism.
There is more than one way of being "'skewed' to the dominant
social wisdom" (Eagleton 1989/90, 46). Ultimately, though, it may
be that the model provided by the 'New York school' is as much a
social as a literary one, showing a way for a group of very different poets
to come together outside prevailing trends, to work together, to
inspire and feed off each other, without ever losing their identities
to a 'school style'. I think we can usefully add one further charac-
teristic. In his highly individual study *Reading Modern Poetry* (1989),
Michael Schmidt (95-6) quotes approvingly Alice Meynell's dis-
tinction in prose fiction "between vivacity and genuine vitality ...
between a language of social energy and a language of imaginative
energy. It is the distinction we can apply to poetry, discriminating
between the work of Kingsley Amis and that of Philip Larkin,
between metaphors of Craig Raine and those of Norman MacCaig".
The work of Ashbery, Koch, O'Hara and Schuyler not only argues
that such a distinction is neither necessary nor advisable: it shows

that an equally distinctive and productive 'voicing' can be made by combining the two. It is this that informs an essential characteristic of much 'Huddersfield' poetry, namely a tension between the conservative and the playful. Peter Sansom — whose influence on certain aspects of recent British poetry through his work as an editor, publisher and teacher is undeniable but still largely unacknowledged — has described his own taste in terms that find immediate echoes in the work of others: "I like writing that has real things, everyday things in it, and makes them vivid. I like texture of language, language that takes risks, and at the same time I love it when poems are well-crafted, so I like formal control" (Interview 1994, 19).

If Sansom's opening remark appears to echo William Carlos Williams's 'no ideas but in things' then that should alert us to the importance of twentieth century American poetry generally to Huddersfield. Simon Armitage has put on record its decisive influence for him: "I particularly remember reading Geoffrey Moore's *Penguin Book of American Verse*, which took the top of my head off. I literally read it until it fell to pieces, then took it back, got another copy and practically did the same again. Poems like, 'The Death of a Ball Turret Gunner', or 'Relating to Robinson', or 'Dirge', suddenly seem to open up great new possibilities. Also Williams, Lowell, Berryman and the rest of that crew ..." (Interview 1991, 93). Of course, it would be ludicrous to suggest that all these poets can forced under the umbrella of some common 'American style' but I think it is possible to say how American poetry — outside the 'New York school' — has been a decisive influence for many contemporary British poets. First, poets such as Williams, cummings, Olson and Creeley show how poetry can follow not literary models but the poet's own voice-patterns, the measure of human breath and common speech. Second, this in its turn creates a poetry which Moore (1989, 40) summarizes as "harsh, direct, ironical, obtaining its effects by timing, catching the cultural echoes and references which the tang of idiom brings with it". It is a description that could be applied to many poets who came to prominence in the 1980s. Thirdly, much twentieth century American poetry seems almost deliberately written to demonstrate the limiting and ludicrous nature of the kind of conventional expectations usefully outlined by Jonathan Culler in *Structuralist Poetics* (1990, 161-188). Briefly, Culler begins with "distance and impersonality" (164) and goes on to say (167) that "even in poems which are ostensibly presented as personal statements made on particular occasions, the conventions of reading enable us to avoid considering the framework as a purely biographical matter" and that (168) "in contemporary poetry ... impersonality is exploited to more disruptive ends". Culler's next convention is "the expectation of totality or coherence" (170) or the expectation "that the richest organization compatible with the data is to be preferred" (174). Culler's final convention is that of "significance" (175), the assumption that a poem contains something that is worthy of attention. Much American poetry throws these conventions into doubt. 'Confessional' poetry by Lowell and others is often 'purely biographical' while O'Hara's work could be said to exploit not impersonality but *the personality* of the poet. Similarly, one might ask of Gary Snyder's 'A Walk' and 'Things to Do Around a Lookout' (Moore [ed.] 1989, 524-5) whether it is useful to describe them in terms of "the richest organization" and what "special formal conventions" (Culler 1990, 175), if any, can be employed to justify their existence. And, as the following examples show, the influence of American poetry on 'Huddersfield poets' has been more a matter of increased flexibility than a basis for radical ruptures.

Geoff Hattersley (b.1956) has clearly been influenced by some of his Northern English contemporaries — Simon Armitage, Ian McMillan and Peter Sansom amongst others — but also acknowledges writers and performers as diverse as Frank O'Hara, Lenny Bruce, Bob Dylan, Pablo Neruda and Charles Bukowski; and named the magazine he founded in 1986, *The Wide Skirt*, after a chapter in Günter Grass's novel *The Tin Drum*. As these two sets of influences might suggest, Hattersley's work can largely be divided between laconic or directly comic personal reminiscence and social reportage, as in 'Untitled, Kibbutz, Late Seventies', 'Elsecar Reservoir' or 'In Phil's Butchers' (1994, 56, 88, 91); and poetry which appears to function as snatches of an ongoing interior monologue. It is on this second aspect of Hattersley's work that the influence of Bukowski and O'Hara has been decisive. Bukowski, particularly, offers a model of poetry which is not about the creation of, say, a cultural or moral space or which invites the reader to admire the operations of a sophisticated sensibility; but which records, without self-pity, a struggle merely to exist, even subsist, and in which a passive voice shares his failures and/or lack of effort:

> I am not aiming high
> I am only trying to keep myself alive
> Just a little longer

* * *

> I wish to hurt nothing, not even a bug

> but sometimes I gather evidence of a kind
> that takes some sorting
> 'don't come around but if you do ...'
>   (Moore [ed.] 1989, 426-7)

What is important here is, firstly, what Simon Armitage calls a difference in "what's considered fair game, what's considered tolerable in a poem" (Interview 1991/2, 264); and, secondly, the particular tone by which "evidence" is less crucial than "sorting". We can hear this tone quite distinctly in a typical Hattersley passage —

> I'm embarrassed about so many things.
> I'm lazy, a weakling, can't even stop smoking.
> My cough gets on my nerves but at least I own it.
>   'Not California' (1994, 107)

— or titles like 'You're Not Even Funny, Not Even Smart' (1994, 62). What accumulates is a kind of narrative of inaction or withdrawal in which 'life' is going on elsewhere. It is an impression reinforced by another element common to both Bukowski and Hattersley, the recurring location of the claustrophobic, impoverished but somehow self-contained interior in which the protagonist struggles to fill in time: "This is a small room. It's true it could be smaller" ('Not California', 1994, 107). However, when this narrative of 'inside looking out' moves from the USA to Northern England it acquires an extra dimension. The background of Hattersley's poetry is generally the urban landscape of post-industrial South Yorkshire and this inevitably suggests that if "Time passes slowly here in South Yorkshire" (1994, 107) then there are particular reasons why it does for so many people. The typical self-deprecating irony of Hattersley's work is most decidedly not about the 'wry self-knowledge' we are so often asked to admire in contemporary poetry; but, rather, it functions as a kind of detachment which results in the self being largely hidden from view. The geographical and social context of the poetry invites the conclusion that for a whole strata of society and a part of the country any other condition of existence has been made unavailable through economic and political circumstance. What, in another time and literature, would be termed an existential 'inability to act' may here be related to deprivation and unemployment. It would be unjust to Hattersley's characteristic reticence about larger issues and to his essential good humour to make too much of this but the number of poems in which fantasy is either thwarted by the banal or shades into paranoia underline the sense of the impossibility of finding firm ground for action or judgement. Here, too, the example of Bukowski is instructive for inaction, withdrawal and passivity become resources to be explored; and a reduced perspective brings its own oblique moments of celebration.

Beyond different permissions of tone and subject, contemporary American poetry offers Hattersley two sets of organising principles. The first of these comes from the poets who take their lead from Charles Olson and his manifesto of 1950, 'Projective Verse', which argues that the poetic line "comes from the breath, from the breathing of the man who writes, at the moment that he writes" (in Moore [ed.] 1989, 38). This, Olson argues, enables the poet to throw off the constraints of both syntax and stress rhythms and to explore both syllabics and syllabic patterning. Osborne and Woodcock (1988, 116-134) have elaborated Olson's ideas through the analysis of Robert Creeley's poem 'Something' (Moore [ed.] 1989, 467) and in what follows I apply their arguments to the opening of Hattersley's poem 'Spock's Brain' (1994, 104):

> The best start to this year
> would be to make a vow
> and break it the minute
> my head clears, something about
> getting myself ship-shape,
> sorted out. I'm not sure
> if I'm drinking tea or
> coffee or something else
> but at least it's liquid.

The line breaks and the absence of end-stops give the passage an agitated, 'stop-start' rhythm and a dynamic which depends on the reader's need to conclude the sentence and thereby answer the questions that seem to hover invisibly at the end of each line: *which year? why this year? what vow? the minute when what?* Indeed, Hattersley's poem exhibits exactly what Osborne and Woodcock (129) describe in Creeley as the registering of "the nervous garrulity of a timorous mind forced, by the pressure of emotion, into reluctant utterance". This is heightened by the way Hattersley makes confident but empty disclosures: "something about / getting myself ship-shape" and "at least it's liquid". The opening of 'Spock's Brain' also shares Projectivist interests in syllabics and internal rhymes. The passage uses six syllable lines composed largely of monosyllables and its most significant deviation — lines 4 and 5 where 4 has seven syllables and the two lines together contain seven of the passage's eleven polysyllabic words — occurs when it approaches but withdraws from revelation, rather like a wave breaking. The passage is not so much organised as numerically configured. Finally, we should note the framework provided by internal rhymes: year / clears, about / out, best / least. The second set of organising principles comes from the example of Frank O'Hara. O'Hara's work is positively oceanic in its currents and variety but a number of aspects have spurred Hattersley — and others — to more than the misinterpretations of the O'Hara style as 'list' which characterises many of his American imitators. O'Hara's work exemplifies "poetry as an intensifier of life's pleasures, a way of participating more fully in what is happening" (Ford 1994, 142). There is a sense throughout Hattersley's work not only of poetry as a part of life but almost as a way of being. O'Hara's comment about his own poetry, "the only decision you can make is that you did it" (*SP*, 149) can be applied equally to his attitude to the other parts of his life and informs Hattersley openings such as "You're waiting for the post, / nothing else is happening" (1994, 72) and "Life makes as much sense to me / as a ripe avocado does to a dog" (1994, 43). This, in turn, makes O'Hara's work a permission to write poetry which is not self-important but occasional, even ephemeral, and to make this a strength. Poetry, as O'Hara put in 'To Gottfried Benn' (*SP*, 141) is a "part of yourself". If poetry is a part of the self, then O'Hara's poetry shows how the self is indivisible from its environment. This is more than a 'sense of place' for O'Hara's poetry celebrates the self's "radical absorption into the cosmos of Manhattan" (Ford 1994, 146) and allows the city to function as "an organizing principle" (Greenhalgh 1992, 75). Hattersley's poetry explores a similar blurring of conventional distinctions between self and place: "Whose mind had cracked open to reveal those // high rise flats?"; "I will be a broken radio / at the bottom of a filled-in mine-shaft"; "If his future was a building it would be demolished ..."; "he'd fall asleep in the chair and dream // he was a city" (1994, 19, 22, 63, 77). And his work shares with O'Hara's the restricted geographical location of an insulated and self-contained area. South Yorkshire, as much as Manhattan, offers the means of insisting "on the incidental and arbitrary nature of experience" (Greenhalgh 1992, 78).

Simon Armitage's use of American poets as models and, indeed, of other poets as models generally is even more comprehensive than Geoff Hattersley's. His comments about 'Poem' ("Frank O'Hara was open on the desk ...")(1989, 33) can usefully be applied throughout his work: "The O'Hara poem ... has his name on the first line — as a kind of homage, really — and yet at the same time I think I'm saying that the lay-out might be his but the sentiment's universal, and *I'm* going to do it" (Interview 1991/92, 263). In fact, reading Armitage's total oeuvre to date it is clear that he is a poet who loves to be excited and inspired by other writers: 'Wintering out' (1992, 10) is obviously a reference to Heaney; 'Canard' (1989, 54) and 'Gooseberry Season' (1992, 1) are partly in the style of Muldoon; and 'At Sea' (1992, 21) is clearly informed by Lowell's 'Man and Wife' (1965, 52) just as 'Hunky Dory' (1989, 66) takes its ending from the American poet's 'Skunk Hour' (1965, 53). Elsewhere — 'Shrove Tuesday' (1992, 9), 'The Catch' (1992, 17) and 'Girl' (1989, 37) — Armitage has found the American method of organising by 'breath unit' as liberating as Geoff Hattersley; but, as this wide spread of models perhaps implies, it is difficult to say whether one poet has been a more decisive influence than another. Eliot's remark that "mature poets steal" is clearly pertinent here and Armitage has remade, remodelled, stolen and borrowed as has seemed appropriate to the development of his own distinctive prosody and syntax. Nevertheless, I want to argue that two American writers have been decisive: Weldon Kees and Robert Lowell.

Much has been made — not least by Armitage himself — of the English poet's debt to the neglected Weldon Kees, poet, painter, jazzman, photographer and art critic, who is presumed to have committed suicide in 1955. An early poem 'The Stuff' (1989, 69) refers to people who "vanished completely like Weldon Kees: / their cars left idle under the rail bridge" and *Kid* (1992) is interleaved with a sequence of poems which resurrects and then reinvents Kees's character Robinson. The poems represent an important stage in Armitage's development for they show him not only exploring a fully developed fictional character in contrast to the various personae which characterise his early work; but also, particularly in a poem such as 'Robinson In Two Cities' (1992, 18), using the model of Kees to experiment both with different cadences and a more detached and formal poetry. However, I feel that Kees's true influence was as much in terms of the image he projects as in the models which individual poems may provide. For just as a characteristic Armitage poem exhibits a self-consciousness about both its occasion and linguistic means and draws attention to its own fictivenss at the same time as it seeks to convince us of its 'reality' and 'truth', so Kees's poetry refuses to be seduced by its own precision and polished formalities. The deliberate 'poeticising' of Kees's work seems designed neither to attract the reader or aid the poet in the pursuit of universal or self-knowledge but to function in the service of a coldly impersonal art. An essential difference, of course, is that Armitage always keeps his eye on making a contract with the reader but Kees has surely taught him much about being wary of the creative impulse. Similarly, just as Armitage's poems are often concerned to get a perspective on a particular event or to notate an inexorable process so Kees despairs of the possibility of intervention in existence. The opening poem of the recently reprinted *Collected Poems* (1993) offers the reader "a movie of death" which will also reveal "the logic of your destiny". Again, there is a difference so that what is apocalyptic in Kees becomes comic in Armitage. Finally, Kees's example is also likely to be instructive in terms of career trajectory from regional origins to the centre of poetic activity.

Kees's work, though, offers an aesthetic of denial or self-denial and this brings us neatly to Lowell whose influence on Armitage has been comprehensive and whose "command" Heaney (1989, 147) locates in his "readiness not to commandeer the poetic event but to let his insights speak their own riddling truths". Without wishing in any way to detract from or to undersell Armitage's originality and versatility, I want to argue that many aspects of his poetry may be traced to hints or definite models in Lowell. Take this unmistakable example of what Morley (1992, 57) calls the "Armitage style-sheet in action" from the 'poem film' *Xanadu* (1992):

> A general point
> I wanted to raise
> about spending time
> in an enclosed space ...
>
> the jack-in-the-box
> who discovered the truth
> stood up for himself
> and hit the roof.
>   (40)

The two stanzas give us many of the Armitage 'hallmarks' in a typical combination: the everyday and/or clichéd language used to push the passage forward, the half-rhymes and internal rhymes, the definite closure delightfully at odds with the nebulous opening, a pleasing sense of formal control rubbing against the apparent sloppiness of the clichés. Behind all these, to some degree, stands not only the Lowell of *Life Studies* but also the late Lowell of *Day by Day* and *For The Union Dead*. First, the playing off of closure and openness. Heaney (1989, 131), writing of such poems as 'Man and Wife', has noted of their endings that "Closing lines like these tremble ... in the centre of the ear like an arrow in a target and set the waves of suggestion rippling. A sense of something utterly completed [vies] with a sense of something startled into scope and freedom". One can take virtually any poem from *Zoom!* or *Kid* and find its closing lines or last words 'trembling' in ways that either invite one to read the poem again to discover their meaning, open up vistas outside the poem or suggest an arbitrariness about the ending which, in turn, brings into question the poem's apparent completeness, its status as a definitive account. "Honest" at the end of 'The Stuff' (1989, 68-70) is perhaps the most obvious example of this but the point is demonstrated just as well by "I assure them. But they will not have it" ('Zoom!', 1989, 80), "Am I making myself transparent?" ('Eyewitness', 1989, 51) or "and in a way that reminds him" ('Mr Robinson's Holiday', 1992, 25). Second, clichés and colloquialisms. Lowell, who to my taste is generally an off-puttingly rhetorical and posturing poet, is in fact rather fond of clichés, puns and making everyday speech function epigrammatically. "We have talked our extinction to death" from 'Fall 1961' (1985, 11) is a particularly apt example which also prefigures a typical Armitage cadence but one could point also to "Absence! My heart grows tense" (1965, 47) and to the many sections of *Notebook* (1969) which attempt to combine or play off cocktail hour chattiness with a self-consciously public discourse. Lowell's "a lioness who ruled the roost" ('Home after Three Months Away', 1965, 49) is similarly a combination typical of Armitage. Third, organisation and form. The late Lowellian stanza common to many of the poems in *For the Union Dead* (1985 edn) — 'Fall 1961', 'Eye and Tooth', 'Buenos Aires' — is the model behind many of the shorter poems in *Kid*. The four and five line stanzas of these poems offer the means of playing control against something so casual and loose as to approach indifference. A stanza may have a pair of end-rhymed lines but those lines may be three and four syllables or eight and ten; one line in a stanza may be only two syllables long; end-rhymes combine with internal rhymes. The result is to draw attention to each line as a unit in itself to see what is set up within it; and to allow the movement between stanzas to veer in a manner that is at once surprising and satisfyingly logical:

> In my room at the Hotel Continentál
> a thousand miles from nowhere,

> I heard
> the bulky, beefy breathing of the herds.
>
> Cattle furnished my new clothes ...
>   Lowell: 'Buenos Aires' (1985, 60)

★ ★ ★

> So from A to B
> we point and counterpoint,
> tread a thin line,
> split hairs so finely
>
> that we lose the thread.
>   Armitage: 'Going West' (1992, 65)

The play of control against indifference is also underlined by the way the pentameter is habitually broken and re-organised as free verse. If the style is one of an apparently formalised indifference to its own effects then it is inseparable from the particular 'voicing' of Lowell's late work. The poems of *Day by Day* and *For the Union Dead* characteristically present highly personal and often very painful material in a way that locates the poet and the reader right at the heart of that material but detaches both of them from it. The personal becomes impersonal. The cool, no-nonsense voice which many have identified in Armitage as something regional and therefore all the more authentic for coming from outside the traditional 'power bases' of literature may in fact be just as much an invaluably flexible strategy borrowed from one of the century's key poets. The passage from *Xanadu* read in the light of Lowell's late poetry suggests that the American poet may be as important in terms of what Armitage has rejected; for while Armitage, like Lowell, wants very small units of language to accumulate into poetry there is very rarely a similar sense of the poet straining to catch our eyes and ears.

I want to close this discussion of specific influences and/or engagements by drawing attention, albeit briefly, to the use of American models beyond Huddersfield and the Northern English scene. Several commentators — e.g. Robinson 1988, 54 — have already remarked on Lowellian characteristics in Michael Hofmann, particularly the tension between ellipsis and disclosure. Lowell is also clearly behind Hofmann's habit of enclosing whole poems in speech marks as in the American's 'To speak of the Woe that is in Marriage' (1965, 53). The influence of Frank O'Hara seems likely to be as widespread. 'Blue' by the promising young Anglophone

Welsh poet Deryn Rees-Jones (1994, 60-1) combines scenes from a relationship with an account of a car breakdown in order to construct a kind of implied elegy for Derek Jarman. O'Hara clearly provides a model for how the poetic consciousness can be organised, as it were, from outside but one can also catch echoes of other New Yorkers: of Koch in the relishing of exotic vocabulary and of Schuyler especially when the narrator goes to "buy groceries — / Oranges and Paracetamol — and it is 12.39 or 12.43". Mark Ford's first collection *Landlocked* (1992) contains a number of poems influenced by O'Hara. 'Christmas' (5) and 'Night Out' (11) come uncomfortably close to impersonations but the excellent and startling 'A Swimming Pool Full of Peanuts' (36) owes O'Hara only a debt of organisation and tone — the rather sinister story is entirely Ford's own creation.

In his introduction to the *Poetry Book Society Anthology 1986/7*, Jonathan Barker highlighted

> the imaginative invention of the newest generation of poets to whom language expresses several things on several levels simultaneously ... It is not easy to pinpoint what has shaped their various styles. Certainly Michael Hofmann, Michael Hulse, Stephen Romer, James Lasdun, Ron Butlin, Jeremy Reed and Oliver Reynolds would seem to be well aware of modern European writing as well as British.

It is perhaps no surprise to find Michael Hulse, in a review-essay published at about the same time (1987, 128-37), quoting Barker approvingly. Hulse adds the name of Charles Boyle to Barker's list and identifies in all eight poets "a perceptual plurality, a core internationalism, and a fascination with bridging that Coleridgean gap between idea and image" (131). Hulse might have added two other comments to his definition: first, that for several poets listed the aspects he refers to are inseparable from either extended travel or residence abroad; and, second, that there are no women poets on the list. In the last section of this chapter, I want to explore 'home thoughts from abroad' in terms of travel and residence abroad; and whether this can be said to have a different meaning and impact for women poets. I shall look briefly at work by Charles Boyle and by Kathleen Jamie.

Michael Hulse (Interview 1994, 47) has described the main advantage of travel and/or the expatriate's life as "the cutting of the umbilical" and has lamented that "so few British poets are willing to cut loose and actually *inhabit* other modes of perception".

Similarly, Charles Boyle (letter to the author) has written of the value of displacement and the usefulness of foreign influences in providing it but adds that "Class, health, religion are at least as arbitrary as where one was born; not without value, but often things start getting interesting only when they're knocked away ... *un*learning things, taking less and less for granted. Abroad can be a short cut". The two sets of remarks are highly suggestive for their terms — "modes of perception", "unlearning", "class, health, religion" — indicate that foreign travel and residence are, in a very important sense, as much as matter of discourse as of personal life-choices. I should point out that I intend 'discourse' here in the sense of pre-existent constructions of identity, both of the English-born poet abroad and of 'abroad' itself. Such constructions are particularly relevant to the poems Charles Boyle has written about Egypt and the Middle East not just because they are present but because they are accompanied by an awareness of their existence and, in more recent poems, a rejection of them. The identity of the poet as a construction has two levels, the first of which is the influence of Keith Douglas. Boyle's poem 'Isis' (1977, 10) pays an explicit debt to Douglas's 'Behaviour of Fish in an Egyptian Tea Garden' (*CP*, 114) and the line "with Mr Mohammed Ebrahim Abdel Hamin, M.Sc." ('Cairo's Poor', 1977, 14) shows clearly that Boyle has learned from Douglas how to pack and extend a line in a way that is at once exact and structurally daring. Elsewhere, Douglas informs a sense of the poem as a casual, almost indifferent glance or snapshot in which something fundamental about the human condition is nevertheless faced and definitively caught. The model of Douglas also provides a way of inserting oneself — Hulse would no doubt say 'inhabiting' — into an alien context, another mode of perception but Boyle's poetry is, I think, alert to the fact that this is only partially satisfactory. This alertness is in fact the second of the two levels of the 'English poet abroad'. Boyle's earliest Egyptian and Middle Eastern poems — collected in *Affinities* (1977) — describe a kind of statelessness or absence that is not only located in the sense of being in a foreign country. Thus, in 'Distances' (1977, 16) distance is at first "a fiction, conspiracy of language / and history" and then "like love a necessary fiction". The same poem is uncertain if old photographs tell the poet he is "a born exile, or they / are tokens of infinity". 'Alex in February' (1977, 20) imagines "this could be somewhere English" and concludes that "Exile's a disease, we catch it being born". The sense of the self constantly changing its position and, indeed, of being in several places at once owes much to Douglas but I think it is possible to read it another way: it is not merely a case of the Douglasian self without its particular context — i.e. the Second World War — but that the condition of exile is also the condition of the post-colonial self. Even Douglas, writing in a sense as the Imperial 'project' was drawing to a close, retained a sense of purpose: "To trust anyone or to admit any hope of a better world is criminally foolish, as foolish as it is to stop working for it" (*CP*, 124). In Boyle this is replaced by the recognition that even such cynical clarity is impossible. One poem refers to "a game that's won or lost" (1977, 8) and in another (1977, 16) "you are / a figure painted on the wall of a tomb / offering or receiving sacrifice / the attitude is not clear". Most telling is the short poem 'Currency' (1977, 18):

> We reckon value now in dollars, the king's piastres
> are trinkets for your neck — souvenirs of an affair
> we missed but have liked to believe in.

If Boyle's poetry recognises the inevitability of engaging with constructions of exile, however questionable, then equally it recognises, engages with and questions the much larger and sophisticated construction which Edward Said (1991) has called Orientalism. This is not the place to attempt to summarize Said's wide-ranging study; instead, I shall highlight Said's definition of Orientalism "as a Western style for dominating, restructuring, and having authority over the Orient" and as the means by which "European culture gained in strength and identity by setting itself off against the Orient as a sort of surrogate and even underground self" (1991, 3). Aspects of the Orient as a constructed identity might be, say, its 'timelessness' or eternality, its patriarchal societies, its cruelty, its sexual licence. As Said points out, however, (1991, 208) it is ideas of time moving more slowly that are fundamental to clichés about the East; and that this 'timelessness' or eternality can be both good and bad. Boyle's early Egyptian poems express this view, albeit residually: "a dark country ... colour of ... age" (9); "Older than stone, older than any politics" (14); "time-warped villages" (19); and "temples unattainably old" (16). What is interesting is how a later group of poems set in North Africa and collected in *Sleeping Rough* (1987, 39-64) not only abandon the earlier poems' search for a position and/or rôle for the self but seek to move beyond constructions of the East. What comes across powerfully from poems such as 'How Did You Get About?' (1987, 47) or 'Under The Light With You' (1987, 58) is the experience being allowed to organise the poem. A tell-tale sign is that the 'I' that is almost always present in the earlier poems is here either replaced with "you" or "we" or is wholly absent. Another difference and a sign of Boyle's rejection of pre-existent constructions is the attention paid to women. Said, again, has drawn attention to the fact that the Orient as a place of sexual energy and licence and the sexualization of the Oriental woman are characteristic of received ideas about the Orient. In the later Boyle, women are often in the foreground of the poems and are generally shown either engaged in work or are portrayed in terms of their position in social structure or sexual politics. It would be easy to dismiss lines like "the women buying and selling, women at women's work / which is most of the work of this world" (1987, 40) as nods to 'political correctness' but this would be a grossly unfair misreading: what such lines inscribe is Boyle's determination to be *responsible* to what he sees. Similarly, to say that the 'self' of the earlier Egyptian poems gives way to the Other would be an overstatement but such a formulation does, I think, catch something of the changed nature of Boyle's views of 'abroad' and his own position there.

Foreign travel is a defining factor in the poetry of Kathleen Jamie (b.1962). At first sight, her work appears to share some of the concerns of Charles Boyle. Just as Charles Boyle has written of the need for 'displacement' and for the cultivation of 'the innocent eye' so Jamie has described travel in terms of "You learn to let go, but you don't fall. It's a holiday from class, identity, mortgages. You learn a sense of proportion" (Interview 1992, 104). Similarly, her work seems to share Boyle's concern with recording moments of self-realisation. The opening poem of the 'Karakoram Highway' sequence (1987, 25-28) portrays this explicitly: "You / are a blip in someone's long night. / About to be born. Into the light". However, such similarities are ultimately deceptive for Jamie shows no interest in exploring the anxieties resulting from being, in Harry Clifton's words, "a child of Europe" (1992, 56):

> Sometimes I feel so constrained with [the] palaver of labelling
> I just bugger off abroad where nobody knows and nobody
> cares.
>   (Interview 1992, 103)

One section of 'Karakoram Highway' observes matter-of-factly that "the river's throughout like a sense of myself" which underlines a conception of the self as process and of the new experiences provided by foreign travel as stages in that process. The thirteen sections of the sequence are concerned not only to register the journey through

northern Pakistan with unexotic accuracy but to show the self, in a
sense, standing aside to let the new experiences through. 'I' appears
only three times in the sequence and is replaced by the collective
self of the group of travellers; the cultural baggage we find in Boyle
finds no room in poetry excited by changes and accommodations.
In one section "thought // gives out to no thought"; in another the
first sight of the mountains is "distance, not menace. White, not
frightening"; and in yet another "Fear passes out into long passive
blue, / a slight smile". The osmotic relationship between 'inside' and
'outside' is even more to the fore in the 1993 collection devoted
exclusively to travels in Amdo and Tibet *The Autonomous Region*.
The largely untitled poems mingle Jamie's own journey with
recreations of the journeys of two historical travellers, the monk
Fa-shien and the Chinese Princess Wen Cheng. Where 'Karakoram
Highway' noted that "this is our world for a time", the poems of
Tibet go even further beyond the limits of the knowable. The word
"rumour" recurs through the book — "Promise or rumour without
author or source / ever keeps us moving" (19); "as if rumours we
repeat to ourselves / converge on truth" (67) — as the poems remain
ever watchful for what the earlier 'Karakoram Highway' called "the
shimmer of joy on the face of uncertainty". However, the most
interesting aspect of *The Autonomous Region* for the current discussion
is that the moment when Jamie's two characters meet — as they
never could have done in reality — coincides with the emergence of
Scots as a poetic language which at first alternates with English and
finally comes to dominate. This may seem to bear out Heaney's
suggestion that "the shortest way to Whitby ... is via Warsaw and
Prague" (1989, 41) but Heaney's remark also implies the existence
of a ready made counter-tradition. If "a woman's tradition and a
woman's discourse are still in the process of construction" (Montefiore
1994, 96) then Jamie's work implies that both tradition and
discourse are likely to be the product of each woman writer's
independent exploration.

It would be ludicrous to argue that all examples of foreign
influences, literary or travel, in recent British poetry could be
recuperated into one model but we can, I think, relate their
commonality to larger forces. First, the changed face of poetry
publishing in Britain must be considered as a decisive factor. The
rise of independent presses such as Bloodaxe Books, Carcanet and
Forest and their commitment to publishing both foreign poetry in
translation and foreign poetry in English means, quite simply, that
there is more of such work available. Similarly, the changed nature

of British bookselling, particularly the rise of chains such as Dillons and Waterstones, means not only that one can purchase books from independent publishers easily but that an increased percentage of imported books is on the market. All this is in marked contrast to the situation ten years ago. Second, and most importantly, British poets coming to maturity in the 1980s will inevitably have been influenced by the combined atmosphere of Thatcherism and the postmodern age with the result that many display a self-consciousness and distrust of the discourses and 'master narratives' of their native culture. In contrast, writers as diverse as, say, Charles Bukowski and Gyorgy Petri appear to offer both a model of writing that is outside any dominant wisdom; and the possibility of writing life — raw, unacculturated — straight onto the page. Finally, foreign influences must be understood against the wider fragmentation of both cultural forms and audience. It may be that just as there is no longer 'pop music' per se but a bewildering array of niche markets — dance, soul, acid jazz, grunge — so there is no longer 'poetry' but 'poetries', not only in terms of what people want to read but also in terms of what they want to write.

7. "Finding an Adequate Measure": Poetry as Media

> The study of modern poetry ... reveals at least one concern which has assumed the status of a widely held conviction: poetry must, in some way, seek to place itself within the collective experience of the society for which it is written.
> (John Williams 1985, 78)

> It is a little known fact that the techniques of the persuaders — government spin doctors, media advisers, advertisers — are very closely allied to poetry. At a time when poetry is sidelined in our culture, a perversion of its techniques has become a powerful tool in shaping our perceptions.
> (Peter Forbes 1993, 2)

Both epigraphs highlight a recurrent twentieth century anxiety over the role and status of poetry; indeed, the second appears to be arguing for 'status by appropriation'. The anxiety may be summarised as follows: poetry is a uniquely 'privileged' discourse but it is not an eccentric and minority activity; if it is to demonstrate this it must be able to make a contribution to and to locate itself in the particular age which produces it and it must be able to reach the largest possible audience; but in seeking an audience poetry must somehow lose none of its uniquely 'privileged' character, the very character which leaves its open to criticism as élitist, obscure, eccentric and marginal. Whether "the persuaders" have in fact been taking their cue from the poets seems to me highly debatable; however, despite the marginal status of poetry, one of the distinctive characteristics of the British since 1980 — and particularly in the late 1980s and early 1990s — has been a willingness to explore the potentialities of public poetry. It is this I intend to discuss here, using the term 'poetry as media' to distinguish not only the fact that poetry has often functioned like the media — as in *Poet's News* and *Poems for Rwanda* on BBC2 — but also to highlight a wider range of activity, commentary and responsiveness than a designation such as 'political poetry' would cover.

Of course, there is nothing new about such activity per se. One can point to poems such as Peter Porter's 'Your Attention Please', Adrian Mitchell's 'On The Beach At Cambridge' and, more recently, work by James Fenton and Tony Harrison. However, the increasing incidence of such writing in the period covered by this book suggests that 'poetry as media' can be related quite specifically to a set of circumstances and factors prevalent in late twentieth century Western culture generally and British culture and society in particular. First, as we saw in the preceding chapter, there has been a greater availability of both foreign poetry in translation and of foreign poetry in English. Whether, as Heaney has argued, this has set new 'benchmarks' for native writers or has merely resulted in the exercise of bad conscience, the exemplary experience of writers from Mandelstam to Mapanje has been unignorable. Second, as the enormous quantity of poetry produced in response to the Gulf War makes plain, the rise of global electronic media in recent years has made possible immediate responses to current events without the necessity for direct participation. Indeed, the Gulf War highlighted that we experience reality at several removes and this has interfused powerfully with poetry's claims to experience the world directly and to be the ultimate discourse of truth. Third, there is the example of two generations of Northern Irish poets. The force of that example resides perhaps not so much in the demonstration that poetry cannot escape bearing witness to the cultural and political circumstances that shape and produce it as in the various strategies poets as different as Heaney and Paulin offer for doing so. As I explained in my foreword, this book does not deal with Northern Irish poets in detail — with the exception of Heaney — but in the context of the present discussion it seems apposite to note, say, Heaney's various "modes of indirection" (Corcoran 1993, 184) in dealing with the Northern Irish experience; and Paulin's and Muldoon's use of "contemporary events without imposing a judgmental shape on them" (Corcoran [ed.] 1992, 186). And whatever the strategies employed, the Northern Irish poets have shown that an unavoidable corollary of such writing is a decision about identifying and exploring the self as part of a particular community or constituency. An engagement with the fraught nature of identity has in Corcoran's words led to a poetry that "seems to fit completely successfully into neither an exclusivist Irish account nor an exclusivist British account" (1992, 8) and it is here that Northern Irish poetry begins to acquire some of its wider relevance. The apparently widening divisions in British society after 1979 between North and South, rich and poor, white and non-white coincide with a shift from what could once be described with certainty as English poetry to what can only properly be described as 'British poetries'. The inelegance of the designation perhaps mirrors both uncertainty over its usefulness as well as the discomfort involved in such a shift but the example of the Northern Irish poets (and of 'the middle generation' — see Chapter One) shows that poetry in English cannot avoid involvement in a what is at once a negotiation and struggle between two polarities: a regional, phonocentric identity and a commodifying, national identity. The impact of the national and, indeed, the global on the local gains primacy as a poetic subject.

If, however, the experience of living in Britain after 1979 and the cultural and social fall-out of fifteen years of non-interventionist, free market politics can be discussed in terms of 'dissolution of consensus', 'fragmentation', 'polarisation' and the assertion of identity through the exploration of difference then these terms suggest a relation between the specific British experience and the condition of postmodernity in Western capitalist societies generally. British cultural and political events can be related to, say, larger currents of distrust of ideas of canon and tradition and impulses to focus attention on the "context of enunciation" (Hutcheon 1988, 184); and to the self-conscious exploration of the marginal and the ex-centric as a mode of discourse through which to contest the power of dominant discourses and structures. To quote Hutcheon again (1988, 202), "Postmodernism ... renegotiates the borders between the public and the personal, but aims to replace individualistic idealism with institutional analysis". I should emphasise at this point that it is certainly not my intention to argue that all recent political or socially responsive poetry is ultimately postmodernist; nor is it my intention to retread the ground already covered in Chapter Three. However, since 'poetry as media' is often political in content and direction I do want to draw on the work of postmodernist commentators and interpreters because it seems to me pointless to proceed without acknowledging that postmodernism has not only helped us to identify and characterise discourse but also because it is prompted a revaluation of 'traditional' political ideas about the self and society.

Postmodernism asks us to consider the potentially contradictory nature of a political or socially engaged text. I want to begin with *commodification*, which I also discuss in Chapter One, and which refers to the process by which an artform or a discourse is made acceptable and therefore consumable by capitalist culture. Since commodification implies "complicity with the dominant" (Hutcheon 1988, 207) and political or socially responsive writing is conventionally understood as a challenge to the dominant, we should be alert to the possibility that 'poetry as media' may seem to pull in a number of different directions or to hold a number of conflicting elements in close relation. This, in turn, relates to the wider impact of postmodernism on the understanding of 'traditional' political positions of Left and Right, liberal and conservative. Hutcheon (1988, 205) argues that "the definitions of those political positions [have become] fluid ones"; Graff (1983, 603) goes further and contends that challenges to the dominant ideology mounted from ex-centric positions are particularly prone to being *ambidextrous* i.e. open to appropriation by either Left or Right. A similar degree of uncertainty can be said to surround the use of self-consciousness or *self-reflexiveness*, the highlighting of conventions within a text. This has, indeed, become such a wide-ranging characteristic of contemporary poetry that to refer to it only in the context of postmodernism starts to seem unnecessarily limiting. We need to ask whether its presence in a particular text may be deemed a liberating strategy, a talisman against delusion or self-delusion, or whether it is merely game-playing for its own sake.

If commodification, ambidexterity and self-reflexiveness suggest the potentially difficult nature of 'poetry as media' they should not, however, be taken to imply that such writing is somehow 'hobbled' or self-cancelling. Several commentators have argued (Sukenick 1985, 236; Russell 1985, 207; and Hutcheon 1988, 217-21) that the example of Brecht teaches that a willingness to embrace contradictions in political or socially engaged writing may be the means of making those contradictions progressive instead of disabling. Sukenick, for example, argues that such a text can offer the reader "models for a creative truth of 'construction' rather than a passive truth of 'correspondence'". For our purposes, the Brechtian model is very usefully summarised by Catherine Belsey's conception of *the interrogative text* (1980, 91; and in Hutcheon 1988, 221), a text which "disrupts the unity of the reader by discouraging identification with a unified subject"; and which, consequently, "[invites] the reader to reproduce answers to the questions it implicitly or explicitly raises". Belsey's idea of disrupted unity and discouraged identification leads beyond immediate textual considerations to postmodernism's wider debate about politics. The assertion by a recent British Prime Minister that 'there is no such thing as society' is, in one sense, merely the most superficial manifestation of a larger, ongoing re-examination — on both the Left and Right — of 'traditional' ideas of self and society. Richard Rorty (in Docherty [ed.] 1993, 323-8), for example, argues that we can no longer think in terms of 'natural rights' or 'moral self' when discussing the individual's relation to power structures. The self is, in fact, "a network of beliefs, desires and emotions with nothing behind it — no sub-strate behind the attributes". Beyond this, there are not absolute values enshrined in institutions but an "overlap" with the particular group with which the individual choses to identify; and "appeals to what [Ronald Dworkin] calls 'conventions and anecdote' ... anecdotes about the past effects of various practices and predictions of what will happen if, or unless, some of these are altered". A view such as this is extreme and highly debatable but it is one that is definitely 'in the air' at the present time and it clearly permeates the work of Michael Hofmann, for example, where a Lowellian identification of private turmoil with public events founders in an inability to make judgements or differentiations, to do very little except mirror the alienation and fetishisation of surfaces which are the products of late capitalism. The background of the debate about the self, politics and society informs two important characteristics of 'poetry as media' which perhaps serve to distinguish it from similar writing in earlier periods. First, such writing in British poetry of the 1980s and early 1990s often involves a concern with how the self is constructed and with how the factors that shape that construction influence political and social engagement. This is not an anxiety one finds in, say, Auden's 'Spain 1937' or in the type of writing fostered by the *Review* in the Sixties and early Seventies (see Corcoran 1993, 146-9); and its presence serves to underline the importance of both Northern Irish writing and of 'the middle generation'. Second, 'poetry as media' often invokes other texts before the subject of its particular engagement, almost as if literary certainties have come to replace political and social ones. Michael Hulse's poem 'Fornicating and Reading The Papers' (1991, 20-3) states this explicitly and shows the liberal conscience, at several removes from raw experience, struggling to accommodate civilisation's 'double encoding' of humanism on the one hand and violence and exploitation on the other. Tony Harrison's Gulf War poem, 'A Cold Coming' (1992, 48-54) invokes Eliot's 'Journey of the Magi'; and W.N. Herbert's sequence of poems on the closure of the Timex factory in Dundee, 'Ticka Ticka' (1994, 84-104) uses the writings and persona of a nineteenth century Scottish Radical Fanny Wright. In what follows I shall discuss a number of examples of 'poetry as media' which are representative of such writing in the 1980s and early 1990s.

W.N. Herbert's poem in Scots 'A Three Year Ode' (1994, 58-62; originally published in a shorter version in *TNP*, 293-7) is a response to one of the twentieth century's most momentous events: the collapse of the Soviet Union and the subsequent struggles with

democracy in the new Russia. The fact that the poem is in Scots
signals that it is 'political' beyond Herbert's immediate response to
world events: 'Russia' as a subject is inextricable from arguments
about British poetry in general and Scottish poetry in particular, the
example of Russian poets and the present political condition of
Scotland inter alia. The 'Ode' is in three sections — 'To Gorbachev
(1991)', 'To Yeltsin (1992)' and 'To Rutskoi (1993)' — which each
begin in the same way: a natural event — light through a window,
the onset of spring, the sound of a horse — becomes a mode of
transition between the poet indoors and events in Russia:

> Eh sit an feel
> licht fill thi hooses in Fife
> an the cheek banes o Tay's waves,
> Eh rowl wi ut lyk this cat owre
>
> thi Baltic. Eh'm oan a trenn a licht
> speedin fur Moscow, bearin Pasternak
> back, shoovelt oot o Zhivago's snaa-cell.
>   'To Gorbachev (1991)'

MacDiarmid — whose 'Hymns to Lenin' provide epigraphs to Parts
I and III — is clearly a presence behind the easy movement from
the natural to the political but the real point of such passages lies in
their very ease. Why should there be anything complex or uncomfort-
able about moving from the personal to the global? Herbert's
remarks in an interview given to Richard Price (1990, 89-95)
suggest that such object lessons are the result of dissatisfactions with
both English and Scottish poetry: "[W]hen I looked at poetry I
realised ... that there were a whole series of subjects that were shut
out". Similarly, Herbert argues that Scottish culture and particularly
poetry in Scots "should continue to meet the frame that the modern
world is putting it in". The appearance of a Russian poet at the point
of transition — here Pasternak and later in the 'Ode' Mandelstam
and Mayakovsky — develops the argument further. On a simple
level they function as notional Virgils to Herbert's Dante but just as
the poem's later invocation of the Italian poet is *political* not artistic
so their presence works against expectation. Pasternak, Mandelstam
and Mayakovsky are not invoked because they have come to symbolise
a particular type of personal and artistic struggle; Herbert is in
interested in their relevance to contemporary Russia not as global
'benchmarks' for poetry. All three poets have, in Mandelstam's
memorable and poignant phrase, found their 'readers in the future'

and in terms of the 'Ode' these 'readers' are the three Russian
leaders the poem addresses:

> As Eh exhaled, trehin tae relax,
> Eh heard thi saulter i thi field ootside
> whinny, and Eh thocht o thon
>
> puir cuddie in Kutznetsky Street
> that Mayakovsky waatcht faa doon,
> be whuppit as ut pechd uts life awa.
>
> That whiz whit yi ettlet tae dae
> tae thon sair forfochen nag
> caad 'Communism' thi ither dey.
>   'To Rutskoi (1993)'

The appearance of Pasternak, Mandelstam and Mayakovsky also
brings into play particular ideas about poetic language which, in
turn, inform Herbert's choice of Scots or, more correctly, Synthetic
Scots. We have already seen that "licht", "buds" and "saulter" (a
show-jumping horse) provide the means of moving from the personal
to the global and I do not think it is an over-interpretation to detect
the influence of Mandelstam here, particularly his rejection of
symbolism: "In Mandelstam's view, Russian words are themselves
symbols. Therefore, symbolism becomes redundant: the word itself
is magic, incantatory, and at the same time creating a humanizing
link with the world of objects" (McDuff 1983, xviii). This invites
connections between the compressed and layered meanings of
Russian poetry and similar possibilities in Scots. The example of
Mandelstam may also inform the 'Ode's' circling round literal and
notional ideas of 'home'; and perhaps even the fact that, for a
non-Scottish reader, the poem must to a large extent be composed
like Mandelstam's own poetry "on the lips" (McDuff 1983, xix) if
it is to be properly understood.

   All this makes clear that 'A Three Year Ode' is almost entirely a
text of 'construction' rather than of 'correspondence' not only in
the way the reader has to work out a complex interweaving of
concerns but also in its tacit argument that events in Russia, even
post-Communism, continue to have implications for radical political
activity elsewhere. Part II refers to "Scoatlan, still stapt ticht / in uts
disunity" and Part III connects the failed counter-revolution of
Rutskoi to the ultimate failure to save jobs at the Timex factory in
Herbert's native Dundee and links both failures to untimely action.
The 'Ode's' 'perspectivism' also demonstrates that it functions

'interrogatively' after Belsey's model. First, its three sections offer the reader a bewildering variety of viewpoints — the poet, Russian poets, the poem's three dedicatees, Krikalev the last Russian cosmonaut — by which to orient his or her reading. Second, the poem quite literally 'discourages identification with a unified subject' through the same means but also because its subject is disunity or, perhaps more correctly, a 'between-state' similar to that found in Northern Irish poetry. At the end of Part I, "fowk" in both Scotland and Russia are portrayed in a state of becoming as they "waatch this licht arrive / fae extink stars, an wait fur this licht // fae thi stars yet tae come". Part II moves from a picture of Krikalev — "thi furst tae cross owre concepts" — via Dante's self-imposed exile from Florence to suggest Scotland's "indecisive noo"; and Part III ends with the poet who began the poem with "loose ... attenshun" imagining himself loosening the harness of the state and ushering in "thi Apocalypse o statelessness". The apparently neat circularity of the 'Ode' should not blind us to the fact that, throughout, its invention and playfulness function as an expression of dissatisfaction. The poem is written against an inherited British poetry whose "intersection with [the] world is attenuated and discourages reading back; transformation is confined within the surprises and routines of rhetoric" (Sinfield 1983, 230); and against political philosophies which preach an obeisance to and repetition of the past. Herbert's 'Ode' reads 'home' — cultural and national — through Russia but it also, in the words of another poem, describes a country for which "there is no passport ... it exists as a quality of the language" ('Dingle Dell',1994, 40).

A different kind of reading of country shapes Ken Smith's poem 'Brady at Saddleworth Moor' (1990, 17). The poem forms part of a triptych about notorious British murderers 'Figures in three landscapes', a work that is characteristic of a substantial oeuvre in poetry and prose that deals with the fall of the Berlin Wall, Smith's experience as a writer-in-residence at Wormwood Scrubs and the impact of fifteen years of laissez faire economic policy. Smith has also co-edited *Klaonica: Poems For Bosnia* (1993) — discussed later in this chapter — which attracted some controversy. Smith's intervention in that controversy serves to describe a more general conception of poetry's role and responsibility:

> But where the alternative is silence, *Nothing will come of nothing*. To refuse to pay attention to the dire anxieties is to deny them by our silence, to listen only to the journalists and let the politicians speak for us. Either we refract the worries

of the world, however off-centre, however intermittently, or
we climb into the attic and haul up the ladder.
    (1993/4, 45)

'Refraction' might be used to describe Smith's strategy in 'Brady at
Saddleworth Moor' which recreates the occasion when the Moors
murderer was taken back by police to the scene of his crimes in an
attempt to solve other murders. Mass murderers, but especially
Brady and his accomplice Myra Hindley, are staples of the tabloid
press and the event furnished copy for several weeks. A recognisable
narrative is retold on such occasions in which the crimes are
reiterated, speculation made about the murderer's possible release,
parents or relatives of his victims canvassed for their reactions and
the involvement of public figures like Lord Longford ridiculed.
Smith, however, chooses to present the poem as the thoughts of
Brady and to make only oblique references to his crimes:

> Out, this is air, abrupt and everywhere,
> the light and sky all one blaze of it.
> Count them: eleven clear hours of wind
> over the world's tops into my face —
>
> this old bleached-out moon always adrift
> through the bad dreams of the neighbourhood.
> In my ten thousand days I count this day:
> *the moor, all its space and vastness*

On one level, then, the poem exists to work against prurience and
sensationalism; but at the same time, Smith is offering his own bit
of sensationalism by suggesting that Brady is 'human like the rest
of us'. What is interesting is how in doing this Smith ends up
producing something as 'unreal' as a tabloid account. First of all,
Smith has Brady speak in a loosely-controlled, emotionally-drained
sub-Shakespearean blank verse. The 'release' of Brady into formal
verse mirrors his day release on the moor and makes a tacit argument
about his humanity and the supposed generosity of the humanistic
tradition. Second, the poem is clearly indebted to the 'new narrative'
poetry of James Fenton, Blake Morrison and Andrew Motion. All
three poets have written about murderers and Smith's stanza has
marked similarities to Fenton's in 'A Staffordshire Murderer' (1992,
58-61). In common with such poems, Brady is the unreliable, dubious
narrator par excellence and may be judged "a voyeur to his own
past" like many of the characters in 'new narrative' poetry (Corcoran
1993, 246). Detachment is emphasised by the deliberate clumsiness

of phrases and juxtapositions such as "days I count this day", "fell I felt" and "I hear them say I say. I find" which, together with the use of internal rhymes and other syntactical clashes, echoes poets such as Simon Armitage and Glyn Maxwell and makes the poem typically Eighties. Smith's poem is also similar to Carol Ann Duffy's monologues in its playing off of aberrancy and criminality against 'expert' behaviour-in-language. His intermingling of various contemporary British poetries emphasises not only Brady's otherness but the way otherness functions as the necessary 'shadow' of culture and society. The second verse makes clear that a 'neighbourhood' is not complete without its "bad dreams" and bogeymen.

While all this highlights how Smith plays with our expectations of 'correspondence' but in fact gives us a text that works largely as a 'construction' it does not mean that 'Brady at Saddleworth Moor' escapes being problematic. Smith's project of writing against prurience and sensationalism is a highly honourable one as is his obvious determination not to produce a text which can in any way appear complicit with the commodification of mass murderers and serial killers in our culture e.g. tabloid coverage and 'partworks' such as *Murder Casebook*. At the same time, it is possible to offer a different reading in which Smith cannot quite avoid commodification. First, 'Brady at Saddleworth Moor' is self-consciously a poem in ways that Smith's persona pieces and plain but acute reportage are generally not. Consequently, the very strategies which Smith uses to describe a relationship with otherness may also be read as ways of suppressing and containing that otherness. The reality of Brady's mind and voice at the particular moment the poem describes seem stifled under a tightly woven blanket of poetries. The result is something that is unsensational but also uncontroversial and therefore 'safe' as poetry. Second, we can say that the practice of putting poetry into the mouths of murderers, sex offenders, racists and the like is, in our period, something of a commodity in itself, one of the ways in which poetry states its reality and relevance and thereby earns its place.

Duncan Bush has made an explicit correlation between 'poetry as media' and anxiety over the status of poetry:

> I think I decided a long time ago that certain poets I admired — Plath, Lowell, Berryman: the 'confessionals' — represented a dead end not only in terms of poetry but in a human sense as well. 'Open-heart surgery' as Berryman referred to it ... I disliked (and still do) the 'occasional' poem, the slightly random published collections of so many delicately-suffering poetical egotists, who really do still believe that their

personalised 'sensitive' responses are an adequate measure
of the problems of the world they live in.
        (Poole 1992, 45)

Poetry, then, is about responsibility to the world at large but there
is a danger that poetry ends up being valued only for how well it
reports on 'the problems of the world' and for what problems it
reports on. The poet — and the critic — can find themselves in the
difficult and unfortunate position of having to make value judgements
about experience. Is a death in Bosnia somehow worse and therefore
a better subject for poetry than a racist attack in Brick Lane? The
poet and the critic can end up little better than ambulance chasers.
It's hardly surprising to find Bush often uncomfortable with his
chosen responsibility and struggling to find 'an adequate measure'.
A comparison of families on Sunday outings with refugees from
Saigon in 'Nausea' (1983, 34) and the superficial reference to Chile
in 'Snow At Dawn' (1983, 35) seem awkward and gratuitous.
Another early poem, 'Movietone' (1983, 56-7) engages with the
dangers inherent in reportage through a response to old newsreels
of the Warsaw ghetto, Nazi concentration camps and "Ypres, the
Rhondda marches, Munich, / the triumvirate at Yalta". Bush's point
is that the old newsreels in a sense become a discourse that conditions
our responses: whatever the subject we are to a degree seduced by
the black and white, the sepia, the graininess. "The past framed"
becomes "familiar"; and "instantaneous cheap nostalgia leaves / no
moral to record" and yet these filmed records are precisely what
history has come to mean to us. It is characteristic of Bush's oeuvre
generally that he is always willing to confront the problems inherent
in a socially responsive poetry. Another early poem, 'To the Memory
of Robert Watson, 37, of Aberdeen, Killed During the Lorry
Driver's Strike of 1979' (1983, 54-5) is a partially successful attempt
to compensate for 'Movietone's' reportage without moral. The
poem's epigraph is the news item from *The Guardian* which inspired
it and Bush's poem is in part an exercise in economy of means as it
teases out the meanings of various words in the report — wheel/s,
driver, driven, driving — to suggest that the event and its aftermath
was something beyond the control of the participants. The poem's
impact is deadened somewhat by the fact that its language is as
limited and flat as the newspaper report and that its excavations of
media 'lego language' often read as a series of rather forced puns.
'To the Memory of Robert Watson' exemplifies one of Bush's
principal concerns: that in the late twentieth century our experience
of anything beyond our own immediate life is almost inevitably

mediated through the mechanically reproduced, electronic or digitised image and report. As 'Movietone' suggests, one response in historical terms is to read old images as closely as texts, a procedure which produces the free verse sequence 'Navvies' (1985, 30-41). Bush mingles his own poetry with quotations from a variety of sources including economic and archaeological studies, Walter Benjamin and Milan Kundera to construct another sort of compensation, this time for the fact that "History is full / of silences" (38). The sequence ends with an evocation of the navvies' world:

> a world
>   warped
> to the sentimentality
> of atavisms, sung
> in stillness,
> hunched, rapt with the eyes
> closed:
>
>   old songs
> sung
> into silence and against it ...
>   (41)

The organisation of the text mimes the difficulty of reconstructing lost history but the key word in the passage is "atavisms". It is a word that appears in two poems that make responses to early Eighties struggles over the coal industry. In 'At the News of Proposed Pit Closures' (1983, 53) mining communities are seen as "shabby vineyards / of industrialism / along some valley's sides, the bare / hills atavistic and / familiar as breast-milk"; and in 'Summer 1984' (1985, 69-70) the rediscovered sense of community resulting from the Miners' Strike is described "as if / an atavistic common memory ... // ... was now being learnt again". What is interesting is that in all three cases, Bush uses the word to suggest continuity and strength when its connotations have come to be perjorative. To write 'poetry as media' Bush seems to be saying might involve taking sides in a class narrative if not in the class struggle itself.

Both poems about the Miners' Strike of 1984 begin with newspaper reports and this leads to other complications inherent in 'poetry as media'. If poetry is an art of responsibility, an art that in a very real sense works to be a corrective to the mediation of experience, what are the implications of the fact that 'poetry as media' is often a direct response to media events? And what are the implications for the way the self is constructed in the world? 'At the News of Proposed Pit

Closures' ends by suggesting that we can't avoid having our
responses structured and commodified for us:

> At home
> I got half-
> drunk on the music of exiles:
> > > Dvorak.
>
> > > > Whom they turned
> to Weltschmaltz film scores,
> aching for the prairies.

The commodified response is explored further in the recent poem
'Living in Real Times' (1994, 28-9) whose punning title hints at the
impossibility of unmediated experience. The poet, watching cricket
in a television shop window, sees a news report from the former
Yugoslavia on another screen and observes that "TV's intimate and
/ generalising eye makes everywhere somewhere else" and "post-
modernism makes all things / present, all things post-reality". Both
cricket and war report can be reshown endlessly — a cricketer with
a "moustache bigger than Nietzsche's" signals that Bush has in
mind the German philosopher's doctrine of the eternal recurrence.
Bush's point has, however, nothing to do with Nietzsche's speculations
whether this made life gruesome or beautiful. The poem ends with
the poet seduced by the repeated images, hooked like an addict
"lingering // to watch them all do it again, in slowmo ... / trained ...
to the destined fact, knowing there's no way out". The media gives
us power through allowing us to enjoy the powerlessness of others.

It might seem from this that 'poetry as media' cannot avoid being
complicit in the discourses of media but Bush's work offers two ways
out. The first of these is the use of personae which is one of Bush's
favoured strategies. By having the poem apparently spoken by
someone else from the midst of their own life the poet can avoid
many of the problems of mediation. Bush's much anthologised
poem 'Pneumonocosis' (1985, 25; and *TNP*, 94), in which a miner
speaks of his wrecked lungs, is a particularly good example. Bush
uses colloquial speech freighted with just the right amount of
rhetoric to produce a compelling mini monodrama; and the distant
echoes of Wilfred Owen's 'Dulce et Decorum Est' in "I saw my own
brother: rising, / dying in panic, gasping / worse than a hooked /
carp drowning in air" allows a larger argument about power and
individuals to hang in the atmosphere of the poem like the "black
diamond dust" itself. The second way of approaching an unmediated

'poetry as media' is through the carefully observed social or urban scene as in 'Near Tilbury Dock' (1983, 36-7) or 'August. Sunday. Gravesend' (1985, 52-4; and *TNP* 95-6). Both poems 'earn' their conclusions about workless individuals through careful observation of the landscapes that contain such figures. Words such as "fallout", "petrifies", "amnesia" and "flaccid" combine with lines like "It is like the moment after an explosion" to imply a post-industrial landscape and, consequently, cause the reader to reflect on the circumstances that brought it into being.

The mediation of experience is the central preoccupation of Carol Ann Duffy's poetry. The early poem 'Poem in Oils' (1985, 47) asks — and answers — a question which defines her engagement with that mediation:

> Is this what I see?
> No, but this is the process of seeing.

The short love poem 'Words, Wide Night' (1990, 47) states the gap between 'seen' and 'process' more explicitly: "For I am in love with you and this // is what it is like or what it is like in words". The conception of language as something that appears to correspond to the world but in fact constructs it is at the heart of Duffy's work. When we come into the world we also enter a number of rôles and relations with others which are defined by the various discourses which structure and order society. Any act of language is at the same time an assertion of identity, a point of orientation with or against the grain of one or more of these discourses. Duffy's preferred form is the monologue or persona poem which allows her to explore the gap between 'what it is like' and 'what it is like in words' by playing with the split between her speakers and what they speak or, more often, what is 'spoken' through them. In 'You Jane' (1985, 34) the speaker is a clichéd macho-man — "I can cope with the ale no problem" — but the poem is structured so that each assertion of male prowess is placed with a statement that either displays contempt for or enacts domination of women. This particular type of maleness, the poem argues, is indivisible from and is indeed founded on objectification of the other. A similar but much more disturbing split runs through 'Psychopath' (1987, 28-9) where the speaker describes himself as a "Ladies' Man" and portrays himself in terms of tough-but-vulnerable movie and rock'n'roll stereotypes. Poems such as these make neither easy nor pleasant reading. Their effect is to make the reader reconsider whole rafts of prevalent

attitudes; to ponder whether he is guilty of similar self-deception or
has his own identity suppressed by a reductive stereotype. Duffy's
titles often signpost that a poem is about to deconstruct a cliché or
investigate the truth behind an appearance: e.g. 'Translating The
English, 1989' (1990, 11), 'Yes Officer' (1987, 31) or 'Weasel
Words' (1990, 14).

The conception of language outlined above is particularly to the
fore in the parts of Duffy's work that can be termed 'poetry as
media'. I am prepared to admit that such a distinction may seem
facile when Duffy herself has remarked (Interview 1988, 70) "What
I am doing is living in the twentieth century in Britain and listening
to the radio news every day and going out every day and reading the
newspapers every day". However, what I want to focus on are poems
that are concerned explicitly with the social and political fabric of
contemporary living and with the pressing problems of our age such
as racism or unemployment. In many of these poems Duffy's
analytical approach to language is turned on the language of politics
and especially the nature of that language in the 1980s and 1990s.
It could be argued that we have travelled a very long way from
expressions of collective will or responsibility embodied in, say, "the
winds of change" or "the white heat of technological change";
through superficial soundbites such as "the lady's not for turning"
or "we remember the Good Samaritan because he had money"; to
the almost anti-language of recent election campaigns exemplifed
by "double whammy" and "nightmare on Kinnock Street". What
is distinctive about contemporary political language is, first, its
highly personal nature and, second, its virtual synonymity with the
'feelgood' slogans of advertising and the media. 'Poet for Our
Times' (1990, 15; and *TNP*, 229) suggests that politics is indistin-
guishable from the way it is reported:

> I write the headlines for a Daily Paper.
> It's just a knack one's born with all-right-Squire.
> You do not have to be an educator,
> just bang the words down like they're screaming *Fire*!
> CECIL-KEAYS ROW SHOCK TELLS EYETIE WAITER.
> ENGLAND FAN CALLS WHINGEING FROG A LIAR.

Duffy's parodies of tabloid press obsessions also ask us to consider
the nature of the society that a) regards such things as newsworthy;
and b) condones such attitudes. If the headline writer is, as he "likes
to think", "a sort of poet for our times" then what are we to say
about such times? We might note here that Duffy's choice of "for"

over "of" carries the implication that we get what we deserve. While Duffy's mock headlines make her poem unmistakably of its time and place, the analysis she puts into the mouth of her journalist is perhaps even more uncomfortable:

> Of course, these days, there's not the sense of panic
> you got a few years back. What with the box
> et cet. I wish I'd been around when the Titanic
> sank.

On one level, the lines argue that we live in a comatose state induced by the electronic media but, on another, their compression of history into what one might term 'before and after' — Empire, industrial power, faith in progress and science — suggest that what the last line of the poem calls "The instant tits and bottom line of art" are symptomatic of a wider loss of certainty and a resultant cynicism. In such a climate, the prejudices and prurient obsessions of the tabloid headline are easily expressed and readily consumed.

The relations between language, consumption, the condition of England and English culture and society as particular kinds of texts are also at the heart of 'Translating The English, 1989' (1990, 11):

> Wheel-clamp. Dogs. Vagrants. A tour of the wonderful
> capital city is not to be missed. The Fergie,
> The Princess Di and the football hooligan, truly you will
> like it here, Squire. Also we can be talking crack, smack
> and Carling Black Label if we are so inclined. Don't
> drink the H_2O.

The voice of the poem is not that of a credulous immigrant but that of a credulous native who portrays England as a kind of Third World state. The apparently random aspects of "my country" are all presented as separate but equally seductive items of consumption and pleasure. The ludicrousness of this allows the poem to exploit the gap between that apparent randomness and the fact that these items also form a system that is recognisable but, in this manifestation, uncomfortable and almost 'other'. Putting the poem into a pidgin voice makes the point that natives of England have only imperfect access to that system and its relationships; and that their only status is as consumers of it. The reader, as a consequence, is prompted to consider his or her own relation to and identity in a culture whose confusions, gaps and apparent randomness suggest a debasement or perhaps even total loss of coherent national identity. A culture which exists as media events, criminality and oppression is, of course, no sort of culture at all and Duffy's poem begs further questions: how and to whom is it supposed to be sustaining? If this is the surface then what lies beneath? Who owns it? What is the glue that holds all these items together? As in 'Poet for Our Times' there is not only an argument that debased language is the product of a wider debasement in culture and society but also the suggestion that culture and society in fact function as debased texts. 'Translating the English, 1989' uses typical postmodernist strategies (McHale 1987, 7) such as discontinuity, randomness, excess and quasi-nonselection to suggest that the equalisation of value and apparently dispersed ownership offered by contemporary culture are symptoms of collapse not indicators of revolution and liberation.

The problematic nature of personal identity in national cultural terms in late twentieth century Britain is one of the central concerns of Carol Rumens's poetry:

> When I think of *British* I think of brass-hatted Britannia, ruling the waves from a coin ... When I think of *English* I think of chalk downs, lager louts, the London underground, the Houses of Parliament and cardboard cities under wet bridges where the hopeless young say over and over, hope-lessly polite: could you spare us a bit of change, please. And I want to kick someone — but I don't know who.
>   (1994/5, 17)

The passage might almost be a fugitive part of Duffy's 'Translating the English, 1989' but Rumens's assessment of Medbh McGuckian's poetry locates her own precarious identification and consequent undirected anger in the landscape of what she herself has labelled — controversially — 'post-feminist' poetry. The strategies of McGuckian's poetry "call into question the whole idea of nation-hood, setting up as counter-state the territory of the home and raising the Woolfian issue of whether a woman can really belong to a nation in any secure way" (1993, 21). However, the setting up of counter-states is a difficult project that always runs the risk of being overrun by nation, a point made explicitly in Rumens's poem 'A Lawn for the English Family' (1989, 31-2). The scene is an English garden with children playing on a climbing frame:

> I did not invent this garden
> though I put the children in it.
> I was not its ruler. I wanted
> only pity and beauty to rule it.

★ ★ ★

> For a while they can sit in the sky,
> laughing at money, its blades
> on all sides, slicing and scouring
> the shapes of pity and beauty.

The impossibility of countering existing structures from within is paralleled by the poem's portrayal of the pastoral — the traditional English retreat from the world, the fiction of a prelapsarian state — as inseparable from politics and economics. Throughout the poem the language of the garden — green, dahlias, rose — is juxtaposed with the discourse of power: strategic, law, dictatorship, official broadcast. This mirrors the fact that, say, the great English garden poems of Jonson and Marvell were written under the patronage of the powerful; or that the original layout of the gardens at Castle Howard reproduced the troop deployments of famous victories.

Being English, it seems, means being written into discourses that preclude "pity and beauty". 'Reconstruction' (1989, 43-4) in which the poet's infant self, learning about the Second World War and English attitudes to the Germans from her father, finds herself unable either to confront the memorializing present or accept the vision of the past that present prompts from her imagination writes this on a larger canvas. It's hardly surprising, then, that Rumens's work, although always circling around the domestic and the personal, engages with the post-war European experience, the Holocaust and recent events in Russia and Eastern Europe. This engagement has produced work like the Auschwitz sequence 'Outside Osweicim' (1985) and the "Russian scrapbook" collection *The Greening Of The Snow Beach* (1988). Read back into Rumens's English poems such work suggests that the oppressiveness of nation and the problematic nature of the project of a counter-state result in Englishness being akin to the statelessness that has been a defining factor of the Western historical experience post-1945. England becomes a place where history has almost literally stopped happening and much of Rumens's recent work enacts a desire to counter this by bearing witness to the way the present is freighted with the past — the past returning "gradually from nowhere" (1989, 38); and by seeking out places where history is either still happening or seems inescapable:

> Czechoslovakia, though I've never seen
> Your cities, I have somehow touched your skin.
> You're all the hurt geography I own.
>   'Geography Lesson' (France [ed.] 1993, 241)

At the same time, however, Rumens's poetry never quite loses a sense of the inadequacy of being English. In 'Stella' (1988, 13) a vigorous discussion about glasnost and the meaning of Russia eventually escapes "Our mild English voices / Scarcely comprehended / By anyone but us". Similarly, 'Last of the Lays' (France [ed.] 1993, 244-5) gives a playful, self-conscious account of Rumens's journeys to history:

> Some tanked-up gun-jabber jogged me: 'Nadezhda Krupskaya?'
> 'Crumbs!' I said. 'Wrong revolution. Julian Clary.'
> He didn't find that funny, which meant, as I'd feared,
> History hadn't happened, it hadn't begun.

Although the poem later comments that "English losers are laughers" there is a wider inadequacy that is being uncomfortably mocked. The "wrong revolution" may be interpreted in a number of ways: as postmodernism, as the struggles to assert, say, sexual difference, the difficult journey from the margin to the centre. The poem implies that in England and Western Europe in the late twentieth century these struggles represent a dissipation of the energies of history. 'Last of the Lays' ends with the poet resolving that "Whoever I am I'll / author an honest tear", which is perhaps another way of locating the self and poetry in a world ruled by "pity and beauty".

Carol Rumens's brand of 'poetry as media' engages with the contemporary out of a need to find out how to live as both an English person and as a woman in history; and thereby counter the English view of history as a past pageant of continual growth. Maura Dooley also uses an awareness of history to comment on the present condition of England and particularly life in the capital. Where Carol Ann Duffy re-imagines England as a Third World nation, Dooley draws parallels between past and present to highlight not only the proximity of rich and poor in the urban landscape but also the ever widening gaps between them. 'Out' (1991, 12) begins "It's a medieval life / in this country's great capital" and 'Mind The Gap' (1991, 13) — which records a suicide by drowning in the Thames — pushes the comparison further: "We have settled on either side of a bridge, under arches, / medieval, Dickensian or twentieth century". Like Rumens, Dooley is concerned with England's inability either to recognise such parallels or intervene positively in the fragmentation of society. 'Apple Pie in Pizzaland' (1991, 22) offers an uneasy satire of complacency:

> On the train here a Canadian told me how
> his province holds a lake the size of England.

> I imagine you and I and Pizzaland, the green tables,
> Doncaster, the fields, motorways, castles and flats,
> churches, factories, corner shops, pylons, Hinkley Point,
> Land's End and all of us dropped
> in that huge lake, *plop*.

Here the compactness of nation is also a ludicrous smallness but the deliberate echoes of Larkin's 'Going, Going' complicate the passage further by introducing a note of nostalgia for the country he foresaw composed of "the tourist parts" and "concrete and tyres". However, all this amounts to only one side of the argument: throughout much of Dooley's work there is the sense of historical consciousness and coherence of nation having been replaced by the bulletins of the media. 'Currency' (1991, 36) describes listening to the radio during a car journey — "the endless bulletins of battle" — and ends with "the radio making fiction of us all". 'Over The Fields' (1991, 41) shows the eternals of the natural world becoming over-powered by the manifestations of human technology and, like 'Currency', suggests that the pastoral is no longer a refuge in the electronic media age: "over the fields wires hum". Most tellingly of all, perhaps, 'Towards Summer' (1991, 51) reflects on a broken weather vane

> What would we gain by restoring *N* and *E?*
> A Pole Star, harsh winds, *NEWS.*
> In a surprising spring we can forget
> about the papers, doze in the sun
>
> under a broken weather vane,
> as if it might always be like this.

and 'Shadow on Her Desk' (1991, 69) portrays childhood and later life blighted by the media's obsession with death and disaster: "Saddleworth, Aberfan, Chernobyl: a kind of litany". If the reference to Chernobyl reflects anxieties over media, it also indicates how Dooley's work functions as media itself. The experience of reading her collection *Explaining Magnetism* (1991) is not dissimilar to reading a week's newspapers or the weekend supplements for in it we find all the most characteristic anxieties and feelings about the way we live now. The same impression may be had from Jackie Kay's *The Adoption Papers* (1991) with poems such as 'Death to Poll Tax', 'Mummy and Donor and Deirdre' and 'Severe Gale 8'. This means that a lot of this poetry will very quickly date but in a very large sense this doesn't matter because, first, such writing is adding to the vitality of poetry in our age; and, second, it's setting an invaluable example to beginning and future poets in English of how a public poetry may be written.

The preceding discussion might suggest that public poetry or 'poetry as media' has, as the century winds down and out, suddenly become unproblematic. However, the small controversy surrounding the anthology *Klaonica: Poems For Bosnia* (Benson and Smith [eds.], 1993) shows that, like anthologies and competitions, public poetry seems destined to remain a point of orientation for highly polarised opinions about the condition of contemporary British poetry. The pros and cons were brought into the open, first, by a verse letter by George Szirtes to *The Independent* newspaper in response to its 'Poems For Bosnia' series run in 1993; and, later, by a debate between Szirtes and Ken Smith in *Poetry Review* under the title 'Paper Wars: Bosnia & Public Poetry' (1993/4, 44-5). Szirtes's argument — or as he called it "quarrel" — was with *The Independent* rather than with the anthology itself and may be summarised as follows: public poetry brings into sharper focus the nature of "the relationship between poetry and others' suffering" and because of this the poet's response must be appropriate. The poet must "be specific, and ... must take responsibility for [his] words". Public poetry must not, Szirtes argued, be the unfocused, undirected emotion of the poet in response to some matter of public anxiety. At the same time, public poetry draws our attention to the nature of experience in the late twentieth century:

> There is one other little question my instincts keep asking. They want to know whether I really think I understand the grief of someone by watching it in a snippet on the TV news? Our ways of obtaining public information are fast, selective, rarely sustained, sensational, conjuring intense but short-lived emotions. One story replaces another very quickly. TV gives us distance, immediacy and safety.
> (1993/4, 44)

Smith's argument was simpler: discussions about ethics are all very well but they may lead to silence; and "where the alternative is silence, *Nothing will come of nothing*". We should not choose silence in the belief that it is not proper to speak or that someone else will speak for us. Once the decision is made to speak, how can we judge if one human being's response to another's suffering is proper or improper?

Szirtes's 'quarrel' and Smith's riposte leave much unsaid. One can, for example, agree with Smith and add that, as electronic media and information networks proliferate, it becomes harder and harder for us to say "we didn't know, we saw nothing". TV certainly gives us "distance, immediacy and safety" but it can also give us new feelings of responsiblity as human beings. Poets are not exempt. David Constantine has written that "Poetry wants to witness; it is instinctive" (1994/5, 21) and goes on to say that

> I have had in my head lately a notion of *the rightful scream.* Suppose Angola, Somalia, Bosnia and all the other kindred killing grounds were empowered to utter a scream of a loudness in proportion to their pain. Then we should hear it. We should hear nothing else. Poetry may be viewed as helping humanity towards its rightful scream.

However, many of the poems discussed in this chapter and Gulf War poems by Michael Hulse and others show that poetry often gives that help by responding to media images. If, as Noam Chomsky argues, even the Left-liberal media are involved in 'manufacturing consent' then what are the implication for the effect and status of such poetry?

8. "Everyone Agrees"
or How British Poetry Joined the Culture Club

> For the last two centuries, Western aesthetic speculation was
> engaged in a tightrope act in which the significance which
> must be ascribed to art in order to justify its importance has
> had to be eliminated from art in order to guarantee its
> authenticity.
>
> Gerald Graff: 'The Myth of the Postmodernist
> Breakthrough' (Bradbury [ed.] 1977, 225)

> The politics of subsidy have meant that art has been required
> to be different things in different environments ... For the
> New Right it is a significant industry. The ... definition takes
> art out of the realm of the Romantic, visionary tradition and
> into a new, more objective, territory.
>
> Bryan Appleyard (1984, 48)

Auden wrote famously that "Poetry makes nothing happen" but
as the 1990s gather momentum something has certainly been
happening to British poetry. Suddenly, the quietist art is hot news.
Poems no longer appear only in the pages of the *TLS* and *The
Spectator* but in the pages of *The Independent, The Guardian* and *The
Observer*. For five nights in October 1993, for five minutes a night,
BBC2 ran *Poet's News*, three or four poems commenting on the day's
events. The Poetry Society's 'New Generation Poets' promotion, a
kind of 'Best of Young British Poets', was accompanied by wide
media coverage and such unprecedented tie-ins as Radio 1 broad-
casting poems everyday throughout May 1994. A Poetry Society
spokesperson was quoted saying that "the influence of rock music"
was crucial to the members of the NGP and *The Guardian's* Arts
Correspondent reported excitedly that "comedy was the new rock
'n' roll; now poetry is staking its claim" (*TLS*, 21.1.94, 13). Finally,
the Forward Poetry Prize (founded 1992) is being puffed as the
poetry Booker and its founder launched a National Poetry Day in
October 1994. The *TLS's* 'NB' column (17.12.93) reported that
"Poetry is booming, everyone agrees" and added, in reference to the
New Generation Poets promotion, that "The efficient publicists
Colman Getty have been hired to help stir up the public appetite
for powerful rhymes". The fact that *Poems On The Underground*
(1993) had sold over 100,000 within six months of publication
suggests that not much stirring was required.

Poetry, then, has started to behave like all the other arts that make up the British arts industry or, in Bryan Appleyard's designation which I shall borrow for this chapter, 'the culture club'. After a long and fraught apprenticeship — or perhaps novitiate — poetry has finally been admitted to the territory of hype and subsidy where people talk in compressed paradoxes: "Within the national family we are very good at arts and that feeds into the national household economy. Quality of life is an industry". Or so remarked Lord Gowrie on taking up Chairmanship of the Arts Council. Membership of the culture club clearly has implications for the ways in which poetry is produced, marketed, perceived and consumed. More crucially, it throws into question many cherished assumptions about poetry and, because poetry is a comparatively small area, brings into sharper focus some of the tacit assumptions that have characterised the British arts industry in recent years. It is these implications and assumptions I intend to examine in this chapter. I shall begin by looking at some external aspects of the poetry world — blurbs, competitions — and relate them to larger forces at work in the 1980s and 1990s. I shall follow this by a discussion of sets of assumptions about poetry and culture and their points of conflict and continuity.

Blurbs and Puffs

A sampling of book jacket blurbs from the past thirty years or so provides a useful barometer of the nature and extent of the changes which poetry in Britain has undergone in its journey from tranquil reflection to the new rock 'n' roll.

> (i) The keynote of the collection is tragic irony. Mr Bell's taste is for clowns and clowning in his own persons ... He suspects all public faces, especially his own; they are all, in his view, clown-masks, and so the deepest honesty lies in self-confessed clowning ... Mr Bell works in many forms, from mock-heroic odes and serious and moving elegies for dead friends, to short epigrammatic poems and unembroidered love poems, while his imitations of Laforgue are some of the best that have yet been written. This is a long-awaited collection and it will be long-remembered.
> Martin Bell: *Collected Poems 1937-1966* (1967)

> (ii) Fisher's *City* is a strange phenomenon. Fisher's *City*, like Williams's, is more than itself: he is not painting its portrait but exploring its moral significance, and through it, himself.
> Roy Fisher: *Collected Poems* (1969)

(iii) For the greater part, the poems in John Hartley Williams's first collection are narratives and character studies: as he puts it, 'fiction by ellipsis'. Among them are poems of love, both manifest and concealed, and poems about places, lived in, suffered in, sported in. The author draws on a variety of techniques, modernist and traditional, but asserts throughout his own idiom and identity.

John Hartley Williams: *Hidden Identities* (1982)

(iv) ...*Corona, Corona* displays to the full Michael Hofmann's gift for compressed and vividly pointed reportage. It offers some of the boldest, frankest and most searching poetry of our time.

Michael Hofmann: *Corona, Corona* (1993)

(v) *Soft Targets* is more than just a book of funny poems and savage squibs: it's a portrait of our present age, the good, the bad and the ugly face of Britain today.

Simon Rae: *Soft Targets* (1991)

(vi) All true journeys are also inner journeys. These parable-poems and declarations of intent bring together deep compassion, irony and humour.

Iain Bamforth: *Sons and Pioneers* (1992)

Clearly, a decisive break has occurred between the first three examples and the the second. In the first three, the emphasis is on form, technique and tone as the means of judging achievement within a particular cultural discourse. The poets' work is judged against a set of norms — poems of love, poems of place, moral sense — and within a kind of lineage. In the second three, the quality of the poetry is located in its likeness to something else: reportage, our present age, parable. The emphasis is almost on quality of information rather than means of expression. We might also note that in the second group of examples the stress — explicitly or implicitly — is on compression. Hofmann's 'reportage' is 'compressed'; the blurb writer of Simon Rae's book of satires pleads self-consciously for its expansiveness; and Iain Bamforth's collection sounds like a cross between a religious text (traditionally in short verses) and the clauses of a contract. What the prospective reader is being offered here is something that is comfortable and disposable. You cannot take or leave tragic irony or explorations of moral significance but you can casually leaf through reportage and just as casually put it down again. What is most interesting, however, in the context of the current emphasis on personality and authenticity as commodities is the way the second group of blurbs imply a detachment of the self from the poetry. The first three, in contrast, give not only an impression of the person behind the poetry but a sense that *this poetry* is an inseparable part of *this person*. These blurbs positively revel in intelligence and difficulty. Poetry is not an expression or a description of being, it is synonymous with it. This difference may be linked partly with the dissolution of 'poetry' into 'poetries' and with a changed perception of the poet's rôle from a position within a tradition to an urgent rôle in the here and now; and partly to an age in which it is increasingly difficult and even ill-advised to attempt to distinguish between high and low culture or between culture, entertainment and leisure pursuits. We can, however, approach this last point from a different direction and say that the first three blurbs seem unconcerned whether their poets are going to have any readers or not; while the second go out of their way to attract the widest possible audience. Hence the move from describing poetry as something like a series of Chinese boxes or a set of Russian dolls, existing in a series of contexts widening out from the metrical and syntactical to the moral and philosophical to describing it as a kind of barely personal commentary. Does Hofmann have a taste for tragic irony? Does Simon Rae's portrait of contemporary Britain have moral significance? Is Iain Bamforth a modernist or a traditionalist or a combination of the two? These questions are, apparently, not at issue; and if they are not then this perhaps relates to the idea that there is an audience for and not readers of poetry — to be a reader is to enact a different kind of commitment and involvement than to be a member of an audience. Finally, moving beyond the aesthetic, it seems that the second group of examples exhibit a curious combination of self-assertion and self-effacement, a combination that the American commentator Christopher Lasch relates in late twentieth century capitalist democracies to "the bafflement of the moral imagination" in the face of contemporary world events and contemporary social life. In the face of an age of extremity and paradox, the artist asserts the smallness and non-uniqueness of self (1985, 130).

Biographical Notes

Self-assertion and self-effacement combined relate to the rise of the biographical note on the cover, inside page or jacket flap of poetry collections. I should stress here that by 'biographical note' I mean not the bald statement of birth and origin but the potted biographies listing everything from the poet's primary school to the names of his or her pet cats that began to appear in the latter half of the 1980s. Again, we need to consider some examples to understand their precise meaning.

(i) Martin Bell was born in 1918. He was educated at Taunton's School, Southampton and graduated from University College, Southampton, with an Honours degree in English. He was a Lance-Corporal in the Royal Engineers from 1939 to 1945, and since then has taught for the London County Council in a variety of schools.

Mr Bell was a founder-member of The Group and was involved in its reincarnation as Writers' Workshop. Some of his poems appeared in *Penguin Modern Poets III*, and in 1964 he was awarded the first Arts Council Poetry Bursary.

Martin Bell: *Collected Poems 1937-1966* (1967)

(ii) He was as unmistakably of his period as he was, in his relaxed gracefulness, obviously apart from it. Though he shared its political preoccupations and general attitudes, his own poetry had a fastidious reserve that communicated on a private rather than a public level.

Bernard Spencer: *Collected Poems* (1965)

(iii) Simon Armitage was born in 1963 in Huddersfield and grew up in West Yorkshire. After taking a degree in Geography at Portsmouth Polytechnic, he worked with young offenders for two years, then went to Manchester University, where he gained a CQSW (Certificate of Qualification in Social Work), and as part of his MA wrote a dissertation on the psychology of television violence. He now works as a probation officer in Oldham, and lives in Marsden, near Huddersfield ...

Simon Armitage: *Xanadu* (1992)

(iv) Maura Dooley organised writer's courses at the Arvon Foundation's Lumb Bank centre in Yorkshire for five years, and in 1987 became Literature Officer of London's South Bank Centre. She won a Gregory Award in 1987, and has published two short collections, *Ivy Leaves & Arrows* from Bloodaxe in 1986, and *Turbulence* from Giant Steps in 1988. *Explaining Magnetism* is her first full-length collection.

Maura Dooley: *Explaining Magnetism* (1991)

(v) Born into a family of Plymouth Brethren in 1959, Iain Bamforth was brought up and educated in Glasgow, where he studied medicine at the University. He worked as a

scientific and technical translator, practised medicine in
Paris, Bavaria, the isolated town of Broken Hill, New South
Wales, and now in Scotland ...
   Iain Bamforth: *Sons and Pioneers* (1992)

(vi) Tony Flynn was born in 1951 in Haslingden, Lancashire,
and lives in Walsall. He read Philosophical Theology at Hull
University, and is now a social worker in Birmingham ...
   Tony Flynn: *Body Politic* (1992)

As with our examination of blurbs, we can see that a decisive break
has occurred between the first two examples and the rest. The
biographical notes for Martin Bell and Bernard Spencer are con-
cerned to disseminate salient facts and to assert their subjects'
identities as poets. What is happening in the other examples is, I
would argue, something entirely different: the creation of a frame
of reference in which the poetry can be judged qualitatively. Taking
examples (iii) to (vi) collectively we can see that in the tightrope act
between significance and authenticity described by Gerald Graff,
authenticity has come to dominate. What is striking is the emphasis
given to the fact that poets are actually other things: a probation
officer, a social worker, a doctor and a literature officer. Similarly,
Neil Astley, founder and managing director of Bloodaxe Books, has
said that "We publish everyone from vicars to punks" (in *P.N. Review*
94, editorial). What such a statement offers us is a kind of guarantee
of significance *through* authenticity. The implication is that poetry
only has value as the product of a properly constructed socio-politi-
cal identity. The poem that comes into being merely as the best
expression of any subject that has a genuinely present meaning for
its author is no longer sufficient. It is but one short step from this
position to the poetics of the extreme which, as poet and editor John
Barnie points out, may be just as partial a view of the art as the
so-called 'élitist' poetry of previous generations:

   ... One of the big mistakes we've been making in the West is
   to think that because poets in, say, Eastern Europe have been
   writing out of political and artistic repression, and have
   produced poetry which we have admired, that therefore it is
   hard in the West to compete, because we lack a similar
   extreme of experience. Envy and guilt are mixed in such
   reactions. This seems to me a complete misconception of
   what significant experience is ...
   (Interview with David Hart)

As in the case of writers from Eastern Europe, an emphasis on the place of origin is also indicative of a conviction, dominant in the discussion and presentation of British poetry in recent years, that truth and value are not only socially but geographically constructed. Neil Astley has also commented that "the provinces are after all where everyone lives" and, in the same interview, characterised poetry of the 1970s as "dull stuff, boringly presented and irrelevant to most people's lives" (in *P.N. Review* 94, as above).

The social and geographical construction of value and the equation of origin with relevance are symptomatic of a wider change in late twentieth century western cultures and societies. Lionel Trilling described this in his study *Sincerity and Authenticity* (1974) as a move from sincerity — being true to one's self as the foundation of moral life — to authenticity in which the extent of one's alienation is paramount and becomes the means of asserting both the truth and value of one's self and of one's experience and perceptions. What Trilling neglected to analyse is the extent to which that alienation becomes a marketable commodity. The poet who is a doctor, a vicar, a probation officer or a social worker is not, of course, alienated per se but, it is understood, lives and works at the cutting edge of everyday experience — we might even say comfortable experience. The experience of such poets is also, it is implied, a predominantly social one and therefore of immediate relevance to 'most people's lives'. Real jobs equate to real poetry. However, the emphasis on poets' professions and the degree of those professions' social reality relates to the move from sincerity to authenticity in another, more complex way. It demonstrates a reversal of Romantic *and* modernist conceptions of the artist. The artist is no longer an isolated individual enacting a painful truth to self or shoring up fragments against cultural collapse and personal ruin. Instead, his or her work is judged increasingly by the degree to which it observes or voices the suffering or painful truth to self of *others*. Reading reviews of contemporary British poetry one could be forgiven for thinking that a phrase like "gives a voice to the disenfranchised" is the highest form of praise available. In fact, what takes place is a curious process in which the poet is deprivileged only to be reprivileged. The poet is no longer an outsider granted access to eternal truths or some transcendental reality and neither is his or her poetry part of a larger cultural project to, say, resist the bourgeois and humanize the materialist spirit: he or she now has a job like everyone else and poetry is actually more like the press or photo-journalism. At the same time, however, the job is not like other people's for it brings him or her into contact with worlds beyond most people's everyday experience and it is here that the authority we have been taught to invest in artists becomes relocated. The 'otherness' of the artist has been transferred from the artist per se to externals: his origins, his profession and his subjects.

The particular construction of value and relevance and the identification of poetry with discourses outside itself have combined in recent years to give poetry both a marketable identity and a visible mark of quality. Identity and quality may both be related to wider socio-economic trends since 1980. A marketable identity is of paramount importance for a book trade which is now geared predominantly to the 'frontlist' — i.e. new books — and which is dominated by large national chains. The director of one independent book distributor comments that Waterstones "have changed bookselling in this country" and "have a very up-market image". The move up-market — a tenet of contemporary business wisdom often heard from gurus such as Tom Peters and John Harvey-Jones — can only be achieved with an instantly recognisable product. The large chains have created a climate in which books should have a conformity of size and spine and should, preferably, be laminated, a climate in which appearance equals recognisable product equals visible quality. Visible quality marks can also be related to trends far beyond poetry and bookselling. Quality standards have become increasingly important during the last ten to fifteen years. Kite marks, charter marks and the like have become the compact sign that to some extent replaces the comforting name of the family firm and enhances and distinguishes virtually synonymous products. And to return to Lord Gowrie for a minute, not only is 'quality of life an industry', quality itself is an industry too. The quality assurance standard BS5750, founded in 1979 and widely used in industry and commerce, can at the time of writing be awarded by any one of thirty-three accredited assessment companies for fees between £10,000 and £30,000. In this context, it is hardly surprising to find the *Citizens' Charter*, published by the Government in July 1991, pledging to "work for better quality in every public service". Similarly, just as British Gas is, on its own account, 'a world class energy company' so the RSC now offers prospective theatre-goers 'world class classical theatre'. The application of business language to the arts does indeed show, in the words of one of our epigraphs, art entering "a new, possibly more objective, territory"; and it also suggests that the price of the ticket is, again, a greater degree of homogenisation.

Competitions and Prizes

Biographical notes also alert us to the increasing importance of prizes and competitions in contemporary British poetry:

> Her many awards include first prize in the 1983 National Poetry Competition, a Scottish Arts Council Book Award of Merit for *Standing Female Nude*, a Somerset Maugham Award in 1988 and the Dylan Thomas Award for 1989.
> (Blurb for Carol Ann Duffy: *The Other Country* [1990])

Awards, competitions and prizes not only bring the issues discussed above into much sharper focus: they also enable us to measure more precisely just how much British poetry has become like the other arts in the culture club. Readers and students of British poetry are now so accustomed to seeing awards emblazoned across book covers that it is quite chastening to remind oneself that such things are very much a 1980s/1990s phenomenon. The Arvon (1st prize £5,000) and the Bridport (1st prize £1,000) date from 1980 while the Leeks Arts Festival and Peterloo Competitions date from 1983 and 1986 respectively. The Forward Poetry Prize (£10,000) — only three years old at the time of writing — is already being puffed as the 'bardic Booker'. And on January 20th 1994, the Poetry Book Society awarded the first T.S. Eliot Poetry Prize of £5,000 to Ciaran Carson for his collection *First Language*. As Nicolas Tredell commented in a paper entitled 'Prizing Poetry' (read at The Poetry Industry conference in Oxford in 1994), "It is of course no coincidence that poetry competitions have burgeoned in an era when the virtues of individual competitiveness and acquisitiveness in the economic and social fields have been so stridently proclaimed by right-wing governments, and where those same governments have cut back on public funding for the arts". As Tredell points out, public subsidy has been reduced, cut completely or replaced with 'challenge funding' in which public grants match private sector contributions. Business sponsorship of the arts has become increasingly important: in 1970, the sponsorship total was £500,000 but the total for 1991/2, according to the Association for Business Sponsorship of the Arts, was £65 million (*The Times*, 9.12.93). The importance of business sponsorship for British poetry is underlined not only by Marks and Spencer's sponsorship of the Peterloo Poets Open Poetry Competition but by these lines from the preface to *The Forward Book of Poetry* (1993):

> We have had help with the Prizes and this anthology from

many sources. In particular, I would like to thank Ellen Hipschman at NASDAQ, an award winner under the Business Sponsorship Incentive Scheme for his support of the Book Trust, the administrator of the Prizes. The BSIS is a government scheme administered by ABSA (Association of Business Sponsorship of the Arts) ...

It seems quite easy to imagine a world in which major collections — the new Ashbery? — have a list of credits like those that appear at the end of James Bond movies thanking The Ford Motor Company, Cartier etc; or in which poetry is used, like films, for product placement.

Awards, competitions and prizes show poetry's increasing similarity to other arts in several ways. First, they represent an equation of monetary with aesthetic value. This is not unusual in the world of, say, fine art where money is always involved in value judgements, whether it is public outcry over the Tate's latest acquisition of bricks or media attention for the latest record price for a painting by Van Gogh or Turner. It is, however, new to the world of British poetry. An idea of an audience may have partly replaced the image of a reader but there is not yet a poetry market. Second, the award of a prize and its subsequent use in marketing a book represent a pre-packaged judgement. It is another version of the visible mark of quality I discussed earlier but like those quality marks it is difficult to say what prizes and awards actually mean. What is a Scottish Arts Council Book Award of Merit exactly and how does it differ from a Dylan Thomas Award? Or, to phrase the question differently, what it is about *this poetry* that allows it to win both? Third, such awards and prizes can contribute to distorted perceptions, as the case of the Booker Prize for novels shows only too well. The story of Keri Hulme's *The Bone People* being the winner that nobody chose is well known but it is also interesting to note that the Prize's twenty-fifth anniversary was marked by a 'Booker of Bookers' to select the best of the winners since 1969. This had a curious effect: "This contest has naturally focused attention primarily on the judges' past fallibility and the novels they missed, rather than on their prescience and those they noticed. It seems easy enough to put together a salon des refusés ... that is the equal of the assembled Booker winners" (*TLS*, 10.9.93, 14). This has the double effect of devaluing both prize and winners. Perceptions may be distorted in another way: as competitions and prizes become increasingly important in British poetry, there is a very real danger that when critical studies and historical surveys come to be written they will focus — outside the unignorable major figures like Heaney — on the prized and the puffed. Finally, when competitions and prizes are used to market books, a strange 'translation' takes place: the preferences of small groups of individuals are sent out into the world as if they were the result of a democratic, populist process. This élite judgement is complicated still further. A panel of judges composed of people such as Stephen Spender and Roger McGough — as was the case with the first Forward Prize — cannot reasonably be expected to agree on anything much. In this light it seems inevitable that the criteria of judgement remain hidden from us. Thom Gunn won the major Forward Prize for *The Man With Night Sweats* (1993) but did the judges make the award in recognition of a 'lifetime achievement' in the manner of the Oscars and the Grammys; a generally agreed return to form; or because his book dealt with one of the pressing concerns of the age? Carol Ann Duffy's winning of the main prize in the second year of the Forward Prize with *Mean Time* (1993) would seem to suggest that the judges look for a kind of socially responsive 'poetry as media'. Similarly, in the case of the new T.S. Eliot Prize for the year's best collection, one puzzles over what common standard can be applied to poets as different in style, subject and voice as Les Murray, Patricia Beer, Don Paterson, Douglas Dunn and Moniza Alvi. What makes these writers better than, say, Charles Boyle, Selima Hill and Simon Armitage who all published new and well-received collections during the same year? The answer is, of course, that nothing does and that competitions and awards appear to be natural but are in effect completely artificial. A similar type of distortion characterises the perceptions competitions and awards produce in the market-place. Frank Brazier, then chief executive of the Pentos Group (owners of the Dillons chain of bookshops) remarked that Douglas Dunn's winning of the Whitbread Book of the Year Award for 1985 with *Elegies* brought "to the attention of the people who make decisions the fact that people might read poetry ... In PR and advertising terms I could go from week to week without thinking about poetry" (Interview with David Hart). The fact that people buy a prize-winning book that has received wide media coverage actually tells us very little about readership and reading habits. No better example of the way prizes distort / are used to distort the perception of a work exists than the paperback reissue of Edith Wharton's novel *The Age of Innocence* to 'tie in' with the 1993 film version. The novel was billed as Pulitzer Prize winner which it was — in 1920.

Three Types of Assumption

Blurbs, biographical notes, competitions, awards and prizes all have more complex meanings than might at first appear and demonstrate an irrevocable change in the ways British poetry is perceived and presented. However, as I argued at the start of this chapter, that change brings into question and into sharper focus three sets of assumptions: what we might call 'traditional' ones about poetry; prevailing ones about poetry; and prevailing assumptions within the arts industry about the function and use of culture in general.

First, here is a selection of 'traditional' assumptions about the meaning and use of poetry:

(i)   Poetry is subversive and oppositional. It does not support the dominant socio-political order. It works for integration and against atomization, alienation and fragmentation.

(ii) Poetry is diachronic as well as synchronic: that it, it has a life beyond the immediate circumstances of its composition and publication, beyond the personal pressure that prompts the writing of it and the cultural context that frames it. At the simplest level, this means that as readers we return to favourite poems over and over again; and in a more complex way, the 'double life' of a poem underlies Eavan Boland's remark that "I want a poem I can grow old in. I want a poem I can die in" (Interview 1993, 56).

(iii) Poetry involves the self; poetry is authentic utterance. No-one believes a novel to be an account of the author's own experience but even when a poet does not write 'I' he or she erects a whole scaffolding of expectation.

(iv) Poetry involves a particular relationship with language where the moral, the technical, the musical, the erotic, the sexual and the philosophical may all interfuse.

(v)   Poetry, similarly, is *totally* sensual; that is, it involves all levels of experience, both physical as well as mental. It involves, say, the rhythm of walking as well as the rhythm of breathing.

(vi) Poetry, consequently, is a sacred space. It connects the common life with the larger cycles of the universe and it places and preserves something essential about humanity outside human systems. As Joseph Brodsky asserted in his inaugural address as U.S. Laureate, poetry "is the only insurance against the vulgarity of the human heart" (1991/2, 5).

(vii)   Poetry, finally, is difficult not only in the sense of Wallace
        Stevens's 'resistance of meaning' but in the sense that it is not
        just entertainment. To quote Brodsky again: "[I]n cultural
        matters, it is not demand that creates supply; it is the other
        way round. You read Dante because he wrote *The Divine
        Comedy*, not because you felt the need for him; and you
        wouldn't be able to do so".

Second, in marked contrast and greatly simplified, here are some
prevailing assumptions about British poetry:

(i)   Poetry started in 1980.

(ii)   Poetry should be relevant to people's lives.

(iii)   Poetry in Britain is no longer 'provincial' or 'academic'; it is
        responding to a fruitful internationalising of form and subject.

(iv)   Poetry is an open space. There is nothing that cannot be
        written about and no-one who cannot write about it.

(v)   Poetry is democratic whereas until fairly recently it was élitist.

(vi)   Poetry, as the remark by the Poetry Society spokesperson
        about the importance of rock music for the members of the
        NGP makes clear, is part of wider culture, both positioned in
        it and formed by it.

(vii)   Poetry is political and on the left.

(viii) Poetry is serious but not boring, witty but not frivolous,
        emotional but tough; and consequently there are some experi-
        ences that are more significant than others.

(ix)   "Innovation, accessibility, humour, appropriation of the ver-
        nacular, political nous and significance, even characterisation
        and skilled narrative, are now to be found, not in new fiction,
        but new verse" (Harry Ritchie, Literary Editor of *The Sunday
        Times*, quoted in publicity for NGP).

Finally, here is a selection, again greatly simplified, of prevailing
arts industry assumptions about culture:

(i)   The arts are international.

(ii)   Art is good and more art is better.

(iii)   Art equals synthesis.

(iv)   Truth has been replaced by sincerity or, at least, authenticity.

(v)   "Variety and quantity equal health and renewal" (Appleyard 1984, 12).

(vi)   Plurality equals virtue.

(vii)   For every art there is an audience.

(viii) Art is not élitist.

(ix)   The lines between arts, entertainment and leisure are useless distinctions and are becoming increasingly blurred.

(x)   The identification of a definite audience dictates the suppression of difficulty and difference.

(xi)   The arts are a "multifarious affair" (Appleyard 1984, 121).

(xii)   Good art enacts relevance and offers accessibility.

(xiii) Good art is founded on a generosity of intent which derives from an anti-modernist impulse (Appleyard 1984, 97).

A comparison of the three groups of assumptions shows how closely British poetry can be identified with the rest of the culture club. There are overt similarities between the second and third groups of assumptions but what is more interesting is that we now regularly hear and read comments from the third group being applied to poetry. For example, we might note how in recent years the plurality and variety of British poetry have come to be taken as synonymous with health, renewal and growth. So is poetry in Britain starting to be viewed in ways that are at odds with what have traditionally been believed to be its fundamental attributes; and does this matter? The assertion by Harry Ritchie suggests that there is an increasing emphasis on what is said rather than how it is said; and Neil Astley's comments quoted above almost imply that there are 'right' things to say just as there appear to be 'right' places to come from and 'right' identities or professions to have. And yet poetry, perhaps more than any other cultural form, is thought to locate its achievements and pleasures, challenges and rewards, in the combination of 'what' and 'how'. If the emphasis has changed in favour of 'what' then there can be no doubt that is closely allied to prevailing ideas about accessibility, democracy and relevance; and that it is symptomatic of the increased importance of marketing in contemporary British poetry. Identification of an audience and a resultant boost to sales need a clearly identified product made to a clearly delineated standard and specification. Harry Ritchie's assertion portrays poetry wanting to keep its options open and describes not its unique identity but its likeness to as many other things as possible. The greater such similarities, the larger the potential audience.

The traditionally oppositional and subversive nature of poetry is also compromised and even undermined by its new status. 'New verse' may not actively support the dominant political and social order but it certainly, in the Ritchie version, owes its first allegiance to the demands of its age; and in doing so it inevitably establishes and perpetuates a dominant order of its own. This order dictates safety and comfort, a place where 'innovation' is to be contained within the frame of 'accessibility'; or as one reviewer of *The New Poetry* (1993) put it "... surely the myth of modernism, progressivism, and the perpetual avant-garde was laid to rest years ago?" (Forbes 1993, 4-5). The tentative, almost anxious phrasing of the question signals that it engages with a number of uncomfortable truths. The most important of these is that British poetry in the 1980s and 1990s can only be fully understood through a 'double reading' which recognises that the dissolution of consensus and the resulting divisions at home take place against the larger context of postmodernism. Such a reading recognises, for example, that the dissolution of the post-war consensus is also an example of the end of the 'master narrative'; and that the increasing prominence of non-standard or alternative Englishes in contemporary British poetry can also be read in wider contexts of 'ex-centricity'. Put simply, this means that for every Simon Armitage there is a John Ash, for every Kathleen Jamie a Frank Kuppner and for every Carol Ann Duffy a Medbh McGuckian. Whatever myths were thought to have been laid to rest years ago, our reviewer knows that not everyone — poets and readers — has received invitations to the funeral; and his rhetorical flourish inscribes both a wish that poetry would stop being 'difficult' and a corresponding awareness that, try as we might, we can't stop it being so. This relates to wider trends in the arts in the 1980s and 1990s where a paradigm shift has occurred from the picture of the intractable genius ahead of his or her time to that of the group of apparently interchangeable artists — Young British Novelists, Best of the Bookers, Dirty Realists, New Generation Poets — chasing the widest possible audience. What such groupings offer is a fiction of inclusivity: if anyone (artist) can be included then anyone (audience) can understand and enjoy the product.

The chase for audience also underlies the recent touting of poetry as 'the new rock 'n' roll'. While the increase in readers and money available to individual poets is to be welcomed, this kind of conception also needs to be recognised as a symptom of a particular kind of failure: "At this particular moment there really is a crisis in values. Nobody knows how to judge" (in Appleyard 1984, 48). And here is Philip Norman sounding a note of dissent about the last 'new rock 'n' roll' comedy:

> I'm surprised no-one has pointed out the great flaw in this "Comedy: the rock 'n' roll of the Nineties" argument. Rock 'n' roll, although seeming a dangerous, iconoclastic medium, actually created a state of mass conformity, where con-artists and twerps could depend on being applauded with exactly the same fervour as genuine talents.
> (1994, 20)

One might recall in this context Leavis's comment in *New Bearings in English Poetry* (1976 edn, 58) that "the Sitwells belong to the history of publicity rather than of poetry". The touting of poetry as rock 'n' roll perhaps demonstrates the increasing breakdown of distinctions between the arts, leisure and entertainment referred to earlier and which, in turn, could be termed the final stage of Gerald Graff's tightrope act. What results is a product with all the cachet of art but none of its more problematic and problematizing characteristics. The painter Georges Braque once wrote that "art is made to trouble but science reassures": it would seem that this binary opposition has now been largely reversed. And the need for reassurance from art is, I would argue, connected to something that underlies and informs several chapters in this book: the consequences of the dissolution of the post-war consensus and of the severing of active, meaningful relations with the past. Bryan Appleyard writes that the past "has offered stability and a system of codes and meanings which provide the illusion of an understandable world" (1984, 101). In recent years, a number of factors have conspired to make this model of the past increasingly dubious and inaccessible. First, free market economic policies and their attendant social philosophy have thrown into question our relation with the past and the idea of continuity with tradition. Second, as the end of the century approaches, the past increasingly becomes the turbulent history of the twentieth century. The past starts to look more and more like a place of instability. Finally, it becomes increasingly difficult to argue for the 'relevance' of the past. We are repelled by its sexual politics, its hierarchies, its conceptions of crime and punishment, its attitudes to non-native races; and we are embarrassed by its ideas of duty, its conceptions of a wider morality. And what happens is that the art of the present is asked to offer stability and the illusion of an understandable world. The poet who is a doctor, a social worker, a probation officer or a vicar stands between us and chaos and his or her work makes a 'translation' of it into something 'relevant' but safe.

Bryan Appleyard wrote in *The Culture Club* that

> The uneasy distance between artist and audience, in which once stood the dandy critic-mediator, has been bridged. This is a profound and complex development which, perhaps initially, can be linked with the rightward swing in politics. No-nonsense petit bourgeois economics finds its correlative, perhaps to the artist's discomfiture, in poems that tell stories or in films with a message.
> (1984, 2)

In an age of relevance what place is there for the privacy and sometimes glorious uselessness of poetry? And what place is there for the poet who writes against the prevailing models of the age? My point throughout this chapter and, indeed, throughout much of this book has been that we should not take the current state of British poetry on its own terms and that we should be able to ask some hard and uncomfortable questions about it. It is important to do so because, perhaps for the very first time, British poetry is starting to respond to demands and pressures which it has traditionally resisted; and is starting to locate its strengths in response and not in resistance. For example, Matthew Francis has pointed out some of the consequences of what his recent essay calls "The Competition Culture" (1993, 7-9). Poems cannot be "more than forty lines long ... In form, poets are pushed towards regular metre and away from free verse"; and "In content, the pressure is away from the personal and towards the political". Similarly, John Bayley has observed that "New poetry today all has ... the same political sub-text" (1993, 15). If we are to do contemporary British poetry critical justice then we need to be able to question and understand what it means that independent publishing is supported by public subsidy; that poetry has become pluralist and more 'democratic' in a period when society has become increasingly fragmented; and that while, according to *Poetry Review* (84.2, 85), the five Faber authors in the NGP promotion increased their sales, large quantities of their books could be found in the remainder shops and New Year sales in January 1995. If we cannot explore such questions then we run the risk of the exciting diversity of British poetry in the 1980s and early 1990s becoming an homogenised blandness where 'everyone agrees'.

Appendix:
The New Poetry — A User's Guide

At this late stage in the century and in the history of English poetry there seems to be little meaning or value in talking about the 'difficulty' or 'obscurity' of contemporary poetry per se. Several years ago G.S. Fraser concluded *A Short History of English Poetry* (1981 edn, 368) with the assertion that "The modern period, in the older senses, is over". More recently, Richard Bradford — a writer I shall return to later — has argued in *A Linguistic History of English Poetry* (1993) that stylistic innovation in English poetry is probably over because the conventions of language and the conventions of poetry have been pushed to the point of maximum divergence. We are well accustomed to the idea that something

      like
      this can
      be
      a
      po-
      em

as well as a sonnet by Shakespeare, an ode by Keats or a ballad by Charles Causley. At the same time, we live in a world where linguistic conventions are constantly being challenged or modified and where, increasingly, expert vocabularies are interfusing with everyday discourse. At its most obvious, this manifests itself in the arguments that continue over the correct way to pronounce 'controversy' or in the simplification of the language of political debate over the past ten to fifteen years that culminated in one of the Conservative Party's slogans during a recent General Election using the term 'double whammy'. At a more sophisticated level, the fact that a computer game is called *Donkey Kong* makes a subtle play with both our linguistic and cultural competencies and our expectations of convention. And what is one to make of a conference given by the Major Energy Users' Council Electricity Group in 1994 which promised a forum in which delegates could debate such questions as "Is the uplift being gamed?". My point here is not that the skills of linguistic competence and literary competence are moving closer together — although they might be — but that we should not be surprised that contemporary British poetry asks us to perform similar acts of decoding and, indeed, expects us to be able to do so.

If there is little point in talking about 'difficulty' or 'obscurity' then there seems to be even less in trying to discuss British poetry after 1980 in terms of schools. Several reviewers of *The New Poetry* attempted to do this and did many of the poets collected in it a great disservice. As Paul Hyland points out in his excellent handbook *Getting Into Poetry* (1992, 27), "It's good to be sceptical about groups and tags and movements". Sometimes poets are similar to one another; sometimes they're not. Poets will often group together at the start of their careers but then quickly diverge as they develop and mature or their ambitions and ideas change. Can we really go on calling Craig Raine and Christopher Reid 'martians' in the light of their recent work? As with 'difficulty' and 'obscurity', schools and groups are, it seems to me, a rather lazy way of avoiding getting to grips with what the poetry is really like. What follows is an attempt to provide both students and teachers with some points of orientation to the poetry contained in *The New Poetry* and to contemporary British poetry in general.

Syntax

Donald Davie wrote over thirty years ago in *Articulate Energy* that "the break with the past is at bottom a change of attitude towards poetic syntax" and that "What is common to all modern poetry is the assertion or assumption (most often the latter) that syntax in poetry is wholly different from syntax as understood by logicians or grammarians"(1976 edn, 148). Many poets of the 1980s and 1990s have developed this to such a degree of sophistication that, as Joseph Brodsky has famously remarked of Glyn Maxwell, there is a "tendency to draw metaphor from the syntax itself". The arrangement of words, their relation and connections, becomes another subject that competes for our attention with an individual poem's ostensible subject. I discuss Maxwell's poetry in detail in Chapter Two but it is worth drawing attention to the title and opening of 'Love Made Yeah' (*TNP*, 324) as a further example. Maxwell uses such strategies habitually but it is the frequency rather than the fact of their use that make them so unique in his work. We can find poets working in similar ways throughout *The New Poetry*; and here are some notable instances:

(i)   John Hartley Williams: 'Song of the Grillbar Restaurant' (*TNP*, 41)

> here is a song that i sang that was
> sung in a place that was not song
> which few are

(ii)   Eavan Boland: 'That the Science of Cartography is Limited' (*TNP*, 52)

(iii)   Tom Leonard: from 'Unrelated Incidents' (*TNP*, 70-3). (The opening of part 2 which wonders if the reader has "wurkt oot / thi diff- / rince tween / yir eyes / n / yir ears" might stand as a motto for many poets' use of syntax and also for the particular competencies they expect in their readers.)

(iv)   Duncan Bush: 'August. Sunday. Gravesend.' (*TNP*, 95-6)

(v)   Charles Boyle: 'Cairo's Poor' (*TNP*, 167)

> — where I am talking with
> Mr Mohammed Ebrahim Abdel Hamin, M.Sc.,
>
> a kind of English.

(vi)   Ian McMillan: 'The er Barnsley Seascapes' (*TNP*, 255-8)

Despite their very wide differences of form and subject matter, all these poems exhibit commonalities in their 'foregrounding' of syntax which relate to wider trends in recent British poetry. If we compare our six examples to poems in *The New Poetry* which are syntactically more conventional we can see that their particular strategies signal that types of difficulty are being enacted or negotiated. All six poems seem to be concerned with how to make an entry into experience, culture, history or language and with finding a position from which to speak. None start in a way that convinces us of their natural authority: all seem determined to earn it. Eavan Boland tells us explicitly that she is going to prove something; John Hartley Williams seems to promise us an archetypal poem as song but simultaneously mocks and undercuts it; and the phrase "a kind of English" in Charles Boyle's poem stands not only for the experience of an Englishman abroad but for a wider consciousness of what Douglas Dunn has called "the post-imperial status of the English language" (Interview 1990, 13). This is clearly part of a wider feeling that no-one has any rights to or guarantees of a place in culture; and this, in its turn, relates to the way many poets have chosen to explore passivity as a resource. Roger Garfitt (1989, 30) wonders

> Can we match our forefathers' active
> speech, that *made* a good marriage
> or a good death,
>
> from the passive registry
> that language has become

but many of the poets in *The New Poetry* — particularly Northern British and Scottish writers — start from an assumption that linguistic passivity, disability or disempowerment are the result of cultural hegemony and Government policy and that to exploit or ironise 'the passive registry' as grounds for poetry and resistance is to avoid 'playing the game'. Beyond unabashed engagement, Leonard, McMillan and others use syntax to contribute to a conception of the poem as linguistic spectacle.

Language

A sense of spectacle also underlies the way many of the poets in *The New Poetry* use language. My co-editor David Morley — in an essay entitled 'What's New About the New Poetry?' (1995) — suggests that a characteristic of much recent poetry is a sense that "the poet's language never takes its 'eye' off the reader, indeed, readers can be placed by the poet in a position of involvement with the play of words as though they, the reader, *were* in the creative posture of the writer"; and he goes on to cite Peter Sansom's '[Insert Title]' (1994, 54) and Ian McMillan's 'Kake Yourself Comfortable' (1994, 9). The first, with its repeated invitation to "[insert details]" asks us to ponder the relation between artificiality and authenticity; while the second, in typical McMillan fashion, appears to offer us what Don Paterson's 'An Elliptical Stylus' (1993, 21) calls "something axiomatic on the nature / of articulacy and inheritance" but mocks our expectations. Turning to the work collected in *The New Poetry*, we can see the same thing happening in poems by Peter Reading, Frank Kuppner (particularly the extract from *A Bad Day For The Sung Dynasty*), Maggie Hannan and Simon Armitage. Sean O'Brien's use of the inclusive pronouns "you" and "us" and Matthew Sweeney's mysteriously incomplete or skewed narratives are subtler examples of the same involvement.

However, just as much recent British poetry demands various kinds of 'double reading' so involvement of this kind is also, paradoxically, a self-conscious distancing similar to that produced by 'foregrounded' syntax. Ian Gregson detects this in Simon Armitage's use of colloquial speech and contemporary idioms, arguing that Armitage

> does not use them simply to evoke an authentic voice. Instead that voice is treated with a detachment that arises from the sense of distance that arises between the colloquial idioms and the poetic form in which they're placed, Armitage's symmetrical stanzaic patterns. *This introduces a poetic voice*

> *speaking alongside the colloquial one — a voice that seems*
> *simultaneously to be identified with and sceptical of the colloquial*
> *voice and which simultaneously mocks its often trivial posturing*
> *and enjoys it.*
> (Gregson 1994, 75 — my italics)

Gregson is describing a particularly sophisticated variation on — or even, perhaps, ironic awareness of — something that several critics have argued is fundamental to English poetry. Anthony Easthope, in *Poetry As Discourse* (1983, 160), points to the tensions and divergences between 'sociolect' (the language of a group) and 'idiolect' (the language of one person) which reaches its climacteric, he thinks, in the High Modernism of Pound's *Cantos*. It is a tension that underlies the conclusion of Armitage's poem 'Zoom!' (*TNP*, 336): "It's just words // I assure them. But they will not have it". Poetry, then, seems to be founded on a paradox which Richard Bradford (1993, 19) usefully summarises as follows:

> ... we communicate with one another through linguistic
> competence, a shared, perhaps intuitive, awareness of how
> sentences work. Yet poets seem able to communicate effects
> to us through techniques that stand outside linguistic
> competence.

This 'standing outside' is made explicit at the end of Ciaran Carson's 'The Irish for No' (*TNP*, 143-4) where "Mish-mash. Hotch-potch" describes the poem's method and encapsulate a criticism of Heaney's early poetry. Bradford argues that we find our way round poetry's essential paradox through developing skills in recognising what he terms — drawing on the work of Roman Jakobson and other linguistic critics — 'the double pattern'. The double pattern describes the relation between the conventions of language and the conventions of poetry and, specifically, what occurs when those aspects of language "which do not relate directly to its conventions of meaning and significance [are] deployed as a regular and persistent feature of the text" (1993, 3). At its most obvious, this manifests itself as the use of rhyme and assonance; the relation between syntax and line; or, for example, the patterning of "-ing" endings in Geoff Hattersley's 'Frank O'Hara Five, Geoffrey Chaucer Nil' (*TNP*, 251). The 'double voice' which Gregson detects in Armitage can also be found in Gerard Woodward's 'To a Power Station' (*TNP*, 302-3), in Sean O'Brien and Peter Reading, in Elizabeth Garrett's 'History Goes to Work' (*TNP*, 273) and Carol

Ann Duffy's 'Adultery' (*TNP*, 230). However, reading Gregson in the light of Bradford, I would suggest that what many of the poets in *The New Poetry* offer are, in fact, species of 'treble pattern'. Like the end of Armitage's 'Zoom!', they are well aware that poetry is and is not "just words" and the 'foregrounding' of the colloquial and the idiomatic more often signals a desire to explore and play with ideas of what is artificial and what is authentic. The distance between the colloquial and the poetic that Gregson analyses also means that the colloquial starts to lose its apparent 'reality' and functions as another discourse that both mediates our condition and is simultaneously a part of it.

The interweaving of the colloquial and the poetic, the apparently real and the artificial is one of the particular pleasures of Ciaran Carson's poetry. In 'Calvin Klein's *Obsession*' (*TNP*, 138-141) and 'The Irish for No' (*TNP*, 143-4) a tradition of oral storytelling organises the products of a sophisticated, at times postmodern, cultural consciousness. The wanderings of a yarn become inseparable from the breakdown or problematizing of various identities — national, personal, poetical. The short poem '33333' (*TNP*, 141) ends "I know this place like the back of my hand, except / My hand is cut off at the wrist. We stop at an open door I never / knew existed" which is, perhaps, another way of saying with Michael Hofmann that "Familiarity breeds mostly the fear of its loss" (*Acrimony*, 1986, 41). Familiarity and loss *or* the end of innovation *or* the post-imperial status of English have all contributed to an aspect of poetic language in the 1980s and 1990s of which Carson's work is paradigmatic: the mixing of different discourses and vocabularies. *Poetry Review* attempted to characterise the work of many of the New Generation Poets by arguing that "whole slabs of historical and cultural reference jostle, butt up against, and slip over each other in a form of linguistic plate tectonics" (Forbes 1994, 5). The most explicit example of this is probably Robert Crawford's short poem 'Scotland' (*TNP*, 278) whose opening stanza mixes "semiconductor", "superlattices", "heterojunctive" and "epitaxies" with the more conventional register of "intimate", "cities" and "farmlands" with the result that the two sets of terms, as it were, perform each other. Further examples can be found in Peter Reading (passim), Maggie Hannan (passim) and in Carol Ann Duffy's 'Poet for Our Times' (*TNP*, 229). Pauline Stainer's interfusing of religious and scientific discourses is also notable — see Chapter Five for a fuller discussion of her work and others'. While each poet's method of and reasons for mixing and juxtaposing vocabularies are very different there are, nevertheless, a number of general points that can be made. First, there has been an increasing concern to write poetry that is properly contemporary; in the words of Robert Crawford "a good poem is faithful to the language of its age" (1994, 40). Second, this has gone hand-in-hand with a desire to locate poetry in the context of a wider culture. Anxieties about the audience for poetry and about its function, rôle and public profile are paralleled by the production of poetry that self-consciously performs its co-existence with rock music, sport, and electronic and printed media. Third, just as Douglas Dunn wrote in 'Young Women in Rollers' (1969, 29-30) that "There are many worlds, there are many laws" so many younger poets begin from the assumption that the self and its experiences are formed by precisely the sort of jostling, butting up and slipping *Poetry Review* observed. Finally, many younger poets look to the achievements of High Modernism for spurs and permissions; but the result is not an apocalyptic shoring of fragments against ruins but an exuberant bricolage.

Linguistic plate tectonics of an altogether subtler variety occur in a line like Glyn Maxwell's "her mouth politicised indignity" ('Tale of the Mayor's Son', *TNP*, 329) or Maggie Hannan's "but not / far from the diktat // of knack" ('Provincial', *TNP*, 315). Unlike our earlier examples, these are at some distance from the "stylistic eclecticism and a desire to re-establish poetry as a platform for social and political comment ... that have effectively dominated British poetry between the 1930s and the 1980s" (Bradford 1993, 185). What both Maxwell and Hannan engage with, I would argue, is the way language is actually being used in our time and how usage is altering and shifting in emphasis; and their engagement is akin to that of Malcolm Bradbury's novel *The History Man* (1976) which describes one of its characters speaking "socially" in an attempt to catch a particular form of behaviour.

Voice and Persona

How one speaks and its relation to what Roland Barthes (see Culler 1980, 135) calls "the idiolect ... of the institution" of literature is a defining preoccupation for many poets who began to publish from 1970 onwards; and, indeed, the problematics of 'articulacy and inheritance' (to quote Don Paterson again) may well turn out to be late twentieth century British poetry's most important concerns. Consequently, much recent poetry can be characterised by an awareness that the inherently contradictory nature of the art —

intimate with breath yet presented in a "monumental, hardened" (Barthes in Culler 1980, 133) mode of writing — is further complicated by the fact that a vernacular language of feeling is devalued as writing; and a resultant antagonism towards or rejection of what are perceived as dominant wisdoms, either in poetry or beyond. I discuss these issues in detail in Chapter One; and what I want to focus on here are the demands an engagement with issues of articulacy and inheritance make on the reader.

The New Poetry contains work in a number of alternative — I hesitate to use the term 'non-standard' — Englishes. Among these we can identify Scottish patois (Liz Lochhead, Tom Leonard); Caribbean Creole (David Dabydeen, Fred D'Aguiar); 'Nation language' (Linton Kwesi Johnson); and 'dictionary' or Synthetic Scots (W.N. Herbert). The reading of such poetry involves a complex method of decoding. As Tony Curtis points out in his analysis of Fred D'Aguiar's 'Mama Dot Warns Against an Easter Rising' (*TNP*, 283), "we consciously decode the language and 'read' it as standard English" (1990, 140). At the same time, however, as Curtis himself points out, a key characteristic of much recent poetry is that the reader is "able to place an accent in [the] mind upon the speech" a poem records (1990, 153). The result is that we experience *and* naturalise difference simultaneously and the effect, I would argue, is that the reader is once again, in Morley's terms, "placed ... in a position of involvement". The difference is that this has both a negative and a positive side. First, the involvement is emphatically not "the creative posture of the writer" but, rather, what Neil Corcoran (1993, 159) reads in Tony Harrison's use of a Latin epigraph to *The School of Eloquence*: "a lesson ... in alienation, incapacity and anxiety which the use of any language may involve for those not privy to its ... cultural encodings". The reader is confronted with language as shibboleth, that which reveals one's true origins, as in Seamus Heaney's poem 'Broagh' (1980, 66) with its "last / *gh* the strangers found / difficult to manage". Language is at once a place of inclusion and exclusion. Second, the reader's involvement is what one might term the first step in a process of re-education by which he or she learns, for example, how Caribbean Creole puts one in "contact with raw matter" and with "the uniqueness of the people, the particularity of their being" (Dabydeen 1984, 14, 15). Alternative Englishes offer an alternative to English poetic language as a place of decorum and subdued awarenesses. What the conventions and rules of RP condemn or marginalise become rich resources and through the combination of alienation and re-education the reader is encouraged to re-evaluate preconceptions about both standard and alternative Englishes. Try an exercise with 'To Yeltsin (1992)', part II of W.N. Herbert's 'A Two Year Ode' (*TNP*, 295-6), and see what happens when you replace words like "camsteery" or "eisenin" with their English equivalents; and, conversely, you could try and answer why Herbert didn't call the poem 'A Twa Yeir Ode'. Another difficult question raised by alternative Englishes is that of audience: who are the poems for? My discussion so far has assumed their reception by contemporary poetry's usual readership but is that correct? And if the effect of such work is to make the majority of readers 'strangers' struggling over "that last *gh*" does this mean that, ultimately, it is only the poet who can truly and comprehensively voice the poem; and, if it does, what are the implications of this when the poem is entered into the cultural system of exchange and valuation? A final comment on voice and alternative Englishes from Peter Sansom's handbook *Writing Poems* (1994, 58):

> ... dialect poems ... force the reader to take on the narrator's voice, to speak the poems in that voice. There's a sudden moment of understanding, when a phrase gives up its meaning; that moment of "translation" seems to me to exemplify what happens in a great deal of poetry ...

If *how* a poem should be spoken is problematic then *who* is speaking it is equally complex. About twenty percent — just over forty-five — of the poems in *The New Poetry* are spoken by clearly differentiated characters or personas. This is not, in itself, especially remarkable: we can say the same thing about approximately fourteen percent (just over twenty) of the poems in *The Penguin Book of Contemporary Poetry* and the use of persona has been an accepted feature of poetry at least since the middle of the last century. What is notable, however, is the way many of the poets in *The New Poetry* use personas or characters. Just as syntax and language can be made to comment on themselves and on the creative moment so many poets have chosen to question the relationship between authenticity and artifice in a poem and our assumptions about it. They do so by locating — or asking the reader to locate — the voice of an individual poem on a sliding scale between the apparent self of the poet and an explicit character or persona. Let's look briefly at some examples.

(i)   *Grace Nichols:* 'Abra-cadabra' (*TNP*, 154) *and Simon Armitage:* 'Night Shift' (*TNP*, 338)
       Both poems seem to leave us in no doubt that it is the poet

speaking, although they are very different poems. This is because they present us with family and domestic scenes we can all recognise — 'real' and therefore 'unpoetic' — but also because they persuade us of their reality in particular ways. The Nichols poem, for example, 'earns' its truth because it brings into relation three different registers of language: colloquial ("incredible", "thumb", "split-pea"); literary ("ritual", "purgative", "symmetry"); and West Indian ("narah", "gaulding"). The repetitive patterns and rhythms give it the truth of a Biblical story. Armitage's poem persuades us because of its accumulation of carefully observed detail and the way its language just slips beyond the colloquial: "spores", "stowed", "clockwork contractions", "lipstick love-notes".

(ii)   *John Ash:*'Visigothic' (*TNP*, 130-1)
It is still 'I' speaking but we have already travelled some considerable distance on our sliding scale from self to other as the poet presents us with a highly acculturated facet of his being. The way the poem relishes its arcane knowledge of the life of the Visigothic kingdom should alert us to the fact that something very subtle and sophisticated is going on; something akin, I would argue, to what Neil Corcoran detects in Seamus Heaney's 'Bog People' poems: "the poet's 'I' is detached from ordinary social circumstance, withdrawn to solipsistic meditation. We might think of it, in fact, as mythologized" (1986, 77). In fact, 'Visigothic' might be read as a slightly camp version of a poem like Heaney's 'The Tollund Man' (1980, 78-9); for just as Heaney relates ancient ritual sacrifice to present day Ireland and its atrocities so Ash compacts the so-called 'dark ages' with the apocalyptic feeling of living in New York at the end of the twentieth century; and just as Heaney's poem enacts feelings of exclusion and displacement by "saying the names // Tollund, Grauballe, Nebelgard" so too does Ash's poem with its "list of names I could barely / pronounce: Leovigild, Recared ...". The speaker in 'Visigothic' feels, in New York, as Heaney imagines himself in Jutland, "lost, / Unhappy and at home".

(iii)   *Glyn Maxwell (passim)*
In Maxwell's poems, we find a similar combination of apparently real and fictional self. Personal experience, anecdote and memory are clearly present but the rhetorical flourishes, self-dramatisation and highly formal structure and intricate

syntactical patterns suggest that it is not the poet who speaks but characterisations of a young British male. Here we have persona as mask, as mechanism that conceals a person's true thoughts and feelings. I discuss Maxwell's play with status in greater detail in Chapter Two but it is worth noting that his speakers habitually move between positions of omniscience and stupidity and that one is often located in terms of the other.

(iv) *Bernard O'Donoghue / Carol Ann Duffy*
In 'A Nun Takes the Veil' (*TNP*, 87), 'Psychopath' (*TNP*, 226) and 'Warming Her Pearls' (*TNP*, 232) we are clearly being asked to listen to fictional characters but these personas are pointing us beyond the immediate stories they tell. O'Donoghue's nun encourages us to consider a number of larger questions: the relation between rural and urban in Ireland, for example, or the tension between material and spiritual or the moment when the innocence of one's first world is shattered by contact with the world at large. 'Warming Her Pearls' is clearly a love poem which begs the question: who is it addressed to?

(v) *Carol Ann Duffy:* 'Adultery' (*TNP*, 230-1) *and Maggie Hannan:* 'Environment' (*TNP*, 313-15)
The voices of these poems are perhaps even harder to identify than that of Glyn Maxwell's 'The Eater' (*TNP*, 331-2). We might even say, in fact, that neither poem is actually spoken by *anyone*; that in the Duffy it is the the experience of adultery, the condition of being adulterous that speaks; and that in the Hannan it is almost as if language itself is speaking to us, as words become a medium to be handled as a painter handles paint or a sculptor moulds clay.

(vi) *Linton Kwesi Johnson*
Here the lines between individual and collective identity are blurred. The voice of the poet enacts a responsibility to the community that gave birth to it; and when "mi" speaks it is always as a part of "wi".

(vii) *John Hartley Williams (passim)*
Each of Williams's poems makes the reader ask 'who is speaking?' and in each case the answer is likely to be different and difficult. Williams has, after all, written a Wild West novel in verse, *Bright River Yonder* (1987), in which narration passes

from character to character like the silver dollar that sets the tale in motion. As this suggests, his primary interests are questions of narrative and perspective. In 'Song of the Grillbar Restaurant' we might at first sight think that we have a fairly conventional poem of lovesickness dressed up in an exuberant syntactical display but a closer reading suggests that the poem is hinting at the possibility that while alienation is the paradigmatic modern urban experience it is in fact the only one we can depend on. The use of lower case evokes the American poet ee cummings and the "garmentless and maimed reprieve" in the last line just as inevitably conjures the Wallace Stevens of 'The Idea of Order at Key West'. A. Alvarez (1961, 133) remarks that Stevens characteristically "seems intent on making the best of a bad philosophical world" which might also describe Williams's subject; and so too might ee cummings's remark that "To be nobody-but-yourself in a world that is doing its best, night and day, to make you everybody else — means to fight the hardest battle which any human being can fight" (in Gray 1991, 194). Williams's poem is, then, both a sort of homage and an attempt to write a different sort of English poem — 'i' is both an allusion and a different sort of convention. The voice of 'The Ideology' (*TNP*, 46-7) is equally complex and, again, it is not possible to say it belongs to a person at all for it is actually the sound of the modern self as it is formed by and in the noise of Western capitalist culture.

(viii) *Pauline Stainer*

In 'Sighting the Slave Ship' (*TNP*, 29) — which is probably one of the finest poems of recent years — we are deep in a fictional realm; the poem reads very much like an extract from a novel or, indeed, like an extract from a ship's journal: we enter *in media res*. Stainer might have written 'they' instead of 'we' but this would have made the poem 'only a story': 'we' includes the reader in the sense of disquiet its anonymous speaker registers and prompts a search through the poem's sixty words for its exact location. This proves elusive or, rather, dynamic for many readings are possible. On one level, for example, the poem asks us to ponder how it is that "divine service", "sacrament" and slavery can exist in the same human and imaginative space. On another, the phrase "something more exotic" voices doubts about the practices of poetry, the responsibilities of the imagination and of art in general.

The use of character and distinct personas by many of the poets in *The New Poetry* can be linked to a wider interest in narrative. As I argued in Chapter Four it is important to distinguish between the narratives of James Fenton or Andrew Motion and those of, say, Duncan Bush and Glyn Maxwell. The emphasis in the narrative poetry identified by Blake Morrison and Andrew Motion in *The Penguin Book of Contemporary British Poetry* is essentially a post-modernist one and its practitioners tend to exploit "paradoxes of revelation and concealment, of confession and deception" (Corcoran 1993, 245) or "self-parody and unremitting self-deconstruction" (Robinson 1988, 1). The poets of *The New Poetry* — of whom ten are also novelists — tend to use narrative in a more conventional way that seems akin to what Peter Reading memorably calls (Interview 1985, 6) "big-scale serious tacklings of things, as in Dickens or Smollett". Even Robert Crawford's superficially parodic and surreal 'Customs' (*TNP*, 279-82) is asking us to think about continuities and defining currents in British culture.

If many poets display a desire to portray the present age and the energies that shape our society then the use of characters and personas also relates to a self-conscious concern with the authority and status of the poet. This concern can be summarised by two comments, one from Duncan Bush and one from Carol Ann Duffy:

> I also disliked (and still do) the 'occasional' poem, the slightly random published collections of so many delicately-suffering poetical egotists, who really do still believe that their person-alised 'sensitive' responses are an adequate measure of the problems of the world they live in.
>
> (in Poole 1992, 45)

> And it's back to the kind of bearing witness thing. I don't want to write the kind of poetry that tells the reader how I feel when I see a rainbow. I don't want to write the kind of poetry that tells the reader that I as a feminist think that this guy should have his prick cut off because he was the York-shire Ripper. What I want to do is present it, as it is. Poets don't have solutions, poets are recording human experience.
>
> (Interview 1988, 72)

Form

Like nearly everything else in contemporary poetry, form is the subject of fierce debate and widely divergent opinions. We can find Carol Rumens (1994/5, 10) referring to "The current crisis — or array of crises — in poetic form". We can read Timothy Steele in *Missing Measures: Modern Poetry and the Revolt against Meter* arguing that free verse is the result of a series of errors and misinterpretations. At a further extreme, we can read the poet Frederick Turner and the scientist Ernst Poppel arguing that there is a correspondence between regular poetic metre and the cognitive cycles of the brain (in Feirstein [ed.] 1991). And on both sides of the Atlantic, we can see the rise of new formalist poets such as Dana Gioia and Marilyn Hacker (USA) and Glyn Maxwell, Michael Donaghy and Elizabeth Garrett (GB). I want to confine my remarks to a couple of points which I hope will suggest approaches to much of the work in *The New Poetry*.

First, in common with large areas of modern poetry, the poems in *The New Poetry* are unlikely to be the sources of quotable lines or memorable couplets. It is not the line that is the most important unit but the way a verse 'paragraph' or the whole of a poem works together. The individual poem is somehow indeterminate, an exploration or process of discovery in which we are asked to accompany the poet. We won't know where we're going until we get there and, even then, the destination may be ambiguous or provisional. At the same time, *The New Poetry* is the product of an age which is sceptical and, some would argue, more or less postmodern. Poets, therefore, are mistrustful of easy effects and self-conscious about poetry and poetic language as discourses that shape experience as much they record it. Earlier, I quoted Ian Gregson describing how in Simon Armitage's poetry a 'poetic' voice seems to co-exist with the ostensible voice of an individual poem. I would argue that another aspect of this, audible throughout *The New Poetry*, is a sense of the poet saying 'I could easily have written *that* but I deliberately chose to write *this*'. Again, what results is a species of 'form in flux'.

Second, I want to conclude by quoting from John Garrett's account of W.H. Auden's poem 'Musée des Beaux Arts' and its description of Brueghel's painting 'Landscape with the fall of Icarus'. Although Auden's influence on younger British poets seems to grow stronger with every passing year I am not trying to argue that his example has been decisive for contemporary conceptions of poetic form. Quite simply, Garrett's account seems to me to be suggestive of much about contemporary poetic form and contemporary poetry in general:

> From Brueghel's painting Auden picks out and emphasises
> the 'centrifugal' aspects — the flight from a common centre
> to a disparate periphery where nothing coheres ... Auden's
> poem, like the painting that inspired it, has no focal centre

around which the less significant events are organised; its most important event occurs in its outskirts, 'by the way' as it were.

(Garrett 1986, 222-3)

The New Poetry and the syllabuses

In the final section of this appendix I shall offer some pointers on using The New Poetry with GCSE and Advanced Level examination syllabuses for 1996 and 1997. The two syllabuses in question are NEAB English Literature 1614 and AEB English 0623. In what follows I shall suggest poems which could be used with the NEAB's Areas of Study; adapt previous AEB examination questions to prescribed authors Pauline Stainer, John Hartley Williams, Grace Nichols, Linton Kwesi Johnson, Paul Durcan, Carol Ann Duffy, Bernard O'Donoghue and Liz Lochhead; and provide notes to some of the more obscure references in their poems. Page references are given in brackets.

NEAB Areas of Study

Images of War
Liz Lochhead: 'After The War' (123); Ciaran Carson: 'Belfast Confetti' (141), '33333' (141), 'Night Patrol' (142); Jo Shapcott: 'Phrasebook' (204).

People and Environment
John Hartley Williams: 'Lament for the Subotica-Palic Tramway' (38-41), 'On The Island' (42-4); Eavan Boland: 'That the Science of Cartography is Limited' (52); Bernard O'Donoghue: 'A Nun Takes The Veil' (87); Duncan Bush: 'The Hook' (90-2), 'Pig Farmer' (92-4), 'August. Sunday, Gravesend.' (95-7); Ciaran Carson: 'Calvin Klein's *Obsession*' (138); Ian McMillan: 'The er Barnsley Seascapes' (255-8); Maggie Hannan: 'Environment' (313).

Heroes and Heroines
John Ennis: 'The Croppy Boy' (68), 'Alice of Daphne, 1799' (69); George Szirtes: 'The Big Sleep' (149); Grace Nichols: 'Those Women' (155), 'My Northern-Sisters' (157); Sebastian Barry: 'Mary Donnelan, Seamstress of the Mad' (216), 'Fanny Hawke Goes to the Mainland Forever' (217); Carol Ann Duffy: 'Psychopath' (226-8); Michael Hofmann: 'My Father at Fifty' (265-6):

Glyn Maxwell: 'Tale of the Mayor's Son' (325-30).

Myth and Symbolism
David Constantine: 'In the ocean room' (57), 'Watching for Dolphins' (58); Selima Hill: 'The Graceful Giraffe of Clot Bey' (79-80); Peter Didsbury: 'That Old-Time Religion' (104-5), 'The Drainage' (110-2); John Ash: 'The Wonderful Tangerines' (132-4); Michèle Roberts: 'The Return' (150), 'Lacrimae Rerum' (152); David Hartnett: 'The Fleece' (181); John Burnside: all three poems (219-221).

The Experience of School
Peter Reading: 'FROM Stet' (112-4); Sean O'Brien: 'A Corridor' (192-3); Carol Ann Duffy: 'The Captain of the 1964 *Top of the Form Team*' (228).

AEB

Pauline Stainer
How does Pauline Stainer guide your responses by the different languages, allusions and cultural references she uses in 'The Ice-Pilot Speaks'? OR Examine the way Stainer presents the natural world.

John Hartley Williams
Write about the variety of technical means by which Williams creates impact in his poetry OR Examine the purposes for which Williams uses humour.

Grace Nichols
Examine the way Nichols uses different varieties of language to create impact in her poetry OR Examine some of the uses she makes of the natural world.

Linton Kwesi Johnson
Examine the effects Johnson achieves by using vernacular speech and discuss how these are different from standard English OR What views of present-day England does Johnson present in his poetry?

Paul Durcan
How does Durcan present the relationship between himself and his father? OR Examine Durcan's uses of humour.

Carol Ann Duffy

Discuss how and why Duffy uses dramatic monologue OR Examine how Duffy shows us the inner world of her speakers.

Bernard O'Donoghue

'A Nun Takes The Veil' refers to "the morning's vision". Examine how all four of O'Donoghue's poems present visions or unusual experiences OR Discuss the uses O'Donoghue makes of the natural world.

Liz Lochhead

Examine the ways in which Liz Lochhead uses simple, everyday language to discuss complex subjects OR Liz Lochhead has elsewhere described her work as the "business of putting new twists to old stories"; discuss her poems in *The New Poetry* in the light of this remark.

Notes

Pauline Stainer: 'The Ice-Pilot Speaks'

ultima thule: Thule was the Greek and Roman name for the most northerly land in the world. The words 'ultima thule' are a famous phrase from the Roman poet Virgil, author of the epic poem *The Aeneid,* and describe the furthest place possible. *Thule culture* is the term used to describe prehistoric Eskimo culture which developed along the Arctic coast of Northern Alaska. The culture was centred around whaling and seals; walruses and polar bears were also hunted.

sterna paradisea: the arctic tern.

terra incognita: unknown land.

Gymnopédies/Satie: Erik Satie (1866-1925). French composer whose highly original music — using unusual chords and unconventional harmonies and notable for its flippancy and wit — marked a break with the traditions of the nineteenth century. *Trois Gymnopédies* (1888) is a typical composition. Many see him as a precursor of minimalist music — hence the opening of section IV.

St Brendan's monks: St Brendan (c.484/6-578) also known as Brendan the Voyager or Brendan the navigator. Celtic saint who was also the hero of legendary voyages.

Yggdrasil: In Norse mythology, the world tree, a giant ash tree supporting the universe. One root went into the underworld, another into the land of the giants and another into the home of the gods. Some argue that the idea of the world tree survives in the maypole and the Christmas tree.

Sleipnir: In Norse mythology, the magical horse of the god Odin. He had eight legs, his teeth were inscribed with runes, and he could gallop through the air and over the sea.

Balder: In Norse mythology, the son of Odin and favourite of the gods. He was immune from harm but was killed when the blind god Höd threw mistletoe at him, the only thing that could hurt him. Some scholars have drawn connections between the figure of Balder and that of Christ.

Borges: Jorge Luis Borges. Argentinian writer noted for his short stories or 'fictions' which describe parallel universes of dreams, labyrinths and imaginary beings. Borges became blind in 1955.

Varèse: Edgard Varèse (1883-1965). Avant-garde composer who conceived of music as blocks of sound located in space. His compositions are typically dissonant, non-thematic and rhythmically asymmetric. Also an early composer (after the early 1950s) of electronic music. Stainer refers here to *Density 21.5* for unaccompanied flute which was premiered on a solid platinum flute; the specific gravity of platinum is 21.5.

Loki: In Norse mythology, a trickster who had the ability to change both shape and sex. Loki was portrayed as the companion of the gods Odin and Thor, assisting them with his cunning and cleverness; but he also appears as an embarrassment and even enemy of the gods. He was the main cause of the death of Balder, having tricked Höd into throwing mistletoe at him. For this, he was punished by being bound in a rock which is the event Stainer refers to here.

Sfumato!: From the Italian *sfumare*, to soften or evaporate like smoke. A term used in painting or drawing to describe the fine shading that produces barely visible transitions between different colours or tones. Used in connection with the work of Leonardo da Vinci.

Sigurd: Or Siegfried. Heroic figure in both ancient Germanic and Norse literature. One of his noted exploits was the slaying of Fafnir the dragon, after which he bathed in the dragon's blood. This made him invisible and able to understand the birds.

Sigrfrida: One of the Valkyries or female spirits attending the god of war who helps decide the course of a battle and conveys the dead to Valhalla. One of the legends of Sigurd or Siegfried tells how he awakened Sigrfrida from a charmed sleep.

John Hartley Williams: 'Lament for the Subotica-Palic Tramway'
Subotica: Town in the Vojvodina region of Serbia in the former
Yugoslavia. An agricultural and industrial centre with a large
population of Hungarian descent. The last town before the Hungarian
frontier.
Palic: Or Lake Palic. A small resort with watersports facilities in a
vast area of park-like country about 8km from Subotica.

John Hartley Williams: 'On The Island'
John Hartley Williams writes that the poem "commemorates a very
short-lived period of transition. West Berlin, of course, was the
island, and was frequently portrayed thus on posters which depicted
the ocean crashing on shores that housed all the familiar landmarks
of the city ... In 1989 a peculiar situation existed whereby Polish
citizens were free to travel anywhere they cared to (as they had
previously not been) whereas the GDR still had closed borders with
the West. The Poles headed straight for West Berlin, despite
encountering a great deal of antagonism from the Ossies (East
Germans), who could not travel ... The Poles set up an ad hoc
market around the National Gallery ... and attracted great crowds
of West Berliners" (Letter to the author).
Krumme Lanke: Lake in the Grunewald or Berlin Forest.
Katowice: Coal mining centre in south central Poland.
Osnowiec: Misprint for Sosnowiec, a town near Katowice.
geliebte: Beloved.
Eck-kneipe: Corner pub.
Westberlin: East German way of describing West Berlin using the
lower case.
Brücke der Einheit: Unity Bridge across the Wannsee linking Berlin
with Potsdam.
Friedrich Schinkel: German architect and painter (1781-1841). State
architect of Prussia (1815) and director of the Prussian Office of
Public Works (1830). Designer of important Berlin buildings in the
Greek Revival style such as the Königschauspielhaus and the Altes
Museum.
Treffendes Angebot: An offer that hits the spot.
Wirtschaftswunder: The West German post-war 'economic miracle'.
Luftschiff: Airshi
Das gläserne Pferd ist unbezahlbar, einfact nict zu bezahlen ... : The
glass horse is priceless, simply unaffordable.

John Hartley Williams: 'The Ideology'
die Pflicht der Freude: the duty of joy.
Zum Ambrosius: Ein Bergriff in Berlin: Zum Ambrosius is the name of a chain of rather downmarket *kneipe* whose motto means 'a well-known name in Berlin' or 'a byword in Berlin'.

Paul Durcan: 'Crinkle, near Birr'
Birr: Urban district and market town in County Offaly, Ireland. A monastery was founded there by St Brendan of Birr.
Galway, City of the Tribes: Town in the province of Connacht. The reference here is to the fact that descendants of the followers of the Norman Richard de Burgh, who assumed rule of Connacht in the 1230s, became known as the tribes of Galway.
Spiddal: Town at the mouth of the Owenboliska. Site of an ancient hospice after which it is named.
Gort: Gort inse Guaire or Field on Guaire's Island. The main town on the road from Galway to Ennis, Shannon, Limerick and the South.
Furbo: Town in County Galway.

Paul Durcan: 'Chips'
O'Connell Street: Famous street in Dublin. Site of the General Post Office from where a free republic was proclaimed in the Easter Rising of 1916.
Hawkins Street to Leeson Street: Just two streets in Dublin of no significance.
Keelogues or Parke: Keelogues is a parish in Mayo where the poet's ancestors lived in the last half of the last century. Parke is another parish in Mayo where the tiny village of Turlough is located, a place where Durcan spent much of his childhood.
Ur of the Chaldees: Ancient city of Babylon.
Melchisedech: Canaanite priest-king in Genesis 14:18-20 who Abraham meets on his return from battle. He gives Abraham bread and wine and, in return, Abraham pays him a tribute.
Carolan of the Moy: Or Turlough O'Carolan. Itinerant composer and singer (1670-1738), known as the last of the bards. The Moy is the River Moy.
Raftery of Turlough: Famous blind poet who walked the roads of Mayo and Galway in the nineteenth century. The poem assumes that he must have passed through Turlough although there is no evidence of this. Turlough is also an old Patrician site with a tenth century round tower.

Bernard O'Donoghue: 'Kindertotenlieder'
The title refers to the song cycle *Songs on the Death of Children* (1901-1904) by the Austrian composer Gustav Mahler.
Hyde life: An allusion to the Jekyll and Hyde story by Robert Louis Stevenson.

Liz Lochhead: 'Bagpipe Muzak, Glasgow 1990'
Liz Lochhead parodies and updates Louis MacNeice's poem 'Bagpipe Music' in order to comment on Glasgow's recent rôle as European City of Culture. Where MacNeice's poem satirised a movement from traditional ways of life to lazy materialism, Lochhead's poem satirises the aestheticisation, commodification and gentrification of tradition and locale.

Grace Nichols: 'Abra-Cadabra'
Narah: "Sometimes also spelt 'narra'. Pain in the stomach or abdomen associated with a twist of the intestines. It may be massaged back into place. Vague term for many intestinal ailments" (*Dictionary of Guyanese Folklore*).
Gauldings: West Indian word for heron.

Linton Kwesi Johnson: 'Mekkin History'
Babylan: The land of oppression; the opposite of Zion, the promised land. By extension, any manifestation of *babylan* such as the police, property, store owners; everything which is viewed as negative or destructive in Western society.

Linton Kwesi Johnson: 'Bass Culture'
blood klaat: Or *blodklaat*. Like the similar *raasklaat,* an obscene swear word derived from cloth used for sanitary towelling.

Suggestions for Further Reading

Richard Bradford: *A Linguistic History of English Poetry* (RKP 1993)
Jonathan Culler: *Structuralist Poetics* (RKP 1980)
Tony Curtis: *How To Study Modern Poetry* (Macmillan 1990)
Anthony Easthope: *Poetry As Discourse* (Methuen 1983)
E.L. Epstein: *Language and Style* (Methuen 1978)
G.S. Fraser: *A Short History of English Poetry* (Open Books 1981)
Metre, Rhyme and Free Verse (Methuen 1983)
John Garrett: *British Poetry Since The Sixteenth Century* (Macmillan 1986)
Paul Hyland: *Getting Into Poetry* (Bloodaxe Books 1992)
Millar and Currie: *The Language of Poetry* (Heinneman 1982)
Clive Probyn: *English Poetry* (Longman 1984)
Peter Sansom: *Writing Poems* (Bloodaxe Books 1994)
David Sutcliffe: *British Black English* (Basil Blackwell 1982)
Denys Thompson: *The Uses of Poetry* (CUP 1978)
Reading and Discrimination (Chatto and Windus 1979)
David Trotter: *The Making of the Reader* (Macmillan 1984)
John Williams: *Reading Poetry: A Contextual Introduction* (Edward Arnold 1985)

As will be clear from their titles all these books are aimed at different aspects and levels of the study of poetry; and some indeed assume a considerable amount of expert knowledge. However, the following recommendations can be made. Anyone interested in what happens linguistically when a poem is written and read should read the relevant sections of Bradford and Culler. Both are very accessibly written and Bradford contains an appendix showing the student how to apply linguistic ideas to the study of poetry. Anthony Easthope shows how English poetry has developed historically as a particular way of looking at the world and of ordering experience but is marred by Easthope's habitual agenda: poetry is dead but it won't lie down. Tony Curtis's book is a useful 'how to' introduction which has the merit of stimulating further thought instead of trying to be either definitive or prescriptive. Paul Hyland's and Peter Sansom's books are aimed primarily at the writer of poetry but both contain useful information on key twentieth century poets, collections and trends; and Sansom is particularly good in providing an idiot's guide to such technical matters as anapestic feet. John Williams attempts to put both the study of poetry as well as the writing of it into a socio-historical frame. Finally, David Sutcliffe's book will be useful to the student of poetry by Afro-Caribbean and Black British poets since it contains a useful glossary of West Indian and British Black English on pages 174-196; and F.G. Cassidy's and R.B. Le Page's *Dictionary of Jamaican English* (CUP 1967) may also be useful.

Acknowledgements

I would like to take this opportunity to acknowledge special debts of gratitude. First, to Mick Felton and Cary Archard at Seren for having faith in this project. Second, to David Hart for allowing me to consult and to quote from his as yet unpublished manuscript *Life Doesn't Rhyme: A documentary survey of current poetry writing, publishing and selling in Britain* which proved invaluable in the writing of Chapter Eight. Third, to Ian Gregson for many stimulating conversations which prompted a late rewriting of the Introduction. Fourth, to all the poets who were kind enough to help with the Appendix; and, finally, to my wife Christine for innumerable conversations and suggestions, unfailing enthusiasm and practical support in the compiling of the Bibliography.

David Kennedy

The publisher gratefully acknowledges permission to make quotations from the following poets:

Simon Armitage: excerpts from *Zoom!* (1989) and *Xanadu* (1992) by permission of Bloodaxe Books; excerpts from *Kid* (1992) by permission of Faber and Faber Ltd.

John Ash: excerpts from *The Goodbyes* (1982), *The Branching Stairs* (1984) and *Disbelief* (1987) by permission of Carcanet Press Ltd.

Eavan Boland: excerpts from *Outside History* (1990) by permission of Carcanet Press Ltd.

Robert Crawford: excerpts from *Talkies* (1992) and *A Scottish Assembly* (1990) by permission of Chatto and Windus.

Peter Didsbury: excerpts from *The Classical Farm* (1987) by permission of Bloodaxe Books.

Maura Dooley: excerpts from *Explaining Magnetism* (1991) by permission of Bloodaxe Books.

Carol Ann Duffy: excerpts from *The Other Country* (1990) by permission of Anvil Press Poetry.

Douglas Dunn: excerpts from *Selected Poems 1964-1983* (1986) and *Northlight* (1988) by permission of Faber and Faber Ltd.

Lavinia Greenlaw: excerpts from *Night Photograph* (1993) by permission of Faber and Faber Ltd.

Geoff Hattersley: excerpts from *Don't Worry* (1994) by permission of Bloodaxe Books.

Seamus Heaney: excerpts from *Field Work* (1979) and *Selected Poems 1965-1975* (1980) by permission of Faber and Faber Ltd. Excerpts from *Selected Poems 1966-1987* by Seamus Heaney. Copyright © 1990. Reprinted by permission of Farrar, Straus and Giroux, Inc.

W.N. Herbert: excerpts from *Forked Tongue* (1994) by permission of Bloodaxe Books.

Michael Hofmann: excerpts from *Acrimony* (1986) by permission of Faber and Faber Ltd.

Glyn Maxwell: excerpts from *Tale of the Mayor's Son* (1990) by permission of Bloodaxe Books.

Ian McMillan: excerpts from *Dad, The Donkey's on Fire* (1994) by permission of Carcanet Press Ltd.

Paul Mills: excerpts from *Half Moon Bay* (1993) by permission of Carcanet Press Ltd.

David Morley: excerpts from *Releasing Stone* (1989) and *A Static Ballroom* (1993) by permission of the author.

Sean O'Brien: excerpts from *The Indoor Park* (1983) and *The Frighteners* (1987) by permission of Bloodaxe Books. Excerpts from *HMS Glasshouse* (1991) by permission of Oxford University Press.

Peter Reading: excerpts from *Collected Poems: 1: 1970-1984* (1995) and *Collected Poems: 2: 1985-1996* (1996) by permission of Bloodaxe Books.

Carol Rumens: excerpts from *From Berlin to Heaven* (Chatto and Windus, 1989) reprinted by permission of the Peters Fraser and Dunlop Group Ltd.

Pauline Stainer: excerpts from *Sighting the Slave Ship* (1992) by permission of Bloodaxe Books.

Ken Smith: excerpts from *the heart, the border* (1990) by permission of Bloodaxe Books.

Bibliography

Abrams, M.H. *The Mirror and The Lamp: Romantic Theory and the Critical Tradition* (Oxford: Oxford University Press, 1971).

Ackroyd, Peter. *Notes For a New Culture* (London: Vision, 1976).

al-Udhari, Abdullah. Introduction to al-Udhari, Abdullah (ed.). *Modern Poetry of the Arab World* (Harmondsworth: Penguin, 1986).

Alvarez, A. *The Shaping Spirit* (London: Chatto and Windus, 1961).

(ed.). *The New Poetry* (Harmondsworth: Penguin, 1962).

Foreword to Holub, Miroslav. *On The Contrary* (Newcastle upon Tyne: Bloodaxe, 1984).

Appleyard, Bryan. *The Culture Club: Crisis in the Arts* (London: Faber and Faber, 1984).

The Pleasures of Peace (London: Faber and Faber, 1989).

Arkell, David. *Looking For Laforgue: an informal biography* (Manchester: Carcanet, 1979).

Armitage, Simon. *Zoom!* (Newcastle upon Tyne: Bloodaxe, 1989).

Interview with Jane Stabler in *Verse*, 8.1 (Spring 1991), 92-99.

Interview, *Bête Noire* 12/13 (Autumn 1991/Spring 1992), 261-275.

Kid (London: Faber and Faber, 1992).

Xanadu (Newcastle upon Tyne: Bloodaxe, 1992).

Ash, John. *The Goodbyes* (Manchester: Carcanet, 1982).

'The Poet's Grandmother and Other Dilemmas', *P.N. Review* 47, 12.3 (1985), 38-40.

'Reading Music', *P.N. Review* 50, 12.6, 45-48.

The Branching Stairs (Manchester: Carcanet, 1984).

Disbelief (Manchester: Carcanet, 1987).

The Burnt Pages (Manchester: Carcanet, 1991).

Ashbery, John. *Selected Poems* (London: Paladin, 1987).

'In conversation with John Ash', *P.N. Review* 46, 12.2, 31-34.

Flow Chart (Manchester: Carcanet, 1991).

Astley, Neil (ed.). *Bloodaxe Critical Anthologies 1: Tony Harrison* (Newcastle upon Tyne: Bloodaxe, 1991).

Introduction to Astley, Neil (ed.). *Poetry With An Edge* (Newcastle upon Tyne: Bloodaxe, 1994), 17-22.

'Is poetry the new rock and roll?', Bloodaxe Catalogue 1994/5, 2-3.

Auden, W.H. *Collected Poems* (London: Faber and Faber, 1976).

Bamforth, Iain. *Sons and Pioneers* (Manchester: Carcanet, 1992).

Bannet, Eve Tavor. 'Marx, God and Praxis' in Berry and Wernick (eds.). *Shadow of Spirit: Postmodernism and Religion* (London: RKP, 1992).

Barker, Jonathan. Introduction to *The Poetry Book Society Anthology 1986-7* (London: Hutchinson, 1987).

Barr, Alfred H., Jr. *Matisse: His Art and His Public* (London: Secker and Warburg, 1975).

Barthes, Roland. *Sade, Fourier, Loyola*. Trans. Richard Miller (New York: Hill and Wang, 1976).

'Style and its Image' in Chatman, S. (ed.). *Literary Style: A Symposium*.

(Oxford, New York: Oxford University Press, 1971), 3-10.

Bayley, John. Untitled contribution to '*The New Poetry* — A Symposium' in *Poetry Review*, 83.2 (Summer 1993), 15.

Beer, John. Introduction to *Coleridge: Poems* (London: Dent/Everyman, 1978), v-xxx.

Bell, Martin. *Collected Poems 1937-1966* (London: Macmillan, 1967).

Belsey, Catherine. *Critical Practice* (London: Methuen, 1980).

Benjamin, Walter. *Illuminations* (London: Fontana, 1973; 1982).

Benson, Judi and Smith, Ken (eds.). *Klaonica: Poems for Bosnia* (Newcastle upon Tyne: Bloodaxe, 1993).

Benson, Gerard; Cherniak, Judith; and Herbert, Cicely (eds). *Poems on the Underground* (London: Cassell, 1993).

Boland, Eavan. Interview, *In Her Own Image* (Dublin: Arlen House, 1980).
Night Feed (Dublin: Arlen House, 1982).
The Journey (Manchester: Carcanet, 1987).
Outside History (Manchester: Carcanet, 1990).
'Outside History', *P.N. Review* 75, 17.1 (September-October 1990), 22-27.
P.N. Review 93, 20.1 (September-October 1993), 52-57.
'Making The Difference: Eroticism and Ageing in the Work of the Woman Poet', *P.N. Review* 96, 20.4 (March-April 1994), 13-24.
'Gods Make Their Own Importance: The Authority of the Poet in our Time.' Text of the Ronald Duncan Lecture 1994. *P.N. Review* 102, 21.4 (March-April 1995), 10-14.

Boyle, Charles. *Affinities* (Manchester: Carcanet, 1977).
Sleeping Rough (Manchester: Carcanet, 1987).

Bradbury, Malcolm. *The History Man* (St Albans: Granada, 1976).
The Novel Today (Glasgow: Fontana, 1977).

Bradford, Richard. *A Linguistic History of English Poetry* (London: RKP, 1993).

Braine, John. *Room at the Top* (London: Mandarin, 1989).

Brodsky, Joseph. 'Laureate of the Supermarkets' — Inaugral Address as Poet Laureate of the USA at the Library of Congress, *Poetry Review*, 81.4 (Winter 1991/2), 5-9.

Bush, Duncan. *Aquarium* (Bridgend: Poetry Wales Press, 1983).
Salt (Bridgend: Poetry Wales Press, 1985).
The Genre of Silence (Bridgend: Poetry Wales Press, 1988).
Interview, *Poetry Wales*, 28.1 (July 1992), 11-22.
Masks (Bridgend: Seren, 1994).

Bush, Douglas. *Science and English Poetry* (Oxford: Oxford University Press, 1950).

'Business and the Arts', Supplement to *The Times*, 9.12.93.

Carson, Ciaran. *The Irish For No* (Newcastle upon Tyne: Bloodaxe, 1988).
Belfast Confetti (Newcastle upon Tyne: Bloodaxe, 1990).

Carver, Raymond. *The Stories of Raymond Carver* (London: Picador, 1985).

Celan, Paul. *Selected Poems*. Trans. Michael Hamburger (Harmondsworth: Penguin, 1990).

Charmley, John. 'The Price of Victory: Churchill and the history of decline',

The Times Literary Supplement 4754, 13.5.94, 8.

Chatman, S. (ed.). *Literary Style: A Symposium.* (Oxford, New York: Oxford University Press, 1971), 3-10.

Checkland, Sarah Jane. 'Infra-red scrutiny of the Arnolfini Marriage leaves an art-historical industry short of a good theory', *The Guardian,* 13.2.95, 20.

Clifton, Harry. *The Desert Route* (Newcastle upon Tyne: Bloodaxe, 1992).

Coleridge, S.T. *Poems.* Selected, edited and with an Introduction by John Beer (London: Dent/Everyman, 1978).

Collie, Michael. *Jules Laforgue* (London: The Athlone Press, 1977).

Connor, Steven. *Postmodernist Culture: An Introduction to Theories of the Contemporary* (Oxford: Basil Blackwell, 1989).

Constantine, David. 'The War Goes On', Bloodaxe Catalogue 1994/5, 20-1.

Corcoran, Neil. *Seamus Heaney* (London: Faber and Faber, 1986).

'One Step Forward, Two Steps Back: Ciaran Carson's *The Irish For No*', in Corcoran, Neil (ed.). *The Chosen Ground* (Bridgend: Seren, 1992), 213-237.

English Poetry since 1940 (Harlow: Longman Group UK, 1993).

Cottrell-Boyce, Frank. 'The Urban Idyll', *Living Marxism* (June 1994), 41.

Crawford, Robert. *A Scottish Assembly* (London: Chatto and Windus, 1990).

Talkies (London: Chatto and Windus, 1992).

Devolving English Literature (Oxford: Oxford University Press, 1993).

Identifying Poets: Self and Territory in Twentieth Century Poetry (Edinburgh: Edinburgh University Press, 1993).

'Robert Crawford writes', *Poetry Review — New Generation Poets Special Issue* (Summer 1994), 40.

Crimp, Douglas. 'On the museum's ruins' in Foster, H. (ed.). *The anti-aesthetic: essays on postmodern culture* (Port Townsend, Washington: Bay Press, 1983).

Crozier, Andrew. 'Thrills and frills: poetry as figures of empirical lyricism' in Sinfield, Alan (ed.). *Society and Literature 1945-1970* (New York: Holmes and Meier Publishers, 1983), 199-235.

Curtis, Tony. *The Last Candles* (Bridgend: Seren, 1989).

How to Study Modern Poetry (Basingstoke: Macmillan, 1990).

Taken For Pearls (Bridgend: Seren, 1993).

Culler, Jonathan. *Structuralist Poetics* (London and Henley: RKP, 1990).

'Jacques Derrida' in Sturrock, John (ed.) *Structuralism and Since* (Oxford: Oxford University Press, 1982), 154-181.

Dabydeen, David. *Slave Song* (Denmark: Dangaroo Press, 1984).

Davie, Donald. *Purity of Diction in English Verse* (Harmondsworth: Penguin, 1966).

Collected Poems 1950-1970 (Manchester: Carcanet, 1972).

Articulate Energy (London: RKP, 1950). Reprinted 1976.

Collected Poems 1971-1983 (Manchester: Carcanet, 1984).

Czeslaw Milosz and The Insufficiency of the Lyric (Knoxville: University of Tennessee Press, 1986).

Day, Gary (ed.). *British Poetry 1950-90: Aspects of Tradition* (Basingstoke: Macmillan, 1995).

Derrida, Jacques. *Positions*. Trans. Alan Bass (London: Athlone Press, 1981).

Didsbury, Peter. *The Butchers of Hull* (Newcastle upon Tyne: Bloodaxe, 1982).

    The Classical Farm (Newcastle upon Tyne: Bloodaxe, 1987).

    That Old-Time Religion (Newcastle upon Tyne: Bloodaxe, 1994).

Dixon, Peter. *Rhetoric* (London: Methuen, 1971; 1987).

Docherty, Thomas (ed.). *Postmodernism: A Reader* (Hemel Hempstead: Harvester Wheatsheaf, 1993).

    'Postmodernism: An Introduction' in Docherty, T. (ed.). (1993), 1-33.

Dooley, Maura. *Explaining Magnetism* (Newcastle upon Tyne: Bloodaxe, 1991).

Douglas, Keith. *The Complete Poems* *(CP)* (Oxford: Oxford University Press, 1987).

Duffy, Carol Ann. *Standing Female Nude* (London: Anvil Press Poetry, 1985).

    Selling Manhattan (London: Anvil Press Poetry, 1987).

    Interview, *Bête Noire* 6 (Winter 1988), 69-78.

    The Other Country (London: Anvil Press Poetry, 1990).

    Mean Time (London: Anvil Press Poetry, 1993).

Duhig, Ian. *The Bradford Count* (Newcastle upon Tyne: Bloodaxe, 1991).

Durcan, Paul. *Jesus, Break His Fall* (Dublin: Raven Arts Press, 1980).

    Ark of The North (Dublin: Raven Arts Press, 1982).

    Jumping The Train Tracks With Angela (Dublin: Raven Arts Press, 1983).

Dunmore, Helen. *The Apple Fall* (Newcastle upon Tyne: Bloodaxe, 1983).

Dunn, Douglas. *Terry Street* (London: Faber and Faber, 1969).

    'The Grudge', Editorial, *Stand* (1975), 4-6.

    Barbarians (London: Faber and Faber, 1979).

    St Kilda's Parliament (London: Faber and Faber, 1981).

    Interview in Haffenden, John. *Viewpoints: Poets in Conversation* (London: Faber and Faber, 1981).

    (ed.). *A Rumoured City* (Newcastle upon Tyne: Bloodaxe, 1982).

    Elegies (London: Faber and Faber, 1985).

    Selected Poems 1964-1983 (London: Faber and Faber, 1986).

    Northlight (London: Faber and Faber, 1988).

    'As A Man Sees ... On Norman MacCaig's Poetry', *Verse*, 7.2 (Summer 1990), 55-68.

    Interview, *The Printer's Devil* 'A' (1990), 12-34.

    Interview, *Acumen*, Thirteen (April 1991), 9-21.

    'The Topical Muse' in Astley (ed.). (1991), 120-132. Extracted as 'Formal Strategies in Tony Harrison's Poetry'.

Eagleton, Terry. 'Literature and History', *Critical Quarterly*, 27.4 (1985), 23-26.

    'Comment', *Poetry Review*, 79.4 (Winter 1989/1990), 46.

    'Antagonisms: Tony Harrison's *V*' in Astley, Neil (ed.). *Tony Harrison* (Newcastle upon Tyne: Bloodaxe, 1991), 348-350.

Easthope, Anthony. *Poetry As Discourse* (London: Methuen, 1983).

Eliot, T.S. *Collected Poems* (London: Faber and Faber, 1974).

    'Tradition and the Individual Talent' in Kermode, Frank (ed.). *Selected Prose of T.S. Eliot* (London: Faber and Faber, 1975).

Ellis, S.J. 'On Geoffrey Hill's Decade of Reticence', *P.N. Review* 98, 20.6 (July-August 1994), 51-54.

Ellis, Steve. *Home And Away* (Newcastle upon Tyne: Bloodaxe, 1986).

Ewart, Gavin. *Penultimate Poems* (London: Hutchinson, 1989).

Fanon, Frantz. *The Wretched of the Earth* (Harmondsworth: Penguin, 1985).

Feinstein, Elaine. 'Words made to last at least a while', *The Guardian*, 6.7.93, Books 10-11.

Feirstein, Frederick (ed.). *Expansive Poetry: Essays on the New Narrative and the New Formalism* (California: Story Line Press, 1991).

Fender, Stephen. 'The novelist as liar', *The Times Literary Supplement*, 27.5.94, 20.

Fenton, James. *The Memory of War and Children in Exile: Poems 1968-1983* (Harmondsworth: Penguin, 1992).

Fisher, Roy. *Collected Poems 1968* (London: Fulcrum press, 1969). Reprinted in *Poems 1955-1987* (Oxford: Oxford University Press, 1988).

Flynn, Tony. *Body Politic* (Newcastle upon Tyne: Bloodaxe, 1992).

Foden, Giles. 'Trawling in cyberspace', *The Times Literary Supplement*, 13.5.95, 11.

Forbes, Peter. 'Going Critical', *Poetry Review*, 82.1 (Spring 1992), 3.
'A Hundred Harms: Poetry & the Gulf War', *Poetry Review*, 82.2 (Summer 1992), 3-6.
'New Ageism', *The Guardian*, 26.5.93, Arts section, 4-5.
'Talking About the New Generation', *Poetry Review — New Generation Poets Special Issue* (Summer 1994), 4-7.

Ford, Mark. *Landlocked* (London: Chatto and Windus, 1992).
'Wanting To Go To Bed With Frank O'Hara', *Scripsi*, 9.2 (June 1994), 141-151.

Frampton, Kenneth. 'Toward a Critical Regionalism: Six points for an architecture of resistance' in Docherty, T. (ed.). (1993).

France, Linda (ed.). *Sixty Women Poets* (Newcastle upon Tyne: Bloodaxe, 1993).

Francis, Matthew. 'The Competition Culture', *P.N. Review* 93, 20.1 (September-October 1993), 7-9.

Fraser, G.S. *A Short History of English Poetry* (Wells: Open Books, 1981 edn).

Fuller, John. *The Mechanical Body* (London: Chatto and Windus, 1991).

Fuller, Peter. *Beyond The Crisis in Art* (London: Writers and Readers, 1980).

Garrett, John. *British Poetry Since the Sixteenth Century* (Basingstoke: Macmillan, 1986).

Garfitt, Roger. *Given Ground* (Manchester: Carcanet, 1989).

Gilbaut, S. *How New York Stole The Idea Of Modern Art* (Chicago: University of Chicago Press, 1985).

Graff, Gerald. 'The Myth of the Postmodernist Breakthrough' in Bradbury, Malcolm (ed.). *The Novel Today* (Glasgow: Fontana, 1977).
'The Pseudo-Politics of Interpretation', *Critical Inquiry* 9, 3 (1983), 597-610.

Gray, John. 'Whatever happened to Englishness?', *The Times Literary Supplement*, 4.11.94, 26.

Gray, Richard. *American Poetry of the Twentieth Century* (Harlow: Longman, 1991).

Greenhalgh, Chris. 'Towards A Postmodern Urban Poetic: The Poetry of
     Frank O'Hara', *Verse*, 9.3 (Winter 1992), 75-87.
Greenlaw, Lavinia. *Night Photograph* (London: Faber and Faber, 1993).
Gregson, Ian. 'Music of the Generous Eye: Roy Fisher's *Poems 1955-1980*',
     Bête Noire 6 (Winter 1988), 186-197.
     Review of *The New Poetry* (1993), *New Welsh Review* 22, VI.2, 78-80.
     '"Grapevine, Barge Pole, Whirlpool, Chloride, Concrete, Bandage,
     Station, Story": Some Versions of Narrative in Contemporary
     British Poetry', *Bête Noire* 14/15 (May 1994), 66-78.
Gunn, Thom. *The Man With Night Sweats* (London: Faber and Faber, 1993).
Haffenden, John. *Viewpoints: Poets in Conversation* (London: Faber and
     Faber, 1981).
Handy, Charles. *The Age of Unreason* (London: Hutchinson, 1990).
     The Empty Raincoat (London: Hutchinson, 1994).
Harris, T.J.G. 'In The Labyrinth', *P.N. Review* 80, 17.6 (July-August 1991),
     70-71.
Harrison, Tony. *The Loiners* (London: London Magazine Editions, 1970).
     From The School of Eloquence and other poems (London: Rex Collings,
     1978).
     Continuous (London: Rex Collings, 1981).
     Selected Poems (Harmondsworth: Penguin, 1984).
     The Blasphemer's Banquet. In Astley (ed.). (1991), 395-406.
     'In conversation' (with Richard Hoggart) in Astley (1991), 36-46.
     Interview, *Verse*, 8.2 (Summer 1991), 84-94.
     The Gaze of the Gorgon (Newcastle upon Tyne: Bloodaxe, 1992).
Hart, Henry. *Seamus Heaney: Poet of Contrary Progressions* (New York: Syracuse
     University Press, 1991).
Harvey, David. *The Condition of Postmodernity* (Oxford: Basil Blackwell,
     1989).
Hattersley, Geoff. *Slouching Towards Rotherham* (Sheffield: Wide Skirt
     Press, 1987). Reprinted in *Don't Worry* (Newcastle upon Tyne:
     Bloodaxe, 1994).
Hawking, Steven. Interview on *Desert Island Discs*, BBC Radio 4, 25.12.92.
Heaney, Seamus. *North* (London: Faber and Faber, 1975).
     Field Work (London: Faber and Faber, 1979).
     Preoccupations: Selected Prose 1968-1978 (London: Faber and Faber,
     1980).
     'Englands of The Mind' in Heaney, Seamus. *Preoccupations: Selected
     Prose 1968-1978*, 150-173.
     Selected Poems 1965-75 (London: Faber and Faber, 1980).
     Interview in Haffenden, J. (1981), 57-76.
     An Open Letter (Derry: Field Day Theatre Company, 1983).
     The Haw Lantern (London: Faber and Faber, 1987).
     The Government of the Tongue (London: Faber and Faber, 1989).
Heath-Stubbs, John and Salmon, Phillips (eds.). *Poems of Science* (Har-
     mondsworth: Penguin, 1984).
Herbert, W.N. Interview in *Verse*, 7.3 (Winter 1990), 89-96.
     Anither Music (London: Vennel Press, 1991). Partially reprinted in

Forked Tongue (Newcastle upon Tyne: Bloodaxe, 1994).

Hewison, Robert. *Too Much: Art and Society in the Sixties 1960-75* (London: Methuen, 1988).

In Anger: Culture in the Cold War 1945-60 (London: Methuen, 1988).

Hill, Geoffrey. *Collected Poems* (Harmondsworth: Penguin, 1985).

Hill, Selima. *Saying Hello At The Station* (London: Chatto and Windus, 1984).

Hofmann, Michael. *Nights in the Iron Hotel* (London: Faber and Faber, 1983).
Acrimony (London: Faber and Faber, 1986).
Corona, Corona (London: Faber and Faber, 1993).

Holub, Miroslav. *On the Contrary* (Newcastle upon Tyne: Bloodaxe, 1984).
Poems Before and After (Newcastle upon Tyne: Bloodaxe, 1990).
Interview with David Morley and Kevan Johnson in *Poetry Review*, 84.2 (Summer 1994), 38-43.

Housman, A.E. *A Shropshire Lad.*

Hughes, Ted. *Selected Poems 1957-1981* (London: Faber and Faber, 1982).

Hulme, T.E. *Speculations.* Read, Herbert (ed.). (London: RKP, 1924).

Hulse, Michael. 'Familiarity and Loss', *Prospice* 22 (1987), 44-51.
Eating Strawberries In The Necropolis (London: Harvill, 1991).
Interview with Annie Greet, *Bête Noire* 14/15 (1994), 44-51.

Hulse, Michael; Kennedy, David; and Morley, David (eds.). *The New Poetry* (*TNP*) (Newcastle upon Tyne: Bloodaxe, 1993).

Hutcheon, Linda. *A Poetics of Postmodernism* (London: Routledge, 1988).

Huxley, Aldous. *After Many A Summer* (St Albans: Triad/Panther, 1976).

Hyland, Paul. *Getting Into Poetry* (Newcastle upon Tyne: Bloodaxe, 1992).

Jamie, Kathleen. *The Way We Live* (Newcastle upon Tyne: Bloodaxe, 1987).
Interview in *Verse*, 8.3 & 9.1 (Winter/Spring 1992), 103-107.
Interview in *Oxford Poetry*, VII.2 (Summer 1993), 57-63.
The Autonomous Region (Newcastle upon Tyne: Bloodaxe, 1993).
The Queen of Sheba (Newcastle upon Tyne: Bloodaxe, 1994).
'Lives of the Poet', *Poetry Review*, 84.4 (Winter 1994/95), 42-44.

Jenkins, Alan. Introduction to Reading, Peter. *Essential Reading* (London: Secker and Warburg, 1986).

Jenkins, Keith. *Rethinking History* (London: RKP, 1991).

Johnstone, Keith. *Impro* (London: Methuen, 1982).

Jonson, Ben. *Poems.* Selected with an Introduction by Thom Gunn. (Harmondsworth: Penguin, 1974).

Juvenal. *The Sixteen Satires.* Translated with an Introduction and notes by Peter Green (Harmondsworth: Penguin Classics, 1970).

Kay, Jackie. *The Adoption Papers* (Newcastle upon Tyne: Bloodaxe, 1991).

Kearney, Richard. *Dialogues with contemporary Continental thinkers: The phenomenological heritage* (Manchester: Manchester University Press, 1986).

Kees, Weldon. *Collected Poems* (London: Faber and Faber, 1993).

Kennedy, David. 'Bogus Journeys', *The Honest Ulsterman* 94 (1993), 89-91.

Kenner, Hugh. *The Pound Era* (London: Faber and Faber, 1971).

Kermode, Frank (ed.). *Selected Prose of T.S. Eliot* (London: Faber and Faber, 1975).

Romantic Image (London: RKP, 1957. Reprinted Glasgow: Collins/ Fontana, 1976).

King-Hele, Desmond. *Erasmus Darwin and the Romantic Poets* (Basingstoke: Macmillan, 1987).

Kroker, Arthur, and Cook, David. *The Postmodern Scene: Excremental Culture and Hyper-Aesthetics* (London: Macmillan, 1988).

Kuppner, Frank. *A Bad Day For The Sung Dynasty* (Manchester: Carcanet, 1984).

Laforgue, Jules. *Poems of Jules Laforgue*. Translated and Introduced by Peter Dale (London: Anvil Press Poetry, 1986).

Larkin, Philip. *Collected Poems* (London: Faber and Faber, 1988).

Larrissy, Edward. *Reading Twentieth-Century Poetry: The Language of Gender and Objects* (Oxford: Basil Blackwell, 1990).

Lasch, Christopher. *The Minimal Self: Psychic Survival in Troubled Times* (London: Picador, 1985).

Leavis, F.R. *New Bearings in English Poetry* (Harmondsworth: Penguin, 1976).

Leonard, Tom. *Intimate Voices: Selected Work 1965-1983* (Newcastle upon Tyne: Galloping Dog Press, 1984).

Lévi-Strauss, Claude. *Tristes Tropiques* (Harmondsworth: Penguin, 1978).

Levin, Harry (ed.). *The Essential James Joyce (EJJ)* (Harmondsworth: Penguin, 1972).

Lowell, Robert. *Selected Poems (SP)* (London: Faber and Faber, 1965; 1973).

For the Union Dead (London: Faber and Faber, 1985 edn).

Luckhurst, Roger. 'Shut(ting) The Fuck Up: Narrating *Blue Velvet* in the Postmodern Frame', *Bête Noire* 8/9 (Autumn 1989/Spring 1990), 170-183.

Lyotard, Jean-François. *The Postmodern Condition: A Report on Knowledge*. Trans. Geoff Bennington and Brian Massumi, Foreword by Frederick Jameson (Manchester: Manchester University Press, 1986). 'Note on the Meaning of "Post-"' in Docherty, Thomas (ed.). (1993), 47-51.

MacDiarmid, Hugh. *Aesthetics in Scotland* (Edinburgh: Mainstream, 1984). *The Complete Poems 1920-1976 (CP)* Vols I & II. Grieve, Michael and Aitken, W.R. (eds.). (Harmondsworth: Penguin, 1985). *Selected Prose* (Manchester: Carcanet, 1993).

Maguire, S. 'Postmodernism', *Poetry Review — New Generation Poets Special Issue* (Summer 1994), 69.

Maxwell, Glyn. Interview, *Verse*, 7.3 (Winter 1990), 79-88. *Tale of the Mayor's Son* (Newcastle upon Tyne: Bloodaxe, 1990). *Out of the Rain* (Newcastle upon Tyne: Bloodaxe, 1992). 'Desperanto' — review of Peter Reading. *Evagatory* and *3 in 1* in *Poetry Review*, 82.2 (Summer 1992), 53-54.

McCorduck, Pamela. 'Artificial Intelligence: An Aperçu' in Grabaud, Stephen R. (ed.). *The Artificial Intelligence Debate: False Starts, Real Foundations* (Cambridge, Mass: MIT Press, 1988).

McCorkle, James. '"The Sigh of History": The Poetry of Derek Walcott', *Verse*, 11.2 (Summer 1994), 104-112.

McDuff, David. Introduction to Mandelstam, Osip. *Selected Poems*. Trans. David McDuff (London: Writers and Readers, 1983).

McGuckian, Mebdh. *The Flower Master* (Oxford: Oxford University Press, 1982).

McHale, Brian. *Postmodernist Fiction* (London: Methuen University Paperbacks, 1987).

McMillan, Ian. *The Changing Problem* (Manchester: Carcanet, 1980).
Now It Can Be Told (Manchester: Carcanet, 1983).
Selected Poems (Manchester: Carcanet, 1987).
More Poems Please, Waiter, And Quickly (Stafford: Sow's Ear Press, 1988).
UNSelected Poems (Huddersfield: Wide Skirt Press, 1988).
A Chin? (Huddersfield: Wide Skirt Press, 1991).
Introduction, *The Wide Skirt 16 — Huddersfield Special* (October 1991).
Dad, The Donkey's on Fire (Manchester: Carcanet, 1994).

McMillan, Ian and Wiley, Martyn. *Yakety Yak* (Retford: A Twist in the Tale, 1993).

Meehan, Paula. *Return and No Blame* (Dublin: Beaver Row, 1984).

Miller, Chris 'Continental and Insular Poets', *Verse*, 11.2 (Summer 1994), 69-78.

Mills, Paul. *Half Moon Bay* (Manchester: Carcanet, 1993).
'The Quantum Uncertainty of the Narrator', *Poetry Review*, 85.1 (Spring 1995), 40-43.

Milner, Ian. Foreword to Holub, Miroslav. *Poems Before and After* (Newcastle upon Tyne: Bloodaxe, 1990), 13-16.

Montefiore, Jan. *Feminism and Poetry* (London: Pandora, 1994).

Moore, Geoffrey (ed.). *The Penguin Book of American Verse* (Harmondsworth: Penguin, 1983; 1989).

Morley, David. *Releasing Stone* (Todmorden: Nanholme Press, 1989).
A Static Ballroom (Stockton-on-Tees: Scratch, 1993).
Untitlws review in *The Wide Skirt*, 19 ()ct0ber 1992), 56-62).
Review of Maxwell, Glyn. *Out of the Rain* in *The Wide Skirt*, 20 (February-May 1993), 55-57.
'Tomlinson's Presences', *Agenda* (Summer 1995).
'What's New About The New Poetry?', *Poetry Wales*, 30.4 (April 1995), 17-24.

Morrison, Blake and Motion, Andrew (eds.). *The Penguin Book of Contemporary British Poetry* (Harmondsworth: Penguin, 1982).

Motion, Andrew. *Dangerous Play: Poems 1974-1984* (Harmondsworth: Penguin, 1984).

Muldoon, Paul. *Selected Poems 1968-1983* (London: Faber and Faber, 1986).

Murray, Les. *Collected Poems (CP)* (London: Minerva, 1992).
The Paperbark Tree (London: Minerva, 1993).

Nancy, Jean-Luc. 'On the threshold', *Paragraph*, 16.2 (July 1993), 111-122.

Nichols, Grace. *i is a long memoried woman* (London: Karnak House, 1983).

Ní Dhomhnaill, Nuala. *An Dealg Droighim* (Ireland: Mercier Press, 1981).

Norman, Phillip. 'Hollow Laughter', *The Guardian Weekend*, 5.2.94, 20-21.

O'Brien, Sean. *The Indoor Park* (Newcastle upon Tyne: Bloodaxe, 1983).

The Frighteners (Newcastle upon Tyne: Bloodaxe, 1987).

'In terms of the ocean', *The Times Literary Supplement*, 14.9.90–29.9.90, 977-978.

H M S Glasshouse (Oxford: Oxford University Press, 1991).

Interview, *Bête Noire* 12/13 (Autumn 1991/Spring 1992), 157-169.

Interview, *Verse*, 9.2 (Summer 1992), 50-64.

O'Donoghue, Bernard. 'Involved Imaginings: Tom Paulin' in Corcoran, Neil (ed.). *The Chosen Ground* (Bridgend: Seren, 1992), 171-191.

O'Hara, Frank. *Selected Poems (SP)* (Manchester: Carcanet, 1991).

Osborne, John. 'The Sage of Ventnor Street' *Bête Noire* 6 (Winter 1988), 7-42. 'Myth and Modern Science in *The Maximus Poems* of Charles Olson', *Bête Noire* 7 (Spring 1989), 116-134.

Osborne, John and Woodcock, Bruce. 'Bunting, Olson and the Modernist Inheritance', *Bête Noire* 5 (1988), 116-134.

Paterson, Don. *Nil Nil* (London: Faber and Faber, 1993).

Interview, *Verse*, 10.2 (Summer 1993), 28-35.

Paulin, Tom. 'Junk Britain: Peter Reading', *Grand Street* (Summer 1988). Reprinted in *Minotaur: Poetry and the Nation State* (London: Faber and Faber, 1992).

Ponting, Clive. *Winston Churchill* (London: Sinclair Stevenson, 1994).

Poole, Richard. 'Duncan Bush's Personae', *Poetry Wales*, 28.1 (July 1992), 33-45.

Porter, Peter. 'Provinces plenty, London nil', *The Independent on Sunday*, 30.5.93, 37. 'The Messiness Of Life', *P.N. Review* 99, 21.1 (September-October 1994).

Porter, Roy. 'A seven-bob surgeon: "Pope" Huxley and the new priesthood of science', *The Times Literary Supplement* 4781, 18.11.94, 3-4.

Potter, Simeon. *Our Language* (Harmondsworth: Penguin, 1982).

Powell, Neil. 'Something Unfixed', *P.N. Review* 92, 19.6 (July-August 1993), 58-59.

Prince, F.T. 'In A Glass Darkly', *P.N. Review* 99, 21.1 (September-October 1994), 37-38.

Pyncheon, Thomas. *The Crying of Lot 49* (London: Picador, 1979).

Raban, Jonathan. *The Society of the Poem* (London: George F. Harrap & Co., 1971).

Rae, Simon and Rushton, Willie. *Soft Targets.* (Newcastle upon Tyne: Bloodaxe, 1991).

Reading, Peter. *For The Municipality's Elderly* (London: Secker and Warburg, 1974).
The Prison Cell & Barrel Mystery (London: Secker and Warburg, 1976).
Nothing For Anyone (London: Secker and Warburg, 1977).
Fiction (London: Secker and Warburg, 1979).
Tom O'Bedlam's Beauties (London: Secker and Warburg, 1981).
Diplopic (London: Secker and Warburg, 1983).
C (London: Secker and Warburg, 1984).
Ukelele Music/Going On (London: Secker and Warburg, 1985).
Interview in *Poetry Review*, 75.1 (1985), 5-13.

Essential Reading (*ER*) (London: Secker and Warburg, 1986).

Stet (London: Secker and Warburg, 1986).

Final Demands (London: Secker and Warburg, 1988).

Perduta Gente (London: Secker and Warburg, 1989).

Interview in *Oxford Poetry*, V.III (Winter 1990/1), 94-99.

Three in One (*3 in 1*)(London: Chatto, 1992).

Evagatory (London: Chatto, 1992).

Last Poems (London: Chatto, 1994).

Redgrove, Peter. *The Weddings at Nether Powers* (London: RKP, 1979).

Interview, *Poetry Review*, 77.2 (June 1987), 4-10.

Under the Reservoir (London: Secker and Warburg, 1992).

Rees-Jones, Deryn. *The Memory Tray* (Bridgend: Seren, 1994).

Riach, Alan. 'The New Poetry in Scotland', *Verse*, 10.2 (Summer 1993), 107-113.

Richards, I.A. *The Philosophy of Rhetoric* (London: Oxford University Press, 1936).

Science and Poetry (London: Oxford University Press, 1926).

Ricks, Christopher. Preface to Sterne, Lawrence. *The Life and Opinions of Tristram Shandy* (Harmondsworth: Penguin, 1985), 7-28.

Roberts, Michèle. *The Mirror of the Mother* (London: Methuen, 1986).

Psyche and the Hurricane (London: Methuen, 1991).

Roberts, Neil. 'Dream and Discourse: Peter Redgrove's New Work', *The North*, 13 (1993), 41-43.

'Poetic Subjects: Tony Harrison and Peter Reading', forthcoming in Day, Gary (ed.). *British Poetry 1950-1990: Aspects of Tradition* (Basingstoke: Macmillan, 1995).

Robinson, Alan. *Instabilities in Contemporary British Poetry* (Basingstoke: Macmillan, 1988).

Rumens, Carol. *Direct Dialling* (London: Chatto and Windus, 1985).

The Greening of the Snow Beach (Newcastle upon Tyne: Bloodaxe, 1988).

From Berlin to Heaven (London: Chatto and Windus, 1989).

'Selves to Recover', *Second Shift* (Spring 1993), 18-21.

'A Railway Child', Bloodaxe Catalogue 1994/5, 16-17.

Russell, Charles. *Poets, Prophets and Revolutionaries: The Literary Avant-garde from Rimbaud through Posmodernism* (Oxford: Oxford University Press, 1985).

Rylance, Rick. 'On Not Being Milton', in Astley, Neil (ed.). *Tony Harrison* (Newcastle upon Tyne: Bloodaxe, 1991), 114-129.

Said, Edward. *Orientalism* (Harmondsworth: Penguin, 1991).

Culture and Imperialism (London: Chatto and Windus, 1993).

Representations of the Intellectual (London: Vintage, 1994).

Sail, Lawrence. 'The Cheshire Cat's Grin', *P.N. Review* 101, 21.3 (January-February 1995), 1-14.

Sansom, Peter. *Writing Poems* (Newcastle upon Tyne: Bloodaxe, 1994).

January (Manchester: Carcanet, 1994).

Interview in *The Wide Skirt*, 24 (June-September 1994), 15-24.

Scammell, William (ed.). *The Poetry Book Society Anthology 3* (London: Hutchinson, 1992).

Schmidt, Michael. *Reading Modern Poetry* (London: Routledge, 1989).

Schultz, Susan M. 'Defiance and Translation in Walcott', *Verse*, 11.2 (Summer 1994), 93-97.

Schuyler, James. *Selected Poems* (Manchester: Carcanet 1990).

Serres, Michel. *Hermes* (Baltimore and London: Johns Hopkins University Press, 1983).

Sinfield, Alan (ed.). *Society and Literature 1945-1970* (New York: Holmes and Meier Publishers, 1983).

Sinner, Alan. 'Frontiers of Writing: A Look At Some Poems in Seamus Heaney's *The Haw Lantern*', *Bête Noire* 10/11 (Autumn 1990/Spring 1991), 409-423.

Smith, Ken. *the heart, the border* (Newcastle upon Tyne: Bloodaxe, 1990). 'Nothing will come of nothing', *Poetry Review*, 83.4 (Winter 1993/4), 45 (Part of 'Paper Wars: Bosnia and Public Poetry', 44-45).

Spencer, Bernard. *Collected Poems* (London: Alan Ross Ltd, 1965).

Spencer, Luke. *The Poetry of Tony Harrison* (Hemel Hempstead: Havester Wheatsheaf, 1994).

Spender, Stephen. 'Remembering Eliot' in Tate, Allen (ed.). *T.S. Eliot: The Man and his Work* (Harmondsworth: Penguin, 1971).

Stainer, Pauline. *The Honeycomb* (Newcastle upon Tyne: Bloodaxe, 1989). *Sighting The Slave Ship* (Newcastle upon Tyne: Bloodaxe, 1992). 'Pauline Stainer writes', *Poetry Review — New Generation Poets Special Issue* (Summer 1994), 82.

Steele, Timothy. *Missing Measures: Modern Poetry and the Revolt against Meter* (Arkansas: University of Arkansas Press, 1990).

Steiner, George. *Language and Silence* (Harmondsworth: Penguin, 1969; 1979).

Stevens, Wallace. *Selected Poems* (London: Faber and Faber, 1970).

Stevenson, Anne. *Correspondences* (Oxford: Oxford University Press, 1974).

Sturrock, John (ed.). *Structuralism and Since: From Lévi-Strauss to Derrida* (Oxford: Oxford University Press, 1982).

Sukenick, Ronald. *In Form: Digressions on the Act of Fiction* (Carbondale and Edwardsville: Southern Illinois University Press, 1985).

Sweeney, Matthew. *A Round House* (Dublin: Raven Arts Press, 1983).

Szirtes, George. 'The Suffering of others', *Poetry Review*, 83.4 (Winter 1993/4), 44-45 (Part of 'Paper Wars: Bosnia and Public Poetry' 44-45).

Tallis, Raymond. 'Newton's Sleep (1): Poets, Scientists and Rainbows', *P.N. Review* 77, 17.3 (January-February 1991), 47-52. 'Newton's Sleep (2): The Eunuch at the Orgy', *P.N. Review* 78, 17.4 (March-April 1991), 48-51. 'Newton's Sleep (3): The Murderousness and Gadgetry of This Age', *P.N. Review* 79, 17.5 (May-June 1991), 39-42. 'Newton's Sleep (4): Anti-Science and Organic Daydreams', *P.N. Review* 80, 17.6 (July-August 1991), 31-36.

Tate, Allen (ed.). *T.S. Eliot: The Man and His Work* (Harmondsworth: Penguin, 1971).

Terada, Rei. *Derek Walcott's Poetry: American Mimicry* (Boston: North-eastern University Press, 1992).

The Citizens' Charter (HMSO, 1991).

The Forward Book of Poetry 1993 (London: Forward Publishing in association with Faber and Faber, 1993).

Thomas, Edward. *Collected Poems* (Oxford: Oxford University Press, 1978).

Thomas, Jane E. 'The Intolerable Wrestle with Words: the Poetry of Carol Ann Duffy', *Bête Noire* 6 (Winter 1988), 78-88.

Tomlinson, Charles. *Some Americans: a Personal Record* (London: University of California Press, 1981).

Eden (Bristol: Recliffe Poetry, 1986).

In conversation with David Morley, *The North* 10 (1991), un-numbered pages.

Tredell, Nicolas. *The Critical Decade: Culture in Crisis* (Manchester: Carcanet, 1993).

Conversations with Critics (Manchester: Carcanet, 1994).

Trilling, Lionel. *Beyond Culture* (London: Secker and Warburg, 1966).

Sincerity and Authenticity (London: Oxford University Press, 1974).

Turner, G.W. *Stylistics* (Harmondsworth: Penguin, 1973).

Tzonis, A. and Lefaivre, L. 'The grid and the pathway', *Architecture in Greece*, 15 (Athens, 1981), 178.

Walcott, Derek. *Collected Poems 1948-1984* (London: Faber and Faber, 1986).

Omeros (London: Faber and Faber, 1990).

Watson, Roderick. *MacDiarmid* (Milton Keynes: Open University Press, 1985).

Waugh, Patricia. 'Feminism and Postmodernism', *Bête Noire* 8/9 (Autumn 1989/Spring 1990), 64-77.

Wedde, Ian. Introduction to Darwish, Mahmoud. *Selected Poems* (Manchester: Carcanet, 1973), 7-17.

Weiner, Norbert. *Cybernetics* (New York; Wiley, 1957).

Westfall, Richard. *Never At Rest: A Biography of Isaac Newton* (Cambridge: Cambridge University Press, 1980).

White, Hayden. *Tropics of Discourse* (London: Johns Hopkins University Press, 1978).

Whitworth, John. 'But What Does He Want?', review of Peter Reading's *Perduta Gente* in *Poetry Review*, 79.3 (Autumn 1989), 40-41.

Williams, John. *Reading Poetry: A Contextual Introduction* (London: Edward Arnold, 1985).

Williams, John Hartley. *Hidden Identities* (London: Chatto and Windus, 1982).

Williams, Raymond. *Keywords* (London: Flamingo, 1983).

Winterson, Jeanette. Interview on *Face to Face*, BBC 2 Television, 28.6.94.

Wittgenstein, Ludwig. *Tractatus Logico-Philosophicus* (London: RKP, 1974).

Woolf, Virginia. *A Room of One's Own* (St Albans: Granada, 1977).

Index

Al Nawab, Mudhafer, 195-196
al-Udhari, Abdullah, 195
Alvarez, A., 24, 27, 34, 168, 188, 264
Alvi, Moniza, 246
Amis, Kingsley, 198
Armitage, Simon, 12-13, 18-19, 20, 55-78 passim, 126, 144-145, 146, 169, 186, 197, 199, 200, 201, 203-207, 223, 240, 246, 250, 255, 256-257, 258, 261-262, 266
Arnold, Matthew, 156, 157
Ash, John, 16-17, 18, 21, 79-119 passim, 131, 250, 262, 268
Ashbery, John, 101-102, 110, 118, 147, 173, 190, 197, 198, 245
Astley, Neil, 10, 187, 241, 242
Auden, W.H., 153, 185, 186, 218, 236, 266-267

Bamforth, Iain, 238, 239, 240
Barnie, John, 241
Barry, Sebastian, 267
Baudelaire, Charles, 127
Beer, Patricia, 246
Bell, Martin, 237, 240, 241
Berryman, John, 199
Blake, William, 155
Boland, Eavan, 46, 53-54, 87, 169, 247, 255, 267
Boyle, Charles, 185, 208-211, 212, 246, 255
Brodsky, Joseph, 28, 73, 247-248, 254
Bukowski, Charles, 200-202, 213
Bunting, Basil, 161
Burnside, John, 268
Bush, Duncan, 191-194, 223-227, 255, 265, 267

Carson, Ciaran, 137, 244, 257, 258, 267
Campbell, Thomas, 155
Causley, Charles, 253

Celan, Paul, 194
Chaucer, Geoffrey, 131, 153
Clifton, Harry, 211
Clough, Arthur Hugh, 128, 189
Coleridge, Samuel Taylor, 92-95, 154, 155, 158, 178
Constantine, David, 235, 268
Crawford, Robert, 118, 137, 170, 176-179, 258, 259, 265
Creeley, Robert, 199, 202-203
cummings, ee, 199, 264
Curnow, Allen, 186
Curtis, Tony, 195-197, 260

Dabydeen, David, 260
D'Aguiar, Fred, 260
Darwin, Erasmus, 154-155
Davidson, John, 177
Davie, Donald, 58, 189, 190, 254
Derrida, Jacques, 147
Dickinson, Emily, 175
Didsbury, Peter, 16-17, 18, 20, 21, 22, 79-119 passim, 268
Donaghy, Michael, 266
Dooley, Maura, 232-233, 240
Douglas, Keith, 188, 209-210
Duffy, Carol Ann, 22, 223, 227-230, 232, 244, 246, 250, 257, 258, 263, 265, 267, 268, 269
Dunn, Douglas, 11, 15-16, 25-54 passim, 87, 103, 106, 108, 109, 110, 119, 126, 246, 259
Durcan, Paul, 267, 268, 272

Eliot, T.S., 45, 55-56, 61, 65, 127, 158-159, 189, 190-191, 204, 218
Ellis, Steve, 98
Ennis, John, 267
Ewart, Gavin, 120

Feinstein, Elaine, 55
Fenton, James, 18, 144, 146, 214, 222, 265

Fisher, Roy, 103-104, 105, 106, 126, 134, 237
Flynn, Tony, 241
Forbes, Peter, 9
Ford, Mark, 208
France, Linda, 186
Fuller, John, 58

Garfitt, Roger, 255
Garrett, Elizabeth, 257, 266
Gioia, Dana, 266
Gray, Thomas, 123, 129, 190
Greenlaw, Lavinia, 149, 169, 170, 179-181
Gunn, Thom, 75, 246

Hacker, Marilyn, 266
Hannan, Maggie, 256, 258, 259, 263, 267
Harrison, Tony, 13, 14-15, 19, 24-54 passim, 61, 87, 119, 129, 138, 186, 214, 218, 260
Hartnett, David, 268
Hattersley, Geoff, 185, 197, 200-203, 204, 257
Heaney, Seamus, 13, 14-15, 17, 24-54 passim, 55-57, 58, 61, 62, 63, 66, 75, 79, 87, 90, 97, 98, 119, 123, 162, 172, 187-188, 194-195, 204, 205, 206, 212, 215, 260, 262
Herbert, W.N., 19-20, 28, 118, 218-221, 260, 261
Herbert, Zbigniew, 174
Hill, Geoffrey, 10, 16, 33, 55, 56-57, 58, 61, 69-70, 123, 129
Hill, Selima, 16-17, 20, 22, 131, 246, 268
Hofmann, Michael, 9, 16-17, 18, 20, 21-22, 79, 169, 207, 218, 238, 239, 258, 267
Holub, Miroslav, 154, 165-167, 168, 170
Housman, A.E., 149
Hughes, Ted, 55, 56-57, 58, 61, 97, 98-99, 172-173, 186
Hulse, Michael, 208, 218, 235

Jamie, Kathleen, 208, 211-212, 250
Johnson, Linton Kwesi, 260, 263, 267, 268, 273
Joyce, James, 35

Kay, Jackie, 144, 233
Keats, John, 18, 25, 34, 38, 40, 154, 155, 172, 253
Kees, Weldon, 186, 204-205
Koch, Kenneth, 197, 198, 208
Kuppner, Frank, 16-17, 21, 118, 250, 256

Laforgue, Jules, 189-191
Larkin, Philip, 14-15, 30, 31, 42, 49, 55, 56-57, 58, 61, 62, 65, 66, 126, 139-142, 189, 198, 235
Leonard, Tom, 255, 256, 260
Lochhead, Liz, 260, 267, 269, 273
Lowell, Robert, 123, 199, 200, 204, 205-207 passim, 218

MacDiarmid, Hugh, 137, 154, 158, 161-163, 164, 165, 167, 170, 175, 177, 219
Maguire, Sarah, 117-118
Mandlestam, Osip, 215, 219-220
Mapanje, Jack, 215
Maxwell, Glyn, 13, 22, 55-78 passim, 96, 126, 144, 145, 149, 186, 223, 254, 259, 262-263, 265, 266, 268
Mayakovsky, Victor, 219-220
McCaig, Norman, 31, 198
McGuckian, Mebdh, 183, 230, 250
McMillan, Ian, 21, 79-119 passim, 197, 200, 255, 256, 267
Middleton, Christopher, 135
Mills, Paul, 149, 170, 171, 173-176
Milosz, Czeslaw, 162, 190
Milton, John, 42, 192-194
Mitchell, Adrian, 214
Morgan, Edwin, 177
Morley, David, 75, 149, 170-173,

174, 179, 205, 256
Morrison, Blake, 16, 46, 143, 144, 186, 222, 265
Motion, Andrew, 16, 18, 46, 143, 144, 186, 222, 265
Muldoon, Paul, 60, 79, 144, 146, 204, 215
Murray, Les, 60, 149, 157, 167, 172, 186, 246

Neruda, Pablo, 200
Nichols, Grace, 261-262, 267, 268, 273

O'Brien, Sean, 16-17, 18, 20, 21, 22, 46-53, 62, 126, 144, 149, 256, 257, 268
O'Donoghue, Bernard, 263, 267, 269, 273
O'Hara, Frank, 169, 197-204 passim, 207-208
Olson, Charles, 199, 202
Owen, Wilfred, 226

Pasternak, Boris, 219-220
Paterson, Don, 246, 256
Paulin, Tom, 120, 122, 146, 149, 215
Petri, Gyorgy, 213
Porter, Peter, 55, 190, 191, 214
Pound, Ezra, 127, 189, 190-191, 257

Rae, Simon, 238, 239
Raine, Craig, 60, 137, 198, 254
Reading, Peter, 16, 23, 120-152, 256, 257, 258, 265, 268
Redgrove, Peter, 154, 163-165, 167, 175
Rees-Jones, Deryn, 208
Reid, Christopher, 254
Rich, Adrienne, 183
Roberts, Michèle, 53, 268
Rumens, Carol, 230-232, 265

Sail, Lawrence, 10
Sansom, Peter, 12, 98, 168, 188, 197, 199, 200, 256, 261

Scammell, William, 14
Schuyler, James, 197-198, 208
Shapcott, Jo, 22, 267
Shelley, Percy Bysshe, 155, 156
Smith, Ken, 221-223, 234-235
Snyder, Gary, 200
Spencer, Bernard, 240, 241
Spenser, Edmund, 37
Stainer, Pauline, 159, 170, 181-184, 258, 264, 267, 268, 269-270
Stannard, Martin, 197
Stevens, Wallace, 169, 170-171, 173, 264
Stevenson, Anne, 16
Sweeney, Matthew, 144, 256
Szirtes, George, 234-235, 267

Tennyson, Alfred, 156
Thomas, Edward, 49, 124
Thomson, James, 154
Tomlinson, Charles, 57, 189, 191, 197

Walcott, Derek, 24, 25, 27, 29, 41, 43
Williams, Hugo, 17
Williams, John Hartley, 238, 254, 255, 263-264, 267, 268, 271-272
Williams, William Carlos, 127, 158, 199
Woodward, Gerard, 257
Woolf, Virginia, 52
Wordsworth, William, 25, 40, 62, 154, 155, 156, 159, 190

Yeats, W.B., 173

Zukofsky, Louis, 127

About the Author

David Kennedy was born in Leicester in 1959 and currently lives in Sheffield where he works in manufacturing industry. He also studies in the Graduate School at Sheffield University where he is researching a doctorate on ideas of community in the work of Douglas Dunn, Tony Harrison and Seamus Heaney. He was a co-editor of *The New Poetry* (Bloodaxe, 1993) and his poems, essays and reviews have been published widely in magazines in the UK and abroad. His first collection of poetry, *The Elephant's Typewriter*, was published by Scratch in 1996. A selection of translations from Max Jacob's *Le Cornet à Dés* (The Dice Cup), in collaboration with Christopher Pilling, is forthcoming from Atlas.

DATE DUE

			Printed in USA

HIGHSMITH #45230